1000 RECIPES

Chicken

igloobooks

Published in 2016
by Igloo Books Ltd
Cottage Farm
Sywell
Northants
NN6 0BJ
www.igloobooks.com

Food photography and recipe development: PhotoCuisine UK
Front cover image © luchezar / Getty Images

Cover designed by Nicholas Gage
Edited by Caroline Icke

HUN001 0716
2 4 6 8 10 9 7 5 3 1
ISBN: 978-1-78557-590-7

Printed and manufactured in China

CONTENTS

LIGHT BITES & STARTERS

1

SERVES 6–8

Thai Vermicelli Soup

PREPARATION TIME:
30 MINUTES

COOKING TIME:
40–45 MINUTES

INGREDIENTS

3 tbsp vegetable oil
4 spring onions (scallions), sliced
1 red pepper, deseeded and diced
2 cloves of garlic, finely chopped
1 red chilli (chili), finely sliced
2 stalks lemon grass, bruised
1 tbsp fresh ginger, grated
1 tsp turmeric
3–4 chicken breasts, skinned and finely
    chopped
2 tsp tamarind paste
2 tbsp fish sauce
400 ml / 14 fl. oz / 1 ½ cups coconut
    milk
200 ml / 7 fl. oz / ¾ cup chicken stock
150 g / 5 oz / ⅔ cup vermicelli noodles
1–2 limes, juiced
½ bunch coriander (cilantro), finely
    chopped, stalks reserved

- Heat the oil in a wok or large pan and fry the onion and pepper until deep gold and sweet. Add the garlic and chilli and cook out for 2 minutes. Add the cubed chicken, lemon grass, ginger and turmeric and allow to colour on all sides.
- Stir in the tamarind and fish sauce, then pour over the coconut milk and chicken stock and add the coriander stalks. Lower the heat and leave to simmer for 15–20 minutes until the chicken is cooked through.
- Adjust the seasoning and stir in the lime juice and chopped coriander just before serving in deep warmed bowls.

Spicy Thai Soup

2

- Add a teaspoon of chilli (chili) powder for an extra kick.

3

SERVES 4

Chicken with Figs and Broad Beans

PREPARATION TIME:
15 MINUTES

COOKING TIME:
30 MINUTES

INGREDIENTS

2 tbsp olive oil
4 chicken thighs, skinned
1 onion, peeled and finely chopped
400 g / 14 oz / 1 ½ cup chopped
    tomatoes
2 sprigs basil leaves
salt and pepper
4 ripe figs
100 g / 3 ½ oz / ½ cup broad beans

- Heat the olive oil in a pan and cook the chicken thighs until golden on all sides. Remove and set aside.
- Add the onion and cook until softened, then add the tomatoes, basil and a little seasoning, return the thighs to the pan and simmer until thickened and the chicken is cooked through.
- Meanwhile blanch the broad beans and pod them, discarding the grey skins.
- Just before serving add the figs and broad beans to the sauce to heat through.

Chicken with Figs and Peas

4

- Fresh peas make a nice substitute for the beans.

5

SERVES 4–6

Chicken Curry Filo Parcels

- Preheat the oven to 200°C (180°C fan) / 400F / gas 6.
- Heat the oil in a pan and sauté the onion for about 10 minutes or until golden-brown. Add the garlic and ginger and fry for another minute.
- Add the spices and stir well, then add 200 ml water and the chicken and cook gently for 10 minutes or so. Once the liquid has mostly evaporated, stir in just enough yogurt to bind and leave to cool.
- Keeping the remaining filo sheets covered with a damp tea towel, remove one at a time from the pack and brush with melted butter before using.
- Place 2 sheets of pastry on a surface, brush each with melted butter, then spoon a little of the chicken mixture into the middle. Wrap the pastry around to enclose the filling. Repeat until all the filling and pastry is used up.
- Brush the tops with a little egg wash, then bake in the oven for 15–20 minutes.

PREPARATION TIME:
45 MINUTES

COOKING TIME:
20 MINUTES

INGREDIENTS

3 tbsp vegetable oil
1 onion, peeled and finely sliced
2 cloves of garlic, chopped
1 tsp fresh ginger, grated
1 tsp ground coriander
½ tsp turmeric
1 tsp ground cumin
1 tbsp garam masala
1 tsp paprika
4 chicken thighs, skinned, deboned and diced
2–3 tbsp plain yogurt
Salt
12–16 sheets filo pastry
120 g / 4 oz / ½ cup butter, melted
2 eggs
1 egg yolk, beaten

Chicken Curry Parcels with Sauce

6

- Serve alongside garlic mayonnaise.

7

SERVES 2

Artichoke and Chicken Salad

- Shred the chicken and place in a salad bowl with the artichoke hearts and tomatoes.
- Whisk together the mustard and vinegar, then whisk in the oil until emulsified. Add 1 tbsp artichoke oil if available. Season.
- Toss the salad ingredients in the dressing, sprinkle with chopped chives and serve.

PREPARATION TIME:
15 MINUTES

INGREDIENTS

2 chicken breasts, cooked
250 g / 9 oz / 1 cup prepared globe artichoke hearts, drained of oil
2 tomatoes, cored and diced
1 tbsp Dijon mustard
1 tbsp red wine vinegar
3 tbsp extra virgin olive oil
salt and pepper
10 chive stems, chopped

Warm Artichoke Salad

8

- Sauté the artichoke hearts in a little oil with the chicken, then toss while still warm with the tomatoes and dressing and serve on thick toast.

9

SERVES 4

Chicken Bites with Fresh Mint

Spicy Chicken Bites

10

- Add a pinch of dried chilli flakes for an extra kick.

Tarragon Chicken Bites

11

- Use fresh tarragon leaves in place of the mint.

PREPARATION TIME:
5 MINUTES + MARINATING TIME

COOKING TIME:
10 MINUTES

INGREDIENTS

4 chicken breasts, skinned and cubed
150ml / 5 fl. oz / ⅔ cup plain yogurt
1 bunch mint leaves, finely chopped
salt and pepper
½ lemon, juiced
½ cucumber, finely sliced
4 pitta breads

- Toss the chicken in the yogurt and mint to marinate in the refrigerator for about 20–30 minutes.
- Heat a griddle or frying pan until hot, then wipe off any excess marinade and cook the chicken until sizzling and golden.
- Season and drizzle on lemon juice, then serve with cucumber and warmed pitta breads.

12

SERVES 4

Chicken Courgette Kebabs

- Thread the chicken, onion chunks and courgette slices alternately onto soaked wooden skewers.
- Drizzle with oil and oregano and griddle over medium heat for 10–12 minutes until golden and cooked through.
- Season well and squeeze over a little lemon juice before serving.

PREPARATION TIME:
10 MINUTES

COOKING TIME:
10–12 MINUTES

INGREDIENTS

4 chicken thighs, skinned, deboned and chopped
½ red onion, peeled and cut into chunks
½ courgette (zucchini), thickly sliced
2 tbsp olive oil
1 tsp dried oregano
½ lemon, juiced
salt and pepper

Turkey Courgette Kebabs

13

- Try using turkey thigh meat for a change, but marinate in oregano or thyme for 30 minutes before cooking to add flavour.

14

SERVES 2

Chicken and Pickled Salad Bagel

- Thickly slice the chicken and set aside.
- Toss the carrot and courgette with the vinegar, sugar and salt and leave to marinate for 5–10 minutes, until still crunchy but starting to soften.
- Toast the bagels.
- Place lettuce leaves on the bottom bagel halves, top with drained pickled vegetables then the sliced chicken and the other bagel half on top.

PREPARATION TIME:
20 MINUTES

INGREDIENTS

2 chicken breasts, skin on, cooked
1 carrot, peeled and cut into matchsticks
1 courgette (zucchini), peeled and cut into matchsticks
2 tbsp rice vinegar
1 tbsp sugar
1 tsp salt
4 lettuce leaves
2–4 bagels, depending on appetite

Chicken and Pickled Salad Pittas

15

- Substitute the bagels for pittas instead.

16

SERVES 4

Honey Soy Chicken Kebabs

PREPARATION TIME:
10 MINUTES

COOKING TIME:
10–12 MINUTES

INGREDIENTS

4 chicken thighs, skinned, deboned and chopped
2 tbsp soy sauce
1 ½ tbsp runny honey
1 tbsp sesame seeds
salt and pepper or chilli (chili) flakes

- Mix together the soy, honey, sesame and chilli or pepper.
- Coat the chicken pieces thoroughly and thread onto soaked wooden skewers.
- Griddle over medium heat for 10–12 minutes until cooked through. Serve hot or cold.

Ginger Honey Soy Kebabs

17

- Add 1 tbsp fresh grated ginger for a kick.

18

SERVES 2

Chicken, Spinach and Mozzarella Rolls

PREPARATION TIME:
10 MINUTES

COOKING TIME:
8–12 MINUTES

INGREDIENTS

2 chicken breasts, skinned
handful baby spinach leaves
1 ball mozzarella, sliced
100 g / 3 ½ oz / ½ cup dried breadcrumbs
salt and pepper

- Place the chicken between 2 pieces of cling film and bash out to about 1 cm (½ in) in thickness.
- Place on a board and cover each with a few slices mozzarella, then top with spinach leaves. Season, then roll up to form a sausage shape.
- Roll cling film around the chicken roll and twist the ends to secure.
- Steam over simmering water for 8–12 minutes until the chicken is cooked.
- Unwrap and sprinkle with breadcrumbs. Grill until golden, then serve hot.

Steamed Tricolore Rolls

19

- Add pieces of sun-dried tomato to add colour and flavour.

20

SERVES 4

Chicken Tikka Bites

Curried Chicken Bites

21

- Use any kind of curry paste, including Thai, for different flavours.

Soy Sauce Dip

22

- Mix together 2 tbsp soy sauce and ½ tbsp lime juice as a dipping sauce.

PREPARATION TIME:
5 MINUTES + MARINATING
TIME

COOKING TIME:
10 MINUTES

INGREDIENTS

4 chicken breasts, skinned
4 tbsp tikka masala paste
100 ml / 3 ½ fl. oz / ½ cup plain yogurt
salt and pepper
½ lemon, juiced

- Cube the chicken, toss with the curry paste and yogurt and leave to marinate in the refrigerator for 30 minutes.
- Griddle or fry the chicken in a pan until golden and sizzling and just cooked through.
- Squeeze over the lemon juice, season and serve hot.

23

SERVES 4

Colombo Style Chicken Legs

PREPARATION TIME:
40 MINUTES

COOKING TIME:
25 MINUTES

INGREDIENTS

1 tbsp vegetable oil
salt and pepper
1 onion, peeled and chopped
3 cloves of garlic, crushed
2 tbsp curry powder
6 sprigs thyme leaves
1 tsp ground allspice
½ tsp ground cinnamon
2 bay leaves
1–2 Scotch Bonnet chillies (chilies)
   (depending on how hot you want it)
8 spring onions (scallions), ends
   trimmed
500 ml / 1 pint / 2 cups chicken stock
400 g / 14 oz / 1 ½ cups canned chopped
   tomatoes
4 chicken legs

- Heat the oil in a large pan and cook the onion and garlic with the spices until softened.
- Add the chillies and spring onions, chicken stock and tomatoes and simmer for 30 minutes or until thick and reduced.
- Leave to cool, then coat the chicken thoroughly in the marinade and leave for 4 hours or overnight.
- Preheat the oven to 190°C (170°C fan) / 375F / gas 5.
- Sit the chicken in a roasting tin and cook in the oven for 25–30 minutes until cooked through.
- Meanwhile simmer any excess marinade to serve alongside.
- Serve the chicken with the sauce.

Colombo Style Chicken Wings

24

- Substitute the chicken legs for chicken wings.

25

SERVES 4

Chicken Tandoori Tomato Salad

PREPARATION TIME:
10 MINUTES

COOKING TIME:
15 MINUTES

INGREDIENTS

4 skinless chicken breasts,
   diced evenly
400 g / 14 oz / 1 ½ cups baby
   spinach leaves
3 tbsp capers, drained

FOR THE MARINADE
1 tsp ground cumin
1 tsp ground coriander
1 tsp garam masala
1 tsp ground cinnamon
1 ½ tsp tandoori chilli (chili) powder
1 tsp paprika
1 tsp caster (superfine) sugar
1 clove garlic, minced
salt and pepper
300 ml / 10 fl. oz / 1 ¼ cups canned
   tomatoes
1 tbsp vegetable oil

- Prepare the tandoori marinade by mixing together all the ingredients for the marinade apart from the tomatoes in a mixing bowl. Add the chicken, mix well, then cover and chill for at least 1 hour.
- Shake off any excess and fry the chicken briskly in the oil until golden and cooked through.
- Meanwhile pour the tomatoes into a pan with the excess marinade and simmer for 10 minutes until thickened.
- Serve the chicken and sauce spooned over baby spinach leaves and topped with the capers.

Tandoori Tomato Chicken with Rice

26

- Stir the spinach into just-cooked rice to wilt, then serve alongside the chicken for a more substantial meal.

SERVES 6–8 27

Chicken and Pistachio Pâté

- Heat the chicken stock in a pan and poach the chicken for 10 minutes until cooked. Remove with a slotted spoon and leave to cool.
- Whisk the gelatine into the hot stock until dissolved.
- Fill a terrine mould with the chicken and scattering over the pistachios, seasoning as you go.
- Pour the liquid over the chicken terrine and refrigerate for at least 4 hours until set.
- Serve in thick slices with sun dried tomatoes and salad.

PREPARATION TIME:
30 MINUTES

COOKING TIME:
30 MINUTES

INGREDIENTS

FOR THE TERRINE
500 g / 1 lb / 2 cups chicken breast, skinned and cut into chunks
400 ml / 14 fl. oz / 1 ½ cups chicken stock
100 g / 3 ½ oz / ½ cup pistachios, chopped
2 leaves gelatine, soaked in cold water
salt and pepper

Chinese Flavoured Pâté   28

- Try using cashew nuts and 2 tbsp soy sauce and 1 star anise in the chicken stock to give a tiny hint of Eastern flavours.

29

SERVES 4

Tunisian Salad

- Preheat the oven to 220°C (200°C fan) / 425F / gas 7
- Place the peppers in a snug roasting tin and drizzle with oil. Roast for 40–45 minutes until blackened. When cooked, place in a freezer bag to cool.
- Cook the potatoes in boiling salted water until tender to the point of a knife. Drain thoroughly.
- Rub the harissa into the chicken on all sides and roast in the oven alongside the peppers for 20 minutes until cooked through.
- When the peppers have cooled enough to handle, peel away the skins to leave the soft flesh. Tip into a large serving bowl with the olives, tomatoes, onion and drizzle over oil, lemon juice and seasoning. Add the potatoes and toss gently.
- Slice the chicken and sit on top of the salad before serving.

PREPARATION TIME:
20 MINUTES

COOKING TIME:
45 MINUTES

INGREDIENTS

2 red peppers, deseeded and halved
2 tbsp olive oil
500 g / 1 lb / 2 cups new potatoes, halved
salt
2 chicken breasts, skin on
2 tbsp harissa paste
60 g / 2 oz black olives
12 cherry tomatoes, halved
½ red onion, finely chopped
2 tbsp extra virgin olive oil
½ lemon, juiced

Tunisian Salad with Eggs   30

- Quartered hard boiled eggs would make a good addition to this salad.

31

SERVES 4

Chicken Tomato Skewers

Chicken and Pepper Skewers

 32

- Replace the tomatoes with green and red pepper chunks.

Chicken and Olive Skewers

33

- Replace the tomato with green and black olives.

PREPARATION TIME:
15 MINUTES

COOKING TIME:
10–12 MINUTES

INGREDIENTS

4 chicken breasts
4 sprigs fresh thyme
2 tbsp olive oil
salt and pepper
4 long rosemary stalks (optional)
8 garlic cloves
8 cherry tomatoes
4 spring onions (scallions), halved
 lengthways

- Chop the chicken into bite-size pieces and toss with the thyme, oil and seasoning.
- Blanch the garlic cloves in their skins in boiling water for 3 minutes. Leave to cool, then remove the skins. This will help them cook on the griddle.
- If using, thread the chicken onto the rosemary stalks, alternating with tomatoes and halved spring onions, pushing the garlic in between.
- Griddle over medium heat for 10–12 minutes until cooked through, watching the tomatoes don't collapse.

34

SERVES 4

Chicken Nuggets

- Bash the chicken breasts between 2 pieces of cling film with a rolling pin until about 2 cm (1 in) thick.
- Cut each piece into thick strips and place in a bowl with the buttermilk. Refrigerate for at least 2 hours or even overnight.
- The next day, dip them one at a time into the flour, egg then breadcrumbs mixed with the flavourings and lay on a rack to dry slightly.
- Heat 1 cm (½ in) depth oil in a pan and fry the chicken in batches until golden on both sides and cooked through. Serve warm.

PREPARATION TIME:
5 MINUTES + MARINATING TIME

COOKING TIME:
10 MINUTES

INGREDIENTS

4 chicken breasts, skinned
300 ml / 10 fl. oz / 1 ¼ cups buttermilk
100 g / 3 ½ oz / ½ cup plain (all-purpose) flour
2 eggs, beaten
200 g / 7 oz / ¾ cup breadcrumbs
1 tsp mustard powder
pinch cayenne
salt and pepper
vegetable oil

Chicken Nuggets with Herbs
35

- Use finely chopped thyme or rosemary in the breadcrumbs for a herbier hit.

36

SERVES 4

Chicken and Lemon Grass Kebabs

- Marinate the chicken with ginger, turmeric and a little seasoning for 30 minutes.
- Strip away the outer leaves of the lemon grass to leave the firm inner core. Push it through the pieces of chicken to skewer them.
- Griddle over medium heat brushed with a little oil for 8–10 minutes until cooked through.

PREPARATION TIME:
10 MINUTES + MARINATING TIME

COOKING TIME:
10 MINUTES

INGREDIENTS

4 chicken breasts, skinned and chopped
1 tsp fresh ginger, grated
1 tsp turmeric
1 tbsp vegetable oil
salt and pepper
4 sticks lemon grass

Chicken and Mushroom Kebabs
37

- Thread a button mushroom between each piece of chicken, before griddling.

38

SERVES 4

Chicken Satay with Coconut Shavings

PREPARATION TIME:
15 MINUTES

COOKING TIME:
10 MINUTES

INGREDIENTS

8 chicken thighs, skinned, deboned and
    cut in half
½ coconut

FOR THE MARINADE/SAUCE

2 shallots, peeled and finely chopped
½–1 red chilli (chili), finely chopped
2 cloves of garlic, finely chopped
1 cm (½ in) piece fresh ginger, grated
5 tbsp peanut butter
1 tbsp tamarind paste
2 tbsp soy sauce
100 ml / 3 ½ fl. oz / ½ cup coconut milk
1 tsp palm or dark brown sugar
1 tbsp fish sauce
1 lime, juiced

- Mix together the marinade ingredients and pour half over the chicken pieces.
- Leave to marinate for at least 4 hours or overnight.
- Skewer with soaked wooden kebab sticks. Griddle over a high heat for 6–8 minutes until blackened in patches and cooked through.
- Meanwhile heat the remaining sauce in a small pan, then squeeze in a little lime juice.
- Carve out shavings of fresh coconut, being very careful with your fingers.
- Serve the chicken sprinkled with fresh coconut and any sauce alongside.

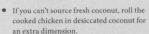

Satay Chicken rolled in Coconut

39

- If you can't source fresh coconut, roll the cooked chicken in desiccated coconut for an extra dimension.

40

SERVES 2

Chicken on Toast with Bearnaise

PREPARATION TIME:
15 MINUTES

COOKING TIME:
30 MINUTES

INGREDIENTS

1 tbsp tarragon, chopped
1 shallot, finely chopped
6 black peppercorns, crushed
2 tbsp white wine vinegar
150 ml / 5 fl. oz / ⅔ cup dry white wine
3 egg yolks
1 tsp mustard powder
25 g / 1 oz butter at room temperature
180 g / 6 oz / ¾ cup butter, melted
salt
1 chicken leg, skin on
1 thick slice sourdough bread, toasted
rosemary, to serve
cherry tomatoes, to serve

- Make the bearnaise: put the tarragon, shallot, peppercorns, vinegar and wine in a pan and reduce by a third, then strain.
- Whisk the egg yolks and mustard together in a bowl over a pan of barely simmering water.
- Whisk in the vinegar reduction, add a tbsp water.
- Beat in the 25 g butter a little at a time, then slowly trickle in the melted butter a drop at a time, continually whisking, until the sauce has emulsified and thickened. Season and keep warm until needed.
- Meanwhile heat a griddle pan until smoking. Rub the chicken with a little oil, season and cook skin-side down on the griddle pan until golden. Turn over and cook on the other side until cooked through.
- Arrange the chicken on top of the toast. Sprinkle over the rosemary, and serve with the sauce and some cherry tomatoes.

Griddled Chicken with Aioli

41

- This would work well with a home-made garlic mayonnaise, or just stir crushed garlic into prepared French-style mayo.

42

SERVES 4

Thyme Chicken with Rosé Wine

Lavender Chicken

 43

- Take this one stage further in summer and substitute the coriander seeds for lavender heads before barbecuing the chicken.

Chicken in White Wine

44

- If it's not quite summery enough, use white wine instead of rosé wine.

PREPARATION TIME:
10 MINUTES

COOKING TIME:
20 MINUTES

INGREDIENTS

4 chicken breasts
100 ml / 3 ½ fl. oz / ½ cup rosé wine
4 sprigs thyme leaves
1 tbsp coriander seeds, lightly crushed
salt and pepper
2 tbsp olive oil
1 cos lettuce
1 tbsp red wine vinegar
2 tbsp extra virgin olive oil

- Marinate the chicken in the wine, thyme, coriander and a little seasoning for at least 30 minutes.
- Preheat the oven to 190°C (170°C fan) / 375F / gas 5.
- Sit the chicken in a roasting tin, drizzle with a little oil and roast for 20 minutes or until just cooked through. Set aside to rest.
- Tear the cos lettuce into separate leaves. Whisk the red wine vinegar with the oil and a little seasoning and lightly coat the lettuce.
- Thickly slice the chicken and serve on top of the lettuce.

45

SERVES 4

Thyme and Garlic Chicken Meatballs

PREPARATION TIME:
20 MINUTES

COOKING TIME:
25 MINUTES

....

INGREDIENTS

300 g / 10 oz / 1 ¼ cups minced chicken
1 tbsp thyme leaves, finely chopped
1 clove of garlic, crushed
½ lemon, zested
salt and pepper
3 tbsp olive oil
sweet chilli (chili) sauce, to serve

- Mix the chicken mince thoroughly with the thyme, garlic, zest and some seasoning. Roll into tiny meatballs and refrigerate for 10 minutes.
- When ready to cook, heat the oil in a pan and fry the meatballs in batches until golden and cooked through.
- Arrange the meatballs on skewers and serve with sweet chilli sauce on the side.

Meatballs with Yogurt **46**

- Try whisking 200 g plain yogurt with a dash of extra virgin olive oil, 1 tsp of crushed garlic and some seasoning to make a yogurt dressing.

47

SERVES 4

Chicken Salad with Courgette and Nuts

PREPARATION TIME:
15 MINUTES

COOKING TIME:
20 MINUTES

....

INGREDIENTS

4 chicken breasts, skin on
2 tbsp olive oil
salt and pepper
250 g / 9 oz / 1 cup mixed nuts, such as
    walnuts, cashews, hazelnuts (cobnuts)
1 courgette (zucchini), thinly sliced
150 g / 5 oz / ⅔ cup rocket (arugula)
    leaves
50 ml / 1 ¾ oz / ¼ cup extra virgin
    olive oil
½ lemon, zested
dried breadcrumbs, to serve

- Preheat the oven to 200°C (180°C fan) / 400F / gas 6.
- Roast the chicken with a little oil and seasoning for about 20 minutes until just cooked through. Leave to rest.
- Toast the nuts in a dry frying pan until lightly golden.
- Toss the salad leaves in a bowl with the nuts and courgette. Whisk together the oil and lemon juice, then season. Drizzle over the salad.
- Slice the chicken in half and place on top of the salad, then sprinkle with breadcrumbs to serve.

Chicken Salad with Pistachios **48**

- Use pistachios and sultanas for a sweeter salad.

49

SERVES 4

Fried Breaded Chicken

- Place the chicken in a bowl with the buttermilk. Refrigerate for at least 2 hours or even overnight.
- Mix the breadcrumbs with the mustard, cayenne and seasoning.
- Dip the chicken pieces one at a time into the flour, egg then breadcrumbs and lay on a rack to dry slightly.
- Heat enough oil in a pan to come two-thirds of the way up the sides until a cube of bread sizzles immediately when dropped in or to 180°C / 350F.
- Fry the chicken in batches until golden on both sides and cooked through – 8–12 minutes, depending on size.

PREPARATION TIME:
10 MINUTES

COOKING TIME:
15–20 MINUTES

INGREDIENTS

4 chicken breasts or thighs, skinned
300 ml / 10 fl. oz / 1 ¼ cups buttermilk
100 g / 3 ½ oz / ½ cup plain
    (all-purpose) flour
2 eggs, beaten
250 g / 9 oz / 1 cup breadcrumbs
1 tsp mustard powder
½ tsp cayenne pepper
salt and pepper
vegetable oil for deep frying

Spicy Breaded Chicken

50

- You can add pretty much what you fancy to the breadcrumbs to add flavour and colour. Try paprika, herbs, fennel seeds, curry powder, or garlic.

51

SERVES 4

Layered Chicken and Courgette Towers

- Preheat the oven to 200°C (180°C fan) / 400F / gas 6.
- Place the chicken breasts between 2 pieces of cling film and bash to flatten out slightly. Drizzle with oil, season and roast in the oven for 15 minutes or until just cooked through. Set aside to rest.
- Meanwhile cut the salsify into cork-size lengths and sauté in a mixture of butter and white wine until tender.
- Brush the courgette rounds with olive oil and griddle on a hot pan until charred and tender.
- Slice the chicken into thick slices.
- Layer the courgettes and chicken on individual plates, starting and ending with courgette. Spoon a little salsify around, then sprinkle over torn basil leaves, Parmesan shavings and a little extra virgin olive oil.

PREPARATION TIME:
25 MINUTES

COOKING TIME:
30 MINUTES

INGREDIENTS

2 chicken breasts, skin on
2 tbsp olive oil
salt and pepper
200 g / 7 oz / ¾ cup salsify peeled,
    scrubbed and tossed with lemon juice
1 tbsp butter
75 ml / 2 ½ fl. oz / ⅓ cup dry
    white wine
2 large courgettes (zucchini), sliced into
    thick rounds
olive oil
½ bunch basil leaves
25 g / 1 oz Parmesan, shaved
extra virgin olive oil

Chicken and Mixed Vegetable Towers

52

- Alternate the courgette with aubergine (eggplant) and/or roasted peppers for colour.

53

SERVES 4

Spanish Chicken with Pearl Barley Risotto

Chicken and Tomato Rolls

54

- You can use diced tomato in place of or in addition to the red pepper for a fresher flavour.

Chicken with Serrano Ham

55

- Layer on a slice of serrano ham for a smoky flavour.

PREPARATION TIME:
20 MINUTES

COOKING TIME:
30 MINUTES

INGREDIENTS

4 chicken escalopes
2 tbsp olive oil
1 red pepper, deseeded and very finely diced
1 clove of garlic, crushed
200 g / 7 oz / ¾ cup cream cheese
8 slices chorizo
salt and pepper
1 onion, peeled and finely chopped
30 g / 1 oz butter
150 g / 5 oz / ⅔ cup pearl barley
100 ml / 3 ½ fl. oz / ½ cup dry white wine
400 ml / 14 fl. oz / 1 ½ cups chicken stock
½ lemon, zested

- Preheat the oven to 180°C (160°C fan) / 350F / gas 4.
- Place the chicken between 2 pieces of cling film and use a saucepan to batten out to about 1cm thick.
- Sauté the peppers and garlic in a little oil until tender, then leave to cool. Mix with the cream cheese.
- Spread the cream cheese mix evenly over the chicken escalopes, then top with 2 slices chorizo and roll into a sausage shape. Secure with toothpicks if necessary. Roast in the oven for about 15–20 minutes until cooked through, then set aside to rest.
- Meanwhile, sweat the onion in the butter, then add the barley. Stir in the white wine, simmer for 5 minutes, then add the chicken stock, Stir well, then simmer for about 20–30 minutes or until the barley is tender and the stock mostly absorbed. Season and add the lemon juice.
- Slice the chicken in half and serve with the risotto alongside.

56

SERVES 2

Thai Chicken and Pear Noodles

- Heat the oil in a wok and stir fry the chicken until golden.
- Add the pears and cook briefly. Whisk together the dressing, pour into the wok and toss to coat.
- Cook the rice noodles according to packet instructions, then drain thoroughly.
- Toss the noodles in the wok and reheat briefly, then serve in deep bowls.

PREPARATION TIME:
10 MINUTES

COOKING TIME:
10–15 MINUTES

INGREDIENTS

1 tbsp vegetable oil
1 tsp sesame oil
2 chicken thighs, skinned, deboned and chopped
2 ripe pears, peeled, cored and chopped
200 g / 7 oz / ¾ cup rice noodles

FOR THE DRESSING
60 ml / 2 fl. oz soy sauce
juice and zest of 1 lime
1 red chilli (chili), finely chopped
1 tsp tamarind paste
2 tsp soft brown sugar

Thai Chicken Noodles with Pineapple

57

- Chunks of refreshing pineapple would make a good foil to the sweet-sharp dressing.

58

SERVES 2

Chicken and Bacon Pancakes

- Heat the oil in a pan and sauté the chicken and bacon until golden.
- Lay out the pancakes on the surface and spoon over the meat, then top with a few spinach leaves. Roll up into sausage shapes and set aside.
- Heat the coconut milk in a small pan and simmer with the spring onions and coriander for 5 minutes. Season with the soy sauce.
- Spoon onto a plate and set the pancakes on top.

PREPARATION TIME:
15 MINUTES

COOKING TIME:
10 MINUTES

INGREDIENTS

2 tbsp olive oil
2 chicken breasts, skinned and cubed
4 rashers streaky bacon, chopped
handful baby spinach leaves
2 pancakes, ready-made
3 spring onions (scallions), finely chopped
¼ bunch fresh coriander (cilantro) chopped
150 ml / 5 fl. oz / ⅔ cup coconut milk
1 tbsp soy sauce

Chicken and Prawn Pancakes

59

- Substitute the bacon for cooked large prawns.

60

SERVES 4

Savoury Autumn Eclair

PREPARATION TIME:
15 MINUTES

COOKING TIME:
15 MINUTES

INGREDIENTS

4 crisp French-style baguettes
30 g / 1 oz butter
2 chicken thighs, deboned and skinned,
    meat cubed
100 g / 3 ½ oz / ½ cup chestnut
    mushrooms, quartered
1 clove of garlic, crushed
½ glass white wine
100 ml / 3 ½ fl. oz / ½ cup crème fraîche
½ lemon, zested
salt and pepper
¼ bunch parsley, chopped

- Slice the baguettes in half horizontally and grill carefully until crisp. Set aside.
- Heat the butter in a pan and sauté the chicken, mushrooms and garlic until golden.
- Add the white wine and deglaze the pan, then add the crème fraîche, a little lemon juice and seasoning, then the parsley and stir well.
- Spoon hot into the crisp baguettes and serve.

Autumn Eclairs with Cheese

 61

- Add a little grated Parmesan and fresh mozzarella for extra depth.

62

SERVES 4

Curried Chicken and Tomato Glasses

PREPARATION TIME:
15 MINUTES

COOKING TIME:
10 MINUTES

INGREDIENTS

2 tbsp groundnut oil
2 chicken thighs, skinned, deboned
    and diced
2 tsp garam masala
salt and pepper
4 ripe tomatoes, cored and diced
2 shallots, peeled and finely sliced
4 tbsp extra virgin olive oil
4 sprigs coriander (cilantro)

- Heat the oil in a pan and fry the chicken briskly, sprinkling over the garam masala and tossing the chicken to coat. Season and set aside when cooked through.
- Spoon the slices of tomato, shallots and chicken into small serving glasses. Drizzle over a little oil and serve decorated with coriander.

Curried Chicken with Diced Lemon

63

- Cut out lemon segments and add the tiny dice to the glasses for instant freshness.

64

SERVES 4

Spicy Chicken Kiwi Coconut Soup

Chicken and Mango Soup

 65

- Substitute the kiwi for diced mango.

Chicken Noodle Soup 66

- Add 2 nests of noodles to cook in the soup.

PREPARATION TIME:
15 MINUTES

COOKING TIME:
25–30 MINUTES

INGREDIENTS

3 tbsp vegetable oil
1 onion, peeled and finely sliced
2 cloves of garlic, finely chopped
2 stalks lemon grass, bruised
2 kaffir lime leaves
1 red chilli (chili), finely sliced
   lengthways
3–4 chicken breasts, skinned and cubed
2 tsp tamarind paste
2 tbsp fish sauce
1 tbsp soft brown sugar or palm sugar
400 ml / 14 fl. oz / 1 ½ cups coconut
   milk
300 ml / 10 fl. oz / 1 ¼ cups chicken
   stock
salt and pepper
1–2 limes, juiced
1 kiwi fruit, peeled and diced

- Heat the oil in a wok or large pan and fry the onion until deep gold and sweet.
- Add the garlic and spices and cook out for 2 minutes.
- Add the cubed chicken and allow to colour on all sides.
- Stir in the tamarind and fish sauce and sugar, then pour over the coconut milk and chicken stock.
- Lower the heat and leave to simmer for 15–20 minutes until the chicken is cooked through.
- Adjust the seasoning and stir in the lime juice just before serving. Sprinkle over diced kiwi once served in the bowls.

67

SERVES 4

Chinese Chicken Soup

PREPARATION TIME:
15 MINUTES

COOKING TIME:
30 MINUTES

INGREDIENTS

2 tbsp vegetable oil
1 onion, peeled and sliced
2 cloves of garlic, finely sliced
1 tsp fresh ginger, grated
1 carrot, peeled and chopped
200 g / 7 oz / ¾ cup mushrooms, sliced
4 chicken thighs, skinned, deboned and
    cut into chunks
500 ml / 1 pint / 2 cups chicken stock
2 tbsp oyster sauce
1 tbsp soy sauce
¼ bunch parsley or coriander (cilantro),
    roughly chopped

- Heat the oil in a large pan and gently cook the onion, garlic and ginger without colouring.
- Add the carrots and mushrooms and cook for 5 minutes until starting to soften.
- Add the chicken, stock and sauces and simmer gently for 20 minutes until cooked.
- Adjust the seasoning and serve with the herbs sprinkled in.

68

SERVES 4

Tex-Mex Chicken Salpicon

PREPARATION TIME:
10 MINUTES

COOKING TIME:
45 MINUTES

INGREDIENTS

2 tbsp olive oil
2 chicken breasts, skinned and cubed
½ cucumber, finely diced
¼ pineapple, finely chopped
½ red onion, peeled and finely diced
1 lime, juiced
1 red chilli (chili), deseeded and finely
    chopped
200 ml / 7 fl. oz / ¾ cup plain yogurt
salt and pepper
fresh coriander (cilantro) leaves

- Heat the oil in a pan and sauté the chicken until golden and cooked through.
- Mix together the cucumber, pineapple, red onion and a little lime juice and season.
- Mix the yogurt with the chilli, more lime juice and seasoning, then spoon into small ramekins.
- Top with the mixed fruit, then the chicken, a little more lime juice and coriander.

69
SERVES 4

Balsamic Chicken Liver Salad

- Heat the butter in a pan and sauté the livers for 4–6 minutes until caramelised and still pink and moussey within. Toss with seasoning and balsamic in the pan.
- Tip the leaves into a bowl and toss with the shallots.
- Spoon the balsamic coated livers onto the leaves. Return the pan to the heat and fry the breadcrumbs quickly until golden.
- Scatter the breadcrumbs over the salad and serve.

PREPARATION TIME:
10 MINUTES

COOKING TIME:
10 MINUTES

INGREDIENTS

40 g / 1 oz butter
500 g / 1 lb / 2 cups chicken livers, trimmed and halved
salt and pepper
2 tbsp balsamic vinegar
500 g / 1 lb / 2 cups baby spinach leaves
2 shallots, peeled and finely sliced into rings
½ bunch chives
4 tbsp breadcrumbs

Chicken Tabbouleh

70
SERVES 4

PREPARATION TIME:
15 MINUTES

COOKING TIME:
20 MINUTES

INGREDIENTS

4 chicken breasts, skin on
2 tbsp olive oil

salt and pepper
1–2 lemons, juiced
300 g / 10 oz / 1 ¼ cups bulghur wheat
400 ml / 14 fl. oz / 1 ½ cups chicken stock
1 bunch parsley, chopped
3 tomatoes, cored and diced
1 red onion, peeled and finely diced

- Preheat the oven to 200°C (180°C fan) / 400F / gas 6.
- Roast the chicken in the oven with a little oil and seasoning for about 20 minutes. Set aside to rest.
- Meanwhile soak the bulghur wheat in the hot stock for 25–30 minutes until tender. Drain off any excess liquid and season. Stir through the parsley, tomatoes and onion and juice of ½ lemon.
- Serve the chicken drizzled with a little lemon juice and the tabbouleh alongside.

Chicken Skewers and Mustard Mayo

71
SERVES 4

PREPARATION TIME:
30 MINUTES

COOKING TIME:
10 MINUTES

INGREDIENTS

4 chicken breasts, skinned and cut into chunks
1 tsp thyme leaves

4 tbsp olive oil
½ lemon, juiced
salt and pepper
1 yellow pepper, deseeded and roughly chopped
1 red pepper, deseeded and roughly chopped
100 g / 3 ½ oz / ½ cup mayonnaise
2–3 tbsp grain mustard
1 tbsp Dijon mustard

- Toss the chicken chunks with thyme, oil, a little lemon juice and seasoning. Leave to marinate for 20 minutes.
- Thread the chicken onto soaked wooden skewers alternating with the peppers.
- Grill or griddle until the chicken is golden and just cooked through – about 8–10 minutes.
- Meanwhile mix the mayo with the mustards and season - you may want a squeeze of lemon juice.
- Serve the hot kebabs with the mustard mayo.

72

SERVES 4

Glazed Chicken Wings

PREPARATION TIME:
10 MINUTES

COOKING TIME:
30–40 MINUTES

....

INGREDIENTS

12–16 chicken wings
2 tbsp soy sauce
1 tbsp paprika
1 tsp cayenne pepper
2–3 tbsp runny honey
salt and pepper
250 g / 9 oz / 1 cup basmati rice, cooked
    and cooled
½ head broccoli, separated into florets
1 carrot, peeled and diced
2 tbsp sesame seeds

- Preheat the oven to 180°C (160°C fan) / 350F / gas 4.
- Tip the wings into a foil-lined roasting tin. Mix together the remaining glaze ingredients and taste – you may want more soy, honey or spice. Pour over the wings and coat thoroughly. Roast in the oven for 30–40 minutes until sticky and cooked.
- Meanwhile cook the rice in boiling salted water according to packet instructions. 3 minutes before the end of cooking time, add the broccoli and carrots to the pan to cook.
- When the rice is tender, drain thoroughly and leave to steam dry.
- Sprinkle the cooked wings with sesame seeds and serve with the rice.

Chicken Wings with Honey Mustard Glaze

73

- Add 1 large tbsp of grain mustard to the glaze for a punch.

74

SERVES 4

Chicken Satay Brochettes

PREPARATION TIME:
15 MINUTES

COOKING TIME:
10 MINUTES

....

INGREDIENTS

8 chicken thighs, boned and skinned
2 shallots, peeled and finely chopped
½ red chilli (chili), finely chopped
2 cloves of garlic, finely chopped
1 cm (½ in) piece fresh ginger, grated
5 tbsp peanut butter
1 tbsp tamarind paste
2 tbsp soy sauce
100 ml / 3 ½ fl. oz / ½ cup coconut milk
1 tsp palm or dark brown sugar
1 tbsp fish sauce
1 lime, juiced
1 carrot, peeled
1 courgette (zucchini)
2 peppers, deseeded and finely sliced
1 tbsp rice vinegar
1 tbsp sugar
1 tsp dried oregano
½ tsp caster (superfine) sugar
salt and pepper

- Halve the chicken pieces.
- Mix together the marinade ingredients and pour half over the chicken pieces.
- Leave to marinate for at least 4 hours or overnight.
- Meanwhile, use a vegetable peeler to cut the carrot and courgette into ribbons and mix with the peppers. Toss with the vinegar, sugar and salt and leave to lightly pickle.
- Skewer with soaked wooden kebab sticks.
- Griddle over a high heat until blackened in patches and cooked through – 6–8 minutes.
- Serve with the pickled vegetables alongside.

Chicken Satay with Rice

75

- Serve the skewers on a bed of boiled rice.

76

SERVES 4

Chicken and Pepper Kebabs

- Toss the chicken chunks with oregano, oil, a little lemon juice and seasoning. Leave to marinate for 20 minutes.
- Thread the chicken onto soaked wooden skewers alternating with the peppers. Add the halved garlic cloves in between the chicken and peppers for extra flavour.
- Grill or griddle until the chicken is golden and just cooked through – about 8–10 minutes.
- Serve with lemon juice squeezed over and a little more salt. Remove the garlic before eating.

PREPARATION TIME:
30 MINUTES

COOKING TIME:
10 MINUTES

INGREDIENTS

4 chicken breasts, skinned and cut into chunks
1 tsp dried oregano
4 tbsp olive oil
½ lemon, juiced
salt and pepper
1 green pepper, deseeded and roughly chopped
1 red pepper, deseeded and roughly chopped
4 garlic cloves, skin on, halved

Chicken Pepper Pittas

77

- Warmed split pitta breads filled with the chicken, peppers and a good dollop of garlic mayo are great for parties.

78

SERVES 4

Chicken, Almond and Coconut Skewers

- Marinate the chicken in the coconut milk, chilli, lime juice and fish sauce for at least 30 minutes.
- Thread onto skewers and barbecue or griddle until cooked – about 8 minutes. Once cooked, roll in the ground almonds.
- Meanwhile whiz the mangos in a liquidiser with the lime juice and a little water to make a smooth sauce.
- Decant into a bowl and sprinkle with a little sea salt, then serve alongside the chicken.

PREPARATION TIME:
5 MINUTES

COOKING TIME:
8–10 MINUTES

INGREDIENTS

4 chicken breasts, skinned and cubed
150 ml / 5 fl. oz / ⅔ cup coconut milk
1 red chilli (chili), chopped
½ lime, juiced
1 tbsp fish sauce
2 tbsp ground almonds
2 mangos, halved, stoned and peeled
1 lime, juiced
sea salt

Chicken Pistachio Coconut Skewers

79

- For extra colour and flavour, roll in finely chopped pistachios.

80

SERVES 4

Stuffed Fennel with Chicken and Raisins

Stuffed Courgettes with Chicken and Raisins

81

- Replace the fennel with courgettes (zucchinis).

Crunchy Stuffed Fennel

82

- Add a few tbsp breadcrumbs before baking to add extra crunch.

PREPARATION TIME:
20 MINUTES

COOKING TIME:
5 MINUTES

INGREDIENTS

4 large fennel bulbs
40 g / 1 oz butter
1 shallot, peeled and finely chopped
2 chicken thighs, deboned and skinned, meat diced
50 g / 1 ¾ oz raisins
80 g / 2 ½ oz / ⅓ cup hazelnuts (cobnuts), chopped
100 ml / 3 ½ fl .oz / ½ cup chicken stock

- Cut the fennel bulbs in half and carefully hollow out the centre, leaving enough leaves intact to make a 'bowl' to put the stuffing in. Finely chop the removed fennel.
- Heat the butter in a pan and sweat the onion and fennel until soft. Add the chicken and cook until golden, then add the raisins, hazelnuts and stock and simmer for 5 minutes.
- Carefully spoon the stuffing into the hollow in each fennel bulb and grill until the hazelnuts are golden.

83

SERVES 4

Chicken with Cantonese Rice

- Slice the chicken into strips. Combine the egg white, cornflour, a pinch of salt and sesame oil in a bowl then thoroughly coat the chicken strips in the mixture.
- Heat the vegetable oil in a wok until smoking, then add the coated chicken and stir fry over a high heat until the chicken turns white.
- Remove the chicken from the pan and set aside. Discard the oil. Add the lemon juice and zest, stock, sugar and soy and cooking wine and bring to a rapid boil.
- Whisk in the cornflour until thickened then return the chicken to the pan for a few minutes to cook through.
- To make the rice: heat the oil in a wok until nearly smoking, then add the onion and garlic and stir fry briskly for 1 minute. Add the eggs and cook for a couple of minutes. Add the rice and meat and combine thoroughly. Stir in some soy sauce and the bean sprouts and peas.
- Serve the Cantonese rice with the chicken.

PREPARATION TIME:
30 MINUTES

COOKING TIME:
20 MINUTES

INGREDIENTS

4 chicken breasts, skinned
1 egg white
2 tsp cornflour (cornstarch)
salt
1 tsp sesame oil
2 tbsp vegetable oil
1 lemon, juiced and zested
100 ml / 3 ½ fl. oz / ½ cup chicken stock
1–2 tsp sugar
splash soy sauce and cooking wine
1 tsp cornflour (cornstarch)
2 tbsp vegetable oil
1 onion, peeled and finely chopped
1 garlic clove, finely chopped
3 eggs, beaten
500 g / 1 lb / 2 cups cooked white rice
3–4 spring onions (scallions), sliced
soy sauce
handful bean sprouts
handful cooked peas

Lemon Chicken with Cantonese Rice

84

- For a real citrus tang, use 3 lemons in the sauce.

85

SERVES 4

Chicken Tomato Roulade

- Preheat the oven to 180°C (160°C fan) / 350F / gas 4
- Whisk the egg whites and lemon juice in a clean bowl to stiff peaks.
- In a separate bowl, whisk together the cornflour, milk, tomato purée and egg yolks until thoroughly combined. Fold carefully into the egg whites with a metal spoon.
- Line a baking tray with greaseproof paper and spoon the mixture onto the tray, spreading it evenly. Cook for 5–10 minutes, until set and golden.
- Meanwhile heat the butter in a pan and sauté the chicken until golden. Stir in the parsley and season.
- When the sponge is cooked, leave to cool. Spread the chicken over the sponge, then use the greaseproof paper to roll into a log shape. Slice and serve with salad.

PREPARATION TIME:
25 MINUTES

COOKING TIME:
10 MINUTES

INGREDIENTS

3 eggs, separated
1 tsp lemon juice
1 tsp cornflour (cornstarch)
200 ml / 7 fl. oz / ¾ cup milk
3–4 tbsp tomato purée
salt and pepper
4 chicken thighs, deboned and skinned, meat diced
30 g / 1 oz butter
½ bunch parsley, finely chopped

Cheesy Roulade

86

- Add mozzarella and wilted spinach to the filling, alongside the chicken.

87

SERVES 2

Lemon Chicken Salad

PREPARATION TIME:
15 MINUTES

....

INGREDIENTS

2 chicken breasts, cooked
2 preserved lemons, chopped
1 tbsp capers, drained
2 tomatoes, cored and chopped
½ bunch parsley, chopped
Small handful sorrel leaves
400 g / 14 oz / 1 ½ cups canned
    chickpeas, drained
salt and pepper
3 tbsp extra virgin olive oil

- Shred the chicken breasts and add to a bowl. Add the lemons, capers, tomatoes, sorrel, parsley and chickpeas and toss to combine.
- Add the oil and season generously and toss, then serve.

Warm Lemon Chicken Salad

 88

- Add the salad to a pan, minus the sorrel leaves, and warm gently, then serve with the sorrel leaves scattered over.

89

MAKES 12

Chicken, Cheese and Herb Empanadas

PREPARATION TIME:
30 MINUTES

COOKING TIME:
15 MINUTES

....

INGREDIENTS

FOR THE PASTRY
350 g / 12 oz / 1 ½ cups plain
    (all-purpose) flour
pinch salt
¼ tsp baking powder
180 g / 6 oz / ¾ cup butter, melted
2 eggs

FOR THE FILLING
2 tbsp olive oil
1 onion, peeled and finely chopped
1 clove of garlic, finely chopped
1 pepper, deseeded and chopped
1 tsp smoked paprika
1 tsp ground cumin
150 g / 5 oz / ⅔ cup mild cheese,
    such as Emmental or Cheddar
200 g / 7 oz / ¾ cup chicken breast,
    cooked and diced
1 bunch parsley, finely chopped
salt and pepper

- Preheat the oven to 200°C (180°C fan) / 400F / gas 6.
- Sieve the flour, salt and baking powder into a bowl and mix in the melted butter and 1 egg, beaten. Gradually stir in 100 ml warm water to make a soft dough. Wrap in cling film and chill for 30 minutes.
- Heat the oil in a pan and sweat the onion until softened. Add the garlic and pepper and cook until softened.
- Add the spices, chicken and a splash of water and cook until hot, season and set aside to cool.
- Roll the pastry out to 3 mm thickness and cut out circles around 15 cm (6 in) in diameter. Divide the filling between the circles, placing it on one half so you can fold the other half over to make a half-moon shape.
- Sprinkle cheese and herbs over the filling, fold the pastry over to enclose the filling and crimp the edges to seal.
- Brush with the remaining egg and bake in the oven for about 15 minutes.

Spicy Chicken Vegetable Empanadas

 90

- Use 1 aubergine (eggplant), diced and 1 finely chopped red chilli (chili) in place of the cheese.

91

SERVES 2

Chicken and Avocado Salad

Chicken Salad with Chicory

 92

- Leaves of chicory would go well with orange, adding a bitter crunch.

Chicken Avocado Salad with Fennel

93

- Add thinly sliced fennel for freshness.

PREPARATION TIME:
10 MINUTES

COOKING TIME:
20 MINUTES

....

INGREDIENTS

2 chicken breasts
1 tbsp olive oil
salt and pepper
1 tsp paprika
1–2 avocadoes, halved and stoned
1 large orange
½ red onion, peeled and finely sliced
    into half moons
2 tbsp extra virgin olive oil

- Preheat the oven to 200°C (180°C fan) / 400F / gas 6.
- Drizzle the chicken with oil, sprinkle with seasoning and paprika and roast for 20 minutes. Leave to rest.
- Chop the avocadoes and tip into a bowl. Peel the orange rind off with a knife, slicing it off to reveal the segments, then cut the segments out of the orange, slicing either side of the white pith, over the bowl to catch any juice. Add the segments to the bowl with the red onion and extra virgin oil and toss gently.
- Spoon carefully onto a plate, slice the chicken and sit on top of the salad. Sprinkle with extra paprika if liked.

94

SERVES 4

Chicken Brochettes with Peach Chutney

PREPARATION TIME:
15 MINUTES

COOKING TIME:
10 MINUTES

....

INGREDIENTS

4 chicken breasts, skinned and cut into
    bite-size pieces
2 tbsp olive oil
1 tsp ground cumin
1 tsp ground coriander
5 peaches, halved and stoned
½ tbsp sugar
6 tbsp extra virgin olive oil
5 basil leaves, finely chopped
10 mint leaves, finely chopped
½ red chilli (chili), finely chopped
    (optional)

- Preheat the oven to 200°C (180°C fan) / 400F / gas 6.
- Toss the chicken cubes in the oil and spices, then coat in
  sesame seeds.
- Thread onto skewers alternating with the red onion and season.
- Cook in the oven on a baking sheet for 8–10 minutes or until the
  chicken is cooked through and juicy.
- Meanwhile place the peaches in a pan with 6 tbsp water and
  the sugar. Simmer gently for 10–15 minutes until tender.
- Leave the peaches to cool, then remove the skins and reserve
  the syrup.
- Whisk the olive oil into the peaches with the herbs and chilli
  if using to give a pulpy-textured chutney.
- Serve with the hot chicken.

Chicken Brochettes with Plum Chutney

95

- Use plums in place of the peaches and add a star
  anise whilst simmering.

96

SERVES 4

Chicken and Vegetable Brochettes

PREPARATION TIME:
30 MINUTES

COOKING TIME:
10 MINUTES

....

INGREDIENTS

4 chicken breasts, skinned and cut into
    chunks
1 tsp dried oregano
4 tbsp olive oil
½ lemon, juiced
salt and pepper
1 yellow pepper, deseeded and roughly
    chopped
1 red pepper, deseeded and roughly
    chopped
1 courgette (zucchini), roughly
    chopped
8–10 cherry tomatoes, halved

- Toss the chicken chunks with oregano, oil, a little lemon juice and
  seasoning. Leave to marinate for 20 minutes.
- Thread the chicken onto soaked wooden skewers alternating with
  the peppers, courgettes and tomatoes.
- Grill or griddle until the chicken is golden and just cooked through
  – about 8–10 minutes.
- Serve with lemon juice squeezed over and a little more salt.

Marinated Chicken Brochettes

97

- Use ready-made curry pastes to marinate the
  chicken before cooking for extra pizzazz.

98

SERVES 4

Chicken Kebabs with Tabbouleh

- Marinate the chicken in oil, thyme, lemon juice and some seasoning for about 30 minutes.
- Meanwhile soak the bulghur wheat in the hot stock for 25–30 minutes until tender. Drain off any excess liquid and season. Stir through the parsley and juice of ½ lemon with the purslane and diced tomatoes.
- Thread the chicken onto skewers and barbecue or griddle for 8–10 minutes until golden and cooked through.
- Serve the chicken drizzled with a little lemon juice and the tabbouleh alongside.

PREPARATION TIME:
10 MINUTES

COOKING TIME:
40 MINUTES

INGREDIENTS

4 chicken breasts, skinned and cubed
2 tbsp olive oil
1 tbsp thyme leaves
1 tbsp lemon juice
salt and pepper
300 g / 10 oz / 1 ¼ cups bulghur wheat
400 ml / 14 fl. oz / 1 ½ cups chicken stock
1 bunch parsley, chopped
½ lemon, juiced
100 g / 3 ½ oz / ½ cup purslane lettuce
2 tomatoes, cored and diced

Chicken Kebabs with Garlic Sauce

99

- Stir 1 clove of crushed garlic and 4 tbsp extra virgin olive oil through 150 ml / 5 fl. oz plain yogurt and drizzle over the chicken.

100

SERVES 4

Crispy Chicken Nuggets

- Cube the chicken and place in a bowl with the buttermilk. Refrigerate for at least 2 hours or even overnight.
- The next day, dip the cubes one at a time into the flour, egg, then cornflakes and lay on a rack to dry slightly.
- Heat 1 cm (½ in) depth oil in a pan and fry the chicken in batches until golden on both sides and cooked through.
- Serve with ketchup for dipping

PREPARATION TIME:
5 MINUTES

COOKING TIME:
10 MINUTES

INGREDIENTS

4 chicken breasts, skinned
300 ml / 10 fl. oz / 1 ¼ cups buttermilk
100 g / 3 ½ oz / ½ cup plain (all-purpose) flour
2 eggs, beaten
200 g / 7 oz / ¾ cup cornflakes, lightly crushed
vegetable oil

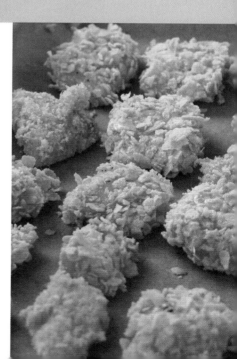

Herby Chicken Nuggets

101

- Sprinkle mixed herbs over the cornflakes for a herby flavour.

102

SERVES 2

Warm Thai Chicken Salad

Thai Pork Salad

 103

- This works well with pork chops, sliced after cooking.

Chicken Salad with Coconut Dressing

104

- Add 2-3 tbsp coconut milk for a rich creamy dressing.

PREPARATION TIME:
10 MINUTES

COOKING TIME:
45 MINUTES

INGREDIENTS

2 chicken breasts
2 tbsp olive oil
salt and pepper
250 g / 9 oz / 1 cup rocket (arugula)
    leaves
10 cherry tomatoes, halved
1 red pepper, deseeded and finely sliced
100 g / 3 ½ oz / ½ cup beansprouts
1 orange, segmented
2 tbsp peanuts or cashew nuts, roughly
    chopped

FOR THE DRESSING

60 ml / 2 fl. oz soy sauce
1 lime, juiced and zested
1 red chilli (chili), finely chopped
1 tsp tamarind paste
2 tsp soft brown sugar

- Heat the oil in a deep-sided frying pan and fry the chicken skin-side down until golden. Turn over and cook for a further 5–6 minutes until cooked through. Set aside, season and keep warm.
- Toss the cold salad ingredients together on a platter.
- Whisk together the ingredients for the dressing, then add to the frying pan and use a wooden spoon to deglaze, scraping any sticky bits into the sauce.
- Shred or slice the chicken and sit on top of the salad. Serve the dressing alongside to spoon over.

105

SERVES 4

Chicken and Tomato Coconut Soup

- Heat the oil in a wok or large pan and fry the onions until deep gold and sweet.
- Add the pepper, garlic and spices and cook out for 2 minutes.
- Add the cubed chicken and allow to colour on all sides.
- Stir in the tamarind and fish sauce and sugar, then pour over the coconut milk and chicken stock.
- Lower the heat and leave to simmer for 15–20 minutes until the chicken is cooked through. Add the tomatoes and simmer for 5 minutes until just collapsing.
- Adjust the seasoning and stir in the lime juice just before serving.

PREPARATION TIME:
15 MINUTES

COOKING TIME:
25–30 MINUTES

INGREDIENTS

3 tbsp vegetable oil
½ bunch spring onions (scallions), finely sliced
1 red pepper, deseeded and chopped
2 cloves of garlic, finely chopped
2 stalks lemon grass, bruised
2 kaffir lime leaves
1 green chilli (chili), finely chopped
1 red chilli (chili), finely chopped
3–4 chicken breasts, skinned and cubed
2 tsp tamarind paste
2 tbsp fish sauce
1 tbsp soft brown sugar
400 ml / 14 fl. oz / 1 ½ cups coconut milk
300 ml / 10 fl. oz / 1 ¼ cups chicken stock
12 cherry tomatoes, halved
salt and pepper
1–2 limes, juiced

Creamy Chicken Soup

106

- Use all stock instead of coconut milk, then stir in 200 ml / 7 fl. oz double (heavy) cream at the end of cooking.

107

SERVES 4

Caramelised Chicken with Date Tabbouleh

- Soak the bulghur wheat in the hot stock for 25–30 minutes until tender. Drain off any excess liquid and season. Stir through the parsley, dates and juice of ½ lemon.
- Heat the oil in a pan and sauté the chicken until white. Add the sugar, vinegar (carefully as it will splutter) and a little seasoning and stir to coat. Bubble up and thicken until sticky.
- Spoon the couscous into serving glasses or ramekins, then top with the sticky chicken. Squeeze over a little lemon juice.

PREPARATION TIME:
5 MINUTES

COOKING TIME:
30 MINUTES

INGREDIENTS

300 g / 10 oz / 1 ¼ cups bulghur wheat
400 ml / 14 fl. oz / 1 ½ cups chicken stock
1 bunch parsley, chopped
150 g / 5 oz / ⅔ cup dates, chopped
2 tbsp olive oil
4 chicken thighs, skinned, deboned and chopped
2 tbsp dark brown sugar
2 tbsp red wine vinegar
salt and pepper
1 lemon, juiced

Apricot Tabbouleh

 108

- Try adding fresh quartered ripe apricots in summer for a fresh tasting tabbouleh.

109

SERVES 4

Chicken Pepper Kebabs

PREPARATION TIME:
30 MINUTES

COOKING TIME:
10 MINUTES

INGREDIENTS

4 chicken breasts, skinned and cut into
  chunks
1 tsp dried oregano
½ bunch parsley, finely chopped
4 tbsp olive oil
½ lemon, juiced
salt and pepper
1 green pepper, deseeded and roughly
  chopped
1 red pepper, deseeded and roughly
  chopped

- Toss the chicken chunks with oregano, parsley, oil, a little lemon juice and seasoning. Leave to marinate for 20 minutes.
- Thread the chicken onto soaked wooden skewers alternating with the peppers.
- Grill or griddle until the chicken is golden and just cooked through – about 8–10 minutes.
- Serve with lemon juice squeezed over and a little more salt.

Chicken Pepper Aubergine Kebabs

110

- Alternate the chicken and peppers with chunks of aubergine (eggplant).

111

SERVES 4

Chicken Meatballs

PREPARATION TIME:
15 MINUTES

COOKING TIME:
20 MINUTES

INGREDIENTS

2 slices stale bread, crusts removed
1 kg / 2 ¼ lbs / 4 ¼ cups minced chicken
1 onion, peeled and grated
1 clove of garlic, crushed
1 lemon, zested
2 tsp dried oregano
salt and pepper
3 tbsp olive oil

- Soak the bread in warm water then squeeze it out. Mix thoroughly with the meat, onions, garlic, lemon zest and oregano and season.
- Form into small balls around 6 cm (2 ½ in) in diameter.
- Heat the oil in a pan and fry the meatballs in batches until golden and cooked through.

Curried Chicken Meatballs

112

- Add 1 tsp garam masala, ground cumin and coriander to the chicken mix instead of the oregano.

113

SERVES 4-8

Tex Mex Chicken Wings

Chicken Wings with Guacamole

114

- A cool creamy guacamole would make a good accompaniment: mash avocadoes with a little hot sauce, lime juice, seasoning and olive oil.

Tex Mex Chicken Nachos

115

- Use chicken thighs instead of wings and shred the meat over nachos to serve.

PREPARATION TIME:
5 MINUTES

COOKING TIME:
30–40 MINUTES

INGREDIENTS

16 chicken wings
2 tbsp smoked paprika
1 lime, juiced
25 ml / 1 fl. oz shot of tequila (optional)
3 jalapeno chillies (chilies), sliced
2 cloves of garlic, crushed
60 ml / 2 fl. oz olive oil

- Mix together all the ingredients for the marinade. Coat the chicken wings thoroughly and marinade for at least 2 hours or overnight.
- Preheat the oven to 200°C (180°C fan) / 400F / gas 6.
- Tip the chicken wings into a foil-lined roasting tin and roast for 30–40 minutes until dark and cooked, turning once during cooking, then serve hot or cold.

116

SERVES 4

Chicken, Olive and Tomato Sandwiches

PREPARATION TIME:
15 MINUTES

COOKING TIME:
10 MINUTES

INGREDIENTS

4 chicken escalopes
2 tbsp olive oil
salt and pepper
4 ripe vine tomatoes, thickly sliced
80 g / 2 ½ oz / ⅓ cup black and green
    olives, stoned and halved
½ cucumber, thinly sliced
1 bunch basil leaves
extra virgin olive oil
4 baguettes, ciabattas or
    submarine rolls

- Heat the oil in a pan and fry the chicken until golden on both sides. When cool, slice into bite-sized pieces.
- Lightly toast the cut insides of the bread.
- Drizzle with extra virgin oil, then lay the chicken slices in the sandwich. Top with tomato and cucumber slices, then season.
- Add a handful of olives and torn basil leaves, drizzle with a little more extra virgin olive oil and lightly press the top of the sandwich on top.
- Char the sandwich in a panini grill, or under the grill for 1 minute.

Crispy Chicken Sandwiches 117

- Coat the chicken in flour, egg and breadcrumbs, then fry for a crisper finish.

118

SERVES 4

Herby Chicken Roulade

PREPARATION TIME:
20 MINUTES

COOKING TIME:
20 MINUTES

INGREDIENTS

4 chicken escalopes, batted out to
    2 cm thick
150 g / 5 oz / ⅔ cup cream cheese
½ bunch parsley, finely chopped
½ bunch tarragon, finely chopped
½ lemon, zested
salt and pepper
30 g / 1 oz butter
12 asparagus spears, trimmed
8 baby carrots, scrubbed
150 g / 5 oz / ⅔ cup mangetout
8 baby turnips, trimmed and scrubbed
400 ml / 14 fl. oz / 1 ½ cups hot
    vegetable stock
salt and pepper

- Spread the chicken escalopes with a thin layer of cream cheese then sprinkle over the chopped herbs, zest and a little seasoning.
- Roll the escalopes tightly into a sausage shape then wrap tightly in cling film.
- Poach in simmering water for about 15 minutes until cooked through.
- Meanwhile, heat the butter in a pan and lightly sweat the vegetables for 5 minutes, then pour over the hot stock and simmer until everything is just tender. You may need to remove vegetables with a slotted spoon as they cook, as the carrots will take longer than the mangetout and asparagus.
- Serve the chicken escalopes sliced with the vegetables and a spoonful or two of the stock.

Spicy Chicken Roulade 119

- Add a teaspoon of chilli powder to the stock for an extra kick.

120

SERVES 4

Chicken and Chive Cream Wraps

- Finely chop or shred the chicken and mix with the shredded vegetables.
- Whisk together the sour cream with chives, lemon juice and seasoning.
- Briefly heat the tortilla wraps to make them more pliable, then fill equally with the chicken mixture.
- Spoon over the chive cream then wrap up and eat.

PREPARATION TIME:
20 MINUTES

....

INGREDIENTS

2 chicken breasts, cooked
2 carrots, peeled and grated
1 cucumber, cut into fine matchsticks
½ iceberg lettuce, shredded
150 ml / 5 fl. oz / ⅔ cup sour cream
1 bunch chives, finely chopped
squeeze of lemon juice
salt and pepper
4 tortilla wraps

Mexican Chicken Wraps

121

- Add lime juice, hot sauce and coriander (cilantro) in the sour cream for a mexican twist.

122

SERVES 8

Chicken Liver and Pine Nut Cake

- Preheat oven to 190°C (170°C fan) / 375F / gas 5.
- Heat the butter in a pan and cook the chicken livers until pink in the centre. Set aside to cool.
- Whisk the eggs and sugar together until pale and thick.
- Sieve the flours, baking powder and salt into a bowl, then fold into the eggs.
- Stir in the oil until incorporated, then add the chicken livers, pine nuts and thyme.
- Grease and line a loaf tin, pour the mixture in, then bake in the oven for about 40 minutes until a skewer inserted into the middle comes out clean.
- Remove to a wire rack and allow to cool.

PREPARATION TIME:
25 MINUTES

COOKING TIME:
40 MINUTES

....

INGREDIENTS

30 g / 1 oz butter
200 g / 6 ½ oz / ¾ cup chicken livers, chopped
3 eggs
1 tsp sugar
235 g / 8 oz /1 cup plain (all-purpose) flour
60 g / 2 oz / ¼ cup potato flour
2 tsp baking powder
½ tsp salt
6 tbsp olive oil
1 tbsp thyme leaves, finely chopped
2 tbsp pine nuts

Chicken Liver and Olive Cake

123

- Replace the pine nuts with sliced, green olives.

124

SERVES 4–6

Chicken and Almond Pastie

Chicken, Pistachio and Fig Pastie

125

- Use chopped pistachios and figs in the parcels instead of almonds and garlic.

Chicken and Basil Pastie

126

- Add 2 tbsp of pesto to the chicken mixture.

PREPARATION TIME:
30 MINUTES

COOKING TIME:
20 MINUTES

INGREDIENTS

4 tbsp olive oil
1 onion, peeled and thickly sliced
2 garlic cloves, finely chopped
2 chicken breasts, skinned and diced
½ tsp ground cinnamon
½ tsp ground cumin
½ tsp ground coriander
100 g / 3 ½ oz / ½ cup almonds, toasted
1 egg yolk
salt and pepper
1 pack filo pastry
120 g / 4 oz / ½ cup butter, melted
2 eggs
1 egg yolk, beaten
icing (confectioners') sugar and ground
    cinnamon, to dust

- Preheat the oven to 200°C (180°C fan) / 400F / gas 6.
- Heat the oil in a pan and sweat the onion and garlic until softened and turning gold. Add the chicken, spices and almonds and sauté until cooked through. Set aside to cool.
- Keeping the remaining filo sheets covered with a damp tea towel, remove one at a time from the pack and brush with melted butter before using.
- Place 2 sheets of pastry on a surface, brush each with melted butter, then top with a little of the chicken mixture. Wrap the pastry around to enclose the filling. Repeat until all the filling and pastry is used up.
- Brush the tops with a little egg wash, then bake in the oven for 15–20 minutes or until the pastry is crisp and golden.
- Lightly dust the top with a little icing sugar and cinnamon before serving.

127

SERVES 4

Chicken and Aubergine Tart

- Preheat the oven to 190°C (170°C fan) / 375F / gas 5.
- Roll the pastry out on a floured surface and use to line 4 individual tart tins. Prick the bottoms with a fork and blind bake for 10 minutes or until pale. Set aside to cool.
- Meanwhile heat the oil in a pan and sweat the shallot and garlic without colouring. Add the aubergine, peppers and chicken, increase the heat and sauté until golden and tender. Season and add the basil.
- Spread the base of the tarts with a little tomato purée, then divide the chicken mixture equally between them.
- Sprinkle over Parmesan, drizzle with extra virgin olive oil and bake for a further 15–20 minutes until golden.

PREPARATION TIME:
20 MINUTES

COOKING TIME:
30 MINUTES

INGREDIENTS

2 sheets ready-rolled shortcrust pastry
3 tbsp olive oil
2 shallots, finely chopped
2 cloves of garlic, crushed
1 aubergine (eggplant), finely diced
1 yellow pepper, deseeded and finely diced
2 chicken breasts, finely diced
¼ bunch basil leaves
salt and pepper
4 tbsp tomato purée
Parmesan, grated
extra virgin olive oil

Chicken Pesto Tarts

128

- Spread the base with pesto for a herby taste.

129

SERVES 4

Chicken Tandoori-Stuffed Potatoes

- Mix the marinade ingredients together and marinade the chicken for at least 1 hour in the refrigerator.
- Meanwhile hollow out the centre of the potatoes to leave room for the stuffing.
- Steam the potatoes over simmering water until just tender to the point of a knife. Set aside.
- Shake off any excess marinade and fry the chicken until cooked and golden, adding excess marinade if it looks dry.
- Using a teaspoon, stuff the tandoori into the hollowed potatoes, then reheat gently in the steamer before serving.

PREPARATION TIME:
15 MINUTES

COOKING TIME:
25 MINUTES

INGREDIENTS

4 skinless chicken breasts, diced evenly
8 large floury potatoes, peeled and turned
FOR THE MARINADE
300 ml / 10 fl. oz / 1 ¼ cups plain yogurt
1 tsp ground cumin
1 tsp ground coriander
1 tsp garam masala
1 tsp ground cinnamon
1 ½ tsp tandoori chilli (chili) powder
1 tsp caster (superfine) sugar
1 clove garlic, minced
salt and pepper

Tandoori-Style Jacket Potatoes

130

- For a quicker supper, try stuffing baked potatoes with the tandoori mixture.

131

MAKES 12

Chicken Mimolette Fondants

PREPARATION TIME:
20 MINUTES

COOKING TIME:
20 MINUTES

INGREDIENTS

2 chicken breasts, skinned and
    finely diced
2 sprigs tarragon, chopped
100 g / 3 ½ oz / ½ cup Mimolette cheese,
    grated
100 ml / 3 ½ fl. oz / ½ cup double
    (heavy) cream
salt and pepper
500 g / 1 lb / 2 cups self-raising flour
80 g / 3 oz / ⅓ cup butter, melted
1 egg, beaten
250 ml / 9 fl. oz / 1 cup milk
30 g / 1 oz butter

- Preheat the oven to 200°C (180°C fan) / 400F / gas 6.
- Heat the butter in a pan and fry the chicken until golden and cooked. Add the tarragon, cheese, cream and seasoning and stir until the cheese has melted and the mixture is hot. Set aside.
- Tip the flour into a bowl and make a well in the centre. Whisk together the wet ingredients and pour into the flour. Mix together roughly until just about incorporated.
- Spoon into a lined muffin tin, filling each hole half full, then top with a generous spoonful of chicken mixture, then another spoonful of the batter to encase it. Bake for about 20 minutes until golden and cooked through at the centre.
- Leave to cool slightly before serving.

Chicken, Cheese and Sun-dried Tomato Fondants

132

- Add chopped sun-dried tomatoes to the mixture for a savoury punch.

133

SERVES 4

Kentucky Corn Chicken

PREPARATION TIME:
5 MINUTES

COOKING TIME:
10 MINUTES

INGREDIENTS

12 chicken wings
300 ml / 10 fl. oz / 1 ¼ cups buttermilk
100 g / 3 ½ oz / ½ cup plain
    (all-purpose) flour
2 eggs, beaten
200 g / 7 oz / ¾ cup cornflakes, lightly
    crushed
1 tsp dried oregano
few drops hot sauce
vegetable oil

- Place the chicken wings in a bowl with the buttermilk. Cool in the fridge for at least 2 hours or even overnight.
- The next day, dip the wings one at a time into the flour, egg then cornflakes and lay on a rack to dry slightly.
- Fill a pan ⅔ full with vegetable oil and heat to 180°C / 350F and fry the chicken wings in batches until golden on both sides and cooked through.
- Serve immediately.

Kentucky Polenta Chicken

134

- Substitute the cornflakes for coarse polenta for a crispy result.

135

MAKES 12

Chicken and Cheese Muffins

Chicken, Cheese and Spinach Muffins

136

- Add 100 g / 3 ½ oz wilted finely chopped spinach to the mix.

Chicken, Tomato and Cheese Muffins

137

- Use chopped sun-dried tomatoes for a richer flavour.

PREPARATION TIME:
15 MINUTES

COOKING TIME:
20–25 MINUTES

INGREDIENTS

225 g / 8 oz / 1 cup self-raising flour
50 g / 1 ¾ oz / ¼ cup rye flour
1 tsp baking powder
½ tsp bicarbonate of (baking) soda
1 tsp salt
1 tsp English mustard powder
pinch cayenne
125 g / 4 oz / ½ cup strong Cheddar, grated
120 g / 4 oz / ½ cup cooked chicken, finely chopped
6 tbsp vegetable oil
150 g / 5 oz / ⅔ cup plain or Greek yogurt
125 ml / 4 fl. oz / ½ cup milk
1 egg

- Preheat the oven to 200°C (180°C fan) / 400F / gas 6.
- Mix together all the dry ingredients in a large bowl, adding the cheese and chicken.
- In another bowl, mix together the liquid ingredients with a fork.
- Pour the liquid ingredients into the dry, mixing with a fork, but don't over-mix – the muffins will be lighter with a lumpy batter.
- Spoon into cases in a muffin tin and bake for 20–25 minutes until golden and risen.
- Allow to cool on a rack before eating.

138

SERVES 4

Coconut Chicken Fondue

PREPARATION TIME:
15 MINUTES

COOKING TIME:
20 MINUTES

....

INGREDIENTS

3 tbsp vegetable oil
1 onion, peeled and finely sliced
2 cloves of garlic, finely chopped
2 stalks lemon grass, bruised
2 kaffir lime leaves
1 red chilli (chili), finely chopped
2 tsp tamarind paste
2 tbsp fish sauce
1 tbsp soft brown sugar or
    palm sugar
400 ml / 14 fl. oz / 1 ½ cups coconut
    milk
300 ml / 10 fl. oz / 1 ¼ cups chicken
    stock
salt and pepper
juice of 1–2 limes
3–4 chicken breasts, skinned
    and cubed
150 g / 5 oz / ⅔ cup peanuts, crushed

- Heat the oil in a wok or large pan and fry the onion until deep gold and sweet.
- Add the garlic and spices and cook out for 2 minutes.
- Stir in the tamarind and fish sauce and sugar, then pour over the coconut milk and chicken stock. Lower the heat and leave to simmer for 10 minutes. Adjust the seasoning and stir in the lime juice just before serving.
- Blanch the chicken in simmering water for 2 minutes just to start the cooking process.
- Pour into fondue bowl set over heat to keep it simmering gently. Dip the chicken pieces in immediately and leave to cook for 5–7 minutes, then retrieve with chopsticks and dip in peanuts before eating.

139

SERVES 4

Chicken and Tomato Terrine

PREPARATION TIME:
1 HOUR

....

INGREDIENTS

2 chicken breasts, steamed and
    finely sliced
1 bunch basil

FOR THE JELLY

1 bunch basil
2 kg / 4 lb ripe tomatoes
knob fresh ginger, peeled and chopped
1 clove of garlic
50 ml / 1 ¾ oz white wine vinegar
salt and pepper
25 g / ¾ oz gelatine, soaked in
    cold water

- Blend the basil, tomatoes, ginger and garlic in a food processor until pulpy then pour into a large bowl lined with muslin. Season generously.
- Carefully lift the corners of the muslin and tie like a knapsack, securing with a hook over the bowl so the liquid can drip through the muslin into the bowl. Leave overnight.
- Squeeze the gelatine dry and stir into the tomato consomme.
- Pour enough consomme into a greased terrine mould to come a third of the way up the sides, then freeze for 10 minutes.
- Layer the chicken and basil on top of the set jelly then pour over the remaining consomme and chill for at least 8 hours or until set.
- Unmould and serve.

140

SERVES 4

Chicken with Breadcrumb Crust

- Place the chicken between 2 pieces of cling film and bat out until a bit thinner with a rolling pin.
- Season, then dunk each chicken into flour, then egg, then the breadcrumbs.
- Heat the oil in a large pan and fry until golden and crisp and the chicken is cooked through – 8–10 minutes.

PREPARATION TIME:
10 MINUTES

COOKING TIME:
10 MINUTES

INGREDIENTS

4 chicken breasts, skinned
salt and pepper
3 tbsp flour
2 eggs, beaten
200 g / 6 ½ oz / ¾ cup dried
  breadcrumbs
olive oil
lemon, sliced

Five-spice Chicken

141

SERVES 4

PREPARATION TIME:
5 MINUTES

COOKING TIME:
10 MINUTES

INGREDIENTS

500 g / 1 lb / 2 cups chicken thigh meat, sliced
2 tsp Chinese 5 spice powder

50 g / 1 ¾ oz / ¼ cup pineapple chunks

FOR THE SAUCE

60 ml / 2 fl. oz cup pineapple juice
splash dry sherry or Shaoxing rice wine
1 tbsp ketchup
1 tbsp soy sauce
1 tbsp Chinese vinegar or red wine
  vinegar
½ tsp cornflour (cornstarch)

- Heat the vegetable oil in a wok until smoking, then add the chicken and 5 spice and stir fry over a high heat until the chicken turns white.
- Add the pineapple and cook briskly until lightly caramelised.
- Mix together the sauce ingredients with the cornflour. Add the chicken back to the pan with the sauce, bubble up until thickened.

Tomato and Chicken Salad

142

SERVES 2

PREPARATION TIME:
15 MINUTES

COOKING TIME:
20 MINUTES

INGREDIENTS

2 chicken breasts, skin on
4 ripe vine tomatoes

salt and pepper
extra virgin olive oil
200 g / 7 oz / ¾ cup cream cheese
½ lemon, juiced
¼ bunch parsley or basil, finely chopped
salt and pepper
1 shallot, sliced

- Preheat the oven to 200°C (180°C fan) / 400F / gas 6.
- Roast the chicken in the oven with a little oil and seasoning until golden and cooked through – about 20 minutes. Set aside to rest.
- Meanwhile quarter the tomatoes and toss with extra virgin olive oil, salt and pepper and leave to macerate.
- Whisk the cream cheese with lemon juice, seasoning and extra virgin olive oil until you make a loose dressing. Stir in the herbs.
- Thickly slice the chicken and toss with the tomatoes and shallot. Drizzle over the dressing and serve.

143

SERVES 4

Chicken and Mushroom Croustade

PREPARATION TIME:
10 MINUTES

COOKING TIME:
15 MINUTES

INGREDIENTS

40 g / 1 oz butter
1 tbsp olive oil
1 shallot, finely chopped
1 clove of garlic, crushed
2 chicken thighs, skinned and deboned,
   cut into chunks
150 g / 5 oz / ⅔ cup chestnut
   mushrooms
100 ml / 3 ½ fl. oz / ½ cup white wine
150 ml / 5 fl. oz / ⅔ cup double (heavy)
   cream
salt and pepper
½ bunch parsley, finely chopped
½ lemon, juiced
4 thick slices sourdough bread
1 spring onion (scallion), sliced

- Heat the butter and oil in a pan and sweat the shallot and garlic.
- Add the chicken and cook briskly for a few minutes, then add the mushrooms and cook until they start to soften.
- Add the white wine and reduce until syrupy, then add the cream and seasoning and simmer until thickened.
- Stir through the parsley.
- Toast the bread. Squeeze a little lemon juice into the chicken mixture and adjust the seasoning, then spoon over the toast. Sprinkle with sliced spring onions and serve.

Chicken and Bacon Croustade 144

- Add 2 rashers of diced and cooked streaky bacon to the chicken.

145

SERVES 4

Chicken with Orange and Sesame Seed

PREPARATION TIME:
5 MINUTES

COOKING TIME:
10 MINUTES

INGREDIENTS

2 tbsp vegetable oil
1 shallot, finely chopped
2 chicken breasts, skinned and chopped
2 oranges, zested and juiced
200 ml / 7 fl. oz / ¾ cup chicken stock
1 tbsp soy sauce
2 tbsp sesame seeds
salt and pepper
1 spring onion (scallion), sliced
cooked white rice, to serve

- Heat the oil in a wok and fry the shallot and chicken briskly until golden.
- Add the orange zest, juice and chicken stock and simmer for 5 minutes until reduced, then stir in the soy.
- Sprinkle over the sesame seeds, season, then serve with white rice and sliced spring onions.

Citrus Chicken with Sesame Seeds 146

- Try adding lime or grapefruit juice with the orange for zing.

147

SERVES 4

Curried Chicken Sandwich

- Cube the chicken, toss with the curry paste and leave to marinate in the refrigerator for 30 minutes.
- Griddle or fry the chicken in a pan until golden and sizzling and just cooked through. Squeeze over the lemon juice, season and set aside.
- Meanwhile whisk the yogurt with the seasoning, lemon juice and mint.
- Slice the bagels in half and spoon the chicken onto the bottom half. Add tomatoes, onion and rocket leaves, then spoon over the dressing. Top with the bagel halves and serve.

PREPARATION TIME:
10 MINUTES

COOKING TIME:
10 MINUTES

INGREDIENTS

4 chicken breasts, skinned
4 tbsp tikka masala paste
100 ml / 3 ½ fl.oz / ½ cup plain yogurt
salt and pepper
½ lemon, juiced
½ bunch mint, finely chopped
2 tomatoes, thickly sliced
8 sun-dried tomatoes
1 red onion, peeled and finely sliced
rocket (arugula) leaves
4 seeded bagels

Spicy Curry Chicken Sandwich 148

- Adding a chopped red chilli to the marinade will add fire to the chicken.

149

SERVES 4

Chicken and Vegetable Salad

- You could leave the cauliflower florets raw if liked but if not, simply steam for a couple of minutes over simmering water.
- Shred the chicken and tip into a bowl with the diced vegetables and cauliflower florets.
- Whisk together the oil, lime and seasoning and toss with the salad.

PREPARATION TIME:
10 MINUTES

INGREDIENTS

2 chicken breasts, cooked
½ head cauliflower, separated
    into florets
250 g / 9 oz / 1 cup sweetcorn
150 g / 5 oz / ⅔ cup green beans, diced .
1 red pepper, deseeded and
    finely chopped
2 tbsp extra virgin olive oil
1 lime, juiced
salt and pepper

Chicken and Bean Salad   150

- Add 400 g / 14 oz / 1 ½ cups canned cannellini beans, drained for bulk.

Chicken and Galangal Soup

151

SERVES 4

Chicken and Pumpkin Soup

152

- Adding diced pumpkin with the chicken adds colour and substance to the dish.

Chicken Soup with Prawns

153

- Add cooked tiger prawns for an extra delicacy.

PREPARATION TIME:
10 MINUTES

COOKING TIME:
25 MINUTES

INGREDIENTS

1 tbsp vegetable oil
1 onion, peeled and finely sliced
2 cloves of garlic, finely sliced
2 cm (1 in) piece galangal, finely sliced
1 stalk lemon grass, bruised
3 curry leaves
1 red chilli (chili), finely sliced
400 ml / 14 fl. oz / 1 ½ cups coconut milk
250 ml / 9 fl. oz / 1 cup chicken stock
2 chicken breasts, skinned and sliced
2 tbsp fish sauce
1 lime, juiced
½ bunch fresh coriander (cilantro), chopped

- Heat the oil in a pan and sweat the onion and garlic without colouring.
- Add the spices and cook for a few minutes until the scent is released, then pour in the coconut milk and stock.
- When simmering, add the chicken pieces and simmer gently for 15 minutes or until the chicken is cooked.
- Season the soup with the fish sauce and lime juice and serve sprinkled with coriander.

154

SERVES 4

Chicken and Feta Pittas

- Heat the oil in a pan and sauté the chicken until golden and cooked through. Season and set aside.
- Lightly toast or grill the pitta breads until puffed up and split in half.
- Mix the yogurt, dill and seasoning in a bowl.
- Fill the pittas with the chicken, tomatoes, shredded lettuce and drizzle over the yogurt before serving.

PREPARATION TIME:
15 MINUTES

COOKING TIME:
10 MINUTES

INGREDIENTS

2 tbsp olive oil
2 chicken breasts, cut into chunks
4 pitta breads
2 ripe tomatoes, cut into chunks
4 lettuce leaves
100 g / 3 ½ oz / ½ cup feta cheese
4 tbsp plain yogurt
½ bunch dill, finely chopped
salt and pepper

Marinated Chicken Pittas

155

- Toss the chicken pieces in lemon juice and chilli (chili) flakes before cooking.

156

SERVES 4

Chicken Quiche

- Preheat the oven to 200°C (180°C fan) / 400F / gas 6 and put in a baking sheet to warm.
- Rub the butter into the flour with the salt until you have coarse breadcrumbs. Add water a little at a time using a round-bladed knife to mix until the mixture just comes together. Form into a ball, cover with cling film and refrigerate for 20–30 minutes.
- Fry the chicken in the butter until golden.
- Roll out the pastry and press it gently into 4 individual lightly greased flan tins. Prick all over with a fork and bake in the oven on the baking sheet for 10 minutes until pale gold.
- Spoon the chicken evenly over the pastry base. Whisk together the eggs, cream, cheese and tarragon and season, then pour in, adding a little pepper but careful on the salt.
- Bake in the oven for 25 minutes until just set.

PREPARATION TIME:
50 MINUTES

COOKING TIME:
35 MINUTES

INGREDIENTS

2 chicken breasts, skinned and diced
30 g / 1 oz butter
½ bunch tarragon, finely chopped
100 g / 3 ½ oz / ½ cup Gruyère cheese, grated
2 eggs, plus 1 egg yolk
300 ml / 10 fl. oz / 1 ¼ cups double (heavy) cream
salt and pepper
FOR THE QUICHE PASTRY
110 g / 3 ½ oz / ½ cup plain (all-purpose) flour
50 g / 1 ¾ oz / ¼ cup cold, diced butter
pinch salt
cold water, to mix

Chicken and Bacon Quiche

157

- Add 2 diced and cooked bacon rashers to the egg mixture, before cooking.

158

MAKES 12

Chicken Cheddar Fondants

PREPARATION TIME:
20 MINUTES

COOKING TIME:
20 MINUTES

....

INGREDIENTS

2 chicken breasts, skinned
    and finely diced
2 sprigs tarragon, chopped
100 g / 3 ½ oz / ½ cup mature Cheddar
    cheese, grated
100 ml / 3 ½ fl. oz / ½ cup double
    (heavy) cream
salt and pepper
500 g / 1 lb / 2 cups self-raising flour
80 g / 3 oz / ⅓ cup butter, melted
1 egg, beaten
250 ml / 9 fl. oz / 1 cup milk
30 g / 1 oz butter

- Preheat the oven to 200°C (180°C fan) / 400F / gas 6.
- Heat the butter in a pan and fry the chicken until golden and cooked. Add the tarragon, cheese, cream and seasoning and stir until the cheese has melted and the mixture is hot. Set aside.
- Tip the flour into a bowl and make a well in the centre. Whisk together the wet ingredients and pour into the flour. Mix together roughly until just about incorporated.
- Spoon into a lined muffin tin, filling each hole half full, then top with a generous spoonful of chicken mixture, then another spoonful of the batter to encase it. Bake for about 20 minutes until golden and cooked through at the centre.
- Leave to cool slightly before serving.

Chicken Rosemary Fondants   159

- Add the same amount of chopped rosemary in place of the tarragon.

160

SERVES 4

Crunchy Chicken Wings with Asparagus

PREPARATION TIME:
10 MINUTES

COOKING TIME:
15 MINUTES

....

INGREDIENTS

8 chicken breasts
300 ml / 10 fl. oz / 1 ¼ cups buttermilk
100 g / 3 ½ oz / ½ cup plain
    (all-purpose) flour
2 eggs, beaten
200 g / 7 oz / ¾ cup breadcrumbs,
vegetable oil
16 asparagus stalks, trimmed
40 g / 1 oz butter
salt and pepper

- Place the chicken in a bowl with the buttermilk. Refrigerate for at least 2 hours or even overnight.
- Dip the chicken wings one at a time into the flour, egg then breadcrumbs and lay on a rack to dry slightly.
- Heat enough oil in a pan to be two-thirds full. It is hot enough when a cube of bread dropped in sizzles immediately. Fry the chicken in batches until golden on both sides and cooked through. Drain on kitchen paper.
- Steam the asparagus for 4–5 minutes until just tender, then toss in butter and seasoning. Serve with the chicken.

Kicking Chicken Wings   161

- Spice up the breadcrumbs with cayenne, mustard and paprika.

162

SERVES 4

Tequila Chicken Kebabs

Bloody Mary Chicken　163

- Try using tomato juice, vodka and parsley in the marinade and cook the same way.

Festival Tequila Chicken　164

- Add chopped red and green peppers to the skewers, between each chunk of chicken.

PREPARATION TIME:
5 MINUTES

COOKING TIME:
10 MINUTES

INGREDIENTS

4 chicken breasts, skinned and cubed
150 ml / 5 fl. oz / ⅔ cup tequila
zest of 1 lime
1 red chilli (chili), sliced
salt and pepper
2 limes, sliced
½ bunch fresh coriander (cilantro)

- Marinate the chicken in tequila, lime zest, chilli and seasoning for 30 minutes.
- Thread onto soaked wooden skewers, alternating with slices of lime.
- Griddle over high heat until golden and cooked through.
- Reduce the marinade in a small pan until syrupy.
- Sprinkle with coriander and serve with the reduced sauce drizzled over.

165

SERVES 4

Chicken Tandoori with Bulghur

PREPARATION TIME:
25 MINUTES

COOKING TIME:
10 MINUTES

INGREDIENTS

4 skinless chicken breasts,
   diced evenly
300 g / 10 oz / 1 ¼ cups bulghur wheat
400 ml / 14 fl. oz / 1 ½ cups chicken
   stock
salt and pepper
FOR THE MARINADE
300 ml / 10 fl. oz /1 ¼ cups plain yogurt
1 tsp ground cumin
1 tsp ground coriander
1 tsp garam masala
1 tsp ground cinnamon
1 ½ tsp tandoori chilli (chili) powder
1 tsp caster (superfine) sugar
1 clove garlic, minced
salt and pepper

- Prepare the tandoori marinade by mixing together all the ingredients for the marinade in a mixing bowl. Add the chicken, mix well, then cover and chill for at least 1 hour.
- Meanwhile soak the bulghur wheat in the hot stock for 25–30 minutes until tender. Drain off any excess liquid and season.
- Preheat the grill to hot. Remove the chicken from the marinade, shaking off any excess, and thread onto the wooden skewers.
- Grill for 8–10 minutes, turning occasionally until lightly charred and cooked through.
- Place the tandoori chicken skewers on top of the bulghur and serve.

Chicken Tandoori with Tzatziki

 166

- Toss ½ grated cucumber with 4 tbsp plain yogurt and ¼ bunch chopped mint leaves and a little seasoning and serve spooned over the chicken.

167

SERVES 4

Chicken and Apple Kebabs

PREPARATION TIME:
10 MINUTES

COOKING TIME:
10 MINUTES

INGREDIENTS

4 chicken breasts, skinned and cut into
   chunks
2 cooking apples, cut into chunks
   (reserve some for the salad)
2 tbsp olive oil
salt and pepper
mixed salad leaves
apple sauce, to serve

- Thread the chicken pieces onto wooden skewers, alternating with the apples, then brush with oil and season.
- Griddle the chicken kebabs over high heat for about 8–10 minutes until the chicken is golden and cooked through.
- Serve the kebabs with the salad leaves, reserved apple and apple sauce.

Sticky Chicken Kebabs

168

- Brush the chicken and figs with a little runny honey during cooking.

169

MAKES 40

Balsamic Chicken and Tomato Crostini

- Preheat the oven to 200°C (180°C fan) / 400F / gas 6.
- Cut the baguette into slices about ½ cm thick. You should get around 40 out of a baguette. Place on baking sheets and brush lightly with olive oil. Bake in the oven for about 5–10 minutes until pale gold. Remove and leave to cool.
- Heat 2–3 tbsp olive oil in a pan and sauté the chicken and garlic until golden. Deglaze with balsamic and thyme leaves and season. Toss in the sesame seeds until coated.
- Toss the chicken with the cherry tomatoes and spoon onto the crostini and serve.

PREPARATION TIME:
20 MINUTES

COOKING TIME:
10 MINUTES

....

INGREDIENTS

1 baguette
olive oil
400 g / 14 oz / 1 ½ cups diced chicken
    meat, preferably from the thighs
1 large clove of garlic, crushed
2–3 tbsp balsamic vinegar
2 tbsp thyme leaves
2 tbsp sesame seeds
salt and pepper
200 g / 7 oz / ¾ cup cherry tomatoes,
    quartered

Persian Chicken Crostini

170

- Twist the recipe by using pomegranate molasses instead of balsamic for a sweet-sour flavour.

171

SERVES 8

Savoury Chicken Carrot Cake

- Preheat oven to 190°C (170°C fan) / 375F / gas 5.
- Whisk the eggs and sugar together until pale and thick.
- Sieve the flours, baking powder and salt into a bowl, then fold into the eggs. Stir in the ricotta and oil until incorporated.
- Fold in the chicken and carrots with the thyme until well combined.
- Grease and line a loaf tin, then pour the mixture in.
- Bake in the oven for about 40 minutes until a skewer inserted into the middle comes out clean.
- Remove to a wire rack and allow to cool before slicing.

PREPARATION TIME:
25 MINUTES

COOKING TIME:
40 MINUTES

....

INGREDIENTS

3 eggs
1 tsp sugar
235 g / 8 oz / 1 cup plain (all-purpose)
    flour
60 g / 2 oz / ¼ cup potato flour
2 tsp baking powder
½ tsp salt
6 tbsp olive oil
2 tbsp ricotta
200 g / 6 ½ oz / ¾ cup cooked chicken,
    finely chopped
2 large carrots, peeled and grated
3 sprigs thyme leaves, chopped

Crunchy Chicken Carrot Cake

172

- 2–3 tbsp finely chopped walnuts stirred into the mix will add crunch.

173

SERVES 4

Thai Chicken Bites

Thai Chicken Bites with Rice

174

- Serve with plain cooked white rice to soak up the sauce.

Chicken Bites in Boats

175

- Serve in little gem lettuce leaves for a carb-free dinner.

PREPARATION TIME:
10 MINUTES

COOKING TIME:
15 MINUTES

INGREDIENTS

4 chicken breasts, skinned and cut into bite-size pieces
1 red chilli (chili), finely chopped
½ bunch spring onions (scallions), sliced
2 cloves of garlic, crushed
2 stalks lemon grass, bruised
2 tsp fresh galangal or ginger, grated
3 tbsp fish sauce
1 lime, zested
1 tbsp dark brown sugar
1 tbsp groundnut oil

- Marinade the chicken in the rest of the ingredients for at least 1 hour.
- Heat the oil in a wok and sauté the chicken in batches if necessary with the marinade until the chicken is cooked, golden and sticky.
- Serve hot.

176

SERVES 4

Pekinese Chicken Soup

- Heat the oils in a wok and stir fry the spring onions, garlic and ginger for 2 minutes.
- Add the chicken and mushrooms and stir fry until golden. Pour over the stock, add the soy and sugar and simmer gently for 20 minutes.
- Stir in the sesame oil, add the chervil and serve in deep bowls.

PREPARATION TIME:
10 MINUTES

COOKING TIME:
25 MINUTES

INGREDIENTS

1 tbsp groundnut oil
1 tsp chilli (chili) oil
1 bunch spring onions (scallions), finely sliced
2 cloves of garlic, finely sliced
1 tbsp fresh ginger, grated
4 chicken thighs, skinned, deboned and cut into large pieces
150 g / 5 oz / ⅔ cup Chinese or wild mushrooms, cleaned and rehydrated if necessary
500 ml / 1 pint / 2 cups chicken stock
2 tbsp soy sauce
1 tsp sugar
2 tsp sesame oil
½ bunch chervil chopped

Pekinese Chicken Noodle Soup

177

- To add heft, cook noodles in the stock for 5 minutes before the end of cooking.

178

SERVES 4–8

Thai Chicken Nems

- Heat the oil in a wok until nearly smoking, then fry the chicken for 2 minutes. Add the fish sauce, then remove with a slotted spoon and set aside to cool. Wipe the wok clean.
- Place the vegetables in a bowl with the mint and chilli, then add the chicken mixture and stir to combine.
- Lay 2 spring roll wrappers on top of one another. Place 2 tbsp filling in the centre then roll the wrapper up, sealing the edges with the cornflour mixed with water to make a paste. Repeat until all the wrappers are used up.
- Fill the wok a quarter-full with oil and heat until a cube of bread turns golden and sizzles when thrown in. Deep fry the spring rolls in batches for 3 minutes, turning carefully, until golden and crisp.
- Drain on kitchen paper and serve.

PREPARATION TIME:
10 MINUTES

COOKING TIME:
20 MINUTES

INGREDIENTS

1 tbsp groundnut oil, plus oil for deep-frying
200 g / 7 oz / ¾ cup chicken breast, skinned and finely chopped
1 tbsp fish sauce
1 carrot, peeled and cut into fine batons
100 g / 3 ½ oz / ½ cup fine green beans, steamed
2 spring onions (scallions), finely sliced lengthways
¼ bunch mint leaves
1 red chilli (chili), finely chopped
16 ready made spring roll wrappers
1 tsp cornflour (cornstarch)
1 tbsp water

Chicken Nems with Dipping Sauce

179

- Mix together 2 tbsp fish sauce, juice of ½ lime, finely chopped red chilli (chili) and 1 tsp sugar for a sweet-sharp contrast.

180

SERVES 4

Chicken, Ham and Apple Bagel

PREPARATION TIME:
10 MINUTES

COOKING TIME:
5 MINUTES

INGREDIENTS

4 bagels
4 slices Parma ham
2 chicken breasts, cooked and sliced
1 red apple, cut into matchsticks
2 tbsp grain or Dijon mustard
salt and pepper

- Split the bagels and toast lightly.
- Heat a dry frying pan and fry the parma ham slices until crisp and darkened on both sides – about 2 minutes per side.
- Spread the bottom bagel halves with a little mustard, then lay the ham slices on top. Place the chicken slices on top and then arrange the apple matchsticks and sandwich with the remaining bagel halves.

Chicken and Blue Cheese Bagels

181

- Slices of Gorgonzola cheese would make a flavoursome addition.

182

SERVES 2

Chicken and Broccoli Salad

PREPARATION TIME:
10 MINUTES

COOKING TIME:
3 MINUTES

INGREDIENTS

2 chicken breasts, cooked
1 head broccoli, separated into florets
1 red pepper, deseeded and sliced
2 ripe tomatoes, cored and cut into
    wedges
200 ml / 7 fl. oz / ¾ cup creme fraîche
1 clove of garlic, crushed
3 tbsp Parmesan, grated
1 tbsp lemon juice
salt and pepper

- Shred the chicken into small pieces and place in a bowl.
- Steam the broccoli florets for 3 minutes until crisp-tender, then add to the chicken with the peppers and tomatoes.
- Mix together the creme fraîche, garlic, Parmesan, lemon and seasoning.
- Toss the salad in the dressing and serve.

Light Chicken Salad

 183

- Use yogurt instead of creme fraîche and forego the Parmesan.

184

SERVES 6–8

Chicken Pâté in Pastry Crust

Chicken and Bacon Terrine

185

- Add 220 g / 8 oz chopped streaky bacon for extra flavour or try using rabbit meat.

Chicken and Pistachio Terrine

186

- Add a handful of shelled pistachios to the mix before cooking.

PREPARATION TIME:
30 MINUTES

COOKING TIME:
40 MINUTES

INGREDIENTS

500 g / 1 lb / 2 cups chicken
3 tbsp olive oil
200 ml / 7 fl. oz / ¾ cup white wine
1 tsp coriander seeds, crushed
1 tbsp thyme leaves
2 tbsp chervil, chopped
2 tbsp parsley, chopped
2 eggs
2 tbsp double (heavy) cream
salt and pepper
500 g / 1 lb puff pastry
flour, for dusting
1 egg, beaten

- Cut the chicken into large chunks and marinate with the wine and oil for 1 hour.
- Preheat the oven to 200°C (180°C fan) / 400F / gas 6.
- Remove the meat from the marinade and place in a food processor, add the herbs and spices, eggs and cream and seasoning and pulse until finely chopped.
- Cut the pastry in half. Roll out on a floured surface to 20 cm x 30 cm (8 in x 11 in) and repeat with the other half. Place one rectangle on a greased baking sheet. Spoon the chicken mixture down the middle, pull the pastry up the sides, then cover with the second rectangle. Cut away any excess, wet the edges with a little water and seal securely all the way round.
- Cut a hole in the top to allow the steam to escape. Brush with eggwash and bake for 20 minutes.
- Reduce the heat to 180°C (160°C fan) / 350F / gas 4 and cook for a further 20 minutes until deep golden brown.
- Leave to rest for at least 30 minutes before slicing.

187

SERVES 2

Indian Chicken Burger

PREPARATION TIME:
15 MINUTES

COOKING TIME:
5 MINUTES

INGREDIENTS

2 chicken escalopes, batted out to 1cm
  thickness
3 tbsp flour, seasoned
2 eggs, beaten
1 tsp ground cumin
1 tsp ground coriander
½ tsp turmeric
1 heaped tsp garam masala
200 g / 6 ½ oz / ¾ cup breadcrumbs
100 ml / 3 ½ fl. oz / ½ cup vegetable oil
½ cucumber, sliced
2 iceberg lettuce leaves
2 focaccia or pitta breads, split
4 tbsp plain yogurt
¼ bunch mint leaves, finely shredded
4 tbsp mango chutney

- Dip the chicken in the flour, eggs and breadcrumbs mixed with
  the spices.
- Heat the oil in a deep-sided pan and shallow-fry the chicken on
  both sides until golden and crisp.
- Fill the split breads with mango chutney, cucumber and lettuce,
  then top with the chicken. Spoon over the yogurt and serve.

Indian Burger with Spicy Yogurt Sauce
188

- Try stirring lime pickle into the yogurt.

189

SERVES 4

Chicken, Mango and Rocket Wrap

PREPARATION TIME:
15 MINUTES

INGREDIENTS

200 g / 7 oz / ¾ cup mild goats' cheese
1 ½ tsp smoked paprika
2 chicken breasts, cooked and sliced
1 ripe mango, peeled, stoned and sliced
salt and black pepper
50 g / 1 ¾ oz / ¼ cup rocket (arugula)
4 tortilla wraps

- Mash the goats' cheese with the paprika.
- Briefly warm the tortillas to make them pliable, then spoon
  equal quantities of the cheese down the middle.
- Top with slices of chicken and mango, then season.
- Top with rocket and wrap to serve.

Chicken, Apple and Rocket Wrap
190

- Slices of crisp tart eating apple make a good foil to
  the cheese and rocket.

191

SERVES 4

Chicken and Mascarpone Soufflé

- Preheat the oven to 200°C (180°C fan) / 400F / gas 6.
- Melt the butter in a pan and stir in the flour. When smooth gradually add the milk, whisking after each addition. Once all the milk has been added, stir in the cheese over a low heat, then season and add the cayenne, a little nutmeg and stir in the chicken.
- Mix the 2 egg yolks into the cheese mixture.
- Whisk the 4 egg whites in a large clean mixing bowl to stiff peaks.
- Fold 1 tbsp of the whites into the cheese mixture to loosen, then, using a metal spoon, carefully fold in the rest in a figure of eight motion to keep the air.
- Spoon the mixture into 4 individual ones and sprinkle with Parmesan. Place in a roasting in and fill the tin with about 4 cm (1 ½ in) of boiling water. Place in the oven and bake for 25–30 minutes. Do not open the door.
- When cooked the soufflé should be risen and golden.

PREPARATION TIME:
25 MINUTES

COOKING TIME:
25–30 MINUTES

....

INGREDIENTS

30 g / 1 oz butter
2 tbsp plain (all-purpose) flour
150 ml / 5 fl. oz / ⅔ cup milk
60 g / 2 oz / ⅓ cup mascarpone cheese
60 g / 2 oz / ⅓ cup strong Cheddar, grated
pinch cayenne pepper
nutmeg
150 g / 5 oz / ⅔ cup cooked chicken, finely chopped
2 large eggs, separated
2 egg whites
salt and pepper
1 tbsp Parmesan, grated

Chicken, Mascarpone and Pancetta Soufflé

192

- Fold in 60 g / 2 oz / ⅓ cup cooked, diced pancetta into the mix for a deeply savoury finish.

193

SERVES 4-8

Chicken Nems

- Heat the oil in a wok until nearly smoking, then fry the chicken for 2 minutes. Add the soy and five spice, then remove with a slotted spoon and set aside to cool. Wipe the wok clean.
- Place the vegetables in a bowl with the ginger, then add the chicken mixture and stir to combine.
- Lay 2 spring roll wrappers on top of one another. Place 2 tbsp filling in the centre then roll the wrapper up, sealing the edges with the cornflour mixed with water to make a paste. Repeat until all the wrappers are used up.
- Fill the wok a quarter-full with oil and heat until a cube of bread turns golden and sizzles when thrown in. Deep fry the spring rolls in batches for 3 minutes, turning carefully, until golden and crisp.
- Drain on kitchen paper and serve.

PREPARATION TIME:
10 MINUTES

COOKING TIME:
20 MINUTES

....

INGREDIENTS

1 tbsp groundnut oil, plus oil for deep-frying
200 g / 7 oz / ¾ cup chicken breast, skinned and finely chopped
1 tbsp soy sauce
½ tbsp five-spice powder
1 carrot, peeled and cut into fine batons
1 red pepper, deseeded and finely sliced
2 spring onions (scallions), finely sliced lengthways
1 tsp fresh ginger, grated
16 ready made spring roll wrappers
1 tsp cornflour (cornstarch)
1 tbsp water

Chicken Nems with Spicy Sauce

194

- Mix together 2 tbsp soy sauce, 1 tbsp rice vinegar, finely chopped red chilli (chili) and 1 tsp sugar for a sweet-sharp contrast.

195

SERVES 4

Chicken, Apple and Peanut Skewers

Chicken and Pear Skewers

196

- This works well with slightly under-ripe pears cut into chunks.

Chicken Goats' Cheese Skewers

197

- Add chunks of goats' cheese to the skewers.

PREPARATION TIME:
15 MINUTES

COOKING TIME:
15 MINUTES

INGREDIENTS

250 g / 9 oz / 1 cup Bramley apples, peeled and roughly chopped
250 g / 9 oz / 1 cup Cox apples, peeled and roughly chopped
1 tbsp sugar (optional, depending on tartness of apples and usage)
2 cloves
2 tbsp water
1 tbsp cider vinegar
2 chicken breasts, skinned and cut into bite-size pieces
1 eating apple, cored and cut into wedges
30 g / 1 oz butter, melted
2 tbsp peanuts, crushed

- Peel and core the apples and cut into chunks. Place in a pan with the sugar, cloves, vinegar and water and cover with a lid.
- Cook over a low heat for 10–15 minutes, checking occasionally, until the apples have 'exploded' to a fine purée and are soft. Beat to a purée and remove the cloves.
- Thread the chicken onto skewers with the apple and brush with melted butter whilst cooking over a medium griddle. Cook until golden and the apple softens.
- Sprinkle with peanuts and serve with the apple sauce to dip.

198

SERVES 4

Sesame Chicken with Mango Chutney

- Roll the chicken pieces in oil, sesame, 5 spice and seasoning.
- Thread onto soaked wooden skewers and griddle over medium heat until cooked through – about 8 minutes.
- Serve with the mango chutney.

PREPARATION TIME:
5 MINUTES

COOKING TIME:
8–10 MINUTES

INGREDIENTS

4 chicken thighs, skinned, deboned and
    cut into chunks
2 tbsp olive oil
2 tbsp sesame seeds
1 tsp dried 5 spice powder
salt and pepper
100 g / 3 ½ oz / ½ cup mango chutney

Indian Sesame Skewers

199

- Substitute the 5 spice for garam masala and serve with hot lime pickle.

200

SERVES 2

Grilled Pepper Chicken

- Coat the chicken with oil, then press peppercorns onto both sides and season.
- Heat a griddle pan and cook for 5 minutes on each side until cooked through. Leave to rest.
- Mix the yogurt with the cucumber and seasoning.
- Serve the chicken sliced , yogurt dressing spooned alongside with some salad.

PREPARATION TIME:
10 MINUTES

COOKING TIME:
10–12 MINUTES

INGREDIENTS

2 chicken breasts, skinned
2 tbsp olive oil
1 tbsp mixed peppercorns, crushed
salt
200 ml / 7 fl. oz / ¾ cup plain yogurt
½ cucumber, cut into fine batons
mixed salad

Grilled Chicken with Hot Peppercorn Sauce

201

- Stir the crushed peppercorns into 200 ml / 7 fl. oz double (heavy) cream and simmer until thickened.

202

SERVES 4

Chicken Tandoori Brochettes

PREPARATION TIME:
25 MINUTES

COOKING TIME:
10 MINUTES

INGREDIENTS

4 chicken thighs, skinned, deboned
   and cubed
1 cucumber, thickly sliced
1 tsp salt
150 ml / 5 fl. oz / ⅔ cup plain yogurt
½ bunch mint leaves, finely sliced
1 clove of garlic, crushed

FOR THE MARINADE

1 tsp ground cumin
1 tsp ground coriander
1 tsp garam masala
1 tsp ground cinnamon
1 ½ tsp tandoori chilli (chili) powder
1 tsp caster (superfine) sugar
1 clove garlic, minced
salt and pepper

- Prepare the tandoori marinade by mixing together all the ingredients for the marinade in a mixing bowl. Add the chicken, mix well, then cover and chill for at least 1 hour.
- Meanwhile toss the cucumber with the salt and leave to drain in a sieve to draw out excess water.
- Mix the yogurt with the mint, garlic and seasoning and set aside.
- Thread the chicken onto skewers and griddle or barbecue for about 10 minutes until cooked through.
- Pat the cucumber dry, then serve alongside the skewers and minted yogurt.

Chicken Tandoori Pittas 203

- Stuff the chicken pieces and cucumber into split pittas and drizzle with the yogurt.

204

SERVES 4

Spicy Chicken Coconut Soup

PREPARATION TIME:
15 MINUTES

COOKING TIME:
25–30 MINUTES

INGREDIENTS

3 tbsp vegetable oil
1 onion, peeled and finely sliced
1 yellow pepper, deseeded and chopped
2 cloves of garlic, finely chopped
2 stalks lemon grass, bruised
2 kaffir lime leaves
1 green chilli (chili), finely chopped
1 red chilli (chili), finely chopped
3–4 chicken breasts, skinned
   and cubed
2 tsp tamarind paste
2 tbsp fish sauce
1 tbsp soft brown sugar or palm sugar
400 ml / 14 fl. oz / 1 ½ cups coconut
   milk
300 ml / 10 fl. oz / 1 ¼ cups chicken
   stock
salt and pepper
1–2 limes, juiced

- Heat the oil in a wok or large pan and fry the onion until deep gold and sweet.
- Add the pepper, garlic and spices and cook out for 2 minutes.
- Add the cubed chicken and allow to colour on all sides.
- Stir in the tamarind and fish sauce and sugar, then pour over the coconut milk and chicken stock.
- Lower the heat and leave to simmer for 15–20 minutes until the chicken is cooked through.
- Adjust the seasoning and stir in the lime juice just before serving.

Quick Coconut Soup 205

- Stir in 2–3 tbsp Thai curry paste instead of the spices for a very fast supper.

206

SERVES 4

Honey and Mustard Chicken with Polenta

Honey Mustard Chicken with Croutons

 207

- For a speedy version on this dish, roast cubed bread croutons around the chicken and toss with the salad.

Honey Mustard Chicken with Noodles

208

- Toss with cooked egg noodles or pasta for a hearty meal.

PREPARATION TIME:
20 MINUTES

COOKING TIME:
1 HOUR

INGREDIENTS

225 g / 9 oz / 1 cup polenta
2 tbsp olive oil
4 tbsp runny honey
2 tbsp grain mustard
salt and pepper
4 drumsticks, skin on
2 tbsp sesame seeds
100 ml / 3 ½ fl. oz / ½ cup olive oil
16 cherry tomatoes, halved
200 g / 7 oz / ¾ cup rocket (arugula)
½ lemon, juiced

- Whisk the polenta slowly into a large pan filled with 1.7 l / 3 pints / 6 cups salted boiling water. As soon as it begins to boil it will start to 'blip', so cover with a lid slightly askew and turn the heat down to minimum.
- When it begins to thicken, stir every 5 minutes or so very thoroughly, ensuring you push the spoon down into the sides of the pan. Cook for about 45 minutes until it begins to have the consistency of mashed potato. Season generously.
- Oil a tray and tip the polenta out onto it. Spread the polenta to about 2 ½ cm (1 in) thick. Leave the polenta to cool for about 30 minutes and then cut out equally-sized cubes. Preheat the oven to 200°C (180°C fan) / 400F / gas 6.
- Meanwhile, mix together the honey, mustard, oil and seasoning and coat the chicken. Roast in a foil-lined roasting tin for about 25 minutes until golden and sticky. Toss in the sesame seeds.
- Heat the oil in a deep-sided pan and shallow-fry the polenta cubes on all sides until golden, turning them frequently. Remove to kitchen paper to drain and season.
- Toss the polenta cubes in a bowl with the tomatoes and rocket and drizzle with a little lemon juice. Serve with the chicken.

209

SERVES 2

Crispy Chicken with Cherry Soup

PREPARATION TIME:
30 MINUTES

COOKING TIME:
15 MINUTES

INGREDIENTS

2 chicken breasts, skinned and thickly
  sliced
3 tbsp flour, seasoned
1 egg, beaten
75 g / 2 ½ oz / ⅓ cup breadcrumbs
1 tsp dried thyme
salt and pepper
2 tbsp vegetable oil
½ cucumber, halved and deseeded
1 green apple, halved and cored
200 g / 7 oz / ¾ cup cherries, stoned
200 ml / 7 fl. oz / ¾ cup light red
  or rosé wine
1–2 tbsp caster (superfine) sugar

- Lay the flour, egg and breadcrumbs out on separate plates. Stir the thyme into the breadcrumbs. Using one hand (to keep the other clean), dip each chicken strip alternately into the flour, egg and breadcrumbs and thoroughly coat.
- Once all have been coated, heat the oil in a pan and fry on all sides until golden and the chicken is cooked through – about 6–8 minutes. Drain on kitchen paper and keep warm in a low oven.
- To make the salad, slice the cucumber into thin half moons. Do the same with the apple halves and mix with the cucumber. Chill until needed.
- To make the soup, simply bring the cherries to a simmer in the wine and add 1 tbsp sugar. Leave to simmer gently for five minutes or until the cherries start to soften. Taste, as you may want more sugar, in which case continue cooking for a few minutes to dissolve the sugar. Chill until needed.
- Serve the warm chicken with the salad and chilled soup.

210

SERVES 4

Tandoori Chicken Salad

PREPARATION TIME:
15 MINUTES

COOKING TIME:
15 MINUTES

INGREDIENTS

4 chicken breasts, skinned
2 tbsp vegetable oil
salt and pepper
1 green pepper, deseeded and
  finely diced
1 yellow pepper, deseeded and
  finely diced
225 g / 8 oz / 1 cup mixed salad leaves
12 cherry tomatoes, halved
1 can sweetcorn, drained
1 carrot, julienned
200 ml / 7 fl. oz / ¾ cup plain yogurt
½ tsp ground cinnamon
1 tsp paprika
1–2 tsp garam masala
pinch cayenne pepper
12 mint leaves, finely shredded

- Pan fry the chicken in the oil with seasoning until cooked through and golden on both sides – about 12–15 minutes. Set aside to rest.
- Toss the salad leaves with the diced peppers, tomatoes, carrot and sweetcorn.
- Mix the yogurt with the spices and mint, then season. Rub into the chicken, then slice thickly.
- Serve the slices of chicken on top of the salad, drizzled with any remaining dressing.

211

SERVES 4

Chicken, Chickpea and Asparagus Salad

- Steam the asparagus over simmering water for 3–4 minutes until the stems are tender to the point of a knife.
- Slice the chicken and toss gently with the chickpeas and onion slices.
- Whisk together the mustard and lemon juice, then whisk in the oil, seasoning and parsley and drizzle over the chicken.
- Serve the salad with the asparagus stems draped over.

PREPARATION TIME:
10 MINUTES

COOKING TIME:
5 MINUTES

INGREDIENTS

4 chicken breasts, cooked
1 bunch asparagus, ends trimmed
400 g / 14 oz / 1 ½ cups canned chickpeas, drained
½ red onion, peeled and finely sliced
½ lemon, juiced
1 tbsp Dijon mustard
80 ml / 2 ½ fl. oz / ⅓ cup extra virgin olive oil
salt and pepper
¼ bunch parsley, finely chopped

Chicken Vol au Vents

212

SERVES 6

PREPARATION TIME:
20 MINUTES

COOKING TIME:
30–35 MINUTES

INGREDIENTS

350 g / 12 oz / 1 ½ cups ready-rolled puff pastry
1 egg, beaten

3 tbsp butter
2 chicken thighs, skinned and deboned, meat chopped
300 g / 10 oz / 1 ½ cups mixed wild mushrooms, chopped
2 sprigs thyme leaves
2 tbsp plain (all-purpose) flour
300 ml / 10 fl. oz / 1 ¼ cups milk
2 tbsp Parmesan, grated
salt and pepper
parsley, to sprinkle

- Roll the pastry out on a floured surface to 2 ½ cm (1 in) in thick. Cut out six 7 cm (3 in) circles with a pastry cutter and score a smaller circle just inside the rim.
- Place on a baking sheet and chill for 30 minutes. Preheat the oven to 200°C (180°C fan) / 400F / gas 6.
- Brush the pastry cases with a little egg and bake for 20 minutes or until risen and golden. Leave to cool, then carefully remove the lids and scoop out the centres.
- Melt the butter in a pan and cook the chicken and mushrooms with thyme and seasoning until any excess liquid has evaporated.
- Stir in the flour and cook out for 2 minutes, then whisk in the milk and simmer for 5–10 minutes until thickened and smooth. Whisk in the Parmesan.
- Spoon into the pastry cases, replace the lids and cook for 10–15 minutes until the filling is bubbling. Sprinkle with parsley and serve.

Oat-crusted Chicken Bites

213

SERVES 4

PREPARATION TIME:
10 MINUTES

COOKING TIME:
10 MINUTES

INGREDIENTS

4 chicken breasts, skinned

salt and pepper
3 tbsp flour
2 eggs, beaten
200 g / 6 ½ oz / ¾ cup coarse oatmeal
½ bunch parsley, finely chopped
olive oil

- Cut the chicken into bite-size pieces. Season, then dunk each chicken into flour, then egg then the oatmeal mixed with the parsley.
- Heat the oil in a large pan and fry in batches until golden and crisp and the chicken cooked through – 8–10 minutes.
- Skewer with toothpicks and serve hot.

214

SERVES 2

Chicken and Gouda Melt

PREPARATION TIME:
5 MINUTES

COOKING TIME:
10 MINUTES

....

INGREDIENTS

2 chicken breasts, skinned and chopped
2 tbsp olive oil
salt and pepper
200 g / 7 oz / ¾ cup Gouda cheese, sliced
4 thick slices bread, lightly toasted

- Heat the oil in a pan and fry the chicken until golden and cooked through. Season.
- Pile onto the toast and top with sliced Gouda.
- Grill until bubbling, then top with the remaining toast slices and serve.

Chicken, Tomato and Gouda Melt

215

- Try adding a handful fresh baby spinach leaves and sliced seasoned tomato underneath the chicken.

216

SERVES 4

Sesame Seed Chicken Balls

PREPARATION TIME:
15 MINUTES

COOKING TIME:
20 MINUTES

....

INGREDIENTS

2 slices stale bread, crusts removed
1 kg / 2 ¼ lbs / 4 ¼ cups minced chicken
1 onion, peeled and grated
1 clove of garlic, crushed
2 tbsp soy sauce
1 tbsp fresh ginger, grated
salt and pepper
3 tbsp olive oil
2 tbsp sesame seeds

- Soak the bread in warm water then squeeze it out. Mix thoroughly with the meat, onions, garlic, soy and ginger and season carefully.
- Form into small balls around 6cm in diameter.
- Heat the oil in a pan and fry the meatballs in batches until golden and cooked through. Toss with the sesame seeds.
- Serve with rice

Honey Soy Chicken Balls

217

- Add 1 tbsp runny honey to the mix for a sweet/ savoury flavour.

218

SERVES 4

Chicken with Prunes and Oranges

- Preheat the oven to 180°C (160°C fan) / 350F / gas 4.
- Soak the prunes in the orange juice for 20 minutes. Drain, reserve the juice, and lay a few in the centre of each chicken escalope, top with a little orange zest and roll up to form a sausage shape. Secure with toothpicks. Drizzle with olive oil, season then bake for 25 minutes.
- Make the sauce: set the sugar and water in a pan over a low heat and swirl until the sugar has melted. Do not stir. Allow to bubble up until golden.
- Once dark golden, remove from the heat and carefully, standing back, add the prune soaking juice, another 150 ml / 5 fl. oz juice and orange zest. Return to the heat and simmer gently for 10–15 minutes until thickened, stir in the marmalade then whisk in the butter a cube at a time.
- Whisk in any chicken resting juices and serve the chicken sliced in half, decorated with candied zest, walnut halves and sauce.

PREPARATION TIME:
30 MINUTES

COOKING TIME:
30 MINUTES

INGREDIENTS

4 chicken breasts, skin on, batted
 out to 1 cm (½ in) thickness
100 g / 3 ½ oz / ½ cup dried prunes
100 ml / 3 ½ fl. oz / ½ cup orange juice
½ orange, zested
olive oil
candied orange zest
walnut halves

FOR THE SAUCE
30 ml / 1 fl. oz / 2 tbsp olive oil
½ tsp caster (superfine) sugar
350 g / 12 oz / 1 ½ cup sliced
basil, to garnish

Chicken with Dates and Oranges

219

- Replace the prunes with dates.

220

SERVES 4

Mixed Brochettes

- Dip the chicken pieces one at a time into the flour, egg then breadcrumbs and lay on a rack to dry slightly.
- Heat 1 cm (½ in) depth oil in a pan and fry the chicken in batches until golden on both sides and cooked through.
- Meanwhile steam the cauliflower florets for 4–5 minutes until just tender.
- Thread the chicken onto skewers alternating with the pineapple. Fold the ham into a small roll and skewer with the cauliflower and prune.
- Serve as a starter.

PREPARATION TIME:
15 MINUTES

COOKING TIME:
10 MINUTES

INGREDIENTS

4 chicken breasts, skinned and
 cut into chunks
100 g / 3 ½ oz / ½ cup plain
 (all-purpose) flour
2 eggs, beaten
200 g / 7 oz / ¾ cup breadcrumbs
100 g / 3 ½ oz / ½ cup pineapple,
 cut into chunks
vegetable oil
4 slices Parma ham or similar
4 prunes
4 large cauliflower florets

Spicy Chicken Brochettes

221

- Pineapple responds well to a kick of heat so sprinkle a little dried chilli flakes on for a punch.

222

SERVES 4

Chicken Yakitori

Chicken and Aubergine Yakitori

223

- Add chunks of aubergine (eggplant) with the chicken to tenderise and soak up the sauces before cooking.

Sweet Chilli Chicken

224

- Use sweet chilli (chili) sauce on half the skewers instead of teriyaki sauce.

PREPARATION TIME:
10 MINUTES

COOKING TIME:
10 MINUTES

INGREDIENTS

4 chicken breasts, skinned
2 tbsp teriyaki sauce
2 tbsp soy sauce
1 tsp fresh ginger, grated
1 clove of garlic, crushed

- Cut the chicken into large chunks.
- Mix together the remaining ingredients and coat the chicken thoroughly. Marinate for 30–60 minutes.
- Thread onto soaked wooden skewers and cook over a medium heat, basting with any remaining marinade until cooked and sticky.
- Serve hot.

225

SERVES 4

Caramelised Chicken Drumsticks

- Preheat the oven to 200°C (180°C fan) / 400F / gas 6
- Mix together the sauce ingredients and simmer in a pan for 5 minutes, then coat the drumsticks thoroughly in the sauce.
- Lay the drumsticks in a foil-lined roasting tin and roast in the oven for about 25 minutes until golden and cooked through. If they look like they are burning, cover with foil.
- Meanwhile arrange the peppers in a bowl and soak the rice noodles according to packet instructions.
- Serve the hot chicken with the cold crunchy peppers and noodles.

PREPARATION TIME:
10 MINUTES

COOKING TIME:
30 MINUTES

INGREDIENTS

8 chicken drumsticks
olive oil
salt and pepper
2 yellow peppers, deseeded and finely sliced
rice noodles, to serve

FOR THE SAUCE
4 tbsp white wine vinegar
3–4 tbsp soy sauce
2–3 tbsp tomato ketchup
1 tbsp soft brown sugar
1 tbsp runny honey
1 tbsp Dijon mustard
1 tsp fresh ginger, grated
1 tsp paprika
pinch dried chilli (chili) flakes
salt and pepper

Caramelised Chicken Wraps

226

- Pull the meat from the cooked drumsticks and wrap in tortillas with the peppers and a little shredded lettuce.

227

SERVES 4

Bollywood Soup

- Heat the oil in a pan and sauté the onion for about 10 minutes or until golden-brown. Add the garlic, chilli and ginger and fry for another minute.
- Add the spices and stir well, then add the chicken and pumpkin to the sauce and pour in the coconut milk and stock. Cook at a simmer for around 20 minutes until the chicken and pumpkin are tender.
- Adjust the seasoning and sprinkle with coriander leaves before serving.

PREPARATION TIME:
15 MINUTES

COOKING TIME:
40 MINUTES

INGREDIENTS

3 tbsp vegetable oil
1 onion, peeled and finely sliced
2 cloves of garlic, chopped
1 red chilli (chili), deseeded and finely chopped
1 tsp fresh ginger, grated
1 tsp ground coriander
pinch turmeric
½ tsp ground cumin
½ tsp garam masala
1 tsp paprika
1 tsp mustard seeds
2 sweet potatoes, peeled and chopped
450 g / 1 lb / 2 cups chicken thigh meat, skinned and diced
400 ml / 14 fl. oz / 1 ½ cups canned coconut milk
300 ml / 10 fl. oz / 1 ¼ cups chicken stock
coriander (cilantro) leaves, to garnish

Jewelled Bollywood Soup

 228

- For extra colour, add some diced peppers.

229

SERVES 2

Courgette Stuffed with Fruity Chicken

PREPARATION TIME:
25 MINUTES

COOKING TIME:
45–60 MINUTES

INGREDIENTS

2 small round courgettes (zucchini)
   or squash
2 tbsp olive oil
2 chicken thighs, skinned, deboned and
   chopped
1 onion, peeled and finely chopped
1 carrot, peeled and diced
100 g / 3 ½ oz / ½ cup sultanas
100 g / 3 ½ oz / ½ cup dried apricots,
   chopped
2 tsp ground cumin
2 tbsp thyme leaves
salt and pepper

- Preheat the oven to 180°C (160°C fan) / 350F / gas 4.
- Cut a 'hat' off the courgette and hollow out the insides, scooping out and discarding the seeds. Finely chop any flesh scooped out.
- Heat the oil in a pan and fry the chicken, onion, carrot and courgette until golden and tender, then add the fruit, cumin, thyme and a splash of water. Season.
- Spoon into the hollowed out courgettes and place the tops back on. Sit in a roasting tin and pour a generous splash of water around to help them cook. Roast for 45–60 minutes until the courgette is tender but not collapsing.
- Serve warm.

Chicken and Rice Courgette   **230**

- 100 g / 3 ½ oz cooked white rice folded into the stuffing ingredients would make this a hearty meal.

231

SERVES 4–6

Chicken Liver Terrine with Gingerbread

PREPARATION TIME:
25 MINUTES

INGREDIENTS

500 g / 1 lb / 2 cups chicken livers,
   trimmed
500 g / 1 lb / 2 cups butter, softened
4 tbsp port
¼ tsp ground mace
1 tsp thyme leaves
1 clove of garlic, crushed
salt and pepper
100 g / 3 ½ oz / ½ cup gingerbread,
   crumbled

- Heat 2 tbsp of butter in a frying pan and cook the chicken livers in batches over a medium heat for 5 minutes, turning them frequently, until golden brown without and just pink within.
- Transfer as they cook with a slotted spoon to a food processor, reserving the frying pan and juices. Pour the port into the pan to deglaze, scraping with a wooden spoon and add the liquid to the processor.
- Melt 300 g butter and pour into the processor. Add the mace, thyme, garlic and salt and pepper. Blend to a smooth purée.
- Spoon into a pot or individual ramekins. Melt the remaining butter in a pan and crumble in the gingerbread. Pour over, leave to cool, then chill for 24 hours before serving with hot toast.

Chicken Liver Terrine
with Pine Nuts   **232**

- Try dry-toasting pine nuts then stir into the melted butter and use to top the terrine.

233

SERVES 4

Chicken and Cherry Tomato Kebabs

Chicken and Button Mushroom Kebabs

234

- Replace the cherry tomatoes with button mushrooms.

Chicken and Red Pepper Skewers

235

- Substitute the tomatoes with chopped red peppers.

PREPARATION TIME:
15 MINUTES

COOKING TIME:
10 MINUTES

INGREDIENTS

4 chicken thighs, skinned, deboned
  and cubed
2 tbsp olive oil
salt and pepper
1 tbsp thyme leaves
12 cherry tomatoes

FOR THE GINGER SAUCE

4 tbsp soy sauce
2 tbsp Dijon mustard
1 tbsp fresh ginger, grated
1 tsp sesame oil
1 tsp honey
salt and pepper

- Toss the chicken with oil, seasoning and thyme and thread onto skewers alternating with the cherry tomatoes.
- Griddle over high heat or barbecue for 8–10 minutes until golden and the tomatoes still holding their shape.
- Meanwhile mix together the ingredients for the sauce and pour into a bowl.
- Serve the hot kebabs with the ginger sauce.

236

SERVES 4

Thai Chicken and Coconut Soup

PREPARATION TIME:
15 MINUTES

COOKING TIME:
25–30 MINUTES

INGREDIENTS

3 tbsp vegetable oil
1 onion, peeled and finely sliced
1 red pepper, deseeded and roughly
    chopped
2 cloves of garlic, finely chopped
1 red chilli (chili), finely sliced
2 stalks lemon grass, bruised
1 tbsp fresh ginger, grated
1 tsp turmeric
3–4 chicken breasts, skinned and cubed
2 tsp tamarind paste
2 tbsp fish sauce
400 ml / 14 fl. oz / 1 ½ cups coconut milk
200 ml / 7 fl. oz / ¾ cup chicken stock
salt and pepper
1–2 limes, juiced
½ bunch coriander (cilantro), finely
    chopped, stalks reserved

- Heat the oil in a wok or large pan and fry the onion and pepper until deep gold and sweet.
- Add the garlic and chilli and cook out for 2 minutes.
- Add the cubed chicken, lemon grass, ginger and turmeric and allow to colour on all sides.
- Stir in the tamarind and fish sauce, then pour over the coconut milk and chicken stock and add the coriander stalks. Lower the heat and leave to simmer for 15–20 minutes until the chicken is cooked through.
- Adjust the seasoning and stir in the lime juice and chopped coriander just before serving in deep warmed bowls.

Thai Chicken Noodle Soup

 237

- Add 1 nest dried egg noodles to cook in the liquid for a more substantial soup.

238

SERVES 4

Chicken and Rice Sesame Salad

PREPARATION TIME:
20 MINUTES

COOKING TIME:
15 MINUTES

INGREDIENTS

240 ml / 8 ½ oz / 1 cup rice
480 ml / 1 pint / 2 cups weak chicken or
    vegetable stock
2 chicken breasts, cooked and shredded
2 sticks celery, finely sliced
2 tbsp lime juice
4 tbsp olive oil
salt and pepper
1 tbsp sesame seeds

- Measure the rice (in volume) into a saucepan and cover with the stock. Cover with a lid and cook for 10 minutes.
- Remove from the heat and leave to sit for 5 minutes with the lid on, then remove the lid and leave to cool a little in a bowl while you prepare the remaining salad.
- Toss the celery and chicken together with the sesame seeds.
- Add the warm rice to the bowl and stir through the lime juice and oil. Season well and serve.

Chicken and Wild Rice Salad 239

- Wild rice will add nutty texture and substance if used in same proportions.

240

SERVES 4

Chicken Vegetable Rice Salad

- Measure the rice (in volume) into a saucepan and cover with the stock. Cover with a lid and cook for 10 minutes.
- Remove from the heat and leave to sit for 5 minutes with the lid on. Then remove the lid and leave to cool a little in a bowl while you prepare the remaining salad
- Meanwhile, mix the carrot, pepper and chicken in a bowl.
- Add the warm rice to the bowl and stir through the vinegar and oil. Season well and serve.

PREPARATION TIME:
20 MINUTES

COOKING TIME:
15 MINUTES

INGREDIENTS

240 ml / 8 ½ oz / 1 cup rice
480 ml / 1 pint / 2 cups weak chicken or vegetable stock
1 carrot, peeled and diced
1 green pepper, deseeded and finely chopped
2 chicken breasts, cooked and shredded
2 tbsp white wine vinegar
4 tbsp olive oil
salt and pepper

Chicken Salad with Courgettes

241

- Try adding sautéed courgettes (zucchini) to the mix for a different texture and colour.

242

SERVES 2

Chicken and Ginger Bites

- Marinate the chicken with the ginger, oil and lemon for at least 2 hours.
- Make the batter: whisk together the beer or water and the egg in a bowl until light and frothy.
- Whisk in the flour. You should have a light batter with a dropping consistency.
- Heat the oil to 180°C / 350F.
- Dip the chicken pieces a few at a time into the batter to coat thoroughly. Drop immediately into the hot oil. Do this in batches so as not to overcrowd the pan.
- Remove with a slotted spoon once golden-brown and drain on kitchen paper.
- Sprinkle with salt before serving and serve with soy sauce to dip.

PREPARATION TIME:
10 MINUTES

COOKING TIME:
15 MINUTES

INGREDIENTS

2 chicken thighs, skinned deboned and cut into chunks
1 tbsp fresh ginger, grated
1 tbsp vegetable oil
2 tbsp lemon juice
vegetable oil, for deep-frying
salt
soy sauce for dipping

FOR THE BATTER

200 ml / 7 fl. oz Japanese beer or lager or sparkling water
1 egg
100 g / 3 ½ oz plain (all-purpose) flour

Spicy Ginger Bites

243

- Add 1 tsp of chilli (chili) powder to the batter for an extra kick.

244

SERVES 4

Chicken Meatballs with Baby Spinach

Meatballs with Hummus

245

- You can make a quick hummus by whizzing a can of drained chickpeas with tahini, crushed garlic, olive oil and lemon juice to serve with the meatballs.

Meatballs with Courgette

246

- Cut 2 courgettes (zucchinis) into thin batons and fry slowly in olive oil with basil and lemon juice to finish.

PREPARATION TIME:
25 MINUTES

COOKING TIME:
40 MINUTES

INGREDIENTS

2 slices stale bread, crusts removed
1 kg / 2 ¼ lbs / 4 ¼ cups minced chicken
1 onion, peeled and grated
1 clove of garlic, crushed
1 lemon, juiced and zested
1 tsp dried oregano
1 red pepper, finely diced
salt and pepper
100 ml / 3 ½ fl. oz / ½ cup olive oil
baby spinach leaves, to serve

- Soak the bread in warm water then squeeze it out. Mix thoroughly with the meat, onions, garlic, zest, oregano and red pepper, then season carefully.
- Form into small balls around 6 cm (2 ½ in) in diameter, then refrigerate for 30 minutes.
- Heat the oil in a pan and fry the meatballs in batches until golden and cooked through.
- Serve with baby spinach leaves.

SERVES 2

Chicken Pittas with Avocado Salad

- Heat the oil in a pan and sauté the chicken and peppers over high heat until golden and tender. Set aside to cool a little.
- Mix the mayonnaise with the spices, lemon juice and spring onions. Tip the chicken and peppers into the bowl and mix thoroughly.
- Warm and split the pitta breads and spoon the chicken mixture into the cavities.
- Halve, stone and scoop out the avocado flesh into a bowl, then add the remaining ingredients and mix well.
- Serve the pittas with the avocado salad alongside.

PREPARATION TIME:
20 MINUTES

COOKING TIME:
10 MINUTES

INGREDIENTS

2 tbsp olive oil
2 chicken breasts, chopped
2 red peppers, deseeded and
   roughly chopped
100 g / 3 ½ oz / ½ cup mayonnaise
2 tsp smoked paprika
1 tbsp lemon juice
½ tsp cayenne pepper
½ bunch spring onions (scallions),
   finely sliced
2 pitta breads
2 avocados
½ lemon, juiced
salt and pepper
2 tbsp extra virgin olive oil
2 tomatoes, cored and diced
1 tsp ground cumin

Chicken Pittas with Guacamole

248

- Take this one step further and mash the avocado with the salad ingredients to make a lumpy mash.

249

SERVES 4–6

Chicken and Prune Parcels

- Preheat the oven to 200°C (180°C fan) / 400F / gas 6.
- Heat the oil in a pan and cook the chicken, spices and prunes until cooked through. Set aside to cool.
- Keeping the remaining filo sheets covered with a damp tea towel, remove one at a time from the pack and brush with melted butter before using.
- Place 2 sheets of pastry on a surface, brush each with melted butter, then top with a little of the chicken mixture. Wrap the pastry around to enclose the filling. Repeat until all the filling and pastry is used up.
- Brush the tops with a little egg wash, then bake in the oven for 15–20 minutes or until the pastry is crisp and golden.
- Serve hot.

PREPARATION TIME:
20 MINUTES

COOKING TIME:
20 MINUTES

INGREDIENTS

4 tbsp olive oil
2 chicken breasts, skinned and diced
½ tsp ground cinnamon
½ tsp ground cumin
½ tsp ground coriander
100 g / 3 ½ oz / ½ cup prunes, chopped
1 egg yolk
salt and pepper
1 pack filo pastry
120 g / 4 oz / ½ cup butter, melted
2 eggs
1 egg yolk, beaten

Savoury Chicken Parcels

250

- Try using diced cooked potato in place of the prunes for a more substantial parcel.

251

SERVES 4–6

Chicken Croquettes with Tomato Sauce

PREPARATION TIME:
40 MINUTES

COOKING TIME:
10–15 MINUTES

INGREDIENTS

1.5 kg / 3 lb / 6 cups floury potatoes, peeled and quartered
50 g / 1 ¾ oz / ¼ cup butter
4 egg yolks, beaten
2 chicken breasts, cooked and shredded finely
¼ bunch parsley, finely chopped
salt and pepper
2 tbsp olive oil
1 clove of garlic, finely chopped
400 g / 14 oz / 1 ½ cups canned tomatoes
½ bunch basil, chopped
6 tbsp flour
2 eggs, beaten
200 g / 7 oz / ¾ cup breadcrumbs, to coat
vegetable oil, for deep frying

- Cook the potatoes in boiling water until tender.
- Drain, then return to the pan and allow to dry.
- Push the potatoes through a sieve or blend to a purée, then add the butter. Work in the egg yolks, then season and add the chicken and parsley. Spread the purée in a greased dish and leave to cool.
- Meanwhile heat the oil in a pan and when very hot, add the garlic and tomatoes all at once, cover immediately with a lid and cook fast for 10 minutes. Remove the lid, stir in the basil and seasoning and set aside.
- Lightly flour your hands, then work the cooled mixture into a ball. Shape into a long cylinder and cut into 5 cm (2 in) logs. Dip each croquette into the flour, egg and then the breadcrumbs to coat.
- Heat the oil to 180°C / 350F. Deep fry the croquettes in batches until golden-brown. Drain on kitchen paper and serve hot with the sauce.

Chicken Croquettes

252

- You can add any kind of flavouring – vary the herbs, add curry powder or chilli (chili) – the choice is endless.

253

SERVES 4

Chicken, Orange and Pepper Kebabs

PREPARATION TIME:
10 MINUTES

COOKING TIME:
10 MINUTES

INGREDIENTS

4 chicken breasts, skinned
2 tbsp thyme leaves
2 tbsp olive oil
salt and pepper
2 oranges, thinly sliced
1 red pepper, deseeded and finely chopped
1 green pepper, deseeded and finely chopped

- Cut the chicken into large cubes and tip into a bowl with the thyme, oil and pepper and mix well.
- Thread onto soaked wooden skewers, alternating with folded slices of orange and pieces of pepper.
- Griddle or barbecue over medium heat for 10 minutes or so, turning every so often, until golden and cooked through.
- Serve hot.

Chicken and Orange Kebabs with Almond Crust

254

- Try rolling the cooked kebabs in 2 tbsp ground almonds for added texture.

255

SERVES 2–4

Chicken Wings with Ginger

Chicken Thighs with Ginger

256

- Replace the chicken wings with chicken thighs.

Chicken Wings with Soy

257

- If cola does not appeal, use 3–4 tbsp soy sauce instead.

PREPARATION TIME:
I HOUR

COOKING TIME:
30–40 MINUTES

INGREDIENTS

8–12 chicken wings
200 ml / 7 fl. oz / ¾ cup full-fat cola
1 tbsp black peppercorns, crushed
1 bunch spring onions (scallions), chopped
1 tbsp fresh ginger, grated
1 tsp salt

- Marinate the chicken wings with the rest of the ingredients for at least 1 hour.
- Preheat the oven to 200°C (180°C fan) / 400F / gas 6.
- Tip the chicken wings and the spring onions into a foil-lined roasting tin and roast for 30–40 minutes until the wings are sticky and dark gold.
- Pour the remaining marinade into a small pan and reduce until syrupy. Taste and adjust the seasoning if necessary – you may want more salt or even a squeeze of lime juice.
- Serve the chicken wings and spring onions with the reduced sauce spooned over.

258

MAKES 12

Chicken and Tomato Crostini

**PREPARATION TIME:
20 MINUTES**

**COOKING TIME:
20 MINUTES**

INGREDIENTS

4 chicken breasts, skin on
12 x 1 cm (½ in) thick slices from a
    baguette
3 tbsp olive oil
6 ripe vine tomatoes
6 tbsp mayonnaise
salt and pepper

- Preheat the oven to 200°C (180°C fan) / 400F / gas 6.
- Drizzle the chicken with a little oil, season and roast in the oven for 20 minutes or until just cooked through. Set aside to rest.
- Brush the baguette slices with a little oil and bake in the oven for 10–12 minutes until crisp and golden.
- Finely dice the tomatoes, coring them first, then toss with the mayonnaise and season generously.
- Slice the chicken breasts. Spoon the tomatoes on top of the crostini and top with chicken.

Spicy Chicken Tomato Crostini

259

- Spice up the mayonnaise with mango chutney, paprika, herbs, mustard – the choice is yours.

260

SERVES 6–8

Chicken and Swiss Chard Terrine

**PREPARATION TIME:
30 MINUTES**

**COOKING TIME:
45 MINUTES**

INGREDIENTS

100 g / 3 ½ oz / ½ cup butter
2 shallots, finely chopped
1 clove of garlic, crushed
2 sprigs thyme
500 g / 1 lb / 2 cups minced chicken
500 g / 1 lb / 2 cups chicken meat, diced
2 tbsp tarragon leaves, chopped
    (optional)
2 eggs, plus 2 egg yolks, lightly beaten
salt and pepper
1 kg / 2 lb / 4 cups Swiss chard leaves

- Preheat the oven to 160°C (140°C fan) / 325F / gas 3.
- Heat the butter in a pan and sweat the shallot and onion with the thyme until softened. Set aside to cool.
- In a large bowl, mix together the chicken and tarragon and mix into the onion mixture once cooled. Add the beaten eggs and incorporate fully, then season.
- Steam the Swiss chard leaves for 3–4 minutes until tender, then pat dry with kitchen towel.
- Line a terrine mould with film, then line with the chard leaves, overlapping each one and leaving plenty hanging over the sides of the mould. Spoon the chicken mixture unto the mould, then fold the chard leaves over to cover.
- Cover the terrine with greaseproof paper, then foil and secure with string. Place in a roasting tin and fill with boiling water to halfway up the sides of the mould. Bake in the oven for 45 minutes.
- Leave to cool in the mould, then remove and slice.

Chicken and Mushroom Terrine

261

- Try adding 250 g / 9 oz / 1 cup mixed wild mushrooms to the shallot mixture for extra flavour.

262

SERVES 4

Chicken Kebabs with Apricots

- Tip the chicken and apricot halves into a bowl and leave to marinate with the remaining ingredients for 30–60 minutes.
- Thread the chicken and apricots alternately onto soaked wooden skewers and griddle or barbecue over a medium heat until golden and cooked through.
- Serve hot or warm.

PREPARATION TIME:
10 MINUTES

COOKING TIME:
10 MINUTES

INGREDIENTS

4 chicken thighs, skinned, deboned and chopped
4 ripe apricots, halved and stoned
½ bunch thyme
2 tbsp olive oil
salt and pepper
½ lemon, zested
1 bunch spring onions (scallions) sliced

Chicken with Plums

263

- Plums work just as well for a late summer barbecue – try adding a little chopped chilli (chili) for kick or hoisin sauce.

264

SERVES 2

Exotic Chicken Salad

- Preheat the oven to 200°C (180°C fan) / 400F / gas 6.
- Drizzle the chicken with oil, season and roast in the oven for 20 minutes or until cooked through. Set aside to rest.
- Meanwhile mix the pineapple, tomatoes and cucumber in a bowl. Rinse, dry and arrange the salad leaves in a serving bowl.
- Whisk together the oil, lime juice and zest, chilli and a little salt, then combine well with the diced fruit. Tip on top of the salad leaves.
- Thickly slice the chicken, arrange on top of the fruit and serve.

PREPARATION TIME:
15 MINUTES

COOKING TIME:
20 MINUTES

INGREDIENTS

2 chicken breasts, skin on
2 tbsp olive oil
salt and pepper
½ pineapple, peeled, cored and diced
2 ripe vine tomatoes, cored and diced
½ cucumber, diced
300 g / 10 oz / 1 ¼ cups Mesclun salad
80 ml / 2 ½ fl. oz / ⅓ cup extra virgin olive oil
1 lime, juiced and zested
½ red chilli (chili), finely chopped

Exotic Salad with Mango

265

- Try adding diced mango, which goes really well with the chilli, and cooked prawns.

266

SERVES 4–6

Chicken and Mushroom Soup

Chicken, Mushroom and Tarragon Soup

267

- Tarragon in place of the thyme would complement the flavours enormously.

Chicken, Mushroom and Leek Soup

268

- Add 2 sliced leeks to the mushrooms for extra sweet flavour.

PREPARATION TIME:
30 MINUTES

COOKING TIME:
40 MINUTES

INGREDIENTS

2 chicken breasts, skinned
1 l / 2 pints / 4 ¼ cups chicken stock
50 g / 1 ¾ oz / ¼ cup unsalted butter
1 onion, peeled and finely chopped
500 g / 1 lb / 2 cups flat or wild mushrooms, finely chopped
1 clove of garlic, crushed
50 g / 1 ¾ oz / ¼ cup plain (all-purpose) flour
1 glass dry white wine or port
salt and pepper
100 ml / 3 ½ fl. oz / ½ cup double (heavy) cream
4 thyme sprigs, plus more for garnish

- Heat the chicken stock in a large pan and poach the chicken breasts for 20 minutes until just cooked through. Remove to a plate with a slotted spoon and reserve the stock.

- Heat the butter in a large deep pan and sweat the onion without colouring for 5–10 minutes or until softened. Add the mushrooms and garlic and cook for a further 5 minutes or until the mushrooms have softened.

- Stir in the flour and cook out for a few minutes, or until the flour has turned a biscuit colour. Add the white wine and simmer until thickened.

- Pour over the stock, add thyme sprigs and bring to the boil, stirring constantly. Reduce to a simmer and cook for 20 minutes. Remove from the heat and allow to cool a little.

- Liquidise the soup in batches, removing the thyme stalks, then return to the pan. Shred the chicken and stir into the soup. Add the seasoning and cream and reheat the soup gently without boiling. Scatter with thyme leaves before serving.

269

SERVES 4–6

Spicy Japanese Kebabs

- Mix together the ingredients for the beef in a bowl, using your hands to make sure everything is combined thoroughly.
- Form into meatballs the size of golf balls and refrigerate for 30 minutes.
- Place the chicken kebab ingredients in a bowl, making sure everything is thoroughly combined and leave to marinate in the refrigerator for 30 minutes.
- Thread the meatballs and chicken pieces onto soaked wooden skewers and griddle over high heat for 4–5 minutes per side until the meat is cooked through.
- Serve hot.

PREPARATION TIME:
15 MINUTES

COOKING TIME:
8–10 MINUTES

INGREDIENTS

400 g / 14 oz / 1 ½ cups beef, minced
3–4 tbsp soy sauce
1 tbsp wasabi paste
black pepper
1 egg, beaten
400 g / 14 oz / 1 ½ cups chicken breast,
    cut into small chunks
1 tbsp fresh ginger, grated
2 tbsp soy sauce
1 tbsp Ume Plum seasoning (optional)
½ red chilli (chili), finely chopped
salt and pepper
1 egg, beaten

Spicy Kebabs with Dipping Sauce

270

- A refreshing dipping sauce can be made from combining soy sauce, lime juice, 1 tsp sugar and a little chilli (chili) sauce.

271

SERVES 4

Chicken Waldorf Salad

- Shred the chicken breasts and place in a bowl with the sultanas and torn-up endive.
- Peel the apples, core and cut into thin batons. Toss with a little lemon juice to prevent browning and add to the bowl.
- Lightly toast the walnuts in a dry frying pan until slightly darkened, then add to the bowl.
- Whisk together the oil and lemon juice with some seasoning and toss with the salad before serving.

PREPARATION TIME:
15–20 MINUTES

INGREDIENTS

4 chicken breasts, cooked
60 g / 2 oz sultanas
250 g / 9 oz / 1 cup curly endive
2 crisp green apples
75 g / 2 ½ oz / ⅓ cup walnuts, chopped
3 tbsp extra virgin olive oil
2 tbsp lemon juice
salt and pepper

Chicken Salad with Mayonnaise

272

- Add 2–3 tbsp of mayonnaise for added richness but keep the lemon juice to cut through.

273

SERVES 4

Chicken Tandoori Kebabs

PREPARATION TIME:
10 MINUTES

COOKING TIME:
8–10 MINUTES

INGREDIENTS

4 skinless chicken breasts,
  diced evenly

FOR THE MARINADE
300 ml / 10 fl. oz / 1 ¼ cups plain yogurt
1 tsp ground cumin
1 tsp ground coriander
1 tsp garam masala
1 tsp ground cinnamon
1 ½ tsp tandoori chilli (chili) powder
1 tsp paprika
1 tsp caster (superfine) sugar
1 clove garlic, minced
salt and pepper

- Prepare the tandoori marinade by mixing together all the ingredients for the marinade in a mixing bowl. Add the chicken, mix well, then cover and chill for at least 1 hour.
- Preheat the grill to hot. Remove the chicken from the marinade, shaking off any excess, and thread onto the wooden skewers.
- Grill for 8–10 minutes, turning occasionally until lightly charred and cooked through.

Curried Chicken Kebabs

274

- Try marinating in any kind of curry paste such as masala, korma or even mango chutney with lime zest.

275

SERVES 8

Chicken and Prawn Open Sandwiches

PREPARATION TIME:
20 MINUTES

INGREDIENTS

16 slices baguette, about 2 cm (1 in)
  thick
2 chicken breasts, cooked and diced
200 g / 7 oz / ¾ cup cooked king prawns
100 g / 3 ½ oz / ½ cup mayonnaise
½ lemon, juiced
salt and pepper

- Place the baguette slices on a baking sheet and grill until lightly toasted.
- Mix the chicken with the prawns, mayonnaise, a squeeze of lemon and seasoning and combine well.
- Pile the mixture onto the baguette slices and serve.

Smoked Fish and Chicken Open Sandwiches

276

- Add smoked mackerel or salmon with the prawns and mayonnaise.

277

SERVES 2

Steamed Lemon Chicken Salad

Lemon Chicken Rice Paper Rolls

 278

- If you shred the steamed chicken finely, you could use it and the salad as a filler for rice paper rolls to serve as a starter.

Vietnamese Ginger Steamed Chicken

279

- Use 2 cm (1 in) piece of fresh ginger, finely sliced, pushed under the chicken in the steaming process.

PREPARATION TIME:
10 MINUTES

COOKING TIME:
20–25 MINUTES

INGREDIENTS

2 chicken breasts, skinned
1 tbsp fish sauce
3 stalks lemon grass, bruised
1 lemon, sliced
1 red chilli (chili), chopped
2 cloves of garlic, sliced
250 g / 9 oz / 1 cup rocket (arugula)
1 bunch radishes, tailed and sliced
1 bunch spring onions (scallions), sliced

- Place a steamer or muslin-lined colander over simmering water and place in it the lemon grass, lemon slices, chilli and garlic. Sit the chicken on top, sprinkle over the fish sauce, put on the lid and steam for 20–25 minutes until cooked through.
- Meanwhile assemble the salad in a bowl ready for serving.
- When the chicken is cooked, remove from the steamer, slice and sit on top of the salad to serve.

280

SERVES 4

Chicken Satay in Pak Choi Boats

PREPARATION TIME:
20 MINUTES

COOKING TIME:
15 MINUTES

INGREDIENTS

8 chicken thighs, boned and skinned
    and cut into large chunks
4–5 heads pak choi, separated into
    leaves
1 nest dried egg noodles
2 tsp sesame oil

FOR THE MARINADE/SAUCE

2 shallots, peeled and finely chopped
½ red chilli (chili), finely chopped
2 cloves of garlic, finely chopped
1 cm (½ in) piece fresh ginger, grated
5 tbsp peanut butter
1 tbsp tamarind paste
2 tbsp soy sauce or kecap manis
100 ml / 3 ½ fl. oz / ½ cup coconut milk
1 tbsp palm or dark brown sugar
1 tbsp fish sauce
1 lime, juiced

- Mix together the marinade ingredients and pour half over the chicken pieces. Leave to marinate for at least 4 hours or overnight.
- Heat a little groundnut oil in a pan and cook in batches until golden and cooked through.
- Meanwhile heat the remaining sauce in a small pan, then squeeze in a little lime juice.
- Steam the pak choi over simmering water for 3 minutes until the stems are tender. Cook the noodles in boiling salted water according to packet instructions then drain and toss in sesame oil.
- Arrange the pak choi leaves on a platter and use a fork to twirl a few noodles into the cup of the leaf. Top with a few chunks of chicken satay and serve.

281

SERVES 4–6

Chicken and Serrano Ham Croquettes

PREPARATION TIME:
40 MINUTES

COOKING TIME:
10–15 MINUTES

INGREDIENTS

1.5 kg / 3 lb / 6 cups floury potatoes,
    peeled and quartered
50 g / 1 ¾ oz / ¼ cup butter
4 egg yolks, beaten
2 chicken breasts, cooked and shredded
    finely
80 g / 2 ½ oz / ⅓ cup Serrano ham, very
    finely chopped
salt and pepper
6 tbsp flour
2 eggs, beaten
200 g / 7 oz / ¾ cup breadcrumbs, to
    coat
vegetable oil, for deep frying
4 slices Serrano ham, finely sliced
salad leaves

- Cook the potatoes in boiling salted water until quite tender – about 20 minutes.
- Drain thoroughly, then return to the pan and allow to dry briefly over a low heat.
- Push the potatoes through a sieve or blend to a purée in a processor (being careful not to over-mix), then add the butter. Work in the egg yolks with a fork, then season and add the chicken and ham. Spread the purée in a greased dish and leave to cool.
- Lightly flour your hands, then work the cooled mixture into a ball. Shape into a long cylinder and cut into 5 cm (2 in) logs. Dip each croquette into the flour, egg and then the breadcrumbs to coat.
- Heat the oil to 180°C / 350F. Deep fry the croquettes in batches until they turn golden-brown – about 3–4 minutes. Drain on kitchen paper and serve hot on top of the shredded ham and salad leaves.

282
SERVES 4

Satay Skewers

- Toss the chicken cubes in the soy, lime, salt and sugar and marinate for 1 hour.
- Meanwhile heat the oil in a pan and gently fry the shallots, garlic and chillies until lightly coloured. Tip into a blender and whizz with the peanuts to a paste.
- Transfer back to the pan, add 150 ml / 5 fl. oz water and honey and cook gently until thickened. Season and set aside.
- Thread the chicken onto wooden skewers and griddle over high heat until golden and cooked through, turning every now and then.
- Serve the kebabs with the peanut sauce to dip.

PREPARATION TIME:
20 MINUTES + MARINATING TIME

COOKING TIME:
10 MINUTES

INGREDIENTS

4 chicken breasts, skinned and cubed
3 tbsp soy sauce or kecap manis
1 tbsp lime juice
1 tsp sugar, 1 tsp salt
2 tbsp groundnut oil
2 shallots, finely chopped
3 cloves of garlic, finely chopped
1–2 red chillies (chilies), deseeded and chopped
100 g / 3 ½ oz / ½ cup peanuts
2 tbsp honey

Chilli Chicken Meatballs

283
MAKES 16–20

PREPARATION TIME:
20 MINUTES

COOKING TIME:
20 MINUTES

INGREDIENTS

500 g / 1 lb / 2 cups chicken, minced
1 onion, peeled and grated

2 cloves of garlic, crushed
salt and pepper
1 egg beaten
8 small red chillies (chilies)
60 g / 2 oz pistachio nuts, chopped

- Tip the chicken mince into a bowl and mix well with the onion, garlic, seasoning and egg.
- Divide the mixture in half and set one half aside. Cut the top off the chilli and roll in between your hands to release the seeds, if you prefer it less hot.
- Form the mixture into small golf-ball sized balls, push a hole into the middle with your thumb and stuff the chilli into the middle.
- Repeat with the remaining mixture, stuffing the centre with pistachio nuts, then reforming the meat around the stuffing.
- Thread onto soaked wooden skewers and griddle or barbecue until golden and cooked through – about 8–10 minutes.
- Serve hot or cold.

Chicken with Lime and Mint

284
SERVES 4

PREPARATION TIME:
10 MINUTES

COOKING TIME:
10–15 MINUTES

INGREDIENTS

4 chicken breasts, skinned and chopped
½ tsp turmeric

2 limes, juiced and zested
½ bunch mint leaves, finely chopped
60 ml / 2 fl. oz olive oil
salt and pepper
lime wedges, to serve
basil, to garnish

- Toss the chicken pieces with the turmeric, juice and zest, mint and oil and a little seasoning and refrigerate for 30 minutes – no longer or the lime juice will start to turn the chicken 'woolly'.
- Heat a pan and fry the chicken until golden and cooked through.
- Sprinkle with a little more salt and serve with the lime wedges.

285

SERVES 4

Chicken Kebabs with Lime Satay

PREPARATION TIME:
15 MINUTES

COOKING TIME:
10 MINUTES

INGREDIENTS

8 chicken thighs, boned and skinned
    and cut in half

FOR THE SAUCE

2 shallots, peeled and finely chopped
½ red chilli (chili), finely chopped
2 cloves of garlic, finely chopped
1 cm (½ in) piece fresh ginger, grated
5 tbsp peanut butter
2 tbsp soy sauce
100 ml / 3 ½ fl. oz / ½ cup coconut milk
1 tsp palm or dark brown sugar
1 tbsp fish sauce
1–2 limes, juiced
coriander (cilantro), finely chopped,
    to serve

- Thread the chicken onto soaked wooden kebab sticks.
- Griddle over a high heat until blackened in patches and cooked through – 6–8 minutes.
- Meanwhile heat the sauce ingredients in a small pan, then squeeze in the lime juice. Taste and adjust the seasoning.
- Serve the satay sauce alongside the chicken, sprinkled with chopped coriander leaves.

Chicken Kebabs with Lemon Satay

286

- Replace the limes with lemons.

287

SERVES 4

Chicken and Pea Cakes

PREPARATION TIME:
20 MINUTES

COOKING TIME:
15–20 MINUTES

INGREDIENTS

500 g / 1 lb / 2 cups cooked potatoes
2 chicken breasts, cooked and shredded
100 g / 3 ½ oz / ½ cup peas, cooked
2 tbsp butter
salt and pepper
2 tbsp plain (all-purpose) flour,
    seasoned
groundnut oil
200 g / 7 oz / ¾ cup purslane
200 ml / 7 fl. oz / ¾ cup creme fraiche
½ lemon, juiced
½ clove of garlic

- Mash the potatoes thoroughly and combine with the chicken, peas and butter. Season and shape into patties.
- Dust both sides with seasoned flour.
- Heat a thin film of oil in a pan and cook the chicken cakes two at a time until golden and crisp on both sides, adding more oil as necessary.
- Whizz the purslane in a food processor with the creme fraiche, a little lemon juice and garlic. Season.
- Serve the hot cakes with the sauce.

Chicken and Pea Cakes with Watercress Sauce

288

- Try whizzing watercress or baby spinach leaves if you find purslane hard to get hold of.

289

SERVES 4

Buffalo Chicken Wings

- Melt the butter in a pan and add the cayenne, hot sauce and salt. Taste and add more sauce if you want it hotter.
- Place the chicken wings in a roasting tin and brush generously with the spiced butter, then grill for 8 minutes. Turn over, brush again with the butter and grill for about 5 minutes until cooked through.
- Crumble the cheese into a bowl and stir in the sour cream, mayonnaise and a few drops Worcestershire. Taste and adjust the seasoning – you may want more Worcestershire and mash with a fork until smooth.
- Serve the hot wings seasoned with salt with the sauce to dip.

PREPARATION TIME:
10 MINUTES

COOKING TIME:
15 MINUTES

INGREDIENTS

16 chicken wings
100 g / 3 ½ oz / ½ cup butter
1 tsp cayenne pepper
1 tsp hot sauce
salt and pepper
200 g / 7 oz / ¾ cup blue cheese, crumbled
200 g / 7 oz / ¾ cup sour cream
200 g / 7 oz / ¾ cup mayonnaise
Worcestershire sauce

Mild Buffalo Wings

290

- Try adding 2 tbsp plain yogurt to the cayenne and hot sauce and marinate for 30 minutes before baking for 30 minutes. You'll get some fire but tempered with yogurt.

291

SERVES 2

Open Chicken Sandwich

- Batten out the chicken breasts between 2 layers of cling film until about 1 cm (½ in) thick.
- Heat the oil in a pan and fry the chicken on both sides until golden.
- Meanwhile, toast the bread. Spread with mayonnaise if using, then top with the ham. Lay a chicken escalope on top, then sit the lettuce and avocado tossed with lemon juice on the chicken and serve.

PREPARATION TIME:
15 MINUTES

COOKING TIME:
10 MINUTES

INGREDIENTS

2 chicken breasts, skinned
2 tbsp olive oil
2 thick slices bread
4 slices Parma ham
1 avocado, halved, stoned and chopped
1 tbsp lemon juice
4 little gem lettuce leaves
4 tbsp mayonnaise (optional)
salt and pepper

Chicken Sandwich with Egg

292

- Add sliced hard-boiled egg to the layers for a more substantial snack.

293

SERVES 2

Chicken, Fig and Mangetout Salad

Crunchy Chicken and Fig Salad

294

- Add pistachios, pine nuts or cashews for crunch and texture.

Chicken Fig Salad with Pomegranate

295

- Add 1 tsp pomegranate molasses or even honey to the dressing.

PREPARATION TIME:
10 MINUTES

COOKING TIME:
4 MINUTES

....

INGREDIENTS

2 chicken breasts, roasted and cooled
4 figs, halved
100 g / 3 ½ oz / ½ cup mangetout
1 shallot, finely chopped
2 tbsp extra virgin olive oil
½ lemon, juiced
salt and pepper

- Finely slice the chicken and toss with the figs in a bowl.
- Steam the mangetout over simmering water until tender – about 4 minutes.
- Whisk the shallot with the oil, lemon and salt and pepper.
- Toss the mangetout with the chicken then coat in the dressing and serve.

SERVES 4

Chicken Caesar Salad with Grapefruit

- Thickly slice the chicken breasts and set aside.
- Tip the salad leaves into a serving bowl with the raw pepper. Steam the baby sweetcorn for about 4 minutes until tender, then add to the bowl.
- Cut away the skin of the grapefruit, using the knife to follow the fruit down the sides, cutting away the white pith as well as the skin. Segment into a bowl to catch any juice, then add the grapefruit to the salad bowl and toss gently to combine.
- For the dressing, mash the anchovy fillets with the garlic to a pulp, then stir in the crème fraîche, lemon juice and Parmesan and season carefully. You may want more lemon juice.
- Add 2 tbsp of the dressing to the salad and coat thoroughly.
- Add the chicken to the salad, then spoon over the remaining dressing.

PREPARATION TIME:
15 MINUTES

COOKING TIME:
5 MINUTES

INGREDIENTS

2 chicken breasts, skinned and roasted
  or bought pre-cooked
200 g / 7 oz / ¾ cup mixed salad leaves
1 red pepper, deseeded and finely sliced
100 g / 3 ½ oz / ½ cup baby sweetcorn
1 grapefruit

FOR THE DRESSING

2 anchovy fillets
½ clove of garlic, crushed
150 ml / 5 fl. oz / ⅔ cup crème fraîche
squeeze of lemon juice
2–3 tbsp Parmesan, grated
salt and pepper

Chicken Caesar with Soft-boiled Egg

297

- Add quarters of soft-boiled egg and 1 tbsp of drained capers for a very grown-up version.

298

SERVES 4–6

Mini Chicken Liver Terrines

- Heat a tbsp of butter in a frying pan and cook the chicken livers over a medium heat for 5 minutes, turning them frequently, until golden brown without and just pink within.
- Transfer with a slotted spoon to a food processor, reserving the frying pan and juices.
- Pour the alcohol into the pan, scraping with a wooden spoon, reduce by half and add to the processor.
- Melt 150 g butter and pour into the processor. Add the mace, thyme, garlic and salt and pepper. Blend to a smooth purée.
- Spoon into individual ramekins. Melt the remaining butter and pour over, leave to cool then chill for 24 hours before serving with hot toast.

PREPARATION TIME:
20 MINUTES

COOKING TIME:
10 MINUTES

INGREDIENTS

225 g / 8 oz / 1 cup chicken livers,
  trimmed
225 g / 8 oz / 1 cup butter, softened
75 ml / 2 ½ fl. oz / ⅓ cup madeira
  or marsala
¼ tsp ground mace
1 tsp thyme leaves
1 clove of garlic, crushed
salt and pepper

Chicken Liver and Caper Terrines

299

- The sharpness of capers nicely offset the richness, so try adding 1 tbsp drained capers to the mix after processing.

300

SERVES 4

Chicken Wings with Lemon and Thyme

PREPARATION TIME:
10 MINUTES

COOKING TIME:
35–40 MINUTES

INGREDIENTS

16 chicken wings
100 g / 3 ½ oz / ½ cup butter
1 lemon, juiced
¼ bunch thyme
salt and pepper

- Preheat the oven to 200°C (180°C fan) / 400F / gas 6.
- Melt the butter in a pan and add the lemon, thyme and seasoning. Brush over the chicken wings and coat thoroughly.
- Place the chicken wings in a roasting tin and roast in the oven for 20 minutes. Turn them over, brush again with the butter, then roast for another 15–20 minutes until sticky, golden and cooked through.
- Serve hot.

Chicken Wings with Rosemary

301

- Use rosemary sprigs to brush on the butter to add extra herby flavour.

302

SERVES 4

Chicken Rice Salad

PREPARATION TIME:
25 MINUTES

COOKING TIME:
25 MINUTES

INGREDIENTS

250 g / 9 oz / 1 cup basmati rice, cooked
    and cooled
2 chicken breasts, skin on
2 tbsp groundnut oil
1 tsp Chinese 5-spice powder
1 red pepper, deseeded and
    finely diced
1 green pepper, deseeded and
    finely diced
2–3 tbsp rice vinegar
1 tbsp groundnut oil
salt and pepper
1 tsp sugar
few sprigs coriander (cilantro)

- Preheat the oven to 200°C (180°C fan) / 400F / gas 6.
- Rub the chicken with oil and 5-spice and roast in the oven for 20 minutes until cooked. Set aside to rest.
- Mix the cooled rice with the peppers. Whisk together the rice vinegar, oil, seasoning and a little sugar, taste and correct the seasoning. Toss with the rice.
- Slice the chicken into chunks and sit on top of the rice salad. Decorate with sprigs of coriander and serve.

Chicken Soy Rice Salad

303

- For a more savoury flavour, add 1 tbsp soy sauce to the dressing.

304

SERVES 4

Chicken Fajitas

Chicken Fajitas with Rice

305

- Serve alongside mexican spiced rice.

Chicken Nachos

306

- Use the crisp boat-shape nachos for a change to tortilla wraps.

PREPARATION TIME:
35 MINUTES

COOKING TIME:
10–15 MINUTES

INGREDIENTS

4 chicken breasts, skinned and
    thinly sliced
2 tsp paprika
2 tsp ground cumin
2 tsp ground coriander
pinch dried chilli (chili) flakes
salt and pepper
4 tbsp olive oil
1 onion, peeled and finely sliced
1 red pepper, deseeded and finely sliced
1 yellow pepper, deseeded and
    finely sliced
1 courgette (zucchini), cut into batons
1 lime, juiced
8 tortilla wraps
sour cream
tomato salsa
guacamole

- Coat the chicken in half the spices and leave to marinate for 30 minutes.
- Heat half the oil in a pan until nearly smoking, then cook the onion, peppers and courgettes until golden and tender. Remove from the pan, keep warm and set aside.
- Add the remaining oil and reheat, then add the meat and sprinkle over the remaining spices.
- Stir briskly for a 2–3 minutes until the chicken is just cooked through. Squeeze over the lime juice. Remove and keep warm.
- Wipe out the pan and use to warm the tortillas through.
- Serve the vegetables with the meat, tortilla wraps and sauces.

307

SERVES 4

Griddled Chicken Pittas

PREPARATION TIME:
10 MINUTES

COOKING TIME:
10 MINUTES

INGREDIENTS

2 tbsp olive oil
4 chicken breasts, cut into thick slices
4 pitta breads
2 ripe tomatoes, cut into chunks
1 red onion, finely sliced
4 lettuce leaves
4 tbsp plain yogurt
½ bunch dill or mint, finely chopped
salt and pepper

- Rub the chicken with oil and cook on a hot griddle pan until golden striped and cooked through. Season and set aside.
- Lightly toast or grill the pitta breads until puffed up and split in half.
- Mix the yogurt, dill and seasoning in a bowl.
- Fill the pittas with the chicken, tomatoes, shredded lettuce and onion and drizzle over the yogurt before serving.

Chicken Feta Pittas

 308

- Add feta cheese either in addition to the chicken or instead of it for a veggie version.

309

SERVES 4–6

Vietnamese Chicken Mango Rolls

PREPARATION TIME:
30 MINUTES

INGREDIENTS

100 g / 3 ½ oz rice vermicelli
1 tbsp rice vinegar
2 tbsp fish sauce
bunch mint, finely chopped
⅓ bunch coriander (cilantro), chopped
½ bunch basil, finely chopped
½ cucumber, cut into matchsticks
2 mangos, stoned, peeled and sliced
2–3 chicken breasts, cooked and
    shredded
1 red chilli (chili), deseeded and
    chopped
12 rice pancakes or sheets
75 ml / 2 ½ fl. oz / ⅓ cup soy sauce
1 tsp fresh ginger, grated
½ red chilli (chili), deseeded and
    chopped
1 lime, juiced
1 tsp dried oregano
½ tsp caster (superfine) sugar
salt and pepper

- Soak the vermicelli according to packet instructions and drain once rehydrated. Place in a bowl and add the vinegar and fish sauce, then add the rest of the filling ingredients and mix carefully.
- Soak the pancakes according to packet instructions then lay on kitchen paper to dry.
- Spoon a narrow strip of filling down the centre of each pancake, fold over one half and then roll up as tightly as possible. Slice each roll in half or quarters and refrigerate.
- Make the dipping sauce by whisking the ingredients together. Serve the chilled rolls with the sauce alongside.

Vietnamese Spring Rolls with Prawns

310

- Large cooked king prawns go really well with mango and spices.

311

SERVES 6

Samosas and Chicken Yakitori

- Make the samosas: cook the potatoes in boiling salted water for about 25 minutes or until tender to the point of a knife. Drain. Roughly crush and add the parsley, curry powder and lime juice. Salt and mix well.
- Lay out the feuilles de brik and brush with melted butter. Using two sheets at a time, lay out on the work surface, place a large tbsp of potato mixture in the centre and fold to form a triangle. Repeat until all the sheets and mixture are used up.
- Heat the oil to temperature, then add the samosas carefully, two at a time. Cook until they are golden and crisp on both sides, then remove to kitchen paper.
- Meanwhile marinate the chicken in the sauces and sugar for 20 minutes, then thread onto soaked wooden skewers. Griddle over a high heat for 6–8 minutes until cooked.
- Serve the samosas in a bowl with the yakitori alongside.

PREPARATION TIME:
30 MINUTES

COOKING TIME:
50 MINUTES

INGREDIENTS

24 sheets of feuilles de brik
  or filo pastry
6 potatoes, peeled
2 bunches parsley, chopped
2 tsp curry powder (or try ground
  ginger, cinnamon or cumin)
juice of 1–2 limes
salt
70 g / 2 ½ oz / ⅓ cup butter, melted
oil for deep frying
4 chicken breasts, skinned and cubed
5 tbsp teriyaki sauce
2 tbsp soy sauce
2 tsp sugar

Samosas and Chicken Yakitori with Yogurt Dip

312

- Stir chopped coriander (cilantro) and crushed garlic through some plain yogurt for a dip to serve with both nibbles.

313

SERVES 4–6

Mini Chicken Pasties

- Preheat the oven to 200°C (180°C fan) / 400F / gas 6.
- Heat the oil in a pan and sweat the onion and garlic until softened and turning gold. Add the chicken, vegetables, spices and sauté until cooked through.
- Keeping the remaining filo sheets covered with a damp tea towel, remove one at a time from the pack and brush with melted butter before using.
- Place 2 sheets of pastry on a surface and cut in half – place half back under the tea towel. Brush each sheet with melted butter, then top with a little of the chicken mixture. Wrap the pastry around to enclose the filling and make a really tiny pastilla. Repeat until all the filling and pastry is used up.
- Brush the tops with a little egg wash, then bake in the oven for 15–20 minutes.
- Lightly dust the top with a little icing sugar and cinnamon before serving.

PREPARATION TIME:
30 MINUTES

COOKING TIME:
20 MINUTES

INGREDIENTS

4 tbsp olive oil
1 onion, peeled and thickly sliced
2 garlic cloves, finely chopped
2 chicken breasts, skinned and diced
1 red pepper, deseeded and finely
  chopped
1 courgette (zucchini), finely diced
½ tsp ground cinnamon
½ tsp ground cumin
½ tsp ground coriander
1 egg yolk
salt and pepper
1 pack filo pastry
120 g / 4 oz butter, melted
2 eggs
1 egg yolk, beaten
icing (confectioners') sugar and ground
  cinnamon, to dust

Cheesy Chicken Pasties

314

- Sprinkle the tops with cheese before baking.

315

SERVES 4

Sweet and Sour Chicken Kebabs

Chicken Vegetable Kebabs

316

- Alternate with chunks of sautéed peppers or aubergine (eggplant) for variety.

Sweet and Sour Chicken with Rice

317

- Serve with plain cooked white rice for a foil to the sweetness.

PREPARATION TIME:
5 MINUTES

COOKING TIME:
20 MINUTES

INGREDIENTS

500 g / 1 lb / 2 cups chicken thigh meat, cut into chunks
50 g / 1 ¾ oz / ¼ cup pineapple chunks

FOR THE SAUCE
125 ml / 4 fl. oz / ½ cup pineapple juice
splash dry sherry or Shaoxing rice wine
2 tbsp ketchup
2 tbsp soy sauce
2 tbsp Chinese vinegar or red wine vinegar
½ tsp chilli (chili) flakes
1 tsp cornflour (cornstarch)

- Heat the vegetable oil in a wok until smoking, then add the chicken and stir fry over a high heat until the chicken turns white.
- Remove the chicken from the pan and set aside.
- Mix together the sauce ingredients with the cornflour. Add to the pan and bubble up until thickened.
- Thread the chicken onto skewers alternating with pineapple and serve covered with the sauce.

SERVES 4

Chicken with Spring Vegetables and Herbs

- Heat the oil in a pan and fry the chicken on all sides until golden.
- Tip the vegetables into the pan and sauté to lightly colour, then add the wine and herbs, then put the lid on and leave to simmer for 10–15 minutes until all is cooked.
- Season and serve decorated with the chives.

PREPARATION TIME:
10 MINUTES

COOKING TIME:
20 MINUTES

INGREDIENTS

2 tbsp olive oil
4 chicken breasts, sliced
1 bunch asparagus, trimmed and
    cut into short lengths
200 g / 7 oz / ²⁄₃ cup mangetout
4 whole garlic cloves, peeled
4 tomatoes, quartered
150 ml / 5 fl. oz / ²⁄₃ cup dry
    white wine
few sprigs thyme or rosemary leaves
salt and pepper
chives to decorate

Chicken and Spring Vegetable Stew

319

- Add 200 ml / 7 fl. oz chicken stock with the wine for a loose stew to serve with crusty bread.

320

SERVES 4–8

Chicken Burger with Avocado

- Mix the chicken with the basil, pepper, salt and lemon zest until thoroughly mixed.
- Pour in enough beaten egg to bind, but don't let the mixture get too wet. With wet hands, form the mixture into 8 small or 4 large burgers.
- Chill in the refrigerator for 30 minutes.
- Meanwhile toss the avocado with a little lemon to prevent browning. Lightly toast the burger buns.
- Cook the burgers in a little oil for 3–4 minutes per side, depending on thickness.
- Serve layered with the avocado and mozzarella in the buns.

PREPARATION TIME:
10 MINUTES

COOKING TIME:
8–10 MINUTES

INGREDIENTS

500 g / 1 lb / 2 cups minced chicken
1 bunch basil leaves, finely chopped
1 tsp Espelette pepper
salt
1 lemon, zested
1 egg, beaten
2 avocadoes, peeled, stoned and sliced
2 balls mozzarella, sliced
burger buns

Chicken and Apple Burgers

321

- Try adding grated peeled apple to the mix for sweetness.

322

SERVES 2

Braised Chicken Balls and Peanuts

PREPARATION TIME:
10 MINUTES

COOKING TIME:
20 MINUTES

INGREDIENTS

1 kg / 2 ¼ lbs / 4 ¼ cups minced chicken
1 onion, peeled and grated
1 clove of garlic, crushed
1 tbsp groundnut oil
1 tsp sesame oil
1 head broccoli, separated into florets
150 g / 5 oz / ⅔ cup peanuts
3 cloves of garlic, finely chopped
1 tsp fresh ginger, grated
2 tbsp soy sauce
2 tbsp oyster sauce
1 tbsp dark brown sugar
2 tbsp rice wine
1 red chilli (chili), chopped, optional

- Combine the minced chicken in a bowl with the onion and garlic and mix well with your hands. Form into small balls and refrigerate for 30 minutes.
- Meanwhile heat the oils in a wok, then sauté the broccoli until starting to catch, the chicken balls and toss until starting to turn golden. Add the peanuts and the rest of the ingredients and add a little water.
- Simmer for 10 minutes or until the chicken is cooked through and the sauce is dark and glossy.
- Serve with noodles, if liked.

Korean Braised Chicken

323

- For an easier version, simply chop chicken thighs and sauté with the broccoli.

324

SERVES 2

Chicken Lollipop Salad

PREPARATION TIME:
20 MINUTES

COOKING TIME:
30–40 MINUTES

INGREDIENTS

8 chicken wings
30 g / 1 oz butter
1 shallot, finely sliced
1 clove of garlic, finely sliced
1 stick celery, finely chopped
150 ml / 5 fl. oz / ⅔ cup white wine
300 ml / 10 fl. oz / 1 ¼ cups strong
  chicken stock
1 tbsp butter, chilled
40 g / 1 oz butter
200 g / 7 oz / ¾ cup wild mushrooms,
  cleaned
mache or corn salad to serve

- Cut and discard the wing tips, then halve the wings at the joint. Working with the smaller joint, remove and discard the thinner bone, then scrape meat down the remaining bone.
- Heat the butter in a pan and cook the chicken wings on all sides until golden. Remove and set aside. Add the shallot, garlic and celery and sweat without colouring. Return the chicken wings to the pan.
- Deglaze with the white wine then reduce. Pour in the stock and reduce until syrupy and the wings are cooked. Use a spoon to baste the wings as they cook.
- Once the wings are cooked, remove and keep warm. Whisk the cold butter into the hot sauce until shiny. Return the wings to the pan.
- Heat the butter and cook the mushrooms until tender.
- To serve, place the salad on a plate, top with chicken wings and mushrooms, then spoon the sauce over.

Chicken and Pepper Salad

325

- Replace the mushrooms with red and green pepper chunks.

326

SERVES 4

Chicken and Tarragon Skewers

Chicken and Mint Skewers

327

- Use chopped mint instead of tarragon.

Chicken Tarragon Bites in Pitta

328

- Serve in warmed split pitta breads with a drizzle of plain yogurt.

PREPARATION TIME:
10 MINUTES

COOKING TIME:
15 MINUTES

INGREDIENTS

4 chicken thighs, deboned and meat cubed
1 tbsp olive oil
salt and pepper
¼ bunch tarragon leaves, chopped
½ turmeric
1 lemon, zested

- Marinate the chicken in the remaining ingredients for 30 minutes.
- Thread onto soaked wooden skewers and griddle over high heat until cooked, turning every so often.
- Serve hot.

MAKES 12

Chicken, Cheese and Bacon Rolls

329

PREPARATION TIME:
15 MINUTES

COOKING TIME:
15 MINUTES

....

INGREDIENTS

4 chicken breasts, skinned
12 streaky bacon rashers
1 ball mozzarella, cubed into
    12 pieces

- Preheat the oven to 200°C (180°C fan) / 400F / gas 6.
- Place the chicken breasts in between 2 layers of cling film and batten out with the base of a saucepan or rolling pin to about 1 cm (½ in) thickness.
- Cut each escalope lengthways into 3.
- Lay the bacon out on a board and use the back of a knife to stretch it slightly. Place a piece of chicken on top, then sit a cube of mozzarella at one end and roll the bacon and chicken around the cheese. Secure with a toothpick and repeat until all the ingredients are used up.
- Cook in the oven on a baking sheet for 15 minutes or until the bacon is crisp. Serve hot.

Spicy Rolls

330

- Sprinkle the mozzarella with a pinch of dried chilli (chili) for a kick.

SERVES 2

Chicken Fruit Salad

331

PREPARATION TIME:
10 MINUTES

....

INGREDIENTS

2 chicken breasts, cooked
mixed salad leaves
1 orange, peeled
2 tbsp extra virgin olive oil
½ lime, juiced (optional)
salt and pepper
½ pomegranate
100 g / 3 ½ oz / ½ cup cherries, stoned

- Shred or chop the chicken and place in a serving bowl with the salad leaves.
- Segment the orange over a bowl to catch the juice, placing the segments in the serving bowl. Squeeze out any excess juice from the pith.
- Whisk in the oil and a little lime juice and seasoning, then toss the salad with the dressing.
- Hold the pomegranate over the bowl cut side down and bash with a wooden spoon to release the seeds. Dot the cherries around and serve.

Citrus Salad

332

- Forego cherries if not in season, but experiment with mango, grapefruit, lemon segments.

333

SERVES 4

Chicken Brochettes and Cannelloni

- Preheat the oven to 200°C (180°C fan) / 400F / gas 6.
- Heat the oil in a pan and add the shallot and onion.
- Add the mushrooms and garlic and cook until the liquid has evaporated. Season, then add the parsley. Remove from the heat.
- Cook the cannelloni tubes in boiling water according to packet instructions. Drain and pat dry.
- Stuff the cannellonis with the mixture. Place in a buttered baking dish, pour over cream and sprinkle with parmesan and butter. Cook in the oven for 20 minutes. Foil over and keep warm.
- Roast the chicken in the oven until golden and cooked.
- Leave the chicken to rest for 5 minutes, then slice into chunks. Thread onto skewers alternating with mozzarella and tomato. Serve the cannelloni with the cream sauce spooned over, topped with a skewer.

PREPARATION TIME:
30 MINUTES

COOKING TIME:
20 MINUTES

INGREDIENTS

3 tbsp olive oil
2 shallots, finely chopped
1 clove of garlic, finely chopped
300 g / 10 oz / 1 ¼ cups morel mushrooms, cleaned
½ bunch parsley, chopped
8 cannelloni tubed
300 ml / 10 fl. oz / 1 ¼ cups double (heavy) cream
40 g /1 oz butter
3 tbsp Parmesan, grated
salt and pepper
2 chicken breasts
1 ball mozzarella, sliced
12 sun-dried tomatoes

Chicken Brochettes and Tomato Cannelloni

334

- Spoon some tomato passata over the cannelloni before baking, for a tangy twist.

335

SERVES 2

Chicken and Pepper Salad

- Heat the oil in a pan and sauté the peppers and chicken until golden and tender.
- Remove with a slotted spoon and keep warm.
- Deglaze the pan with the white wine, scraping at the base with a wooden spoon, then stir in the mustard, seasoning and olive oil.
- Toss the chicken and peppers in the warm dressing then serve on salad leaves.

PREPARATION TIME:
10 MINUTES

COOKING TIME:
15 MINUTES

INGREDIENTS

2 tbsp olive oil
2 red peppers, deseeded and roughly chopped
2 chicken breasts, chopped
100 ml / 3 ½ fl oz / ½ cup dry white wine
1 tbsp grain mustard
2 tbsp extra virgin olive oil
salt and pepper
salad leaves

Chicken and Honey Salad

336

- Add 1 tbsp runny honey to the pan for a sweeter edge.

337

SERVES 2

Chicken Salad with Chicory and Avocado

Chicken Salad Sandwich

338

- Mix the chicory and avocado with a little mayonnaise, then pile all the ingredients between thick white sandwich bread.

Citrus Chicken Salad

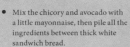

339

- Add segments of pink grapefruit for zing.

PREPARATION TIME:
15 MINUTES

COOKING TIME:
10 MINUTES

INGREDIENTS

2 tbsp olive oil
2 chicken breasts, skinned and cubed
pinch saffron infused in 2 tbsp water
salt and pepper
1 head chicory leaves, separated
1 avocado, stoned and flesh chopped,
    tossed with 1 tsp lemon juice
2 tbsp pine nuts, toasted
2 tbsp raisins
2 tbsp sesame seeds
2 tbsp extra virgin olive oil

- Heat the oil in a pan and fry the chicken until golden. Add the saffron-infused water and toss to coat, then season.
- In a serving bowl arrange the chicory, avocado, pine nuts and raisins and drizzle with extra virgin olive oil.
- Sit the chicken on top and sprinkle over the sesame seeds.

340

SERVES 4

Chicken and Lentil Coconut Soup

- Wash the lentils and pick over for any small stones. Cook in the vegetable stock for about 25 minutes or until tender. Drain the lentils, reserving the cooking liquor.
- In a pan, heat the oil and cook the onions and garlic until golden.
- Add the chicken and spices and cook until golden.
- Return the lentils to the pan and stir well, then stir in the coconut milk, adding a little lentil cooking liquid to loosen. Simmer for 10 minutes.
- Serve decorated with fresh coriander.

PREPARATION TIME:
15 MINUTES

COOKING TIME:
45 MINUTES

....

INGREDIENTS

400 g / 13 ½ oz / 1 ½ cups puy
  or red lentils
750 ml / 1 ⅓ pints / 3 cups vegetable
  stock
2 tbsp olive oil
1 onion, peeled and finely chopped
2 cloves of garlic, finely chopped
1 yellow pepper, deseeded and finely
  chopped
4 chicken thighs, skinned, deboned and
  roughly chopped
1 tsp ground cumin
1 tsp paprika
½ tsp chilli (chili) powder (optional)
400 ml / 14 fl. oz / 1 ½ cups coconut
  milk
salt and pepper
fresh coriander (cilantro)

Lentil Dal

341

- You can make a simple dal by cooking the lentils as above then adding half the coconut milk to make it less liquid. Serve with nan.

342

SERVES 4

Chicken and Red Pepper Meatballs

- Soak the bread in warm water then squeeze it out. Mix thoroughly with the meat.
- Heat the oil in a pan and gently fry the onions, garlic, peppers and rosemary until soft then stir into the meat. Combine well with the paprika and season.
- Form into small balls around 6 cm (2 ½ in) in diameter.
- Heat the oil in a pan and fry the meatballs in batches until golden and cooked through.

PREPARATION TIME:
15 MINUTES

COOKING TIME:
20 MINUTES

....

INGREDIENTS

2 slices stale bread, crusts removed
1 kg / 2 ¼ lbs / 4 ¼ cups minced chicken
2 tbsp olive oil
1 onion, peeled and grated
1 clove of garlic, crushed
1 red pepper, deseeded and very finely
  chopped
1 tbsp rosemary leaves, finely chopped
1 heaped tsp smoked paprika
salt and pepper
3 tbsp olive oil

Meatballs in Tomato Sauce

343

- Fry a chopped onion and some garlic in olive oil, then add 400 g / 14 oz can of chopped tomatoes and simmer until thickened. Season and serve with meatballs.

344

SERVES 4

Chicken with Saffron Rice

PREPARATION TIME:
10 MINUTES

COOKING TIME:
30 MINUTES

INGREDIENTS

4 chicken legs
2 tbsp runny honey
2 tbsp grain mustard
1 tbsp vegetable oil
salt and pepper
1 courgette (zucchini), diced
2 tomatoes, cored and diced
250 g / 9 oz / 1 cup basmati rice
2 cups water infused with pinch saffron

- Preheat the oven to 190°C (170°C fan) / 375F / gas 5.
- Mix together the honey, mustard, oil and seasoning and coat the chicken. Roast in a foil-lined tray for 30 minutes or until golden and sticky.
- Tip the rice into a pan with the water and cook covered with a lid for 10 minutes. Remove from the heat and leave covered for 5 minutes.
- Sauté the courgette briefly in a little oil then add to the rice with the tomatoes. Fork through.
- Serve the chicken with the rice alongside.

Sticky Chicken Pittas   **345**

- This would sit well in split warmed pitta breads for a lunchtime treat.

346

SERVES 6

Chicken and Goats' Cheese Ravioli

PREPARATION TIME:
45 MINUTES COOKING TIME:
3 MINUTES

INGREDIENTS

FOR THE PASTA
500g / 1 lb / 2 cups '00' flour
6 eggs

FOR THE FILLING
200 g / 7 oz / ¾ cup chicken breast, cooked and finely shredded
100 g / 3 ½ oz / ½ cup goats' cheese, chopped
100 g / 3 ½ oz / ½ cup ricotta
8 chive stalks, finely chopped
salt and pepper
butter
Parmesan, grated

- Place the flour in a bowl and make a well in the centre. Crack the eggs into the well. Beat the eggs, then draw in the flour a little at a time.
- Remove the dough from the bowl and knead for 5 minutes. Cover with cling film and refrigerate for 30 minutes.
- Meanwhile make the filling: mix together all the ingredients until thoroughly combined.
- Remove the pasta dough from the fridge. Roll the dough into sheets on a floured surface.
- Place a heaped teaspoon of filling in the middle of the sheet at one end. Repeat all the way along at 5 cm (2 in) intervals.
- Place another sheet of pasta on top, then, working from one end to the other push the sheets together and around each mound of filling. Press down gently to push out all the air. Cut the ravioli into shapes.
- Bring a pan of water to the boil and cook for 3 minutes. Remove then toss with butter and Parmesan cheese.

Spinach and Ricotta Ravioli   **347**

- Use 300 g / 10 oz wilted spinach squeezed dry mixed with the cheeses for a vegetarian version.

348

SERVES 2

Grilled Chicken and Spring Vegetables

Spring Vegetable Salad

349

- Try scrubbed baby carrots, quartered fennel bulbs, halved baby beetroot for variation.

Chicken and Spring Vegetable Pasta

350

- Serve tossed with cooked fusilli pasta.

PREPARATION TIME:
15 MINUTES

COOKING TIME:
20 MINUTES

....

INGREDIENTS

2 chicken breasts, skin on
1 tbsp olive oil
salt and pepper
100 g / 3 ½ oz / ½ cup broad beans, podded
100 g / 3 ½ oz / ½ cup peas
1 bunch asparagus, trimmed
2 ripe tomatoes, cored and cut into wedges
3 tbsp extra virgin olive oil
½ lemon, juiced

- Rub the chicken with oil and seasoning and cook on a griddle pan over medium heat skin side down until golden and crisp. Turn over and cook on the other side for 4 minutes or until cooked through. Set aside to rest.

- Meanwhile cook the bean and peas in salted boiling water for 4 minutes, then drain. Pop the broad beans out of their grey shells; discard the shells and tip peas and beans into a bowl.

- Steam the asparagus spears over simmering water for 3–4 minutes until tender to the point of a knife. Cut into short lengths and add to the bowl with the tomatoes.

- Whisk the oil, lemon juice and seasoning together and toss the vegetables in it gently.

- Slice the chicken and serve with the salad.

SERVES 2

Chicken Aubergine Cannelloni

PREPARATION TIME:
20 MINUTES

COOKING TIME:
20–30 MINUTES

INGREDIENTS

2 tbsp olive oil
2 chicken breasts, thickly sliced
   at an angle
2 red peppers, deseeded and sliced
1 aubergine (eggplant), sliced
   lengthways
olive oil
½ bunch basil
salt and pepper

- Heat the oil in a pan and fry the chicken in batches until golden and sizzling. Remove from the pan with a slotted spoon, then add the peppers and cook until softened.
- Brush the aubergine slices with olive oil, season and griddle in batches on both sides until golden and tender.
- Lay the aubergine slices on the surface and place a little chicken, some peppers and basil in the centre then wrap the aubergine around to form a roll.
- Grill briefly to reheat and serve.

352

SERVES 2

Asian Chicken Salad

PREPARATION TIME:
15 MINUTES

INGREDIENTS

2 chicken breasts, poached and
   shredded
2 carrots, peeled and grated
1 cucumber, cut into fine batons
1 bunch radishes, finely sliced
2–3 tbsp soy sauce
1 lime, juiced
2 tsp fresh ginger, grated
small handful coriander (cilantro),
   chopped
black pepper

- Toss the chicken with the vegetables in a bowl.
- Whisk the soy, lime juice, ginger and coriander in a bowl and add the pepper.
- Toss the chicken and vegetables in the dressing and serve.

353

SERVES 4–6 # Chicken Vegetable Soup with Basil

- Heat the oil or butter in a large pan and sweat the onion, carrot and celery without colouring until softened – about 10 minutes.
- Add the potatoes and chicken, stir well and cook for a few minutes, then add the herbs and stock and simmer for 20 minutes or until the potatoes are tender.
- Season well, sprinkle with torn basil and serve hot.

PREPARATION TIME:
10 MINUTES

COOKING TIME:
35 MINUTES

INGREDIENTS

2 tbsp olive oil or butter
1 onion, peeled and finely chopped
2 carrots, peeled and finely chopped
2 sticks celery, finely chopped
12–16 new potatoes, halved
2–3 chicken breasts, skinned and chopped
1 sprig rosemary or thyme
1 1 / 2 pints / 3 ⅓ cups chicken stock
salt and pepper
½ bunch basil leaves

Chicken and Sage Terrine

354

SERVES 6-8

PREPARATION TIME:
1 HOUR

COOKING TIME:
15 MINUTES

INGREDIENTS

FOR THE TERRINE

500 g / 1 lb / 2 cups chicken breast, skinned and cut into chunks

400 ml / 14 fl. oz / 1 ½ cups chicken stock
1 courgette (zucchini), diced
2 yellow peppers, deseeded and finely chopped
2 leaves gelatine, soaked in cold water
6 sage leaves, finely chopped
salt and pepper

- Heat the chicken stock in a pan and poach the chicken for 10 minutes until cooked. Remove with a slotted spoon and leave to cool.
- Poach the courgette and peppers in the stock for 3–5 minutes until crisp-tender, then remove with a slotted spoon.
- Whisk the gelatine into the hot stock until dissolved.
- Fill a terrine mould with the chicken and vegetables, seasoning as you go and adding sage leaves.
- Pour the liquid over the chicken terrine and refrigerate for at least 4 hours until set.
- Serve in thick slices with chutney.

Chicken Spring Rolls

355

SERVES 4-8

PREPARATION TIME:
10 MINUTES

COOKING TIME:
20 MINUTES

INGREDIENTS

1 tbsp groundnut oil, plus oil for deep-frying
200 g / 7 oz / ¾ cup chicken breast

1 tbsp soy sauce
½ tbsp 5-spice powder
1 carrot, peeled and sliced
1 courgette (zucchini), peeled and sliced
1 red pepper, deseeded and sliced
2 spring onions (scallions), finely sliced lengthways
1 tsp fresh ginger, grated
16 ready-made spring roll wrappers
1 tsp cornflour (cornstarch)
1 tbsp water

- Skin and finely chop the chicken.
- Heat the oil in a wok until nearly smoking, then fry the chicken for 2 minutes. Add the soy and 5-spice, then remove with a slotted spoon and set aside to cool. Wipe the wok clean.
- Place the vegetables in a bowl with the ginger, then add the chicken mixture and stir to combine.
- Lay 2 spring roll wrappers on top of one another. Place 2 tbsp filling in the centre then roll the wrapper up, sealing the edges with the cornflour mixed with water to make a paste. Repeat until all the wrappers are used up.
- Fill the wok a quarter-full with oil and heat until a cube of bread turns golden and sizzles when thrown in. Deep fry the spring rolls in batches for 3 minutes, turning carefully, until golden and crisp.
- Drain on kitchen paper and serve.

356

SERVES 4

Chicken, Raisin and Almond Salad

PREPARATION TIME:
15 MINUTES

COOKING TIME:
15 MINUTES

INGREDIENTS

4 chicken breasts, skin on
1 tbsp olive oil
salt and pepper
80 g / 2 ½ oz / ⅓ cup raisins
80 g / 2 ½ oz / ⅓ cup whole almonds, skinned
2 heads red chicory, leaves separated
2 tsp honey
1 tbsp grain mustard
60 ml / 2 fl. oz extra virgin olive oil

- Rub the chicken with oil and seasoning and cook on a griddle pan over medium heat skin side down until golden and crisp. Turn over and cook on the other side for 4 minutes or until cooked through. Set aside to rest.
- Place the almonds, raisins and chicory in a serving bowl.
- Whisk together the honey and mustard, then whisk in the oil to make an emulsion. Season.
- Slice the chicken and sit on top of the salad. Spoon over the dressing and serve.

Chicken Orange Almond Salad 357

- Add orange segments and use a drop of rose water in the dressing for a hint of the Middle East.

358

SERVES 2

Salmon and Corn Chowder

PREPARATION TIME:
20 MINUTES

COOKING TIME:
25 MINUTES

INGREDIENTS

30 g / 1 oz butter
1 shallot, finely chopped
100 ml / 3 ½ fl. oz / ½ cup white wine
200 ml / 7 fl. oz / ¾ cup creme fraiche
200 g / 7 oz / ¾ cup smoked salmon trimmings
100 g / 3 ½ oz / ½ cup sweetcorn
½ lemon, juiced
4 king prawns, cooked

- Heat the butter in a pan and sweat the shallot without colouring. Add the white wine, reduce by half, then add the creme fraiche.
- When hot, stir in the salmon and sweetcorn, season, then add a squeeze of lemon juice. Stir in the prawns and serve.

Pasta with Salmon Chowder 359

- Boil 2 portions of pasta, according to the packet instructions. Toss the pasta in the sauce and serve.

360

SERVES 4

Chicken and Grapefruit Salad

- Shred or finely slice the chicken and place in a bowl.
- Segment the grapefruit holding it over a bowl then squeeze any excess juice into the bowl as well. Tip the segments in with the chicken.
- Whisk the grapefruit juice with the oil and some seasoning.
- Add the lettuce leaves, onion, artichokes and walnuts to the chicken and toss everything lightly in the dressing, then serve.

PREPARATION TIME:
20 MINUTES

INGREDIENTS

4 chicken breasts, cooked
1 grapefruit, peeled
3 tbsp extra virgin olive oil
salt and pepper
1 head little gem lettuce, leaves
    separated
1 red onion, peeled and finely sliced
4 artichoke bottoms, cooked (from
    a jar), and sliced
2 tbsp walnuts, crushed

Chicken and Blood Orange Salad

361

- This would work well with blood oranges in season, or try normal oranges pepped up with a little lime or lemon juice.

362

SERVES 4

Chicken Nuggets with Tartare Sauce

- Bash the chicken breasts between 2 pieces cling film with a rolling pin until about 2 cm (1 in) thick.
- Cut each piece into thick strips and place in a bowl with the buttermilk. Refrigerate for at least 2 hours or even overnight.
- To make the sauce, mix the mayonnaise with the rest of the ingredients. Taste, adjust the seasoning and chill until needed.
- The next day, dip them one at a time into the flour, egg then breadcrumbs mixed with the flavourings and lay on a rack to dry slightly.
- Heat 1 cm (½ in) depth oil in a pan and fry the chicken in batches until golden on both sides and cooked through.
- Serve with the sauce on the side to dunk.

PREPARATION TIME:
5 MINUTES

COOKING TIME:
15 MINUTES

INGREDIENTS

4 chicken breasts, skinned
300 ml / 10 fl. oz / 1 ¼ cups buttermilk
100 g / 3 ½ oz / ½ cup plain
    (all-purpose) flour
2 eggs, beaten
200 g / 7 oz / ¾ cup breadcrumbs
1 tsp mustard powder
pinch cayenne
salt and pepper
vegetable oil
200 g / 7 oz / ¾ cup mayonnaise
1 shallot, finely chopped
2 gherkins or cornichons, chopped
2 tbsp capers, drained
½ bunch parsley, chopped
½ lemon, juiced
salt and pepper

Chicken Nuggets and Spicy Sauce

363

- Try mixing tomato ketchup, Dijon mustard, lime pickle and Worcestershire sauce in a small bowl, tasting as you go to achieve a piquant dipping sauce for nuggets.

CLASSIC MAINS

364

SERVES 4

Tapenade Chicken with Sautéed Potatoes

PREPARATION TIME:
10 MINUTES

COOKING TIME:
40 MINUTES

INGREDIENTS

80 g / 2 ½ oz / ⅓ cup black olive
  tapenade
4 chicken thighs, skin on, bone in
salt and pepper
olive oil
1 kg / 2 lb / 4 cups waxy potatoes,
  quartered
1 kg / 2 lb / 4 cups baby spinach leaves,
  washed
½ lemon, juiced

- Preheat the oven to 200°C (180°C fan) / 400F / gas 6
- Rub the tapenade over the chicken thighs, then place in a roasting tin, drizzle with a little oil and cook for 30–40 minutes, until cooked through.
- Heat 4 tbsp olive oil in a deep-sided pan and cook the potatoes, turning occasionally, until crisp and cooked through. Season.
- Toss the spinach leaves with a little oil, lemon juice and seasoning.
- Serve the chicken thighs with the potatoes and spinach leaves.

Sun-dried Tomato Tapenade Chicken

365

- You could use sun dried tomato or normal pesto in place of the tapenade.

366

SERVES 4

Poached Chicken with Chanterelles

PREPARATION TIME:
10 MINUTES

COOKING TIME:
45 MINUTES

INGREDIENTS

4 chicken breasts
1 celery stick, chopped
1 carrot, chopped
½ onion
6 black peppercorns
1 bay leaf
50 g / 1 ¾ oz / ¼ cup butter
50 g / 1 ¾ oz / ¼ cup plain
  (all-purpose) flour
40 g / 1 oz butter
100 g / 3 ½ oz / ½ cup chanterelle
  mushrooms, brushed
100 ml / 3 ½ fl. oz / ½ cup double
  (heavy) cream
salt and pepper

- Place the chicken in a pan with the vegetables, peppercorns and bay leaf. Cover with water, simmer and skim any scum from the top.
- Leave to poach at barely a 'blip' for about 20 minutes, or until just cooked through. Remove the chicken from the pan, reserving the poaching liquor.
- Melt the butter in a pan and stir in the flour to make a 'roux'. Slowly whisk in 300 ml of the poaching liquid to make a smooth thick velouté. Season and leave to simmer gently for about 10 minutes to cook out the flour.
- Meanwhile melt the butter in a pan and sauté the mushrooms until just cooked.
- Slice the cooked chicken, then stir into the pan with the cooked mushrooms.
- Stir the cream into the velouté and adjust the seasoning, then serve.

Poached Chicken with Courgettes

367

- Sauté diced courgettes (zucchinis) to serve alongside when chanterelles are not in season.

368

SERVES 4

Creamy Chicken

- Preheat the oven to 220°C (200°C fan) / 425F / gas 7.
- Season the chicken pieces, then dredge lightly in flour.
- Heat a little oil in a pan with the butter and sauté the chicken until golden brown on all sides. Transfer the pan to the oven and cook for a further 10–15 minutes or until cooked through.
- Remove the chicken to a dish and place the pan back on the heat. Add the shallots and cook until softened, then add the white wine, stirring to deglaze the pan.
- When reduced by two thirds, add the tomato, tarragon and chicken stock and reduce by half. Whisk in the cream, adjust the seasoning and cook until thickened.
- Serve the sauce over the chicken.

PREPARATION TIME:
10 MINUTES

COOKING TIME:
35–40 MINUTES

....

INGREDIENTS

4 chicken breasts, cut into large pieces
salt and pepper
2 tbsp plain (all-purpose) flour
olive oil
50 g / 1 ¾ oz / ¼ cup butter
2 shallots, finely chopped
1 tomato, skinned, deseeded and finely chopped
2 sprigs tarragon
200 ml / 7 fl. oz / ¾ cup dry white wine
200 ml / 7 fl. oz / ¾ cup chicken stock
75 ml / 2 ½ fl. oz / ⅓ cup double (heavy) cream

Creamy Chicken with Crème Fraîche

369

- Try using crème fraîche for a fresher tasting sauce.

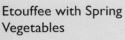

370

SERVES 4

Slow Cooked Chicken Etouffee

- Heat the oil in a deep sided pan and fry the chicken on all sides until golden.
- Add the onion and garlic with the bacon and continue to cook until deep gold and sweet.
- Meanwhile blanch the broad beans in boiling water for 4 minutes. Drain, cool slightly then pop out of the grey skins to leave the bright green beans.
- Add the potatoes and fennel and cook for a few minutes, then add the thyme, beans and wine, season and cover with a lid.
- Cook over a low heat for 20–25 minutes until the chicken is cooked through.
- Serve with crusty bread.

PREPARATION TIME:
10 MINUTES

COOKING TIME:
45–50 MINUTES

....

INGREDIENTS

2 tbsp olive oil
4 chicken legs
1 onion, peeled and finely sliced
2 cloves of garlic, finely sliced
4 rashers smoked streaky bacon, diced
200 g / 7 oz / ¾ cup broad beans
1 bulb fennel, cored and thickly sliced
8 waxy potatoes, quartered lengthways
4 sprigs thyme
200 ml / 7 fl. oz / ¾ cup white wine
salt and pepper

Etouffee with Spring Vegetables

371

- Add baby turnips, peas, baby carrots and courgettes (zucchinis) to ring the changes.

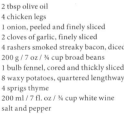

372

SERVES 4

Chicken and Apricot Tagine

Pork and Apricot Tagine

 373

- Try using cubed pork fillet instead of the chicken.

Chicken and Plum Tagine

 374

- In autumn, use halved stoned fresh plums in season.

PREPARATION TIME:
10 MINUTES

COOKING TIME:
45 MINUTES

INGREDIENTS

2 tbsp olive oil
1 onion, peeled and finely sliced
2 cloves of garlic, finely sliced
4 chicken thighs, skinned
1 tsp ras-el-hanout spice mix
1 tsp ground (cilantro) coriander seeds
1 large pinch dried chilli (chili) flakes
400 ml / 14 fl. oz / 1 ½ cups
    chicken stock
200 g / 7 oz / ¾ cup dried apricots
salt and pepper
basmati rice, cooked, to serve

- Heat the oil in a large pan and cook the onions until golden and tender.
- Add the garlic and cook for a few minutes, then remove all from the pan with a slotted spoon.
- Increase the heat and brown the chicken thighs on all sides, then tip the onions back into the pan and sprinkle over the spices.
- Pour over the stock, add the apricots and season, lower the heat and cook gently for about 45 minutes or until the sauce has thickened and the chicken is cooked.
- Serve with the basmati rice.

West Indian Roast Chicken

375

SERVES 4–6

- Preheat the oven to 220°C (200°C fan) / 425F / gas 7.
- Place the chicken in a roasting tin and stuff the cavity with 2 pieces celery, herbs. Run the breast with butter and season. Roast in the oven for 20 minutes.
- Reduce the heat to 180°C (160°C fan) / 350F / gas 4
- After 30 minutes, add the pineapple and the spices and cook for another 30–40 minutes or until the juices run clear when pierced with a toothpick.
- Leave to rest for 20 minutes before carving and serve with the spiced pineapple.

PREPARATION TIME:
10 MINUTES

COOKING TIME:
1 HOUR 30 MINUTES

INGREDIENTS

1 oven ready chicken
3 sticks celery, chopped in half
small bunch thyme
2 bay leaves
salt and pepper
2 tbsp butter
1 cinnamon stick
2 star anise
½ pineapple, peeled and sliced
  into thick rings
1 tsp brown sugar

Roast Chicken with Pears

376

- Replace the slices of pineapple with pears.

Roast Chicken with Persillade Tomatoes

377

SERVES 4–6

- Preheat the oven to 160°C (140°C fan) / 325F / gas 3.
- Place the tomatoes cut side up in a roasting tin, drizzle with oil, season and roast for 2 hours or even longer until shrivelled and deeply savoury. Set aside.
- Increase the oven to 220°C (200°C fan) / 425F / gas 7.
- Place the chicken in a roasting tin, smear with oil and season generously, stuff the cavity with rosemary. Roast in the oven for 20 minutes.
- Reduce the heat to 180°C (160°C fan) / 350F / gas 4 and cook for 1 hour or until the juices run clear when pierced with a toothpick. Leave to rest for 20 minutes.
- Place the parsley, garlic, 1 tsp salt and zest on a board and very finely chop with a sharp knife. Smear on top of the roasted tomatoes and return to the oven for 5 minutes to heat through.
- Serve the chicken carved with the persillade tomatoes alongside.

PREPARATION TIME:
10 MINUTES

COOKING TIME:
3 HOURS 30 MINUTES

INGREDIENTS

4 ripe tomatoes
2 tbsp olive oil
salt and pepper
1 oven-ready chicken
3 sprigs rosemary
1 bunch parsley, chopped
2 cloves of garlic, chopped
zest of 1 lemon

Roast Chicken with Balsamic Tomatoes

378

- Drizzle Balsamic vinegar over the tomatoes for an extra tang.

379

SERVES 4–6

Bacon Wrapped Roast Chicken

PREPARATION TIME:
10 MINUTES

COOKING TIME:
1 HOUR 30 MINUTES

INGREDIENTS

1 oven ready chicken
1 tbsp fennel seeds, lightly crushed
2 tbsp olive oil
salt and pepper
4 rashers smoked streaky bacon
2–3 tbsp olive oil
4 carrots, peeled and cut into short
    lengths
1 onion, quartered
4 garlic cloves, lightly bruised
4 sprigs thyme

- Preheat the oven to 220°C (200°C fan) / 425F / gas 7.
- Mix together the fennel seeds, oil and seasoning and rub over the skin of the chicken. Place the chicken in a roasting tin and cover the breast with the bacon, pressing to keep in place. Roast in the oven for 20 minutes.
- Reduce the heat to 180°C (160°C fan) / 350F / gas 4.
- Tip the carrots into the roasting tin around the chicken with the onion and toss with oil and garlic, tucking the thyme sprigs around. Season and cook for 1 hour or until the juices run clear when pierced with a toothpick.
- Leave the chicken to rest for 20 minutes before carving and serving with the vegetables.

Prosciutto Wrapped Chicken   380

- Thin slices of cured ham such as prosciutto can be substituted for the bacon, giving a very crisp savoury result.

381

SERVES 4

Roast Chicken with Lemon Thyme Mousse

PREPARATION TIME:
40 MINUTES

COOKING TIME:
45 MINUTES

INGREDIENTS

4 chicken legs
2 tbsp olive oil
1 tbsp thyme leaves
½ lemon, juiced
200 ml / 7 fl. oz / ¾ cup white wine

FOR THE MOUSSE

500 g / 1 lb / 2 cups chicken breast,
    skinned
2–3 egg whites
salt and pepper
600 ml / 1 pint / 2 ½ cups double (heavy)
    cream
zest of 1 lemon
3 tbsp thyme leaves, chopped

- Poach the chicken breasts for 15–18 minutes in a pan of barely simmering, lightly salted water. Leave to cool.
- Once cool, place in a food processor and process until finely chopped. Add the egg whites one at a time. Press the mixture through a sieve then refrigerate for 2 hours.
- Preheat the oven to 190°C (170°C fan) / 375F / gas 5. Place the chicken in a tin, rub with oil, thyme and lemon juice and roast for 40 minutes.
- Place the mousse bowl in another bowl filled with ice and stir in the cream until smooth. Stir in the zest and thyme.
- Pour the mousse into a greased mould and place in a tin. Fill halfway with boiling water and bake for 20 minutes, then leave to cool for 10 minutes.
- Set the roasting tin from the chicken legs on the heat and add the white wine, scraping with a wooden spoon to make a sauce. Reduce until syrupy and season.
- Serve chicken with the mousse and sauce spooned over.

Mousse with Tarragon and Mushrooms   382

- You could add tarragon in place of the thyme, and try adding very finely chopped cooked mushrooms.

383

SERVES 4

Chicken and Red Wine Fricassee

Chicken and Red Wine with Croutons

384

- Tear baguette or ciabatta into bite size pieces and toss with olive oil. Grill or bake for a few minutes until golden and crunchy, then sprinkle on the fricassee to serve.

Chicken and White Wine Fricassee

385

- Use white wine in place of the red for a lighter summer dish.

PREPARATION TIME:
10 MINUTES

COOKING TIME:
45–50 MINUTES

INGREDIENTS

2 tbsp olive oil
4 chicken thighs
1 onion, peeled and finely sliced
2 cloves of garlic, finely sliced
4 rashers smoked streaky bacon, diced
200 g / 7 oz / ¾ cup chestnut
   mushrooms, thickly sliced
4 sprigs thyme
200 ml / 7 fl. oz / ¾ cup red wine
salt and pepper

- Heat the oil in a deep sided pan and fry the chicken on all sides until golden.
- Add the onion and garlic and continue to cook until deep gold and sweet.
- Add the bacon and mushrooms and cook for a few minutes, then add the thyme and wine, season and cover with a lid.
- Cook over a low heat for 20–25 minutes until the chicken is cooked through.
- Serve with crusty bread.

386

SERVES 4

Chicken and Pea Pie

PREPARATION TIME:
30 MINUTES

COOKING TIME:
25 MINUTES

INGREDIENTS

40 g / 1 oz butter
4 chicken thighs, skinned, deboned and
   chopped
150 g / 5 oz / ⅔ cup pancetta or diced
   streaky bacon
200 g / 7 oz / ¾ cup chestnut
   mushrooms, quartered
1 clove of garlic, finely chopped
250 g / 9 oz / 1 cup peas
350 ml / 12 fl. oz / 1 ½ cups double
   (heavy) cream
4 sprigs tarragon or thyme
salt and pepper
1 sheet ready-rolled puff pastry
1 egg, beaten

- Preheat the oven to 190°C (170°C fan) / 375F / gas 5.
- Heat the butter in a pan and fry the chicken and bacon until golden
  and the fat starts to run.
- Add the mushrooms and garlic and cook until the liquid
  evaporates, then add the cream and herbs, season and bubble up
  to thicken.
- Tip into a pie dish. Roll out the pastry on a floured surface, then
  place carefully over the pie filling.
- Brush with beaten egg and bake for 25 minutes or until the pastry
  is golden and risen.

Mini Chicken and Pea Pies 387

- If you have little gratin dishes make small pies for
  each person, just cook them slightly less – about
  20 minutes.

388

SERVES 4

Chicken with Mashed Potatoes

PREPARATION TIME:
15 MINUTES

COOKING TIME:
30 MINUTES

INGREDIENTS

4 chicken legs
salt and pepper
1.5 kg / 3 lb / 6 ⅓ cups floury potatoes,
   peeled and cubed
100 g / 3 ½ oz / ½ cup butter
100 ml / 3 ½ fl. oz / ½ cup milk
basil leaves, to serve

- Season the chicken legs well, then steam over simmering water
  until cooked through and the juices run clear – about 20 minutes.
- Meanwhile cook the potatoes in boiling salted water until tender.
  Drain thoroughly and return to the heat briefly to dry out.
- Mash well with the butter and a splash of milk until completely
  smooth. Season well.
- Grill the cooked chicken legs until golden on top.
- Serve the chicken with a spoon of mashed potato alongside,
  scattered with the basil leaves.

Chicken with Ham and Basil 389

- Try wrapping the chicken legs in basil, then
  in cured ham for a stronger flavour.

390

SERVES 4

Chicken Tagliatelle with Peppers

- Heat the butter in a pan, then add the chicken. Sauté until golden, then remove from the pan with a slotted spoon.
- Add the peppers and sauté over high heat until tender, then add the chopped tomatoes.
- Meanwhile cook the tagliatelle according to packet instructions, then drain, reserving a cupful of the cooking water.
- Add a little of the water to the peppers to loosen, then add the baby spinach and allow to wilt. Stir in the chicken
- Toss the sauce and chicken with the tagliatelle, then serve.

PREPARATION TIME:
10 MINUTES

COOKING TIME:
20 MINUTES

INGREDIENTS

40 g / 1 oz butter
200 g / 7 oz / ¾ cup chicken breast, cut into slices
2 red (bell) peppers, deseeded and sliced
1 can chopped tomatoes
handful of baby spinach leaves
salt and pepper
350 g / 12 oz / 1 ⅓ cups tagliatelle

Chicken Tagliatelle with Cream

391

- Add 200 ml / 7 fl. oz / ½ cup double (heavy) cream with the chopped tomatoes, for a creamier dish.

392

SERVES 4

Griddled Chicken with Penne

- Cook the pasta in boiling salted water according to packet instructions. Drain, reserving a little of the water.
- Meanwhile heat the oil in a pan and fry the chicken until golden and cooked through. Add the asparagus spears and season, then reduce the heat until needed.
- Toss the pasta with the extra virgin olive oil and lemon juice, adding a little cooking water to lubricate and season.
- Toss with the cherry tomatoes, onion, asparagus and chicken slices. Serve sprinkled with Parmesan.

PREPARATION TIME:
5 MINUTES

COOKING TIME:
15 MINUTES

INGREDIENTS

500 g / 1 lb / 2 cups penne pasta
2 chicken breasts, sliced into 3 pieces
2 tbsp olive oil
salt and pepper
handful asparagus spears, halved
2 tbsp extra virgin olive oil
1 tbsp lemon juice
16 cherry tomatoes, halved
1 red onion, sliced
25 g / 1 oz Parmesan, grated

Griddled Chicken with Penne and Artichokes

393

- Try adding bottled artichokes to the pasta instead of the asparagus.

394

SERVES 4–6

Roast Chicken with Wild Rice

Spicy Roast Chicken

395

- Try experimenting with lemon juice, hot sauce, white wine, sugar and bay leaves in the rub for the chicken, all of which will really boost its flavour.

Roast Chicken with Vegetable Rice

396

- Replace the wild rice with vegetable or jasmine rice.

PREPARATION TIME:
15 MINUTES

COOKING TIME:
1 HOUR 30 MINUTES

INGREDIENTS

1 oven ready chicken
1 tbsp red wine vinegar
2 cloves of garlic, crushed
1 tsp smoked paprika
1 tsp dried oregano
1 tsp cayenne pepper
2 tbsp olive oil
salt
250 g / 9 oz / 1 cup wild rice
2 tbsp olive oil
1 onion, peeled and finely chopped
4 ripe tomatoes, cored and diced
¼ bunch parsley, chopped

- Preheat the oven to 220°C (200°C fan) / 425F / gas 7.
- Mix together vinegar, garlic, paprika, oregano and cayenne and whisk with the oil and salt to an emulsion. Rub over the skin of the chicken. Place the chicken in a roasting tin and roast in the oven for 20 minutes.
- Reduce the heat to 180°C (160°C fan) / 350F / gas 4 and cook for 1 hour or until the juices run clear when pierced with a toothpick.
- Meanwhile, cook the wild rice according to packet instructions, then drain.
- Heat the oil in a pan and fry the onion and tomato until softened and toss with the wild rice.
- Leave the chicken to rest for 15 minutes before carving and serving with the rice.

397

SERVES 4

Chicken with Homardine Sauce

- Heat the oil in a large pan and sauté the lobster shells for a few minutes. Add the stock and water, simmer and reduce by half. Use a slotted spoon to skim the surface, removing any impurities.
- Once reduced, strain through a large sieve, pressing down to extract maximum flavour, then strain again through a fine sieve for a really smooth sauce.
- Return to the heat and reduce again until reduced by half. Add the cream and simmer for 15 minutes, then whisk in the butter.
- Steam the chicken breasts over simmering water for 10–12 minutes until cooked through. Season.
- Slice the chicken and serve the homardine sauce spooned over.

PREPARATION TIME:
15 MINUTES

COOKING TIME:
1–1 HOUR 30 MINUTES

INGREDIENTS

2 tbsp vegetable oil
350 g / 12 oz / 1 ½ cups lobster carcass, chopped up (ask your fishmonger)
950 ml / 1 quart / 4 cups chicken or veal stock
500 ml / 1 pint / 2 cups water
700 ml / 1 ⅓ pints / 3 cups double (heavy) cream
60 g / 2 oz butter
4 chicken supremes
salt and pepper

Chicken with Crab Shells

398

- If your budget doesn't stretch to lobster, use crab shells instead.

399

SERVES 4

Chicken Pie

- Preheat the oven to 200°C (180°C fan) / 400F / gas 6.
- Heat the butter in a pan and fry the chicken pieces until golden in patches. Remove with a slotted spoon.
- Sweat the shallot with the herbs until softened and the shallot is translucent. Stir in the flour to make a paste, then whisk in the milk a little at a time to make a smooth sauce. Return the chicken to the pan, season and leave to simmer for 10 minutes until thickened.
- Tip the chicken into a pie dish. Roll the pastry out on a floured surface to slightly larger than the pie dish and sit on top of the filling, using an upturned egg cup if necessary to hold it above the filling.
- Brush with beaten egg, make a hole in the pastry to let the steam escape and bake in the oven for about 30 minutes, until the pastry is golden.

PREPARATION TIME:
20 MINUTES

COOKING TIME:
30 MINUTES

INGREDIENTS

1 sheet (225 g / 8 oz) puff pastry, ready rolled
2 tbsp butter
3–4 chicken thighs, deboned and skinned, cut into chunks
1 shallot, finely chopped
3 sprigs thyme
2 sprigs tarragon leaves
1 ½ tbsp plain (all-purpose) flour
300 ml / 10 fl. oz / 1 ¼ cups milk
salt and pepper
1 egg, beaten

Chicken and Ham Pie

400

- Add a handful of cubed ham to the pie mix for a savoury depth of flavour.

401

SERVES 4–6

Roast Chicken with Orange and Fennel

PREPARATION TIME:
10 MINUTES

COOKING TIME:
1 HOUR 30 MINUTES

INGREDIENTS

1 oven ready chicken
1 tbsp fennel seeds, lightly crushed
2 tbsp olive oil
1 orange, zested
salt and pepper
2–3 tbsp olive oil
1 orange
4 carrots, peeled and cut into short
    lengths
1 onion, quartered
4 sprigs thyme

- Preheat the oven to 220°C (200°C fan) / 425F / gas 7.
- Mix together the fennel seeds, oil, zest and seasoning and rub over the skin of the chicken. Place the chicken in a roasting tin. Roast in the oven for 20 minutes.
- Reduce the heat to 180°C (160°C fan) / 350F / gas 4.
- Cut the orange into thick slices. Tip into the roasting tin around the chicken with the carrots and onion and toss with oil, tucking the thyme sprigs around. Season and cook for 1 hour or until the juices run clear when pierced with a toothpick.
- Leave the chicken to rest for 20 minutes before carving and serving with the vegetables.

Roast Chicken with Coriander and Orange

402

- Coriander seeds have a citrus hint to them and work well with the orange.

403

SERVES 2

Pan-fried Chicory, Chicken and Peanuts

PREPARATION TIME:
10 MINUTES

COOKING TIME:
10 MINUTES

INGREDIENTS

2 tbsp olive oil
2 chicken thighs, skinned, deboned and
    chopped
2 heads of chicory, separated into leaves
    and chopped
½ orange, juiced
2 tomatoes, cored and diced
2 tbsp peanuts
salt and pepper

- Heat the oil in a pan and briskly fry the chicken until golden.
- Add the chicory and cook until wilted, then stir in the orange juice and tomatoes.
- Spoon onto plates and sprinkle over peanuts and seasoning, then serve.

Pan-fried Chicory

404

- Halve the chicory and core, then fry cut side down gently in butter and white wine with a lid on until tender.

405

SERVES 4

Chicken with Potatoes and Pumpkin

Chicken With
Sautéed Fennel

406

- Try using a thickly sliced fennel bulb in place of the pumpkin for a cleaner flavour.

Chicken with
Sautéed Turnips

407

- Sweet baby turnips would be perfect in early spring.

PREPARATION TIME:
15 MINUTES

COOKING TIME:
30 MINUTES

....

INGREDIENTS

4 chicken supremes, bone-in, skin on
3 tbsp olive oil
salt and pepper
30 g / 1 oz butter
1 kg / 2 lb / 4 ¼ cups new potatoes, scrubbed
1 small pumpkin or butternut squash, peeled, deseeded and cubed
2 sprigs thyme
100 ml / 3 ½ fl. oz / ½ cup chicken stock

- Preheat the oven to 200°C (180°C fan) / 400F / gas 6.
- Drizzle the chicken with oil, season and roast in the oven for 25 minutes or until just cooked.
- Meanwhile, heat the butter in a pan and sauté the potatoes and pumpkin, adding the chicken stock once they are golden in patches. Add the thyme, season and leave to cook until tender – about 15 minutes.
- Slice the chicken thickly and serve with the sautéed potatoes and pumpkin.

408

SERVES 4

Stuffed Chicken with Risotto

**PREPARATION TIME:
20 MINUTES**

**COOKING TIME:
40 MINUTES**

INGREDIENTS

4 chicken escalopes, 1 cm (½ in) thick
2 tbsp olive oil
2 peppers, chopped
1 shallot, finely chopped
salt and pepper
40 g / 1 oz butter
1 onion, peeled and finely chopped
1 celery stalk, peeled and finely sliced
320 g / 11 oz / 1 ⅓ cups risotto rice
100 ml / 3 ½ fl.oz / ½ cup white wine
1 l / 2 ¼ pints / 4 ¼ cups chicken
    or vegetable stock
150 g / 5 oz / ⅔ cup Parmesan, grated
2 tbsp olive oil
1 onion, peeled and chopped
1 red pepper, chopped
1 clove of garlic, finely sliced
1 tsp smoked paprika
400 g / 14 oz / 1 ½ cups tomatoes

- Heat the oil in a pan and sauté the shallot and peppers.
  Spoon along the middle of each chicken escalope, then roll
  up and wrap tightly in cling film. Steam chicken over simmering
  water for 20–25 minutes.
- Heat the oil and butter in a large pan and add the onion and celery.
  Cook until soft.
- Add the rice and stir to coat in the butter. Pour in the wine and stir
  the rice while the wine is absorbed.
- Reduce the heat a little and add hot stock, a ladleful at a time.
  After about 15–20 minutes the rice should be soft but with a slight
  bite. Season and remove from the heat. Add the Parmesan and
  set aside.
- In another pan, heat oil and cook the onions, pepper and garlic.
  Add tomatoes and paprika, simmer for 10 minutes, then blend.
  Return to pan, and reheat.
- Serve the chicken sliced with the risotto and sauce alongside.

Creamy Stuffed Chicken

409

- Add 2 tbsp cream cheese to the stuffing for a more
  indulgent finish.

410

SERVES 4

Chicken with Creamy Chestnut Sauce

**PREPARATION TIME:
5 MINUTES**

**COOKING TIME:
25 MINUTES**

INGREDIENTS

4 chicken supremes, skin on
2 tbsp olive oil
salt and pepper
30 g / 1 oz butter
1 shallot, finely chopped
1 clove of garlic, crushed
75 ml / 2 ½ fl. oz / ⅓ cup dry white wine
150 ml / 5 fl. oz / ⅔ cup chicken stock
300 ml / 10 fl. oz / ½ cup double (heavy)
    cream
150 g / 5 oz / ⅔ cup vacuum-packed
    cooked chestnuts
salt and pepper
nutmeg, grated
basmati rice, to serve

- Preheat the oven to 200°C (180°C fan) / 400F / gas 6
- Drizzle the chicken with oil, season and roast in the oven for
  25 minutes or until cooked through.
- Meanwhile heat the butter in a pan and sweat the shallot and garlic.
  Deglaze with the wine and reduce to almost nothing, then add the
  stock and reduce by half.
- Add the cream and chestnuts and simmer for 5 minutes then whiz
  in a blender until smooth. Return to the pan, reheat, season and
  add a little grated nutmeg.
- Leave the chicken to rest for 5 minutes before serving with the
  sauce and basmati rice.

Chicken with Creamy
Mushroom Sauce

411

- You could use 100 g chestnut mushrooms as well
  as or in place of the chestnuts.

412

SERVES 4

Chicken and Summer Fruit Tagine

- Heat the oil in a large pan and cook the onions until golden and tender.
- Add the garlic and cook for a few minutes, then remove all from the pan with a slotted spoon.
- Increase the heat and brown the chicken thighs on all sides, then tip the onions back into the pan and sprinkle over the spices.
- Pour over the stock, season, lower the heat and cook gently for about 45 minutes or until the sauce has thickened and the chicken is cooked.
- Stir in the mango and dragon fruit and heat through.
- Serve with the basmati rice.

PREPARATION TIME:
10 MINUTES

COOKING TIME:
45 MINUTES

INGREDIENTS

2 tbsp olive oil
1 onion, peeled and finely sliced
2 cloves of garlic, finely sliced
4 chicken thighs, skinned
1 tsp ras-el-hanout spice mix
1 tsp ground (cilantro) coriander seeds
1 large pinch dried chilli (chili) flakes
400 ml / 14 fl. oz / 1 ½ cups chicken stock
200 g / 7 oz / ¾ cup mango, sliced
2 dragon fruit, cubed
salt and pepper
basmati rice, cooked, to serve

Chicken and Winter Fruit Tagine

413

- You could use pineapple, papaya and sultanas in the colder months.

414

SERVES 4

Creole Chicken with Bananas

- Heat the oil in a large pan and cook the drumsticks on all sides until golden then remove and set aside. Sauté the onion, peppers and celery until softened.
- Add the garlic and flour and cook out for a few seconds, then add the chicken back to the pan.
- Sprinkle over the paprika, then pour in coconut milk and stock. Add the bay leaf and season, then simmer for about 20 minutes over a low heat until the sauce has thickened and the chicken is cooked.
- 5 minutes before the end of cooking, add the bananas to heat through.
- Serve sprinkled with coriander.

PREPARATION TIME:
10 MINUTES

COOKING TIME:
30 MINUTES

INGREDIENTS

2 tbsp olive oil
4 chicken drumsticks
1 onion, peeled and chopped
1 green (bell) pepper, seeded and chopped
1 stick celery, finely chopped
2 cloves of garlic, finely chopped
1 tbsp flour
1 tsp paprika
400 g / 14 oz / 1 ½ cups coconut milk
100 ml / 3 ½ fl. oz / ½ cup chicken stock
1 bay leaf
salt and pepper
2 bananas, peeled and chopped
¼ bunch coriander (cilantro), chopped

Creole Chicken with Pineapple

415

- Replace the banana with pineapple for a tropical twist.

416

SERVES 4

Chicken with Stuffed Roasted Peppers

Cheesy Stuffed Peppers

 417

- Add a chunk of mozzarella or bocconcini to the pepper for the last 10 minutes.

Chicken with Roasted Vegetables

418

- If time is short, simply roast cubed aubergine (eggplant) and peppers.

PREPARATION TIME:
15 MINUTES

COOKING TIME:
40 MINUTES

INGREDIENTS

4 red peppers, halved and deseeded
8 cherry tomatoes
8 anchovy fillets
150 ml / 5 fl. oz / ⅔ cup extra virgin olive oil
4 chicken breasts, skin on
2 tbsp olive oil
salt and pepper
150 ml / 5 fl. oz / ⅔ cup passata
1 clove of garlic, crushed

- Preheat the oven to 220°C (200°C fan) / 425F / gas 7.
- Sit the halved peppers in a roasting tin, then fill the cavities with tomatoes, tucking the anchovy underneath them and a good drizzle of oil. Roast in the oven for 30–40 minutes until the peppers are tender and collapsing.
- Meanwhile roast the chicken alongside, drizzled with oil and seasoned for the last 20 minutes.
- Heat the passata in a small pan with the garlic and season.
- Serve the halved roasted peppers on a plate, slice the chicken and arrange alongside then spoon the sauce around.

419

SERVES 4–6

Chicken with Vanilla and Carrot Mash

- Preheat the oven to 200°C (180°C fan) / 400F / gas 6.
- Drizzle the chicken with oil, season and pour the wine into the bottom of the roasting tin. Roast in the oven for about 30 minutes or until the chicken is cooked through, covering with foil if they look too brown.
- Meanwhile, cook the carrots in the vegetable stock until tender. You may need to add more water if it looks too dry. Drain, reserving the cooking liquid and mash with butter. Season well and keep hot.
- When the chicken is cooked, remove to a serving platter and place the roasting tin over the heat. Split the vanilla pods in half, scrape out the seeds and add with the pods to the tin. Add the thyme and a little carrot cooking liquid and deglaze to make a sauce. Simmer until reduced, season and add a little lemon juice.
- Serve with chicken with the carrot mash and spoon over the sauce.

PREPARATION TIME:
10 MINUTES

COOKING TIME:
30–40 MINUTES

INGREDIENTS

1 chicken, jointed
4 tbsp olive oil
200 ml / 7 fl. oz / ¾ cup white wine
salt and pepper
1 kg / 2 lb / 4 ¼ cups carrots, peeled and chopped
300 ml / 10 fl. oz / 1 ¼ cups vegetable stock
30 g / 1 oz butter
3 vanilla pods
3 sprigs thyme
½ lemon, juiced

420

Chicken with Mixed Vegetable Mash

- Sweet root vegetables go well with the vanilla, so use swede or parsnip for a change.

421

SERVES 4

Chicken, Courgette and Walnut Crumble

- Poach the chicken in the stock for 5 minutes until just cooked through. Drain, reserving the stock.
- Heat the butter in a pan and sauté the onion and courgette until golden, then add the chicken. Add the cream and basil and enough poaching liquor to loosen a little, then season and set aside.
- Meanwhile rub the butter and flour together with your fingertips to resemble breadcrumbs, then stir through the walnuts and season well.
- Spoon the chicken mixture into a gratin dish, then top lightly with the crumble. Grill or bake until bubbling and the topping is golden and crunchy.

PREPARATION TIME:
20 MINUTES

COOKING TIME:
10–20 MINUTES

INGREDIENTS

4 chicken breasts, skinned and cubed
500 ml / 1 pint / 2 cups chicken stock
40 g / 1 oz butter
1 onion, peeled and chopped
2 courgettes (zucchinis), roughly chopped
200 ml / 7 fl. oz / ¾ cup double (heavy) cream
½ bunch basil leaves
salt and pepper
120 g / 4 oz / ½ cup plain (all-purpose) flour
100 g / 3 ½ oz / ½ cup butter, cold and cubed
50 g / 1 ¾ oz / ¼ cup walnuts, chopped

422

Chicken Crumble with Hazelnuts and Pumpkin

- Autumnal hazelnuts (cobnuts) complement the sweetness of pumpkin.

423

SERVES 4–6

Parma Ham Wrapped Chicken

PREPARATION TIME:
20 MINUTES

COOKING TIME:
1 HOUR
30 MINUTES

INGREDIENTS

1 oven-ready chicken
30 g / 1 oz butter, softened
4 slices Parma ham
200 g / 7 oz / ¾ cup white pudding
2 sprigs thyme

FOR THE ROSTI

500 g / 1 lb / 2 cups floury potatoes,
   peeled
2 tbsp butter, melted
2 tbsp vegetable oil
salt and pepper

- Preheat the oven to 220°C (200°C fan) / 425F / gas 7.
- Take the white pudding out of its casing, then stuff into the cavity of the chicken with the thyme. Smear the skin with butter, then cover with the Parma ham. Place in a roasting tin, roast for 20 minutes, then turn the heat down to 180°C (160°C fan) / 350F / gas 4 and cook for a further hour until cooked through.
- Grate the potatoes. Toss with the melted butter and seasoning, ensuring they are thoroughly coated.
- Heat the oil in a large frying pan, then add the mixture to the pan, pressing it down flat with a spatula. Cook over a medium heat for about 10 minutes.
- Run the spatula underneath to loosen, then cook the other side. Cook for a further 10 minutes until browned and crisp.
- After the chicken has rested for 15 minutes, serve with the potato rösti.

Potato and Celeriac Rösti

424

- Use half potatoes and half celeriac (celery root) for an earthy accompaniment.

425

SERVES 4

Chicken in White Wine Sauce

PREPARATION TIME:
10 MINUTES

COOKING TIME:
20 MINUTES

INGREDIENTS

4 chicken breasts
2 tbsp olive oil
4 tbsp thyme leaves
salt and pepper
30 g / 1 oz butter
1 shallot, peeled and finely diced
1 clove of garlic, finely sliced
2 sprigs thyme
200 ml / 7 fl. oz / ¾ cup dry white wine
300 ml / 10 fl. oz / 1 ¼ cups double
   (heavy) cream
salad, to serve

- Preheat the oven to 200°C (180°C fan) / 400F / gas 6.
- Sit the chicken in a roasting tin, drizzle with oil, sprinkle with thyme and seasoning and roast for 20 minutes.
- Heat the butter in a pan and sweat the shallot and garlic without colouring. Add the thyme and wine and reduce until the wine is syrupy, then stir in the cream. Season and simmer for a few minutes until thickened. Strain, discarding the onion, garlic and thyme.
- Serve the chicken with the salad and the sauce spooned over.

Chicken with Cheesy White Wine Sauce

426

- A sprinkle of Gruyère cheese will add depth to the sauce and help to thicken.

427

SERVES 4

Caramel Chicken with Courgette Ribbons

Chicken with Spicy Caramel Sauce

428

- A red chilli (chili), finely chopped, will add a kick.

Chicken with Ginger Caramel Sauce

429

- Add 1 tsp grated fresh ginger for heat without too much fire.

PREPARATION TIME:
5 MINUTES

COOKING TIME:
15 MINUTES

INGREDIENTS

4 chicken breasts, thickly sliced
2 tbsp vegetable oil
1 red onion, peeled and finely sliced
60 ml / 2 fl. oz / ¼ cup dark soy sauce
100 g / 3 ½ oz / ½ cup brown sugar
black pepper
60 ml / 2 fl. oz / ¼ cup fish sauce
½ lime, juiced
2 courgettes (zucchinis)

- Heat the oil in a pan until nearly smoking, then cook the chicken until golden, in batches if necessary.
- Reduce the heat and add the onion and a little more oil if necessary and cook until softened. Add the soy and simmer for 5 minutes or until reduced by half.
- Add the sugar and generously season with pepper and stir to make a caramel sauce. Cook until syrupy then add the fish sauce and lime juice, a little at a time.
- Use a vegetable peeler to slice the courgettes into ribbons.
- Twist and pile the ribbons onto a plate to make a tower and top with the chicken. Spoon the sauce around.

430

SERVES 4

Sesame Seed Chicken

PREPARATION TIME:
10 MINUTES

COOKING TIME:
15 MINUTES

INGREDIENTS

4 chicken pieces, bone in
4 tbsp olive oil
2 cloves of garlic, crushed
½ bunch parsley, finely chopped
1 tbsp Dijon mustard
salt and pepper
4 tbsp sesame seeds
½ lemon, juiced

- Whisk together the oil, garlic, parsley, mustard and some seasoning and coat the chicken pieces thoroughly in the marinade.
- Heat a deep sided pan with a little oil and cook the chicken in batches until golden and cooked through – about 15 minutes.
- Coat in the sesame seeds, squeeze over a little lemon juice and serve hot or cold.

431

SERVES 4

Chicken with Prawns and Spaghetti

PREPARATION TIME:
5 MINUTES

COOKING TIME:
30 MINUTES

INGREDIENTS

4 chicken thighs
2 tbsp olive oil
1 tsp dried oregano or rosemary leaves, chopped
salt and pepper
320 g / 11 oz / 1 ⅓ cups spaghetti pasta
225 g / 8 oz / 1 cup raw king prawns
pinch dried chilli (chili) flakes
1 clove of garlic, crushed
2 tbsp olive oil

- Preheat the oven to 200°C (180°C fan) / 400F / gas 6.
- Drizzle the chicken thighs with oil, sprinkle with herbs and seasoning and roast in the oven for 25 minutes or until golden and cooked through.
- Meanwhile cook the pasta in boiling salted water according to packet instructions. Drain, reserving a little of the pasta cooking water.
- While the chicken is resting, heat the oil in a pan with chilli and garlic and add the prawns. Toss and cook for a few minutes until pink, then add the spaghetti and any roasting juices from the chicken. Toss to coat, then add a splash of pasta cooking water to emulsify the sauce.
- Serve the pasta and prawns in deep warmed bowls, topped with chicken.

432

SERVES 4–6 Chicken with Courgette and Olives

- Preheat the oven to 200°C (180°C fan) / 400F / gas 6.
- Marinate the chicken in the lemon zest, juice, oregano, garlic and oil for 30 minutes.
- Tip the chicken into a large roasting tin and add the onions, courgettes, oil, white wine and season well. Roast for 30 minutes, or until just cooked through.
- Add the olives for the last 5 minutes of cooking, so they don't harden in the heat of the oven.
- Serve with all the pan juices and basil torn over.

PREPARATION TIME:
40 MINUTES

COOKING TIME:
30–35 MINUTES

INGREDIENTS

1 chicken, jointed into 6 pieces
zest and juice of ½ lemon
1 tbsp dried oregano
2 cloves of garlic, crushed
3 tbsp olive oil
4 red onions, peeled and quartered
4 courgettes (zucchinis)
4 tbsp olive oil
splash white wine
salt and pepper
50 g / 1 ¾ oz / ¼ cup olives
1 bunch basil

433

Mediterranean Chicken

SERVES 4–6

PREPARATION TIME:
40 MINUTES

COOKING TIME:
30–35 MINUTES

INGREDIENTS

1 chicken, jointed into 6 pieces
½ lemon, juiced and zested
1 tbsp dried oregano
2 cloves of garlic, crushed

3 tbsp olive oil
2 red peppers, deseeded and roughly chopped
2 yellow peppers, deseeded and roughly chopped
1 green pepper, deseeded and roughly chopped
2 red onions, sliced
4 tbsp olive oil
splash white wine
salt and pepper

- Preheat the oven to 200°C (180°C fan) / 400F / gas 6.
- Marinate the chicken in the lemon zest, juice, oregano, garlic and oil for 30 minutes.
- Tip the chicken into a large roasting tin and add the peppers, onion, oil, white wine and some seasoning. Roast for 30 minutes, or until just cooked through.
- Remove from the roasting tin, slice the chicken and serve on a hot skillet.

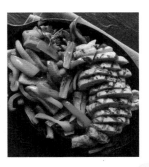

434

Vanilla Chicken with Figs

SERVES 4

PREPARATION TIME:
20 MINUTES

COOKING TIME:
20 MINUTES

INGREDIENTS

4 chicken breasts
100 ml / 3 ½ fl. oz / ½ cup cider or white wine vinegar

100 ml / 3 ½ fl. oz / ½ cup rum
100 g / 3 ½ oz / ½ cup soft brown sugar
1 vanilla pod
salt and pepper
250 g / 9 oz / 1 cup couscous
250 ml / 9 fl. oz / 1 cup chicken or vegetable stock
squeeze of lemon juice
8 figs, halved

- Mix together the vinegar, alcohol, sugar. Split the vanilla pod in half down the middle and scrape out the seeds. Add to the marinade with seasoning. Simmer in a small pan for 5 minutes until the sugar has dissolved. Leave to cool.
- Coat the chicken in the marinade and refrigerate for at least 1 hour.
- Preheat the oven to 190°C (170°C fan) / 375F / gas 5.
- Sit the chicken in a foil-lined roasting tin and roast for 20–25 minutes until cooked through and golden. Reserve any remaining marinade.
- Tip the reserved marinade into a small pan and simmer gently for 5 minutes.
- Tip the couscous into a bowl, cover with the hot stock and cover over with cling film. Leave for 10 minutes or so until tender, then fork through and season and add lemon juice.
- Serve the chicken with the sauce knapped over, the figs and couscous alongside.

435

SERVES 4

Chicken with Olives and Preserved Lemons

PREPARATION TIME:
15 MINUTES

COOKING TIME:
35 MINUTES

······································

INGREDIENTS

2 tbsp olive oil
4 chicken joints, skin on
1 onion, peeled and finely chopped
1 clove of garlic, chopped
1 tsp ground coriander
1 tsp ground cumin
pinch dried chilli (chili) flakes
1 tsp fennel seeds
4 preserved lemons, chopped
100 g / 3 ½ oz / ½ cup almonds
3 bay leaves
400 ml / 14 fl. oz / 1 ½ cups
   chicken stock
large handful green olives
salt and pepper

- Heat the oil in a large pan and fry the chicken on all sides until golden.
- Remove from the pan, add the onion and garlic and cook until golden. Return the chicken to the pan, then add the spices, preserved lemons, almonds, bay and stock and simmer for 30 minutes or until cooked.
- Add the olives, cook for 5 minutes and adjust the seasoning.
- Serve with couscous or rice.

Chicken Vegetable Stew   436

- Halved tomatoes add freshness; chopped courgettes (zucchinis) or cauliflower go well with the spices.

437

SERVES 4

Crispy Chicken with Pistachio Pesto

PREPARATION TIME:
10 MINUTES

COOKING TIME:
10 MINUTES

······································

INGREDIENTS

4 chicken breasts, skinned
salt and pepper
3 tbsp flour
2 eggs, beaten
200 g / 6 ½ oz / ¾ cup breadcrumbs
olive oil
80 g / 2 ½ oz / ⅓ cup pistachio nuts
1 clove of garlic, peeled and chopped
2 bunches basil
80 g / 3 oz / ⅓ cup Parmesan, grated
extra virgin olive oil
salt and pepper

- Place the chicken between 2 pieces of cling film and bat out until a bit thinner with a rolling pin.
- Season, then dunk each chicken into flour, then egg then the breadcrumbs.
- Heat the oil in a large pan and fry until golden and crisp and the chicken cooked through – 8–10 minutes.
- Meanwhile add the pistachio nuts to a frying pan over medium heat and lightly toast for a few seconds until golden.
- Place in a food processor with the garlic, basil and Parmesan.
- Whiz the ingredients in a food processor until roughly blended, stirring in enough olive oil to loosen.
- Serve the chicken with the pistachio pesto and a salad.

Chicken with Walnut Pesto   438

- You can use any nuts, such as walnuts, almonds or hazelnuts (cobnuts) to achieve different seasonal pestos.

439

SERVES 4

Chicken with Mushrooms

- In a large pan heat the butter and brown the chicken skin side down until golden, then turn over and cook until the juices run clear. Remove from the pan, set aside and keep warm.
- Remove any burnt butter and replace if necessary then sweat the shallot and garlic, then add the mushrooms and tarragon. Cook for a few minutes then deglaze with white wine.
- Reduce until syrupy, then add the cream and simmer until thickened – add any resting juices from the chicken and season.
- Meanwhile, steam the celeriac until completely tender, then whiz in a food processor with the butter, cream and seasoning until completely smooth.
- Serve the chicken with the sauce knapped over and the celeriac purée turned out of a ring mold.

PREPARATION TIME:
20 MINUTES

COOKING TIME:
45 MINUTES

....

INGREDIENTS

4 chicken supremes, skin on
50 g / 1 ¾ oz / ¼ cup butter
1 shallot, finely chopped
1 clove of garlic, finely chopped
2 sprigs tarragon, chopped
150 g / 5 oz / ⅔ cup wild mushrooms, cleaned
150 ml / 5 fl. oz / ⅔ cup dry white wine
300 ml / 10 fl. oz / 1 ¼ cups double (heavy) cream
salt and pepper
1 celeriac (celery root) peeled and chopped
50 g / 1 ¾ oz butter, melted
50–75 ml / 1 ¾ fl. oz–2 ½ fl. oz / ¼–⅓ cup double (heavy) cream

Chicken with Curried Celeriac Purée

440

- A pinch of ground cumin or turmeric lifts the purée.

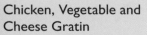

441

SERVES 4–6

Chicken, Vegetable and Cheese Wok-Bake

- Heat the oil in a wok or deep sided pan and sauté the onion and garlic until golden.
- Add the remaining vegetables and cook for a few minutes, then add the chicken and toss and stir until all is patchily golden.
- Pour in the stock and simmer for 5 minutes until everything is tender. Season.
- Place slices of the cheese on top, cover with a lid, turn off the heat and leave to ooze and melt.
- Serve in great heaping spoonfuls with slices of good bread.

PREPARATION TIME:
15 MINUTES

COOKING TIME:
20–25 MINUTES

....

INGREDIENTS

3 tbsp olive oil
1 large onion, peeled and sliced
2 cloves of garlic, finely chopped
1 head broccoli, cut into chunky florets
150 g / 5 oz / ⅔ cup mangetout
2 red peppers, deseeded and sliced
2 yellow peppers, deseeded and sliced
4 chicken breasts, skinned
200 ml / 7 fl. oz / ¾ cup chicken stock
200 g / 7 oz / ¾ cup Pont L'Eveque cheese
salt and pepper

Chicken, Vegetable and Cheese Gratin

 442

- Alternatively tip everything into a gratin dish, top with breadcrumbs and grill until sizzling.

443

SERVES 6

Chicken Stuffed with Mushrooms

Chestnut Bacon and Mushroom Stuffing

444

- Add 2 rashers finely chopped smoky streaky bacon for oomph and a smoky taste.

Pheasant with Chestnut Stuffing

445

- Try using pheasant in season – it will take less cooking – just under an hour.

PREPARATION TIME:
20 MINUTES

COOKING TIME:
1 HOUR 30 MINUTES

....

INGREDIENTS

1 oven ready chicken
1.5 kg / 3 lb / 6 cups potatoes, peeled and
    cut into chunks
150 ml / 5 fl. oz / ⅔ cup milk
100 g / 3 ½ oz / ½ cup butter
3 eggs, beaten
salt and pepper

FOR THE STUFFING

2 tbsp butter
500 g / 1 lb / 2 cups cep or other wild
    mushrooms, chopped
1 onion, finely chopped
1 clove of garlic, chopped
10 vacuum packed chestnuts, chopped
½ bunch tarragon
1 slice bread, soaked in milk
1 egg, beaten

- Preheat the oven to 220°C (200°C fan) / 425F / gas 7.
- Heat the butter in a pan and cook the mushrooms, onion and garlic until tender. Leave to cool.
- Once cool, mix with the chestnuts, tarragon, crumbled bread and egg to form a cohesive mixture, then stuff into the cavity of the chicken.
- Season the chicken all over, drizzle with oil and roast in the oven for 20 minutes.
- Reduce the heat to 180°C (160°C fan) / 350F / gas 4 .
- Meanwhile cook the potatoes in boiling salted water until tender to the point of a knife. Drain thoroughly and return briefly to the heat to drive off any excess water. Mash the potatoes thoroughly with a potato ricer or hand-held masher.
- Heat the milk and butter until the butter has melted, then stir into the potatoes with 2 of the beaten eggs and season well.
- Spoon into a piping bag with a 1.25 cm (½ in) star nozzle and pipe into pyramid shapes onto a greased baking tray. Brush with the remaining egg and sprinkle on the almonds, patting them on to help them stick.
- When the chicken has cooked turn the oven back up to 220°C (200°C fan) / 425F / gas 7 and bake in the oven for 15 minutes or until golden while the chicken is resting.

446

SERVES 4

Pan-fried Chicken with Vegetables

- Heat the oil in a pan and fry the chicken on both sides until golden.
- Tip the vegetables into the pan and sauté to lightly colour, then add the wine and sage, then put the lid on and leave to simmer for 10–15 minutes until all is cooked.
- Season and serve.

PREPARATION TIME:
10 MINUTES

COOKING TIME:
30 MINUTES

INGREDIENTS

2 tbsp olive oil
4 chicken legs
4 carrots, peeled and cut
   into short lengths
2 leeks, trimmed and cut
   into short lengths
4 whole garlic cloves, peeled
150 ml / 5 fl. oz / ⅔ cup dry
   white wine
few sprigs sage leaves
salt and pepper

Pan-fried Chicken with Fennel and Potatoes

447

- Try substituting the leeks and carrots with quartered fennel, new potatoes and a tsp of fennel seeds.

448

SERVES 4

Chicken with Wild Mushrooms

- Preheat the oven to 180°C (160°C fan) / 350F / gas 4.
- Mix together the honey, mustard, oil and seasoning and roll the chicken thoroughly to coat. Place in a foil-lined roasting tin and roast in the oven, turning once, for 30 minutes until sticky and cooked through.
- Meanwhile heat the butter in a pan and sweat the shallot rings and garlic without colouring. Add the mushrooms and sauté briskly until the liquid has evaporated. Season.
- Serve the drumsticks with the mushrooms and shallots spooned around.

PREPARATION TIME:
10 MINUTES

COOKING TIME:
30 MINUTES

INGREDIENTS

4 chicken drumsticks
2 tbsp runny honey
1 ½ tbsp grain mustard
1 tbsp olive oil
salt and pepper
40 g / 1 oz butter
2 shallots, finely sliced into rings
2 cloves of garlic, chopped
250 g / 9 oz / 1 cup wild mushrooms,
   cleaned

Chicken with Wild Mushroom Mash

 449

- To make a substantial side dish, try folding the mushroom mix into creamy mashed potato.

450

SERVES 4

Chicken with Chanterelles and Tarragon

PREPARATION TIME:
10 MINUTES

COOKING TIME:
40 MINUTES

....

INGREDIENTS

40 g / 1 oz butter
1 tbsp olive oil
4 chicken legs
1 shallot, finely chopped
1 clove of garlic, crushed
200 g / 7 oz / ¾ cup chanterelle
   mushrooms, cleaned
1 can chickpeas
4 sprigs tarragon
150 ml / 5 fl. oz / ⅔ cup dry
   white wine
salt and pepper

- Heat the butter and oil in a large pan and brown the chicken legs on all sides, then remove.
- Sweat the shallot and garlic without colouring for a few minutes, then add the mushrooms, chickpeas and tarragon. Season and cook for 5–7 minutes until tender.
- Deglaze with the white wine, then add the chicken back to the pan, cover with a lid and leave to simmer gently for 20–25 minutes until the chicken is cooked.
- Adjust the seasoning and serve.

Chicken with Tarragon Cream Sauce

451

- Add a few tbsp double (heavy) cream for a richer sauce.

452

SERVES 4

Chicken with Thyme Yogurt Sauce

PREPARATION TIME:
5 MINUTES

COOKING TIME:
25 MINUTES

....

INGREDIENTS

4 chicken breasts, skinned
salt and pepper
2 shallots, finely sliced
200 ml / 7 fl. oz / ¾ cup plain yogurt
handful fresh thyme leaves

- Steam the chicken above simmering water for about 20–25 minutes until just cooked through.
- Meanwhile mix the yogurt with the thyme and seasoning.
- Place the chicken on a plate with the sliced shallots and spoon over the yogurt sauce.

Chicken with Garlic Sauce

453

- Roast some garlic and squeeze into the yogurt sauce before serving.

454

SERVES 6

Chicken Fromage Frais Quiche

Chicken Vegetable Quiche

455

- Grated courgettes, cooked briefly with the chicken, are a good addition.

Chicken Broccoli Quiche

456

- Add small partly-steamed broccoli florets for crunch and colour.

PREPARATION TIME:
50 MINUTES

COOKING TIME:
1 HOUR

INGREDIENTS

2 chicken breasts, skinned and diced
30 g / 1 oz butter
100 g / 3 ½ oz / ½ cup Gruyère cheese, grated
2 eggs + 1 egg yolk
300 ml / 10 fl. oz / 1 ¼ cups fromage frais
salt and pepper

FOR THE QUICHE PASTRY

110 g / 3 ½ oz / ½ cup plain (all-purpose) flour
50 g / 1 ¾ oz / ¼ cup cold, diced butter
pinch salt
cold water, to mix

- Preheat the oven to 200°C (180°C fan) / 400F / gas 6 and put in a baking sheet to warm.
- Rub the butter into the flour with the salt until you have coarse breadcrumbs. Add water a little at a time using a round-bladed knife to mix until the mixture just comes together. Form into a ball, cover with cling film and refrigerate for 20–30 minutes.
- Fry the chicken in the butter until golden. Set aside to cool.
- Roll out the pastry and press it gently into a lightly greased flan tin. Prick all over with a fork and bake in the oven on the baking sheet for 20 minutes until pale gold.
- Place the cheese and chicken evenly over the pastry base. Whisk together the eggs and fromage frais and season, then pour in, adding a little pepper but careful on the salt.
- Bake in the oven for 25-30 minutes until just set. Leave to cool before serving.

457

SERVES 2

Lemon and Chervil Chicken

PREPARATION TIME:
5 MINUTES

COOKING TIME:
15–20 MINUTES

INGREDIENTS

2 tbsp butter
2 chicken breasts, skin on
1 lemon
½ bunch chervil, chopped
200 ml / 7 fl. oz / ¾ cup white wine
250 g / 9 oz / 1 cup green beans,
    trimmed
salt and pepper

- Heat the butter in a pan and cook the chicken gently skin side down until golden and crisp.
- Turn over and cook on the other side for 5 minutes.
- Meanwhile remove the zest from the lemon and finely shred.
- When the chicken is cooked, remove to a plate to rest and deglaze with the white wine. Add the zest and chervil, season and reduce until syrupy. Adjust the acidity with a little lemon juice.
- Meanwhile steam the green beans for 4 minutes over some simmering water.
- Serve the chicken with the sauce and green beans.

Orange Turkey Escalopes 458

- Substitute the lemon for orange.

459

SERVES 4

Chicken Aubergine Colombo

PREPARATION TIME:
15 MINUTES

COOKING TIME:
30 MINUTES

INGREDIENTS

1 tbsp vegetable oil
4 chicken thighs, skinned, deboned
    and cubed
salt and pepper
1 onion, peeled and chopped
1 aubergine (eggplant), diced
3 cloves of garlic, crushed
2 tbsp curry powder
6 sprigs thyme leaves
1 tsp ground allspice
½ tsp ground cinnamon
2 bay leaves
1–2 Scotch Bonnet chillies (chilies)
    (depending on how hot you want it)
500 ml / 1 pint / 2 cups chicken stock
400 g / 14 oz / 1 ½ cups chopped
    tomatoes
coriander (cilantro) leaves, to serve
handful chopped almonds, to serve

- Heat the oil and sear the chicken on all sides until golden. Remove with a slotted spoon and set aside.
- Add the onion and aubergines and cook until softened, then add the garlic and spices and cook for 2 minutes.
- Add the chillies, stock and tomatoes and bring to a simmer. Add the chicken back to the pan, reduce the heat, cover with a lid and cook for 20 minutes until the chicken is cooked.
- Remove the chillies, adjust the seasoning, then top with coriander leaves and sprinkle with almonds.

Chicken and
Sweet Potato Colombo   460

- Add diced sweet potatoes to make this more substantial.

461

SERVES 4

Chicken and Leek Parcels

- Preheat the oven to 200°C (180°C fan) / 400F / gas 6.
- Lay out 4 pieces of greaseproof paper and place a chicken breast in the centre of each one.
- Top with the leeks, tomatoes, some lemon zest and juice, a splash of white wine and a tarragon sprig. Season.
- Fold the paper into parcels, scrunching to seal and bake in the oven on a baking sheet for about 25 minutes.
- Serve at the table for everyone to open their own parcels.

PREPARATION TIME:
10 MINUTES

COOKING TIME:
25 MINUTES

....

INGREDIENTS

4 chicken breasts, skinned
1 leek, trimmed and sliced lengthways
4 tomatoes, thickly sliced
1 lemon, juiced and zested
4 sprigs tarragon
100 ml / 3 ½ fl. oz / ½ cup white wine
salt and pepper

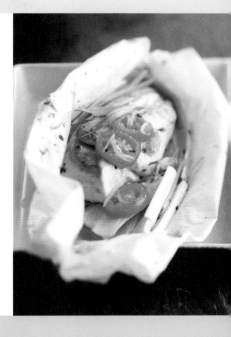

Fragrant Chicken Parcels   462

- Try adding a little lemon grass, lime or curry leaves and fennel seeds for a curry version.

463

SERVES 4

Cider Chicken with Apples

- Preheat the oven to 220°C (200°C fan) / 425F / gas 7.
- Place the chicken in a roasting tin and smear with the butter. Season well and push the thyme sprigs into the cavity. Place in the oven and roast for 20 minutes.
- Turn the heat down to 180°C (160°C fan) / 350F / gas 4.
- Add the potatoes to the pan and roast the chicken for another 30 minutes.
- Pour 200 ml of cider into the pan, add the apples and roast for another 30–40 minutes.
- Remove the chicken, potatoes and apples to a serving platter to rest, loosely covered with foil, then place the roasting tin back on the hob. Add enough cider to make a sauce, scraping at the base of the pan with a wooden spoon and simmer until reduced to your liking. Season.
- Serve the chicken with the apples and potatoes, with the sauce drizzled over.

PREPARATION TIME:
10 MINUTES

COOKING TIME:
1 HOUR 45 MINUTES

....

INGREDIENTS

1 oven ready chicken
30 g / 1 oz butter, softened
salt and pepper
4 sprigs thyme
500 ml / 1 pint / 2 cups dry cider
2 crisp eating apples, sliced into wedges
1 kg / 2 lb / 4 cups waxy potatoes,
   cut into wedges

Creamy Cider Chicken   464

- 2 tbsp creme fraîche added to the sauce once reduced makes for a creamier indulgent sauce.

465

SERVES 4

Basque Chicken with Bacon

Meaty Basque Chicken

466

- Add chopped chorizo or even spicy sausages cut into chunks for extra protein punch.

Sweet Potato Wedges

467

- Roast wedges of unpeeled sweet potato with oil and seasoning for 30 minutes to serve alongside.

PREPARATION TIME:
10 MINUTES

COOKING TIME:
30 MINUTES

....

INGREDIENTS

2 tbsp olive oil
4 chicken drumsticks
1 onion, chopped
2 cloves of garlic, chopped
150 g / 5 oz / ⅔ cup pancetta or smoked
    streaky bacon, chopped
1 red pepper, deseeded and sliced
1 green pepper, deseeded and sliced
6 ripe vine tomatoes, cored and chopped
2 bay leaves
1 tsp sugar
1 tsp smoked paprika
salt and pepper

- Heat the oil in a pan and brown the drumsticks until golden. Remove to a plate and set aside.
- Add the onion and garlic with the pancetta and cook gently until golden, then add the chicken back to the pan and add the peppers and tomatoes, bay leaves, sugar, paprika and seasoning and allow to simmer for about 10-15 minutes until all is combined. Adjust the seasoning to taste.

468
SERVES 4

Chicken Pea and Herb Stew

- Heat the oil and butter in a large pan and brown the chicken thighs on all sides, then remove to a plate and set aside.
- Add the onion and bacon and cook until golden and the fat runs from the bacon. Add the garlic and cook for another minute, then return the chicken to the pan.
- Add the peas, stock and simmer gently for 25 minutes or so, until the chicken is cooked through and the sauce a little reduced.
- Season well, stir through the parsley and serve with crusty bread.

PREPARATION TIME:
10 MINUTES

COOKING TIME:
45 MINUTES

INGREDIENTS

40 g / 1 oz butter
1 tbsp oil
4 chicken thighs
4 rashers streaky smoked bacon
1 onion, peeled and finely sliced
1 clove of garlic, finely sliced
400 g / 14 oz / 1 ½ cups fresh or frozen peas
500 ml / 1 pint / 2 cups chicken stock
salt and pepper
1 bunch parsley, chopped

Chicken and Potato Stew   469
- Adding chunks of floury potato with the chicken will thicken the sauce and make the stew go further.

470
SERVES 4

Basque Chicken Casserole

- Preheat the oven to 180°C (160°C fan) / 350F / gas 4.
- Heat the oil in a pan and brown the thighs until golden. Remove to a plate and set aside.
- Add the onion and garlic and cook gently until golden, then add the chicken back to the pan and add the peppers, tomatoes, sugar, paprika and seasoning and cook for 5 minutes.
- Pour over the wine and stock, add the bay leaves and some salt, cover with a lid and cook in the oven for 45 minutes until the chicken is cooked.

PREPARATION TIME:
10 MINUTES

COOKING TIME:
55 MINUTES

INGREDIENTS

2 tbsp olive oil
4–6 chicken thighs
1 onion, chopped
2 cloves of garlic, chopped
1 red pepper, deseeded and sliced
1 green pepper, deseeded and sliced
1 tsp sugar
2 tsp smoked paprika
8 ripe tomatoes, cored and cut into wedges
300 ml / 10 fl. oz / 1 ¼ cups white wine
250 ml / 9 fl. oz / 1 cup chicken stock
2 bay leaves
salt and pepper

Punchy Basque Casserole   471
- Substitute the white wine for red for a winter's night dish with a punch.

472

SERVES 4

Chicken Broth with Mushrooms

PREPARATION TIME:
30 MINUTES

COOKING TIME:
25 MINUTES

INGREDIENTS

150 g / 5 oz / ⅔ cup dried wild
    mushrooms
750 ml / 1 ⅓ pints / 3 cups chicken stock
4 chicken breasts, skinned
salt and pepper
2 bulbs pak choi, leaves separated
½ bunch chervil sprigs
¼ bunch chives

- Rehydrate the mushrooms in the hot stock for up to 30 minutes.
- Remove the mushrooms with a slotted spoon and set aside. Drain carefully through a lined sieve, reserving the liquid, and discarding any grit at the bottom.
- Pour the stock into a pan and simmer gently, then add the mushrooms and chicken breasts, partially cover with a lid and poach very gently for about 20–25 minutes until the chicken is cooked through.
- Meanwhile steam the pak choi until the white stems are just tender.
- Transfer the chicken to a plate and keep warm. Carefully season the broth.
- Serve the broth in warmed bowls with the pak choi and sliced chicken. Decorate with the herbs.

Chicken Broth with Mixed Greens

473

- Winter or spring greens, shredded, would go well with this dish.

474

SERVES 4

Corn-fed Chicken with Tagliatelle

PREPARATION TIME:
5 MINUTES

COOKING TIME:
30 MINUTES

INGREDIENTS

40 g / 1 oz butter
1 tbsp olive oil
4 corn-fed chicken breasts, skin on
2 shallots, finely sliced
2 cloves of garlic, finely sliced
200 g / 7 oz / ¾ cup morel mushrooms
    or other wild mushrooms, cleaned
200 ml / 7 fl. oz / ¾ cup dry white wine
200 ml / 7 fl. oz / ¾ cup chicken stock
½ bunch tarragon, finely chopped
salt and pepper
320 g / 11 oz tagliatelle pasta
40 g / 1 oz butter

- Heat the butter and oil in a pan and sear the chicken skin side down until golden. Turn over and cook the other side for 3–4 minutes. Remove and set aside.
- Add the shallots and garlic and sweat for 3 minutes, then add the morels and cook for 5 minutes.
- Deglaze the pan with white wine and reduce until syrupy, then add the stock and chicken and simmer for 15 minutes.
- Meanwhile cook the pasta in boiling salted water according to packet instructions. Drain, reserving a little pasta water, and toss with butter.
- Remove the chicken from the pan and slice thickly. Add tarragon and seasoning to the sauce and a little pasta water if too thick.
- Toss the pasta with the sauce and serve with the sliced chicken on top.

Chicken with Ravioli

475

- Replace the tagliatelle with filled ravioli.

476

SERVES 4

Grilled Chicken with Raspberry Vinegar

Chicken with Blackberry Vinegar Sauce

477

- The sauce works equally well with fresh blackberries in autumn.

BBQ Raspberry Chicken

478

- Marinade the chicken in the sauce for 30 minutes, then barbecue for a sweet-sharp flavour.

PREPARATION TIME:
15 MINUTES

COOKING TIME:
30 MINUTES

INGREDIENTS

4 chicken thighs
2 tbsp olive oil
salt and pepper
1 kg / 2 lb / 4 ¼ cups floury potatoes,
   peeled and cut into chunks
50 g / 1 ¾ oz / ¼ cup butter
100 ml / 3 ½ fl. oz / ½ cup milk
½ bunch parsley, finely chopped
½ bunch chives, finely chopped
60 g / 2 oz / ¼ cup raspberries
75 ml / 2 ½ fl. oz / ⅓ cup raspberry or
   red wine vinegar
1 tbsp caster (superfine) sugar

- Preheat the oven to 200°C (180°C fan) / 400F / gas 6.
- Roast the chicken thighs in a little oil and seasoning for 25–30 minutes until crisp and golden. If the skin is not quite crisp set under a hot grill until brown. Remove and keep warm.
- Meanwhile cook the potatoes in boiling salted water until tender – about 15–20 minutes. Drain and dry thoroughly.
- Mash the potatoes with butter, a little milk, seasoning and herbs, until smooth.
- Heat the vinegar in a small pan and dissolve the sugar. Add the raspberries and cook for about 10 minutes over a low heat until reduced to a syrupy consistency. Whiz in a blender and then pass through a sieve to remove any seeds. Reheat gently with a little salt.
- Serve with the chicken sprinkled with a little sea salt and drizzled with the sauce and the herby mashed potato to one side.

479

SERVES 4

Citrus Chicken with Cantonese Rice

**PREPARATION TIME:
30 MINUTES**

COOKING TIME: 20 MINUTES

INGREDIENTS

2 tbsp vegetable oil
3–4 lemons, juiced and zested
100 ml / 3 ½ fl. oz / ½ cup chicken stock
1–2 tsp sugar
splash soy sauce
splash dry sherry
1 tsp cornflour (cornstarch)
4 chicken breasts, skinned
1 egg white
2 tsp cornflour (cornstarch)
1 tsp sesame oil
2 tbsp vegetable oil
1 onion, peeled and finely chopped
1 garlic clove, finely chopped
3 eggs, beaten
200 g / 7 oz / ¾ cup cooked ham
500 g / 1 lb / 2 cups cooked white rice
3–4 spring onions (scallions), sliced
soy sauce
handful bean sprouts
handful cooked peas

- Slice the chicken into strips. Combine the egg white, cornflour, a pinch of salt and sesame oil in a bowl then thoroughly coat the chicken strips in the mixture.
- Heat the vegetable oil in a wok then add the coated chicken and stir fry until the chicken turns white. Remove the chicken from the pan. Discard the oil.
- Add the lemon juice and zest, stock, sugar, soy and sherry and bring to a rapid boil. Whisk in the cornflour until thickened then return the chicken to the pan to cook through. Set aside.
- To make the rice: heat the oil in a wok then add the onion and garlic and stir fry for 1 minute. Push to one side and add the eggs and cook for a couple of minutes until starting to set. Add the rice and meat and combine thoroughly.
- Stir in some soy sauce and the bean sprouts and peas and combine.
- Serve with the lemon chicken.

Lemon Ginger Chicken 480

- Try adding 1 tbsp grated fresh ginger for added spice.

481

SERVES 3-4

Chicken and Vegetable Pizza

**PREPARATION TIME:
45 MINUTES**

**COOKING TIME:
8–10 MINUTES**

INGREDIENTS

2 ready made pizza bases

FOR THE TOPPING

4 tbsp passata
½ courgette (zucchini), thickly sliced
¼ aubergine (eggplant), diced
1 chicken breast, cooked
1 yellow pepper, deseeded and finely chopped
1 tbsp thyme or rosemary leaves
1 ball mozzarella (optional)

- Spread the base of each pizza with passata, then top with the vegetables and chicken. Tear the mozzarella into small pieces and add to the pizza.
- Place either directly on the bars of the oven or on a preheated baking sheet for 8–10 minutes until golden and crisp.

Chicken and Prawn Pizza 482

- Add raw prawns and chopped chilli (chili) to ratchet up the flavour before cooking.

483

SERVES 4

Chicken Colombo with Basmati Rice

- Heat the oil and sear the chicken until golden. Remove with a slotted spoon and set aside.
- Add the onions and carrots and cook until softened, then add the garlic and spices and cook for 2 minutes.
- Add the chillies, spring onions stock and tomatoes and bring to a simmer. Return the chicken to the pan.
- Reduce the heat, cover with a lid and cook for 25 minutes until the potatoes are tender.
- Meanwhile tip the rice into a pan and cook in boiling salted water according to packet instructions. Drain well.

PREPARATION TIME:
20 MINUTES

COOKING TIME:
35 MINUTES

INGREDIENTS

1 tbsp vegetable oil
4 chicken thighs, skinned, deboned and chopped
salt and pepper
1 onion, peeled and chopped
2 carrots, peeled and cut into batons
3 cloves of garlic, crushed
2 tbsp curry powder
6 sprigs thyme leaves
1 tsp ground allspice
½ tsp ground cinnamon
2 bay leaves
1–2 Scotch Bonnet chillies (chilies) (depending on how hot you want it)
8 spring onions, ends trimmed
500 ml / 1 pint / 2 cups chicken stock
400 g / 14 oz / 1 ½ cups canned chopped tomatoes
250 g / 9 oz / 1 cup basmati rice
chive stems, to serve

Chicken Colombo with Green Beans

484

- Add steamed green beans to the curry mix for crunch.

485

SERVES 4

Tagliatelle with Chicken and Vegetables

- Preheat the oven to 200°C (180°C fan) / 400F / gas 6.
- Tip the chicken, aubergine, courgette and tomatoes into a roasting tin, drizzle with oil, thyme and season. Roast for 20 minutes until cooked and tender.
- Meanwhile cook the pasta in boiling salted water according to packet instructions. Drain, reserving a cupful of cooking water.
- Toss the pasta in the roasting tin with the cooked chicken and vegetables and cooking water and serve.

PREPARATION TIME:
10 MINUTES

COOKING TIME:
20 MINUTES

INGREDIENTS

2 tbsp olive oil
2 chicken breasts, cut into chunks
1 aubergine (eggplant), cut into small chunks
2 courgettes (zucchini), cut into small chunks
4 tomatoes, cored and cut into wedges
1 tbsp thyme leaves
salt and pepper
320 g / 11 oz tagliatelle pasta

Cheesy Tagliatelle with Chicken

486

- Add cubes of mozzarella to the roasting tin when tossing the pasta in it.

487

SERVES 4–6

Chicken and Tomato Fromage Frais Pie

Mediterranean Chicken Pie

488

- This pie lends itself to any filling you can think of, but try cooked courgettes and peppers with the chicken and tomatoes.

Cold Picnic Pie

489

- Serve cold for picnics or packed lunches.

PREPARATION TIME:
15 MINUTES

COOKING TIME:
25 MINUTES

INGREDIENTS

2 sheets ready rolled puff pastry
40 g / 1 oz butter
1 onion, peeled and finely chopped
4 chicken thighs, skinned and deboned, cut into small chunks
6–8 ripe vine tomatoes, thickly sliced
2 sprigs thyme leaves
200 g / 7 oz / ¾ cup fromage frais
salt and pepper

- Preheat the oven to 190°C (170°C fan) / 375F / gas 5.
- Lay a sheet of pastry on a lined baking sheet, prick all over with a fork and bake in the oven for 10 minutes or until starting to puff and golden.
- Remove and leave to cool. Meanwhile heat the butter in a pan and cook the onion gently until golden and softened.
- Increase the heat a little and fry the chicken pieces until golden and cooked through. Leave to cool for 5 minutes.
- Spoon the chicken and onion over the base of the cooled pastry. Top with slices of tomato and thyme leaves then season generously. Spoon over blobs of fromage frais, then top with the remaining pastry sheet.
- Crimp around the edges to seal, cut a small cross in the top and bake for 20–25 minutes until puffed and deep gold. Remove from the oven and leave to cool for 5–10 minutes before serving.

490

SERVES 4

Chicken with Broccoli Crust

- Tip the breadcrumbs into a food processor with the broccoli and Parmesan and process until well combined.
- Dip the chicken breasts one at a time into the flour, egg then broccoli breadcrumbs and lay on a rack to dry slightly.
- Heat 1 cm depth oil in a pan and fry the chicken in batches until golden on both sides and cooked through.
- Serve with steamed broccoli and sun-dried tomatoes

PREPARATION TIME:
10 MINUTES

COOKING TIME:
20 MINUTES

INGREDIENTS

200 g / 7 oz / ¾ cup breadcrumbs
½ head broccoli florets
2 tbsp Parmesan cheese, grated
4 chicken breasts, skinned
100 g / 3 ½ oz / ½ cup plain
   (all-purpose) flour
2 eggs, beaten
vegetable oil
steamed broccoli
handful sun dried tomatoes, chopped

Broccoli and Blue Cheese Chicken

491

- Use gorgonzola or similar in place of the Parmesan.

492

SERVES 4

Chicken Cooked in Coconut

- Heat the oil in a wok or large pan and fry the chicken on all sides until golden. Remove and set aside.
- Add the onion and cook until deep gold and sweet.
- Add the garlic and curry paste and cook out for 2 minutes, then add the chicken back to the pan with the curry leaves.
- Pour over the coconut milk and chicken stock, lower the heat and leave to simmer for 20 minutes until the chicken is cooked through.
- Adjust the seasoning and stir in the lime juice just before serving with the rice.

PREPARATION TIME:
15 MINUTES

COOKING TIME:
25–30 MINUTES

INGREDIENTS

3 tbsp vegetable oil
4 chicken drumsticks
1 onion, peeled and finely sliced
2 cloves of garlic, finely chopped
2 tbsp Goan curry paste
4 curry leaves
1 tsp mustard seeds
400 ml / 14 fl. oz / 1 ½ cups coconut
   milk
200 ml / 7 fl. oz / ¾ cup chicken stock
salt and pepper
1 lime, juiced
boiled rice to serve

Coconut Chicken Pasta

493

- Serve the chicken on a bed of tagliatelle instead of rice.

494

SERVES 4

Pan-fried Chicken with Baby Vegetables

PREPARATION TIME:
10 MINUTES

COOKING TIME:
20–30 MINUTES

....

INGREDIENTS

4 chicken pieces, skin on
1 tbsp olive oil
40 g / 1 oz butter
150 g / 5 oz / ⅔ cup mangetout
100 g / 3 ½ oz / ½ cup frozen peas
100 g / 3 ½ oz / ½ cup broad beans,
    double podded
8 baby carrots, scrubbed
200 ml / 7 fl. oz / ¾ cup chicken stock
150 ml / 5 fl. oz / ⅔ cup double (heavy)
    cream
salt and pepper

- Heat the oil and butter in a casserole and fry the chicken skin side down until golden. Turn over and cook the other side.
- Add the vegetables and coat in the butter, then add the stock and simmer, lid off, for 10 minutes or until the vegetables are just tender and the chicken is cooked through.
- Stir in the cream, season and simmer for 5 minutes, then serve in deep bowls.

Chicken with Spring Vegetables

495

- Baby courgettes (zucchini), baby turnips, baby fennel would all make good additions.

496

SERVES 4

Chicken Galettes

PREPARATION TIME:
10 MINUTES

COOKING TIME:
8–10 MINUTES

....

INGREDIENTS

500 g / 1 lb / 2 cups chicken, minced
1 bunch chervil leaves, finely chopped
salt and pepper
1 lemon, zested
1 egg, beaten
1 tbsp flour

- Mix the chicken with the herbs, pepper, salt and lemon zest until thoroughly mixed.
- Pour in enough beaten egg to bind the mixture, but don't let the mixture get too wet.
- With wet hands, form the mixture into 4 large patties. Chill in the refrigerator for 30 minutes.
- Dredge lightly in flour, then cook in a little oil for 3–4 minutes per side, depending on thickness.

Mini Chicken Meatballs

497

- Form the mixture into small balls to make child-sized meatballs for supper.

498

SERVES 4

Chinese Chicken Stir Fry

Chinese
Chicken Baguettes

499

- Spoon the hot stir fry into hot baguettes.

Chicken Squid
Stir Fry

500

- Add frozen defrosted squid rings to the stir fry for texture.

PREPARATION TIME:
10 MINUTES

COOKING TIME:
10–12 MINUTES

....

INGREDIENTS

2 tbsp vegetable oil
350 g / 12 oz / 1 ½ cups chicken
    thigh meat, diced
1 onion, peeled and finely sliced
2 cloves of garlic, finely sliced
1 tsp fresh ginger, grated
1 red pepper, deseeded and finely sliced
½ bunch spring onions (scallions), sliced
200 g / 7 oz / ¾ cup baby sweetcorn
75–100 ml / 2 ½–3 ½ fl. oz / ⅓–½ cup
    soy sauce
2 tbsp rice wine (mirin)
2–3 tbsp sweet chilli (chili) sauce
salt and pepper

- Heat the oil in a wok until nearly smoking, then add the chicken. Stir fry over a high heat until golden all over and the fat crisp. Remove from the pan with a slotted spoon.

- Add the onion, garlic and ginger and stir fry for 2 minutes. Add the vegetables and cook until crisp-tender. Add the meat back to the pan and stir in the sauces.

- Leave to bubble for a few minutes then check and adjust the seasoning if necessary.

501

SERVES 8

Chicken and Tarragon Cake

PREPARATION TIME:
20 MINUTES

COOKING TIME:
40 MINUTES

....

INGREDIENTS

3 eggs
½ tsp sugar
235 g / 8 oz / 1 cup plain flour
60 g / 2 oz / ¼ cup potato flour
2 tsp baking powder
½ tsp salt
6 tbsp olive oil
2 tbsp sour cream
2 chicken breasts, cooked and
    finely chopped
280 g / 9 ½ oz / 1 and a bit cups
    sun-dried tomatoes, chopped
1 tbsp tarragon leaves, finely chopped
2 handfuls mache (corn salad)
2 handfuls rocket (arugula)
2 tbsp Parmesan shavings

- Preheat oven to 190°C (170°C fan) / 375F / gas 5.
- Whisk the eggs and sugar together until pale and thick.
- Sieve the flours, baking powder and salt into a bowl, then fold into the eggs. Stir in the sour cream and oil until incorporated. Stir in the tomatoes, chicken and tarragon leaves.
- Grease and line a 900 g / 1 lb loaf tin, then pour in the mixture, bake in the oven for about 40 minutes until a skewer inserted into the middle comes out clean.
- Remove to a wire rack and allow to cool.
- Serve with the salad and Parmesan.

502

SERVES 4

Chicken, Pepper and Bacon Tagine

PREPARATION TIME:
15 MINUTES

COOKING TIME:
45 MINUTES

....

INGREDIENTS

2 tbsp olive oil
1 onion, peeled and thickly sliced
2 cloves of garlic, finely sliced
4 rashers streaky bacon, diced
4 chicken legs, skinned
2 yellow peppers, deseeded and chopped
1 tsp curry powder
1 tsp ground (cilantro) coriander seeds
1 tsp cumin
4 preserved lemons, chopped
400 g / 14 oz / 1 ½ cups canned tomatoes
200 ml / 7 fl. oz / ¾ cup chicken stock
2 tbsp green olives
½ bunch parsley, chopped
salt and pepper

- Heat the oil in a large pan and cook the onions until golden and tender.
- Add the bacon and garlic and cook for a few minutes, then remove all from the pan with a slotted spoon. Add the peppers and cook for a few minutes.
- Increase the heat and brown the chicken on all sides, then tip the onions back into the pan and sprinkle over the spices.
- Pour over the canned tomatoes and stock and season, lower the heat and cook gently for about 45 minutes or until the sauce has thickened and the chicken is cooked.
- Add the olives to warm through, adjust the seasoning and sprinkle with parsley.

503

SERVES 4

Crispy Chicken with Sweet Potato Mash

- Slice the chicken into strips and place in a bowl with the buttermilk. Refrigerate for at least 2 hours or even overnight.
- Cut the potatoes into large chunks and cook in boiling salted water until tender – about 10–12 minutes. Drain thoroughly, then set the pan over a low heat and shake the pan to drive off any excess moisture.
- Mash thoroughly with the butter until smooth then season generously, stir through the herbs and keep warm.
- Dip the chicken strips one at a time into the flour, egg then breadcrumbs and lay on a rack to dry slightly.
- Heat 1 cm (½ in) depth oil in a pan and fry the chicken in batches until golden on both sides and cooked through.
- Serve the chicken with the warm mash, with green leaves to make a tasty starter.

PREPARATION TIME:
15 MINUTES + MARINATING TIME

COOKING TIME: 20 MINUTES

INGREDIENTS

4 chicken breasts, skinned
300 ml / 10 fl.oz / 1 ¼ cups buttermilk
100 g / 3 ½ oz / ½ cup plain
   (all-purpose) flour
2 eggs, beaten
200 g / 7 oz / ¾ cup breadcrumbs,
vegetable oil
4 large sweet potatoes, peeled
salt and pepper
50 g / 1 ¾ oz butter

504

SERVES 4

Chicken Pasanda

PREPARATION TIME:
15 MINUTES

COOKING TIME:
1 HOUR 15 MINUTES

INGREDIENTS

2 tbsp vegetable oil
1 onion, peeled and finely chopped
1 cinnamon stick
2 cardamom pods, lightly crushed
3 cm (1 in) piece ginger
2 cloves of garlic, finely sliced
1 tsp turmeric, 1 tsp ground cumin
1 tsp ground coriander, 1 tsp paprika
½–1 tsp chilli (chili) powder
150 ml / 5 fl. oz / ⅔ cup plain yogurt
2 tbsp tomato purée
2 chicken breasts, skinned
4 tbsp flaked (slivered) almonds
rice to serve

- Heat the oil in a pan and fry the onion until golden. Add the cinnamon and cardamom, ginger and garlic and cook gently for another 5–10 minutes until soft.
- Add the turmeric, cumin, coriander and chilli and fry for 1 minute, then add 1 tbsp yogurt and cook so it sizzles and starts to dry out – don't worry if it splits or looks odd.
- Repeat until all the yogurt is incorporated then add the tomato purée and around 250 ml / 9 fl. oz / 1 cup hot water and simmer for 20–30 minutes until the sauce thickens.
- Chop the chicken.
- Toast the almonds in a dry frying pan, then crush and stir into the sauce with the chicken and simmer for 20 minutes until the chicken is cooked. Add more water if the sauce looks too dry. Adjust the seasoning.
- Remove the cinnamon stick and cardamom and serve with the rice.

505

SERVES 4

Mediterranean Tray Bake

PREPARATION TIME:
10 MINUTES

COOKING TIME:
30–40 MINUTES

INGREDIENTS

4 chicken breasts, skin on
2 courgettes (zucchini), thickly sliced
2 red peppers, deseeded and roughly chopped
2 orange peppers, deseeded and roughly chopped
2 red onions, peeled and cut into eighths
400 g / 14 oz / 1 ½ cups canned tomatoes
2 tbsp dried Herbes de Provence
salt and pepper
100 g / 3 ½ oz / ½ cup green olives

- Preheat the oven to 180°C (160°C fan) / 350F / gas 4.
- Place the chicken and vegetables in a roasting tin, pour over the tomatoes, sprinkle over herbs, oil and seasoning and roast for 30–40 minutes until the chicken is cooked.
- Add the olives for the last 5 minutes of cooking.
- Serve at the table for everyone to help themselves.

506

SERVES 4

Stuffed Chicken with Monkfish Bites

**PREPARATION TIME:
45 MINUTES**

COOKING TIME: 45–50 MINUTES

INGREDIENTS

100 g / 3 ½ oz / ½ cup dried figs
200 ml / 7 fl. oz / ¾ cup marsala
2 tbsp olive oil
1 onion, peeled and finely diced
2 rashers streaky bacon, diced
100 g / 3 ½ oz / ½ cup pistachios, chopped
1 tbsp parsley, chopped
½ orange, zested
150 g / 5 oz / ⅔ cup breadcrumbs
salt and pepper
4 chicken legs, deboned, skin on
8 dates
400 g / 14 oz monkfish tail, boned
3 tbsp flour
2 eggs, beaten
200 g / 7 oz / ¾ cup breadcrumbs
1 tsp dried thyme
75 ml / 2 ½ fl. oz / ⅓ cup olive oil
rice
slivered pistachios

- Preheat the oven to 180°C (160°C fan) / 350F / gas 4.
- Halve the figs, then soak in the marsala for 20 minutes.
- Fry the onion, bacon and pistachios in oil until golden, then add the parsley, orange zest and leave to cool.
- Lift the figs from the alcohol, reserving the liquid, and finely chop then add to the stuffing mix with the breadcrumbs and mix well.
- Lay chicken legs skin-side down and divide the stuffing between them. Truss with cook's string, to make round parcel. Place in a tin and roast for 45 minutes.
- Meanwhile cut the monkfish into chunks, coat in flour, egg and breadcrumbs mixed with thyme, then shallow fry in the oil until golden on all sides.
- Pour the reserved marsala into a pan, add the dates and reduce. Serve the chicken cushions with the rice and slivered pistachios and monkfish.

Chicken Cushions with Pistachio Couscous

507

- Stir the pistachios into steamed couscous for a change from rice.

508

SERVES 4

Caramelised Chicken, Griddled Corn and Rice

**PREPARATION TIME:
10 MINUTES**

**COOKING TIME:
30 MINUTES**

INGREDIENTS

8 chicken drumsticks
olive oil
salt and pepper
4 sweetcorn, peeled
100 g / 3 ½ oz / ½ cup green beans, trimmed
rice to serve

FOR THE BARBECUE SAUCE

4 tbsp white wine vinegar
3–4 tbsp soy sauce
2–3 tbsp tomato ketchup
1 tbsp soft brown sugar
2 tsp English mustard powder
1 tsp paprika
pinch dried chilli (chili) flakes
salt and pepper

- Preheat the oven to 200°C (180°C fan) / 400F / gas 6.
- Mix together the sauce ingredients and simmer in a pan for 5 minutes, then coat the drumsticks thoroughly in the sauce.
- Lay the drumsticks in a foil-lined roasting tin and roast in the oven for about 25 minutes until golden and cooked through. If they look like they are burning, cover with foil.
- Meanwhile heat a griddle or barbecue until smoking and cook the sweetcorn, turning frequently until lightly charred and tender.
- Steam the green beans over simmering water for 4–5 minutes until crisp-tender.
- Serve the hot chicken with the rice, corn and beans and any sauce spooned over.

Chicken, Corn and Vegetable Rice

509

- Add cooked peas and drained canned black-eye beans to the rice.

510

SERVES 4

Breaded Chicken Breast with Salad

- Place the chicken between 2 pieces of cling film and bash out a little with a rolling pin to about 2 cm thickness.
- Place the chicken in a bowl with the buttermilk. Refrigerate for at least 2 hours or even overnight.
- Dip the chicken breasts one at a time into the flour, egg then breadcrumbs mixed with mustard powder and lay on a rack to dry slightly.
- Heat 1 cm (½ in) depth oil in a pan and fry the chicken in batches until golden on both sides and cooked through.
- Serve with salad and lemon wedges.

PREPARATION TIME:
10 MINUTES

COOKING TIME:
15–20 MINUTES

INGREDIENTS

4 chicken breasts, skinned
300 ml / 10 fl. oz / 1 ¼ cups buttermilk
100 g / 3 ½ oz / ½ cup plain
    (all-purpose) flour
2 eggs, beaten
200 g / 7 oz / ¾ cup breadcrumbs
1 tsp mustard powder
vegetable oil
mixed salad, to serve

Crispy Chicken Muffins

511

- Toast English muffins and top with mayonnaise, tomatoes and crisp chicken cut into slices.

512

SERVES 4

Chicken with Apple Sauce

- Preheat the oven to 200°C (180°C fan) / 400F / gas 6.
- Cook the wild rice according to packet instructions, drain and keep warm.
- Meanwhile drizzle the chicken with oil, season well and roast in the oven for 25 minutes.
- Peel and core the apples and cut into chunks. Place in a pan with the sugar, cloves, vinegar and water and cover with a lid.
- Cook over a low heat for 10–15 minutes, checking occasionally, until the apples have 'exploded' to a fine purée and are soft. Beat to a purée and remove the cloves.
- Cook the Brussels tops briefly in boiling salted water, then drain thoroughly.
- Serve the chicken with the apple sauce, rice and Brussel tops.

PREPARATION TIME:
15 MINUTES

COOKING TIME:
50 MINUTES

INGREDIENTS

4 chicken supremes, skin on
2 tbsp olive oil
salt and pepper
250 g / 9 oz / 1 cup Bramley apples,
    peeled and roughly chopped
250 g / 9 oz / 1 cup Cox apples,
    peeled and roughly chopped
1 tbsp sugar (optional, depending
    on tartness of apples and usage)
2 cloves
2 tbsp water
1 tbsp cider vinegar
250 g / 9 oz / 1 cup Brussels
    sprout tops
250 g / 9 oz / 1 cup wild rice

Chicken with Carrots and Apple Sauce

513

- Replace the brussels with carrots.

514

SERVES 4

Cheesy Chicken with Spiced Carrot Sauce

Chicken with Spiced Parsnip Sauce

515

- Try this sauce using parsnips instead of the carrots for a real winter warmer.

Chicken with Carrot Sauce and Pasta

516

- Toss the chopped chicken and sauce with wholewheat pasta or gnocchi.

PREPARATION TIME:
20 MINUTES

COOKING TIME:
30–35 MINUTES

....

INGREDIENTS

4 chicken thighs
2 tbsp olive oil
salt and pepper
2 tbsp olive oil
1 onion, peeled and chopped
1 stick celery, peeled and sliced
2 carrots, peeled and chopped
2 cloves of garlic, finely sliced
4 sprigs thyme
1 tsp ground cumin
1 tsp ground coriander
400 ml / 14 fl. oz / 1 ½ cups vegetable
    stock or water
150 ml / 5 fl. oz / ⅔ cup double (heavy)
    cream
150 g / 5 oz / ⅔ cup Cheddar, grated

- Preheat the oven to 200°C (180°C fan) / 400F / gas 6.
- Roast the chicken in the oven with oil and seasoning until golden and cooked through. Set aside to rest.
- Meanwhile heat the oil in a large pan and sweat the onion, celery and carrot without colouring for 10 minutes until softened. Add the garlic, thyme and spices and cook for a few minutes, then pour in the stock and simmer for 20 minutes or until the carrot is tender.
- Drain, reserving the cooking liquor and tip the vegetables into a food processor, discarding the thyme stems. Pour in enough cooking liquid to make a smooth thick sauce.
- Pour back into the pan and reheat gently with the cream. Adjust the seasoning.
- Place the chicken in a gratin dish, pour the carrot sauce around and top generously with grated cheese. Grill until bubbling, then serve with greens and crusty bread.

Chicken and Pepper Crumble

517

SERVES 4

- Poach the chicken in the stock for 5 minutes until just cooked through. Drain, reserving the stock.
- Heat the butter in a pan and sauté the onion and peppers until golden, then add the chicken. Add the boursin and enough poaching liquor to loosen a little, then season and set aside.
- Meanwhile rub the butter and flour together with your fingertips to resemble breadcrumbs, then stir through the pine nuts and season well.
- Spoon the chicken mixture into a gratin dish, then top lightly with the crumble. Grill or bake until bubbling and the topping is golden and crunchy.

PREPARATION TIME:
20 MINUTES

COOKING TIME:
10–20 MINUTES

INGREDIENTS

4 chicken breasts, skinned and cubed
500 ml / 1 pint / 2 cups chicken stock
40 g / 1 oz butter
1 onion, peeled and chopped
1 yellow pepper, deseeded and roughly chopped
1 green pepper, deseeded and roughly chopped
1 red pepper, deseeded and roughly chopped
200 g / 7 oz / ¾ cup Boursin cheese
salt and pepper
120 g / 4 oz / ½ cup plain (all-purpose) flour
100 g / 3 ½ oz / ½ cup butter, cold and cubed
50 g / 1 ¾ oz / ¼ cup pine nuts, chopped

Mediterranean Chicken Crumble

518

- Experiment with different vegetables that would hold their shape in the crumble – cooked courgettes (zucchini), broccoli, peas would all work.

Chicken with Tabbouleh

519

SERVES 4

- Preheat the oven to 200°C (180°C fan) / 400F / gas 6.
- Roast the chicken in the oven with a little oil and seasoning for about 20 minutes. Set aside to rest.
- Meanwhile soak the bulghur wheat in the hot stock for 25–30 minutes until tender. Drain off any excess liquid and season. Stir through the parsley and juice of ½ lemon.
- Steam or griddle the asparagus until tender – 4–5 minutes, then chop into short lengths and stir through the tabbouleh.
- Serve the chicken drizzled with a little lemon juice and the tabbouleh alongside.

PREPARATION TIME:
5 MINUTES

COOKING TIME:
30 MINUTES

INGREDIENTS

4 chicken breasts, skin on
2 tbsp olive oil
salt and pepper
1–2 lemons, juiced
300 g / 10 oz / 1 ¼ cups bulghur wheat
400 ml / 14 fl. oz / 1 ½ cups chicken stock
1 bunch parsley, chopped
1 bunch asparagus

Spicy Chicken with Tabbouleh

520

- Add half a teaspoon to the tabbouleh for an extra kick.

521

SERVES 4

Caramel Star Anise Chicken

PREPARATION TIME:
5 MINUTES

COOKING TIME:
25 MINUTES

INGREDIENTS

4 chicken drumsticks
2 tbsp vegetable oil
1 red onion, peeled and finely sliced
2 star anise
60 ml / 2 fl. oz / ¼ cup dark soy sauce
100 g / 3 ½ oz / ½ cup brown sugar
black pepper
60 ml / 2 fl. oz / ¼ cup fish sauce
½ lime, juiced (optional)

- Heat the oil in a pan until nearly smoking, then cook the chicken until golden.
- Reduce the heat and add the onion and a little more oil if necessary and cook until softened. Add the soy and simmer for 5 minutes or until reduced by half.
- Add the sugar and generously season with pepper and stir to make a caramel sauce. Cook until syrupy then add the fish sauce and lime juice if using, a little at a time.
- Serve the chicken with something bland such as white rice.

Sticky Chicken Rolls

522

- Crusty French baguette would make an excellent vehicle for any leftovers – it's worth cooking double.

523

MAKES 16

Chicken and Nori Dumplings

PREPARATION TIME:
1 HOUR

COOKING TIME:
15–20 MINUTES

INGREDIENTS

100 g / 3 ½ oz / ½ cup minced chicken
75 g / 2 ½ oz / ⅓ cup nori seaweed
   or finely shredded spinach
1 tsp ginger, finely chopped
1 clove of garlic, crushed
1 tbsp Shaoxing rice wine or
   dry sherry
1 tbsp dark soy sauce
salt and pepper
4 spring onions (scallions),
   finely chopped
1 tsp sesame oil
½ tsp sugar
100 g / 3 ½ oz / ½ cup mayonnaise
1 lime, juiced and zested

FOR THE DOUGH

150 g / 5 oz / ⅔ cup plain
   (all-purpose) flour
125 ml / 4 fl. oz / ½ cup very hot water

- To make the dough, tip the flour into a large bowl and stir the hot water gradually in until thoroughly mixed.
- Tip onto a floured work surface and knead for 6–8 minutes. Place in the bowl, cover with a damp tea towel.
- Meanwhile combine the filling ingredients in a bowl.
- Knead the dough again for about 5 minutes and shape into a sausage. Slice into 16 equal pieces. Roll each slice into a ball, then roll into a circle 9 cm (3 ½ in) wide. Place on a floured tray and cover with a damp tea towel.
- Place 2 tsp of filling in the centre of each circle and fold the dough over and seal, crimping the edges.
- Heat a large pan, add the oil and place the dumplings in the pan. Cook for 2 minutes, add 100 ml water, cover the pan and simmer for 12–14 minutes. Take the lid off and cook for another few minutes.
- Stir the lime juice and zest into the mayonnaise and serve with the dumplings.

Dumplings with Chinese Dipping Sauce

524

- Mix together 4 tbsp soy sauce, 1 tsp sugar, juice of ½ lime and a little chilli (chili) and serve alongside the dumplings.

525

SERVES 6

Chicken and Goats' Cheese Tart

Chicken Pizza Tart 526

- Add oozing mozzarella for a pizza-like tart.

Chicken Feta Tart 527

- Use feta cheese instead of goats' cheese for a mediterranean twist.

PREPARATION TIME:
10 MINUTES

COOKING TIME:
35–40 MINUTES

INGREDIENTS

1 x 320 g / 11 oz sheet ready-rolled shortcrust pastry
1 egg, beaten

FOR THE FILLING

olive oil
1 onion, peeled and finely chopped
2 cloves of garlic, finely sliced
2 chicken thighs, skinned, deboned and chopped
4–6 ripe tomatoes, thickly sliced
200 g / 7 oz / ¾ cup goats' cheese log, sliced
1 tbsp thyme leaves
salt and pepper

- Preheat the oven to 180°C (160°C fan) / 350F / gas 4.
- Roll out the pastry and use to line a pie dish. Blind bake in the oven for 10 minutes until pale gold. Remove and leave to cool.
- Heat the oil in a pan and cook the onion and garlic until slightly golden. Remove from the pan to a bowl with a slotted spoon.
- Add the chicken and cook until golden.
- Spoon the onion into the base of the tart, then top with sliced tomatoes. Place the chicken pieces on top and dot the goats' cheese around. Sprinkle with thyme leaves.
- Bake in the oven for about 20 minutes until the pastry is golden. Serve warm.

528

SERVES 4

Roast Chicken with Garlic and Tomatoes

PREPARATION TIME:
10 MINUTES

COOKING TIME:
40–55 MINUTES

INGREDIENTS

4 chicken legs
2 onions, peeled and thickly sliced
1 head of garlic, separated into cloves
8 tomatoes, halved
2 tbsp olive oil
salt and pepper
½ bunch thyme or rosemary leaves
2 tbsp balsamic vinegar

- Preheat the oven to 200°C (180°C fan) / 400F / gas 6.
- Place the chicken legs in a large roasting tin and arrange the garlic, onions and tomatoes around. Drizzle with oil, season and sprinkle over the herbs and balsamic.
- Roast for 40 minutes or until the chicken legs are cooked. Add a little water to loosen the sauce.
- If the vegetables look like they need longer to become appetisingly charred and golden, remove the chicken to a plate to rest covered with foil and roast the vegetables for a further 15–20 minutes.
- Serve hot or warm with crusty bread.

Chicken and Tomato Pasta 529

- Toss the contents of the roasting tin and the chicken meat pulled from the bone with your choice of cooked pasta.

530

SERVES 4

Chicken Persillade with Sautéed Vegetables

PREPARATION TIME:
15 MINUTES

COOKING TIME:
20 MINUTES

INGREDIENTS

4 chicken breasts, skinned
1 bunch parsley, chopped
2 cloves of garlic, chopped
1 lemon, zested
80 ml / 2 ½ fl. oz / ⅓ cup olive oil
2 courgettes (zucchini), roughly chopped
2 red peppers, deseeded and roughly chopped
2 yellow peppers, deseeded and roughly chopped
4 asparagus spears
salt and pepper

- Place the chicken breasts between 2 pieces of cling film and bash out slightly with a rolling pin to an even thickness of about 2–3 cm (1–1 ½ in).
- Place the parsley, garlic, 1 tsp salt and zest on a board and very finely chop with a sharp knife to make a dark green almost-paste. Smear the paste onto the top of the chicken breasts.
- Heat half the oil in one pan, add the chicken persillade-side down and cook gently for 5 minutes or so.
- Meanwhile heat the remaining oil in a separate pan and sauté the vegetables until golden and tender. Season.
- Turn the chicken over carefully with a spatula and cook the other side for about 5 minutes until cooked through.
- Serve the chicken on top of a bed of sautéed vegetables.

Persillade Chicken with Sautéed Root Vegetables 531

- Sauté diced celeriac (celery root), potato and swede for an earthy variation.

532

SERVES 6–8

Duck and Chicken Liver Terrine

- Heat a tbsp of butter in a frying pan and cook the duck livers over a medium heat for 5 minutes, turning them frequently. Transfer to a food processor, reserving the frying pan and juices.
- Pour the port into the pan and add to the processor. Melt 250 g butter. Add the butter, mace, thyme, garlic and seasoning. Blend to a smooth purée.
- Heat the oil in a pan and add the shallots. Cook until translucent. Halve the chicken livers and sauté briskly for 6–7 minutes until just pink in the centre.
- Season, then pour in the port. Reduce for 2 minutes.
- Tip the chicken livers and their juices into the bottom of a serving dish. Spread over the duck liver pâté as evenly as possible. Pour over the melted butter. Refrigerate for 12–24 hours until the butter has set. Sprinkle with redcurrants and seeds to serve.

PREPARATION TIME:
30 MINUTES

COOKING TIME:
12 MINUTES

INGREDIENTS

500 g / 1 lb / 2 cups duck livers, trimmed
300 g / 10 oz / 1 ½ cups butter, softened
100 ml / 3 ½ fl. oz / ½ cup port
¼ tsp ground mace
1 tsp thyme leaves
1 clove of garlic, crushed
salt and pepper
1 tbsp olive oil
2 shallots, peeled and finely chopped
400 g / 13 ½ oz / 1 ½ cups chicken livers, trimmed and cleaned
100 ml / 3 ½ fl. oz / ½ cup port
salt and pepper
150 g / 5 oz / ⅔ cup butter, melted
redcurrants, to sprinkle
mixed seeds, to sprinkle

Duck and Chicken Pâté on Toast

533

- Serve alongside toasted bread for a great starter.

534

SERVES 2

Honey-soy Chicken with Mushrooms

- Heat the oil in a wok and sauté the chicken and mushrooms until the chicken turns white.
- Add the garlic, honey and soy and spoon the sauce over the chicken as it cooks to coat and caramelise.
- Once the sauce is sticky and reduced, serve spooned over cooked rice. Sprinkle over the peppercorns.

PREPARATION TIME:
10 MINUTES

COOKING TIME:
10–15 MINUTES

INGREDIENTS

2 chicken breasts, sliced
1 tbsp groundnut oil
2 field mushrooms, thickly sliced
1 clove of garlic, crushed
2 tbsp soy sauce
1 tbsp honey
1 tbsp Szechuan peppercorns, crushed
cooked rice, to serve

Honey-soy Chicken with Aubergine

535

- Add cubes of aubergine (eggplant) with the chicken to cook and tenderise.

536

SERVES 4

Roast Chicken with Figs and Rösti

Roast Chicken with Pears and Rösti

537

- Replace the figs with pear slices.

Apple Potato Rösti

538

- Add grated eating apple to the mix – just one – for a slightly sweet twist.

PREPARATION TIME:
20 MINUTES

COOKING TIME:
30–35 MINUTES

INGREDIENTS

4 chicken supremes, skin on
2 tbsp olive oil
salt and pepper
2 tbsp thyme leaves
500 g / 1 lb / 2 cups floury potatoes, peeled
2 tbsp butter, melted
2 tbsp vegetable oil
salt and pepper
8 figs
coriander (cilantro) sprigs, to decorate

- Preheat the oven to 200°C (180°C fan) / 400F / gas 6.
- Place the chicken in a roasting tin, season well, drizzle with oil and roast for 25–30 minutes until golden and cooked.
- Grate the potatoes. Toss with the melted butter and seasoning, ensuring they are thoroughly coated.
- Heat the oil in a large frying pan, then divide the mixture roughly into 8. Add the mixture in heaped spoonfuls a few at a time to the pan, pressing them down flat with a spatula. Cook over a medium heat for about 10 minutes until the base is brown.
- Run the spatula or a palette knife underneath to loosen, then turn the rösti over to cook the other side. Cook for a further 5–10 minutes until browned and crisp, then remove to kitchen towel to drain and repeat until all the rösti are cooked. Keep warm in the oven.
- For the last 5 minutes of cooking, add halved figs to the roasting tin with the chicken to warm through, then remove and leave to rest for 5 minutes.
- Place 2 rösti on each plate. Slice the chicken at an angle and sit on top, then spoon round the figs and roasting juices. Decorate with coriander sprigs.

539

SERVES 6

Indian Chicken Frittata

- Preheat the oven to 180°C (160°C fan) / 350F / gas 4.
- Combine the chopped chicken and cooked peas in a bowl.
- Beat the eggs with the creme fraiche in a large bowl.
- Add the eggs into the chicken and peas and season, then mix together carefully. Add the spices and feta if using.
- Oil a large frying pan, then pour the mixture in and bake in the oven for about 35 minutes until puffed and golden. The egg should be cooked through.
- Cut the frittata into wedges and serve warm or cold.

PREPARATION TIME:
10 MINUTES

COOKING TIME:
35 MINUTES

INGREDIENTS

2 chicken breasts, cooked and chopped
150 g / 5 oz / ⅔ cup frozen peas, cooked
8 eggs
1 tbsp creme fraiche
100 g / 3 ½ oz / ½ cup feta, optional
½ bunch coriander (cilantro), chopped
½ tsp turmeric
½ tbsp garam masala
olive oil
salt and pepper

Indian Chicken and Potato Frittata

540

- Bulk this up by adding 2 potatoes, chopped and steamed, but try adding steamed chopped green beans or even steamed cauliflower florets as well.

541

SERVES 2–4

Herby Chicken Salad

- Poach the chicken breasts in simmering water for about 20 minutes until cooked through. Set aside to rest, then shred finely.
- Tip the chicken into a large salad bowl and toss with the herbs, capers and seasoning.
- Whisk together the lemon juice and mustard, then whisk in the oil to make an emulsion.
- Toss the salad with the dressing and serve while still warm.

PREPARATION TIME:
10 MINUTES

COOKING TIME:
20 MINUTES

INGREDIENTS

4 chicken breasts, skinned
1 bunch parsley, roughly chopped
60 g / 2 oz / ¼ cup capers, drained
1 bunch chives, chopped
salt and pepper
½ lemon, juiced
1 tbsp Dijon mustard
80 ml / 2 ½ fl. oz / ⅓ cup extra
   virgin olive oil

Herby Chicken and Potato Salad

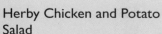

542

- Add boiled potatoes to the salad.

543

SERVES 4

Chicken and Vegetable Tagliatelle

PREPARATION TIME:
15 MINUTES

COOKING TIME:
15 MINUTES

··

INGREDIENTS

4 chicken breasts, skin on
2 tbsp olive oil
salt and pepper
½ lemon, juiced
1 orange, segmented
½ grapefruit, juiced
3 tbsp extra virgin olive oil
1 courgette (zucchini)
1 carrot, peeled
1 red pepper, deseeded and
    finely sliced
8 asparagus, trimmed
320 g / 11 oz / 1 ½ cups fresh tagliatelle
    pasta

- Heat a griddle pan until nearly smoking. Rub the chicken with oil and seasoning and cook skin-side down until striped and golden, then reduce the heat, turn and cook on the other side for 5–6 minutes until cooked through. Set aside to rest.
- Place the orange segments in a bowl with the grapefruit juice and oil. Use a vegetable peeler run down the length of the courgette and carrot to make ribbons and add to the bowl with the pepper.
- Cook the pasta and asparagus in boiling salted water according to packet instructions. Drain, reserving a little cooking water.
- Toss the pasta with the citrus-marinated vegetables and cooking water, then serve topped with sliced chicken.

Chicken and Vegetable Penne 544

- Replace the Tagliatelle with Penne.

545

SERVES 4–6

Chicken and Lemon Pie

PREPARATION TIME:
15 MINUTES

COOKING TIME:
55 MINUTES

··

INGREDIENTS

3 tbsp olive oil
500 g / 1 lb / 2 cups diced
    chicken meat
1 onion, peeled and sliced
2 cloves of garlic, finely sliced
250 g / 9 oz / 1 cup chestnut mushrooms,
    quartered
1 tsp ground cumin
3 preserved lemons, chopped
300 ml / 10 fl. oz / 1 ¼ cups
    chicken stock
100 g / 3 ½ oz / ½ cup green olives
salt and pepper
250 g / 9 oz shortcrust pastry

- Preheat the oven to 190°C (170°C fan) / 375F / gas 5.
- Heat the oil in a pan and brown the chicken meat in batches until golden then remove to a plate with a slotted spoon.
- Add the onion and garlic to the pan and cook gently until softened and gold. Add the mushrooms and cook for 5 minutes, before adding the cumin, lemons and chicken back to the pan. Cover with the stock, reduce the heat and simmer gently for 20 minutes until the chicken has cooked through. Spoon into a pie dish.
- Lightly flour a work surface and roll out the pastry large enough to fit over the pie dish. Lay over the filling, crimping the edges to seal, then make a cross in the top to let out the steam. Bake in the oven for 25 minutes or until the pastry is golden.
- Leave to rest for 5 minutes before serving.

Traditional Chicken Pie 546

- Leave out the preserved lemons and mushrooms and stir 100 ml / 3 ½ oz cream into the sauce at the end before topping with the pastry.

547

SERVES 6

Chicken with Chestnut Stuffing

Stuffed Chicken with Prunes

548

- Adding 200 g / 7 oz chopped prunes to the stuffing will add festive richness.

Chicken Breast with Chestnuts and Stuffing

549

- Any excess stuffing can be rolled into balls and roasted around the meat.

PREPARATION TIME:
20 MINUTES

COOKING TIME:
1 HOUR 30 MINUTES

INGREDIENTS

1 whole chicken, deboned (ask your butcher)
200 g / 7 oz / ¾ cup fresh cep mushrooms, thickly sliced
40 g / 1 oz butter

FOR THE STUFFING
2 tbsp butter
500 g / 1 lb / 2 cups cep or other wild mushrooms
1 onion, finely chopped
1 clove of garlic, chopped
10 vacuum packed chestnuts, chopped
½ bunch parsley
1 slice bread, soaked in milk
1 egg, beaten

- Preheat the oven to 190°C (170°C fan) / 375F / gas 5.
- Heat the butter in a pan and cook the mushrooms and onions until soft. Add the garlic and chestnuts and stir well.
- Transfer to a bowl and mix in the parsley, crumble in the bread then mix in the egg. Use your hands to combine everything.
- Lay the chicken skin-side down on a work surface and spoon the stuffing into the centre. Truss with kitchen string and place in a roasting tin. Season and roast in the oven for about 1 ½ hours until the juices run clear when pierced with a toothpick.
- Leave the chicken to rest for 10 minutes. Heat the butter in a pan and fry the cep slices until golden and tender.
- Serve the chicken in slices with the mushrooms alongside.

550

SERVES 4–6

Almond Chicken with Potatoes

PREPARATION TIME:
20 MINUTES

COOKING TIME:
40–45 MINUTES

INGREDIENTS

4 tbsp olive oil
4 carrots, peeled and cut lengthways
   into batons
400 g / 14 oz / 1 ½ cups waxy potatoes,
   halved
1 chicken, jointed
60 g / 2 oz whole almonds
250 ml / 9 fl. oz / 1 cup chicken stock
salt and pepper
chive stalks, to garnish

- Preheat the oven to 200°C (180°C fan) / 400F / gas 6.
- Toss the carrots and potatoes with the oil and tip into a roasting tin and season. Sit the chicken joints on top, season the skin and roast in the oven for about 20 minutes until the skin is starting to turn gold.
- Pour in the stock and the almonds and return to the oven for 25 minutes until the chicken is cooked and the sauce syrupy and reduced.
- Serve garnished with chives.

Chicken Tray Bake   **551**

- This recipe works well in a tray bake – try adding halved tomatoes, courgette chunks or sweet potato for different combinations.

552

SERVES 4

Chicken Burger

PREPARATION TIME:
10 MINUTES

COOKING TIME:
8–10 MINUTES

INGREDIENTS

500 g / 1 lb / 2 cups chicken, minced
2 tbsp thyme leaves, chopped
salt and pepper
1 clove of garlic, crushed
1 lemon, zested
1 egg, beaten
4 burger buns
4 tomatoes, sliced
½ head iceberg lettuce, shredded
4 tbsp mayonnaise

- Mix the chicken with the thyme, seasoning, garlic and lemon zest until thoroughly mixed.
- Pour in enough beaten egg to bin, but don't let the mixture get too wet. With wet hands, form the mixture into 8 small or 4 large burgers. Chill in the refrigerator for 30 minutes.
- Cook in a little oil for 3–4 minutes per side, depending on thickness.
- Lightly toast the buns and spread with mayonnaise.
- Layer tomatoes, lettuce and chicken burger and top with the toasted top. Serve.

Chicken Sandwich   **553**

- Replace the bun for sliced bread.

SERVES 4–6

Chicken with Garlic Cloves

- Preheat the oven to 180°C (160°C fan) / 350F / gas 4.
- Place the chicken in a roasting tin and smear with the butter, seasoning liberally. Push the tarragon into the cavity.
- Arrange the carrots and garlic around the chicken and pour over the wine. Roast in the oven for 1 ½ hours until the chicken is golden and the juices run clear when pierced with a toothpick. Cover with foil if it looks like burning.
- Transfer the chicken and carrots to a serving platter and leave to rest for 15 minutes. Squeeze the garlic from the cloves into the tin and remove as many skins as possible. Simmer gently over a low heat, stirring with a spoon to make a creamy sauce.
- Serve the chicken carved with the sauce to pour over.

PREPARATION TIME:
10 MINUTES

COOKING TIME:
1 HOUR 30 MINUTES

INGREDIENTS

1 oven-ready chicken
40 g / 1 oz butter
4 sprigs tarragon
4–5 carrots, peeled and chopped
40 cloves of garlic
200 ml / 7 fl. oz / ¾ cup dry white wine
salt and pepper

Garlic Chicken with Salad

555

- This chicken really needs nothing more than a fresh watercress salad with a little lemon juice for dressing.

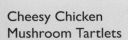

556

SERVES 4

Chicken and Mushroom Tartlets

- Preheat the oven to 200°C (180°C fan) / 400F / gas 6.
- Roll out the pastry on a lightly floured surface to about 1 cm (½ in) thickness. Cut out 4 circles and use to line 4 individual tart cases. Prick the bases with a fork and bake in the oven for 10 minutes until pale gold. Leave to cool.
- Meanwhile heat the butter in a pan and fry the chicken and mushrooms until golden and the mushrooms start to exude juices. Sprinkle in the thyme and garlic and cook until the liquid evaporates, then season and stir in the cream.
- Once the tart cases have cooked and cooled, fill with equal quantities of the chicken mixture, return to the oven and bake for a further 15–20 minutes until the pastry is golden and the filling bubbling. Serve hot or warm.

PREPARATION TIME:
25 MINUTES

COOKING TIME:
15–20 MINUTES

INGREDIENTS

375 g / 13 oz ready-rolled puff pastry
40 g / 1 oz butter
4 chicken thighs, deboned and meat chopped
250 g / 9 oz / 1 cup mixed wild mushrooms, cleaned
2 sprigs thyme leaves
1 clove of garlic, crushed
salt and pepper
150 ml / 5 fl. oz / ⅔ cup double (heavy) cream or crème fraiche

Cheesy Chicken Mushroom Tartlets

557

- Shavings of Parmesan over the top of the filling before baking will melt and add deep savour.

558

SERVES 2

Chicken with Mango

Exotic Fruity Chicken   559

- Experiment with different fruit – pineapple, grapefruit, oranges and melon would all work well with the herbs and spices.

Chicken with Rice Noodles   560

- Soak rice noodles according to packet instructions and toss with the sauce.

PREPARATION TIME:
15 MINUTES

COOKING TIME:
30 MINUTES

INGREDIENTS

2 chicken legs
2 tbsp olive oil
1 tsp ground coriander
1 tbsp thyme leaves
½ tsp cayenne pepper
salt
2 mangoes, very ripe, peeled and stoned
1 lime, juiced
1 red chilli (chili), deseeded and finely chopped
250 g / 9 oz / 1 cup baby spinach leaves

- Preheat the oven to 200°C (180°C fan) / 400F / gas 6.
- Rub the chicken legs with coriander, thyme, cayenne and a little oil. Sprinkle over the salt and roast in the oven for 30 minutes or until golden and cooked through.
- While the chicken is resting, slice the mango thickly and toss with lime juice and chilli. Arrange on a plate with spinach leaves.
- Sit the chicken legs on top and serve.

561

SERVES 4

Rolled Chicken Breasts

- Preheat the oven to 190°C (170°C fan) / 375F / gas 5. Pulse together the spinach, garlic, seasoning and olive oil save for 1 tbsp in a food processor until almost smooth.
- Butterfly the chicken, then spread them with spinach and garlic paste. Tightly roll chicken before rubbing their outsides with olive oil, seasoning with mixed dried herbs.
- Secure with wooden toothpicks and arranging on a baking tray. Roast for 22–25 minutes until firm yet slightly springy to the touch.
- Remove the chicken breasts and discard the toothpicks before slicing and serving.

PREPARATION TIME:
10 MINUTES

COOKING TIME:
40–45 MINUTES

**INGREDIENTS
FOR THE CHICKEN**

4 skinless chicken breasts
4 cloves of garlic, finely chopped
55 ml / 2 fl. oz / ¼ cup olive oil
1 tsp mixed dried herbs
a small bunch of spinach leaves, chopped
salt and pepper

Pine Nut Chicken Breasts

562

- Add 55 g / 2 oz / ½ cup pine nuts to the food processor before blitzing and spreading on the chicken breasts.

563

SERVES 4

Chicken and Salsify Pie

- Preheat the oven to 200°C (180°C fan) / 400F / gas 6.
- Steam the salsify for 20–25 minutes. Drain.
- Heat the butter in a pan and fry the chicken pieces until golden in patches. Remove with a slotted spoon.
- Sweat the shallots with the herbs. Stir in the flour to make a paste, then whisk in the milk. Return the chicken to the pan, season and simmer for 10 minutes.
- Divide the pastry in half. Roll pastry out on a floured surface, cut out 4 circles slightly larger than individual pie dishes and sit in the bases, pushing it into the corners. Prick bases and bake for 10–15 minutes, then leave to cool.
- Tip the chicken mixture into the pastry base, add the salsify. Roll remaining pastry out and cut out to slightly larger than the pie dishes. Sit circles on top of the filling.
- Brush with beaten egg, make a hole in the pastry to let steam escape and bake in the oven for 20–25 minutes.

PREPARATION TIME:
40 MINUTES

COOKING TIME:
30 MINUTES

INGREDIENTS

1 salsify, peeled, chopped and in acidulated water
2 tbsp butter
6 chicken thighs, deboned and skinned, cut into chunks
2 shallots, finely chopped
6 sprigs thyme
2 sprigs tarragon leaves
1 ½ tbsp plain (all-purpose) flour
300 ml / 10 fl. oz / 1 ¼ cups milk
salt and pepper
1 sheet (200 g / 7 oz) shortcrust pastry, ready rolled
1 egg, beaten

Chicken Carrot and Salsify Pie

564

- Carrot add a sweetness to offset the earthiness of salsify – add 2 diced carrots to the shallots when cooking.

565

SERVES 4

Roast Chicken Legs with Sugar Snaps

PREPARATION TIME:
10 MINUTES

COOKING TIME:
30 MINUTES

INGREDIENTS

4 chicken legs
2 tbsp thyme leaves
2 tbsp olive oil
salt and pepper
250 g / 9 oz / 1 cup sugar snap peas
150 g / 5 oz / ⅔ cup pancetta, diced
2 tbsp olive oil
1 clove of garlic, finely sliced
½ lemon, zested
1 tbsp tarragon leaves

- Preheat the oven to 200°C (180°C fan) / 400F / gas 6.
- Rub the chicken legs with thyme and seasoning, drizzle with oil and roast in the oven for about 30 minutes until golden and cooked through.
- Meanwhile steam the sugar snap peas over simmering water for 4–5 minutes until crisp–tender.
- Heat the oil in a pan and fry the pancetta until the fat starts to run, then add the garlic and cook for 1 minute. Add the steamed sugar snaps, lemon zest and tarragon and toss to coat.
- Serve the chicken legs on top of the sugar snap pea mix.

Roast Chicken Legs with Croutons

566

- Add 1 ciabatta loaf torn into bite-size pieces around the chicken legs to soak up all the juices.

567

SERVES 4–6

Fruity Roast Chicken

PREPARATION TIME:
15 MINUTES

COOKING TIME:
1 HOUR 30 MINUTES

INGREDIENTS

1 oven ready chicken
500 g / 1 lb / 2 cups highly-flavoured sausages, such as Tuscan, chilli (chili) etc.
75 g / 2 ½ oz / ⅓ cup breadcrumbs
1 apple, peeled and cored
150 g / 5 oz / ⅔ cup dried apricots, chopped
2 tbsp thyme leaves
3 cloves of garlic, crushed
salt and pepper
40 g / 1 oz butter, softened
250 g / 9 oz / 1 cup couscous
250 ml / 9 fl. oz / 1 cup chicken or vegetable stock
60 g / 2 oz flaked (slivered) almonds
squeeze of lemon juice

- Preheat the oven to 220°C (200°C fan) / 425F / gas 7.
- Slit the skins of the sausage and squeeze the flesh into a bowl. Mix well with the breadcrumbs, apple, apricots, thyme, garlic and a little seasoning and spoon into the cavity of the chicken.
- Place the chicken in a roasting tin. Season, drizzle with oil and roast in the oven for 20 minutes then reduce the heat to 180°C (160°C fan) / 350F / gas 4 and cook for 1 hour or until the juices run clear.
- While the chicken is resting place the couscous in a bowl, add the raisins, cover with the hot stock and cling film the bowl. Leave for 10 minutes or so until tender, then fork through the grains and add the lemon.

Fruity Roast Chicken with Rice

568

- Serve on a bed of boiled rice instead of couscous.

569

SERVES 4

Chicken and Coleslaw Burger

Chicken and Coleslaw Pitta

570

- Replace the burger bun with a pitta bread.

Indian Chicken Burgers

571

- Add a little chopped green chilli and a tsp of garam masala to the mix.

PREPARATION TIME:
20 MINUTES

COOKING TIME:
8–10 MINUTES

INGREDIENTS

500 g / 1 lb / 2 cups minced chicken
1 bunch basil leaves, finely chopped
salt and pepper
1 lemon, zested
1 egg, beaten
½ red cabbage, cored
1 carrot, peeled and chopped
1 red onion, peeled and chopped
180 g / 6 oz / ¾ cup mayonnaise
2 tbsp olive oil
4 burger buns
4 iceberg lettuce leaves

- Mix the chicken with the basil, pepper, salt and lemon zest until thoroughly mixed. Pour in enough beaten egg to bin, but don't let the mixture get too wet. With wet hands, form the mixture into 8 small or 4 large burgers.
- Chill in the refrigerator for 30 minutes.
- Meanwhile process the cabbage, carrot and onion in a food processor until finely shredded. Tip into a bowl, mix with the mayonnaise and plenty of seasoning.
- Cook the burgers in a little oil for 3–4 minutes per side, depending on thickness.
- Split and lightly toast the burger buns, then spoon the slaw onto the bottom half of each bun. Top with a burger, sandwich and eat.

SERVES 2

Chicken and Mushroom Pancakes

PREPARATION TIME:
10 MINUTES

COOKING TIME:
15 MINUTES

INGREDIENTS

40 g / 1 oz butter
2 chicken breasts, skin on
200 g / 7 oz / ¾ cup chestnut
   mushrooms, quartered
1 clove of garlic, crushed
4 sprigs tarragon
200 ml / 7 fl. oz / ¾ cup double (heavy)
   cream
1–2 tbsp grain or Dijon mustard
½ lemon, juiced
salt and pepper
2 galettes or Breton pancakes

- Heat the butter in a pan and fry the chicken for 3 minutes until golden.
- Add the mushrooms and cook until they start to exude juice, then add the garlic and cook until the liquid evaporates. Add the tarragon, cream, mustard and a squeeze of lemon juice and season, then taste and adjust any of the elements if necessary.
- Warm the pancakes briefly in a dry pan, then lay on plates. Spoon the filling into the centre, roll the pancakes up and serve.

SERVES 4

Tropical Chicken Salad

PREPARATION TIME:
20 MINUTES

COOKING TIME:
10 MINUTES

INGREDIENTS

3 tbsp olive oil
500 g / 1 lb / 2 cups chicken, diced
salt and pepper
60 g / 2 oz sesame seeds
1 pineapple, peeled, cored and diced
2 oranges, peeled and segmented
½ fresh coconut, shaved or prepared
   coconut shavings
1 pomegranate
2 limes, juiced
pinch dried chilli (chili) flakes
   (optional)

- Heat the oil in a pan and fry the chicken quickly until golden and cooked through. Season, coat in the sesame seeds and set aside.
- Combine the pineapple and oranges in a serving bowl with the coconut. Halve the pomegranate and hold it cut side down over the bowl. Bash with a wooden spoon to release the seeds – be careful, the juice does spurt out. Stir in the lime juice, a pinch of salt and the chilli if using.
- Sit the chicken pieces on top and serve.

574

SERVES 4

Pesto Chicken with Roasted Peppers

- Preheat the oven to 200°C (180°C fan) / 400F / gas 6.
- Place the peppers in a roasting tin, drizzle with oil and balsamic, season and roast for about 30–40 minutes until charred and tender. Set aside.
- Rub the chicken with oil and seasoning and griddle over medium heat on both sides until cooked through – 12 minutes or so.
- Meanwhile add the pine nuts to a frying pan over medium heat and lightly toast for a few seconds until golden. Place in a food processor with the garlic, basil and Parmesan. Whiz the ingredients in a food processor until roughly blended, stirring in enough olive oil to loosen.
- Serve the chicken with the pesto spooned over sitting on a bed of roasted peppers.

**PREPARATION TIME:
15 MINUTES**

COOKING TIME: 30–40 MINUTES

INGREDIENTS

4 peppers, 'cheeks' cut off
2 tbsp olive oil
salt and pepper
1 tbsp balsamic vinegar (optional)
4 chicken breasts, 2 tbsp olive oil

FOR THE PESTO

2 handfuls pine nuts
1 clove of garlic, peeled and chopped
2 bunches basil
80 g / 3 oz / ⅓ cup Parmesan, grated
extra virgin olive oil
salt and pepper

Chicken Caesar Tuiles

575

SERVES 4

**PREPARATION TIME:
20 MINUTES**

INGREDIENTS

2 chicken breasts, roasted
12 anchovies, from a tin
1 Cos lettuce, separated into leaves
1 ripe avocado, halved, peeled, stoned and chopped

FOR THE DRESSING

150 g / 5 oz / ⅔ cup Parmesan, grated
2 tbsp white wine vinegar

200 g / 7 oz / ¾ cup mayonnaise
2–3 tbsp Dijon mustard
2 anchovy fillets
1 clove of garlic, crushed
2–3 tbsp extra virgin olive oil
salt and pepper

FOR THE PARMESAN TUILES

150 g / 5 oz / ⅔ cup Parmesan, grated

Chicken with Mozzarella Salad

576

SERVES 2

**PREPARATION TIME:
10 MINUTES**

**COOKING TIME:
20 MINUTES**

INGREDIENTS

2 chicken breasts, skin on
2 tbsp olive oil
salt and pepper
2 tsp dried oregano

1 tbsp rosemary leaves, finely chopped
1 tbsp balsamic vinegar
2 ripe tomatoes, cored and cut into wedges
3 tbsp extra virgin olive oil
1 tbsp balsamic vinegar
1 ball mozzarella
½ bunch basil leaves

- Make the dressing. Place all the ingredients in a food processor and pulse until combined. Taste and adjust the seasoning – you may want a squeeze of lemon juice or a little more pepper.
- Place the lettuce and avocado in a bowl. Shred the chicken and add to the bowl with the anchovies. Gently toss in ¾ of the dressing.
- Place tbsps of the grated Parmesan on a baking sheet and grill – watching like a hawk – until melted and bubbling. Remove from the heat and leave to cool and harden.
- Decorate the salad with Parmesan tuiles and topped with a little more dressing.

- Preheat the oven to 190°C (170°C fan) / 375F / gas 5.
- Mix together the oil, seasoning, herbs and vinegar and massage into the chicken. Place in a roasting tin and roast for 20 minutes or until cooked through.
- Meanwhile macerate the tomatoes in the oil and vinegar with a little salt and pepper.
- Set the chicken aside to rest and assemble the salad. Tear the mozzarella into chunks and place on a serving plate. Spoon the tomatoes and dressing around, scattering over torn basil and more seasoning. Thickly slice the chicken and sit on top of the salad.

577

SERVES 4–6

Chicken Pastries

PREPARATION TIME:
30 MINUTES

COOKING TIME:
20 MINUTES

INGREDIENTS

4 tbsp olive oil
1 onion, peeled and thickly sliced
2 garlic cloves, finely chopped
2 chicken breasts, skinned and diced
½ tsp ground cinnamon
½ tsp ground cumin
½ tsp ground coriander
100 g / 3 ½ oz / ½ cup almonds, toasted
2 red peppers, 'cheeks' cut off and
    roasted
1 egg yolk
salt and pepper
12–16 sheets filo pastry
120 g / 4 oz / ½ cup butter, melted
2 eggs
1 egg yolk, beaten
icing sugar and ground cinnamon,
    to dust

- Preheat the oven to 200°C (180°C fan) / 400F / gas 6.
- Heat the oil in a pan and sweat the onion and garlic until softened and turning gold. Add the chicken, spices and almonds and sauté until cooked through. Set aside to cool.
- Keeping the remaining filo sheets covered with a damp tea towel, remove one at a time from the pack and brush with melted butter before using.
- Place 2 sheets of pastry on a surface, brush each with melted butter, then place a roasted pepper piece on top. Spoon a little of the chicken mixture onto the pepper. Wrap the pastry around to enclose the filling. Repeat until all the filling and pastry is used up.
- Brush the tops with a little egg wash, then bake in the oven for 15–20 minutes or until the pastry is crisp and golden.
- Lightly dust the top with a little icing sugar and cinnamon before serving.

Chicken Aubergine Pastries

 578

- You could use the same method with long tender slices of cooked aubergine instead of the peppers.

579

SERVES 4–6

Roast Chicken with Pastis and Fennel

PREPARATION TIME:
20 MINUTES

COOKING TIME:
I HOUR 30 MINUTES

INGREDIENTS

1 oven-ready chicken
40 g / 1 oz butter, softened
salt and pepper
4 thyme sprigs
½ lemon
3 fennel bulbs, halved
1 head garlic, halved
60 ml / 2 fl. oz olive oil
100 ml / 3 ½ fl. oz / ½ cup Pastis
    (or vermouth if you can't find it)
200 ml / 7 fl. oz / ¾ cup chicken stock
handful black olives

- Preheat oven to 220°C (200°C fan) / 425F / gas 7.
- Smear the chicken with the butter and season generously. Stuff the cavity with thyme and the lemon half, place in a roasting tin and roast for 20 minutes.
- After 20 minutes lower the heat to 180°C (160°C fan) / 350F / gas 4 and add the fennel, garlic and drizzle over the oil and Pastis. Return to the oven for another hour or until the chicken is cooked through and the juices run clear when pierced with a toothpick.
- Transfer the chicken and vegetables to a serving platter and loosely cover with foil. Place the roasting in on the hob and deglaze the pan with a wooden spoon, adding the stock. Simmer for 10–15 minutes until reduced and syrupy, adjust the seasoning and add the olives.
- Serve the chicken with the vegetables and the sauce in a warmed sauce boat.

Lemony Chicken with Fennel

580

- Adding a halved lemon to the roasting tin will really intensify the lemon flavours in this dish and you won't need the stock. Good in the summer.

581

SERVES 4

Chicken with Honey, Tomato and Almonds

- Heat the oil and cook the chicken briskly until golden, then reduce the heat and add the onion and spices and cook until the onion has softened.
- Stir in the tomatoes, stock and honey and simmer uncovered for 10–15 minutes until the sauce has reduced and the chicken has cooked.
- Stir through the almonds.

PREPARATION TIME:
10 MINUTES

COOKING TIME:
20 MINUTES

INGREDIENTS

3 tbsp olive oil
4 chicken thighs, skinned, deboned
   and diced
1 onion, peeled and finely sliced
1 tsp ground cumin
1 tsp ground coriander
1 tsp paprika
3 ripe tomatoes, thickly sliced
250 ml / 9 fl. oz / 1 cup chicken stock
2–3 tbsp runny honey
60 g / 2 oz whole skinned almonds
salt and pepper

Chicken with Aubergine and Almonds

582

- Aubergines go well with all the main flavourings in this dish and would add bulk and flavour.

583

SERVES 4

Baked Chicken with Yogurt and Lemon

- Preheat the oven to 180°C (160°C fan) / 350F / gas 4.
- Place the chicken thighs skin side up in a roasting tin, surround with the lemon slices, drizzle with oil and season. Pour in the stock and wine and roast for 30 minutes or until the chicken is cooked through and the liquid reduced.
- Remove the chicken and lemon slices to a plate then tip the sauce into a pan. Simmer until reduced by a third or to your liking – taste and see how intense you want the flavours, then remove from the heat and stir in the yogurt. Do not reheat. Season and pour over the chicken.

PREPARATION TIME:
5 MINUTES

COOKING TIME:
40 MINUTES

INGREDIENTS

4–6 chicken thighs, skin on
4 tbsp olive oil
salt and pepper
½ lemon, sliced
200 ml / 7 fl. oz / ¾ cup
   chicken stock
100 ml / 3 ½ fl. oz / ½ cup
   dry white wine
150 ml / 5 fl. oz / ⅔ cup plain yogurt

Herby Baked Chicken

584

- Parsley, basil, thyme and tarragon would all work well finely chopped and added to the sauce with the yogurt.

SERVES 2

Honey Lime Chicken

Lime Chicken with Vegetable Rosette

586

- Try adding roasted pepper, griddled aubergine or even steamed slices of potato for colour and variation.

Honey Lime Chicken Kebabs

587

- Thread chunks of chicken marinated the same way onto skewers and barbecue.

PREPARATION TIME:
10 MINUTES

COOKING TIME:
20 MINUTES

INGREDIENTS

2 chicken breasts
1 tbsp olive oil
2 tbsp runny honey
1 lime, juiced
salt and pepper
2 beef tomatoes, thickly sliced
1 courgette (zucchini), thickly sliced
2 tbsp olive oil
1 lime, thinly sliced

- Preheat the oven to 200°C (180°C fan) / 400F / gas 6.
- Coat the chicken in the oil, honey and lime juice and season, then roast in the oven for 20 minutes until cooked through. Set aside to rest.
- Meanwhile heat a griddle pan to hot. Brush the tomatoes and courgette with oil and griddle over high heat until tender, but try to keep the tomatoes holding their shape.
- Thickly slice the chicken and serve on a plate interleaved with lime slices. Layer the courgette and tomato slices into a tower and serve.

588

SERVES 4

Chicken with Raisin Couscous

- Heat the oil in a pan and cook the chicken with the garlic until golden and cooked through. Season and set aside.
- Place the couscous in a bowl, add the raisins, cover with the hot stock and cling film the bowl. Leave for 10 minutes or so until tender, then fork through the grains and add the lemon, parsley and pine nuts.
- Serve the couscous on a large serving platter topped with the cooked chicken.

PREPARATION TIME:
10 MINUTES

COOKING TIME:
10–15 MINUTES

INGREDIENTS

4 chicken thighs, skinned, deboned and
    cut into chunks
2 tbsp olive oil
1 clove of garlic, crushed
salt and pepper
250 g / 9 oz / 1 cup couscous
250 ml / 9 fl. oz / 1 cup chicken or
    vegetable stock
60 g / 2 oz raisins
squeeze of lemon juice
1 bunch parsley, roughly chopped
2 tbsp pine nuts (kernels), toasted

Chicken with Mushroom Couscous

589

- Replace the raisins with mushrooms.

590

SERVES 2

Grilled Chicken with Bananas and Lime Rice

- Tip the rice into a pan with the lime zest and cover with water. Cook with the lid on for 12–14 minutes until cooked and tender, then drain thoroughly. Return to the pan, toss with lime juice, almonds and salt.
- Brush the chicken breasts with honey, oil and seasoning and griddle over high heat skin side down until golden and stripy. Turn over, reduce the heat and cook for another 6–8 minutes until cooked through.
- Griddle the bananas in their skins until blackened and the insides softened. Carefully peel and slice.
- Serve the chicken with the rice and top with the bananas.

PREPARATION TIME:
5 MINUTES

COOKING TIME:
15 MINUTES

INGREDIENTS

120 g / 4 oz / ½ cup basmati rice
juice and zest of 1 lime
60 g / 2 oz flaked (slivered) almonds,
    toasted
2 chicken breasts, skin on
1 tbsp honey
2 tbsp olive oil
salt and pepper
2 bananas, in their peel

Chicken with Grilled Courgette

591

- Try substituting the bananas for courgettes and cook in the same way.

592

SERVES 2

Chicken, Feta and Beetroot Salad

PREPARATION TIME:
10 MINUTES

COOKING TIME:
20 MINUTES

....

INGREDIENTS

2 chicken breasts, skin on
salt and pepper
2 tbsp olive oil
1 tbsp rosemary leaves, finely chopped
2 whole beetroot, ready cooked
    and peeled (not in vinegar)
150 g / 5 oz / ⅔ cup feta cheese,
    crumbled
1 tbsp balsamic vinegar
3 tbsp extra virgin olive oil
½ orange, zested
mixed salad leaves

- Preheat the oven to 200°C (180°C fan) / 400F / gas 6.
- Season the chicken and rub in the rosemary leaves, drizzle with oil and roast in the oven for 20 minutes until cooked. Set aside to rest for 10 minutes.
- Meanwhile, slice the beetroot into wedges and place in a bowl with the salad leaves.
- Whisk together the balsamic, oil, orange zest and seasoning and toss the salad lightly in the dressing.
- Slice the chicken, sit on top of the salad and crumble over the feta cheese.

Chicken Salad with Mustard Dressing

593

- A sharper mustard dressing would also go well: whisk 1 tbsp Dijon with 1 tbsp red wine vinegar, olive oil and seasoning.

594

SERVES 4

Japanese Fried Chicken

PREPARATION TIME:
10 MINUTES

COOKING TIME:
15–20 MINUTES

....

INGREDIENTS

4 chicken breasts, skinned
3 tbsp soy sauce
1 tbsp teriyaki sauce
100 g / 3 ½ oz / ½ cup plain
    (all-purpose) flour
2 eggs, beaten
200 g / 7 oz / ¾ cup panko crumbs
vegetable oil

- Place the chicken in a bowl with the soy and teriyaki. Refrigerate for at least 2 hours or even overnight.
- Dip the chicken breasts one at a time into the flour, egg then panko crumbs and lay on a rack to dry slightly.
- Heat 1 cm (½ in) depth oil in a pan and fry the chicken in batches until golden on both sides and cooked through.
- Serve hot or cold.

Fried Chicken with Dipping Sauce

595

- Try mixing a little rice wine (mirin) with teriyaki and soy sauce and a little chilli.

596

SERVES 4

Chicken Roasted with Thyme and Lemon

Chicken with Thyme and Lime

597

- Replace the lemon with a lime.

Thyme Chicken with Basil Mash

598

- Stir chopped basil into very creamy mashed potato to serve alongside.

PREPARATION TIME:
5 MINUTES

COOKING TIME:
30–35 MINUTES

INGREDIENTS

4 chicken legs, skin on
2–3 tbsp olive oil
1 tbsp butter
1 lemon
½ bunch thyme
salt and pepper
100 ml / 3 ½ fl. oz / ½ cup white wine

- Preheat the oven to 200°C (180°C fan) / 400F / gas 6.
- Place the chicken legs in a snug–fitting roasting tin. Smear over the oil and butter and season generously. Halve the lemon, squeeze over the chicken and add the empty halves to the tin. Push the thyme around and under the chicken.
- Roast in the oven for about 30–35 minutes until golden and cooked through.
- Transfer the chicken to a plate to rest, loosely covered with foil. Place the tin on the hob, deglaze with the white wine and simmer the juices for a couple of minutes to reduce and intensify. Season.
- Serve the legs with the roasting juices spooned over.

599

SERVES 4

Coq au Vin

PREPARATION TIME:
20 MINUTES

COOKING TIME:
1 HOUR

INGREDIENTS

50 g / 1 ¾ oz / ¼ cup butter
6 rashers smoked streaky bacon or
    pancetta, diced
2 red onions, peeled and finely sliced
1 carrot, sliced
3 cloves of garlic, finely sliced
2 sprigs thyme
1 chicken, jointed
2 tbsp seasoned flour
300 g / 10 oz / 1 ¼ cups chestnut
    mushrooms, quartered
500 ml / 1 pint / 2 cups red wine
200 ml / 7 fl. oz / ¾ cup chicken stock
salt and pepper
2 tbsp parsley, chopped

- Heat the butter in a casserole and fry the bacon until starting to colour.
- Add the onion, carrot and garlic and cook until lightly gold. Add the thyme. Using a slotted spoon, remove the bacon and onions from the pan to a bowl.
- Add a little oil. Lightly dust the chicken joints with flour, shake off any excess and brown on all sides in the pan.
- Add the mushrooms and cook until golden, then return the bacon and onions to the pan.
- Pour over the wine and stock, bubble up and cook gently for about 30 minutes until the chicken is cooked through.
- Add the parsley and season. Serve hot.

Coq au Vin Blanc

600

- You can make this stew in exactly the same way with white wine for a lighter dish.

601

SERVES 4

Chicken and Mimolette Cheese Crumble

PREPARATION TIME:
20 MINUTES

COOKING TIME:
10–20 MINUTES

INGREDIENTS

4 chicken breasts, skinned and cubed
500 ml / 1 pint / 2 cups chicken stock
40 g / 1 oz butter
1 onion, peeled and chopped
200 g / 7 oz / ¾ cup chestnut
    mushrooms, chopped (optional)
200 g / 7 oz / ¾ cup Boursin cheese
salt and pepper
120 g / 4 oz / ½ cup plain
    (all-purpose) flour
100 g / 3 ½ oz / ½ cup butter,
    cold and cubed
50 g / 1 ¾ oz / ¼ cup Mimolette cheese,
    grated

- Poach the chicken in the stock for 5 minutes until just cooked through. Drain, reserving the stock.
- Heat the butter in a pan and sauté the onion and mushrooms until golden, then add the chicken. Add the boursin and enough poaching liquor to loosen a little, then season and set aside.
- Meanwhile rub the butter and flour together with your fingertips to resemble breadcrumbs, then season well.
- Spoon the chicken mixture into a gratin dish, then top lightly with the crumble. Sprinkle over the cheese. Grill or bake until bubbling and the topping is golden and crunchy.

Chicken and Ham Crumble

602

- Add chopped ham to the chicken mixture or add a layer of sliced tomatoes under the crumble to ring the changes.

603

SERVES 4

Mexican-style Chicken and Pork Stew

- Heat the oil in a pan and fry the pork, then the chicken in batches until golden. Remove from the pan with a slotted spoon before proceeding with the next batch.
- Add the onion, sweetcorn and chilli and fry for 5 minutes, then return the meat and any juices to the pan, pour over the stock and simmer for 5 minutes.
- Season, stir through the banana and serve hot.

PREPARATION TIME:
10 MINUTES

COOKING TIME:
25 MINUTES

INGREDIENTS

2 tbsp olive oil
200 g / 7 oz pork fillet, cubed
2 chicken breasts, skinned and cubed
1 red onion, peeled and sliced
100 g / 3 ½ oz / ½ cup canned sweetcorn, drained
1 red chilli (chili), finely chopped
200 ml / 7 fl. oz / ¾ cup chicken stock
salt and pepper
1 banana, peeled and sliced

Chicken and Pork Stew with Beans

604

- Simply steamed green beans would make a fresh accompaniment.

605

SERVES 2

Chicken Escalope with Caperberries

- Preheat the oven to 180°C (160°C fan) / 350F / gas 4.
- Cut the carrot into short batons, then turn and shape into lozenge shapes. Cut the salsify into short batons. Simmer in boiling water until just tender – the salsify may take longer.
- Dip the escalopes into the flour, then the egg then the breadcrumbs thoroughly coating both sides. Roast in the oven for 15–20 minutes, turning once.
- Meanwhile, heat the butter in a small pan and fry the shallot until golden. Deglaze with the wine and reduce until syrupy, then add the stock and rosemary and simmer until reduced. Season.
- Heat the second amount of butter in a pan and toss the carrot to coat and cook gently until lightly golden.
- Serve the chicken with the carrots and salsify arranged around, spoon over the sauce and dot with caperberries.

PREPARATION TIME:
20 MINUTES

COOKING TIME:
30–40 MINUTES

INGREDIENTS

1 carrot, peeled
1 salsify, peeled and held in acidulated water
2 chicken escalopes
2 tbsp flour, seasoned
1 egg, beaten
100 g / 3 ½ oz / ½ cup breadcrumbs
40 g / 1 oz butter
2 tbsp caperberries, drained

FOR THE SAUCE

30 g / 1 oz butter
1 shallot, finely chopped
100 ml / 3 ½ fl. oz / ½ cup white wine
200 ml / 7 fl. oz / ¾ cup chicken or veal stock
1 sprig rosemary

Stuffed Chicken Escalope

606

- Slit a small pocket in the chicken and add a knob of butter and some chopped parsley. Proceed as above.

607

SERVES 4

Chicken Escalope with Exotic Kebabs

Grilled Exotic Kebabs **608**

- Place the kebabs on the griddle at the same time as the chicken and turn frequently.

Stuffed Cherry **609**
Tomatoes and Chicken Escalope

- Hollow out the tomatoes and stuff a little cheese inside before cooking.

PREPARATION TIME:
5 MINUTES

COOKING TIME:
6–10 MINUTES

INGREDIENTS

4 chicken breasts, skinned
salt and pepper
2 tbsp olive oil
½ lemon, juiced
16 cherry tomatoes
3–4 star fruit, sliced

- Place the chicken breasts one at a time between 2 pieces of cling film and bash with a rolling pin until about 1 cm (½ in) thick. Transfer to a plate, rub with oil and season.
- Heat a griddle pan until very hot and cook the escalopes 2 at a time until stripy and golden, then turn and cook the other side – about 2–3 minutes per side. Transfer to a plate and keep warm.
- Meanwhile thread cherry tomatoes and sliced star fruit onto wooden skewers.
- Squeeze a little lemon juice over the chicken and serve with the skewers.

Parsley-stuffed Chicken with Chips

610

SERVES 2

- Preheat the oven to 190°C (170°C fan) / 375F / gas 5.
- Place the chicken between 2 pieces of cling film and bash out with a rolling pin to about 1.5 cm (1 in) thick.
- Pulse the parsley, pine nuts garlic and oil in a processor until combined but not mushy. Divide equally between the chicken breasts, spooning the filling down the centre. Roll the chicken into a sausage shape and tie with string to secure. Place in a roasting tin, season and roast for about 15 minutes until cooked.
- To make the fries, soak well in cold water to remove the starch, then dry thoroughly.
- Bring a pan a third full of oil to 140°C / 275F and plunge in the fries, and cook for 10 minutes until pale. Remove, drain on kitchen paper.
- Heat the oil to 180°C / 350F and plunge the fries back in until golden and crisp. Remove to kitchen paper, season well and serve with the sliced stuffed chicken.

PREPARATION TIME:
20 MINUTES

COOKING TIME:
20 MINUTES

INGREDIENTS

2 chicken breasts, skinned
1 bunch parsley, chopped
4 tbsp pine nuts, lightly toasted
1 clove of garlic, crushed
2–3 tbsp extra virgin olive oil
4 large baking potatoes, peeled
   and cut into 1cm thick batons
vegetable oil
salt

Pesto Stuffed Chicken

611

- Replace the stuffing with Pesto.

All-in-one Roast Chicken

612

SERVES 4–6

- Preheat the oven to 200°C (180°C fan) / 400F / gas 6.
- Place the chicken in a roasting tin. Using the handle of a teaspoon, gently loosen the skin from the meat, using the spoon to create pockets.
- Mix the butter with the parsley, seasoning and lemon zest.
- Push the butter into the pockets under the skin, using your fingers to massage it out and cover the breast.
- Drizzle the skin with oil and season, then roast in the oven for 20 minutes.
- Reduce the heat to 180°C (160°C fan) / 350F / gas 4.
- Toss the cubes with the chicken juices in the bottom of the tray, drizzle with a little oil and roast for 1 hour or until the juices run clear when pierced with a toothpick. 5 minutes before the end of cooking, toss in the olives.
- Leave to rest for 10 minutes before carving.

PREPARATION TIME:
10 MINUTES

COOKING TIME:
1 HOUR 30 MINUTES

INGREDIENTS

1 oven-ready chicken
½ bunch parsley, finely chopped
150 g / 5 oz / ⅔ cup butter, softened
salt and pepper
½ lemon, zested
1 baguette, torn into small-ish pieces
olive oil
60 g / 2 oz green olives, stoned

Chicken with Roast Tomatoes

 613

- Halve a few tomatoes and roast alongside the chicken for extra flavour.

614

SERVES 4

Chicken Burgers with Pepper and Basil

PREPARATION TIME:
10 MINUTES

COOKING TIME:
8–10 MINUTES

INGREDIENTS

500 g / 1 lb / 2 cups minced chicken
1 bunch basil leaves, finely chopped
1 tsp Espelette pepper
salt
1 lemon, zested
1 egg, beaten

- Mix the chicken with the basil, pepper, salt and lemon zest until thoroughly mixed.
- Pour in enough beaten egg to bind, but don't let the mixture get too wet. With wet hands, form the mixture into 8 small or 4 large burgers.
- Chill in the refrigerator for 30 minutes.
- Cook in a little oil for 3–4 minutes per side, depending on thickness.

Cheesy Chicken Burgers with Peppers

615

- Add a handful of grated cheese to the burger mix.

616

SERVES 4

Grilled Mustard Chicken Legs

PREPARATION TIME:
5 MINUTES

COOKING TIME:
10–15 MINUTES

INGREDIENTS

4 chicken legs, skin on, boned out
2 tbsp olive oil
2 tbsp Dijon mustard
small handful thyme leaves
½ lemon, juiced
salt and pepper

- Mix together the oil, mustard, thyme and some seasoning and thoroughly coat the chicken legs in the mixture.
- Grill or griddle, turning regularly, until the chicken is golden and cooked through – 10–15 minutes.
- Squeeze over a little lemon and serve.

Grilled Honey Mustard Chicken

617

- Use any kind of mustard to ring the changes – honey is especially tasty.

618

SERVES 2

Chicken with Mushroom Sauce

Chicken with Dried Mushrooms

619

- Soak dried wild mushrooms in hot water for 15 minutes before hand and use a little of the water in the sauce to intensify the flavour.

Chicken with Cheese Polenta

620

- Serve with cooked polenta mixed with 200 g / 7 oz grated Cheddar cheese.

PREPARATION TIME:
10 MINUTES

COOKING TIME:
40 MINUTES

INGREDIENTS

40 g / 1 oz butter
2 chicken breasts
1 shallot, finely chopped
2 cloves of garlic, finely sliced
100 g / 3 ½ oz / ½ cup button or chestnut mushrooms, sliced
100 g / 3 ½ oz / ½ cup wild mushrooms, cleaned
100 ml / 3 ½ fl. oz / ½ cup dry white wine
150 ml / 5 fl. oz / ⅔ cup double (heavy) cream
salt and pepper
120 g / 4 oz / ½ cup wild rice, to serve

- Cook the wild rice according to packet instructions, drain and keep warm.
- Heat the butter in a pan and cook the chicken skin side down until golden. Turn over and cook on the other side for 5–6 minutes until cooked through. Remove from the pan with a slotted spoon and keep warm.
- If the butter has burnt, wipe out the pan and replace with more. Sweat the shallot and garlic without colouring. Add the mushrooms and season, then sauté until any excess liquid has evaporated, then deglaze the pan with the white wine. Reduce until syrupy then add the cream and bubble up.
- Serve the chicken sliced with sauce spooned over and wild rice to accompany.

621 · SERVES 6

Chicken and Courgette Quiche

PREPARATION TIME: 50 MINUTES

COOKING TIME: 1 HOUR

INGREDIENTS

2 chicken breasts, skinned and diced
30 g / 1 oz butter
1 courgette (zucchini), finely diced
½ bunch tarragon, finely chopped
100 g / 3 ½ oz / ½ cup Gruyère cheese, grated
2 eggs + 1 egg yolk
300ml / 10 fl. oz / 1 ¼ cups double (heavy) cream
salt and pepper

FOR THE QUICHE PASTRY

110 g / 3 ½ oz / ½ cup plain (all-purpose) flour
50 g / 1 ¾ oz / ¼ cup cold, diced butter
pinch salt
cold water, to mix

- Preheat the oven to 200°C (180°C fan) / 400F / gas 6.
- Rub the butter into the flour with the salt until you have coarse breadcrumbs. Add water a little at a time and mix until the mixture just comes together. Form into a ball, cover with cling film and refrigerate for 20–30 minutes.
- Fry the chicken and courgettes in the butter until golden. Set aside to cool.
- Roll out the pastry and press it gently into a lightly greased flan tin. Prick all over with a fork and bake in the oven on the baking sheet for 20 minutes until pale gold.
- Spoon the chicken and courgettes evenly over the pastry base. Whisk together the eggs, cream, cheese and tarragon and season, then pour in, adding a little pepper but careful on the salt.
- Bake in the oven for 25–30 minutes until just set. Leave to cool before serving.

Chicken and Ham Quiche — 622

- Chopped ham adds depth of flavour.

623 · SERVES 4

Chicken Basquaise

PREPARATION TIME: 10 MINUTES

COOKING TIME: 30 MINUTES

INGREDIENTS

2 tbsp olive oil
4 chicken thighs
1 onion, chopped
2 cloves of garlic, chopped
1 red pepper, deseeded and sliced
1 green pepper, deseeded and sliced
1 yellow pepper, deseeded and sliced
6 ripe vine tomatoes, cored and chopped
2 bay leaves
1 tsp sugar
2 tsp smoked paprika
salt and pepper

- Heat the oil in a pan and brown the drumsticks until golden. Remove to a plate and set aside.
- Add the onion and garlic and cook gently until golden, then add the chicken back to the pan and add the peppers and tomatoes, bay leaves, sugar, paprika and seasoning and allow to simmer for about 10–15 minutes until all is combined. Adjust the seasoning.
- Serve hot with rice or crusty bread.

Chicken and Chorizo Basquaise — 624

- Add 100 g / 3 ½ oz chopped chorizo with the vegetables for a real punch of smoky flavour.

625

SERVES 4–6 # Creamy Chicken Lasagne

- Heat the butter in a pan and add the vegetables and chicken and cook gently for 10 minutes. Season.
- Add the wine and stir for about 5 minutes until it has evaporated. Add the herbs and set aside.
- Meanwhile make the béchamel sauce: heat the butter in a pan until foaming, then stir in the flour to make a paste. Whisk in the milk a little at a time.
- Add the bay leaf and simmer for 10 minutes, whisking frequently. Season and add a little freshly grated nutmeg. Stir the chicken mixture into the bechamel.
- Preheat the oven to 190°C (170°C fan) / 375F / gas 5.
- Spread a third of the sauce in the bottom of a baking dish, then 4 sheets of lasagne. Repeat twice more, then cover the top layer of lasagne with béchamel and sprinkle over the parmesan.
- Bake in the oven for about 40 minutes until the pasta is tender.

Chicken and Tomato Lasagne   626

- Add 6 chopped tomatoes to the mix for fresh flavour.

PREPARATION TIME:
30 MINUTES

COOKING TIME: 40 MINUTES

....

INGREDIENTS

40 g / 1 oz butter
1 onion, peeled and finely chopped
1 carrot, peeled and diced
1 celery stick, finely chopped
250 g / 9 oz / 1 cup mushrooms, chopped
500 g / 1 lb / 2 cups chicken
    meat, diced
200 ml / 7 fl. oz / ¾ cup dry
    white wine
1 bunch tarragon or parsley, chopped
salt and pepper
12 fresh lasagne sheets
2 tbsp Parmesan, grated

FOR THE BÉCHAMEL SAUCE

2 tbsp butter
2 tbsp plain (all-purpose) flour
700 ml / 1 ¼ pints / 2 ¾ cups milk
1 bay leaf
nutmeg

627

SERVES 4 # Chicken, Lemon and Olive Fricassee

- Heat the olive oil in a casserole and brown the chicken thighs until golden all over.
- Add the onions and carrots to the pan and cook for 10 minutes until softened. Add the bay, lemons and stock, cover with a lid and cook for 30 minutes or until the chicken is cooked through and the carrots are tender.
- Stir through the olives, season carefully and serve.

PREPARATION TIME:
10 MINUTES

COOKING TIME:
45 MINUTES

....

INGREDIENTS

2 tbsp olive oil
4 chicken thighs, skin on
1 onion, peeled and chopped
8 baby carrots, scrubbed
2 bay leaves
2 preserved lemons, chopped
300 ml / 10 fl. oz / 1 ½ cups chicken
    stock
60 g / 2 oz green olives
salt and pepper

Chicken Fricassee
with Green Beans   628

- Add 100 g / 3 ½ oz / ½ cup green beans to the stock for added colour.

629

SERVES 4

Chicken Canneberg

Creamy Chicken Canneberg

630

- A couple of tbsp double (heavy) cream will add richness.

Chicken with Port and Red Wine Sauce

631

- Substitute 50 ml / 1 ¾ fl. oz of port and 150 ml / 5 fl. oz red wine for a richer sauce.

PREPARATION TIME:
10 MINUTES

COOKING TIME:
45 MINUTES

INGREDIENTS

2 tbsp olive oil
4 chicken legs, skin on
1 onion, peeled and finely chopped
1 stick celery, finely sliced
100 g / 3 ½ oz / ½ cup chestnut
    mushrooms, sliced
200 ml / 7 fl. oz / ¾ cup red wine
300 ml / 10 fl. oz / 1 ¼ cups chicken
    stock
¼ bunch thyme
2 tbsp dried cranberries
salt and pepper
mashed potato, to serve

- Heat the oil in a pan and brown the chicken legs on both sides, then remove and set aside.
- Add the onion and celery and cook until softened, then add the mushrooms.
- Deglaze with the red wine and reduce by half, then add the chicken stock. Add the thyme and chicken back to the pan and simmer for 30 minutes until the chicken is cooked through.
- Stir in the dried cranberries to the sauce and adjust the seasoning. Serve hot with creamy mashed potato.

632

SERVES 4

Sticky Chicken and French Fries

- Mix together the oil, paprika, honey, soy and ginger and coat the chicken thoroughly. Marinate for at least 1 hour.
- Preheat the oven to 190°C (170°C fan) / 375F / gas 5.
- Tip the drumsticks into a foil–lined roasting tin and roast for 30–40 minutes, turning once, until sticky. Remove and keep warm.
- To make the fries, soak the potato batons well in cold water to remove the starch then dry thoroughly.
- Bring a pan a third full of oil to 140°C / 275F.
- Plunge in the fries, in batches if necessary and cook for 10 minutes until pale but starting to look 'cooked'. Remove, then drain on kitchen paper.
- Heat the oil to 180°C / 350F and plunge the fries back in until golden and crisp. Remove to kitchen paper, season well and serve with the chicken.

PREPARATION TIME:
10 MINUTES + MARINATING TIME

COOKING TIME:
30–40 MINUTES

INGREDIENTS

8 drumsticks
1 tbsp vegetable oil
1 tsp paprika
2 tbsp runny honey
2 tbsp soy sauce
1 tsp ground ginger
salt and pepper
4 large baking potatoes, peeled and cut into 1 cm (½ in) thick batons
vegetable oil

Treacle Chicken

633

- Try using black treacle instead of honey for a really dark sticky grown-up glaze.

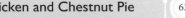
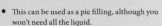

634

SERVES 4

Chicken and Chestnut Blancquette

- Place the chicken in a pan with the aromatics and cover with weak chicken stock. Poach the chicken very gently for about 20 minutes until cooked, then remove and reserve meat and stock.
- Melt the butter in a pan and cook the shallot and mushrooms until tender. Stir in the flour to make a paste, cook out for 2 minutes, then whisk in the measured amount of reserved chicken stock. Simmer gently for 20 minutes.
- Shred the chicken and add to the soup with the chestnuts. Season and serve hot.

PREPARATION TIME:
15 MINUTES

COOKING TIME:
45 MINUTES

INGREDIENTS

2 chicken breasts, skinned
1 carrot, chopped
1 celery stick, chopped
1 bay leaf
6 black peppercorns
40 g / 1 oz butter
1 shallot, finely chopped
200 g / 7 oz / ¾ cup chestnut mushrooms, chopped
40 g / 1 oz flour
500 ml / 1 pint / 2 cups reserved chicken stock
150 g / 5 oz / 2/3 cup vacuum–packed chestnuts, chopped
salt and pepper

Chicken and Chestnut Pie

635

- This can be used as a pie filling, although you won't need all the liquid.

636

SERVES 2

Chicken Noodles

PREPARATION TIME:
10 MINUTES

COOKING TIME:
10 MINUTES

....

INGREDIENTS

2 tbsp vegetable oil
1 onion, peeled and (scallions)
  finely sliced
1 clove of garlic, finely sliced
1cm piece fresh ginger, finely sliced
1 red pepper, deseeded and
  finely sliced
1 green pepper, deseeded and
  finely sliced
2 chicken thighs, skinned, deboned and
  chopped
3–4 tbsp soy sauce
2 tbsp oyster sauce
100 ml / 3 ½ fl. oz / ½ cup chicken stock
2 nests noodles
1 tbsp sesame oil
1 tbsp Szechuan peppercorns, crushed
  (optional)

- Heat the oil in a wok until nearly smoking then stir fry the onion, ginger and garlic until golden.
- Add the vegetables and stir fry until just tender, then add the chicken and cook through.
- Meanwhile cook the noodles in boiling salted water according to packet instructions, then drain.
- Add the sauces to the pan and bubble up, then add the cooked noodles and sesame oil.
- Serve topped with the crushed peppercorns.

Quick Chicken Noodles   **637**

- This is already pretty speedy, but for a quicker version use grated carrot and courgette in place of the peppers and pre-cooked chicken.

638

SERVES 6

Roast Chicken with Stuffing and Apples

PREPARATION TIME:
20 MINUTES

COOKING TIME:
1 HOUR 30 MINUTES

....

INGREDIENTS

1 oven-ready chicken
2 tbsp oil
salt and pepper
6 eating apples, halved

FOR THE STUFFING

2 tbsp butter
250 g / 9 oz / 1 cup mushrooms, finely
  chopped
1 onion, finely chopped
1 clove of garlic, chopped
1 lemon, zested
½ bunch parsley
1 slice bread, soaked in milk
1 egg, beaten

- Preheat the oven to 190°C (170°C fan) / 375F / gas 5.
- Heat the butter in a pan and cook the mushrooms and onions until soft. Add the garlic and stir well.
- Transfer to a bowl and mix in the zest, parsley, crumble in the bread then mix in the egg. Use your hands to combine everything.
- Spoon the stuffing into the cavity of the chicken and place in a roasting tin. Place the apple halves around the outside. Season, drizzle with oil and roast in the oven for about 1 ½ hours until the juices run clear when pierced with a toothpick.
- Leave the chicken to rest for 10 minutes before carving.

Roast Chicken with Pears   **639**

- Replace the apples with pears.

640

SERVES 4

Chicken with Herby Tortilla

Tomato and Herb Tortilla

641

- Halved cherry tomatoes would add colour and freshness to the tortilla and make a good foil to the savoury chicken.

Chicken and Potato Tortilla

642

- Add diced steamed white or sweet potato to the mix before baking.

PREPARATION TIME:
15 MINUTES

COOKING TIME:
35 MINUTES

INGREDIENTS

6 eggs
1 tbsp crème fraiche
½ bunch coriander (cilantro) chopped
½ bunch parsley, chopped
olive oil
salt and pepper
4 chicken legs
2 tbsp olive oil
½ bunch tarragon, chopped
200 ml / 7 fl. oz / ⅔ cup dry
     white wine

- Preheat the oven to 190°C (170°C fan) / 375F / gas 5.
- Beat the eggs with the crème fraiche in a large bowl. Add the herbs and season then mix together carefully.
- Oil a large frying pan, then pour the mixture in and bake for about 35 minutes until puffed and golden. The egg should be cooked through.
- Meanwhile, roast the chicken legs in the oven alongside drizzled with oil and seasoned. They should take the same amount of time.
- Remove the legs to a plate to rest. Place the tin on the hob and deglaze with the white wine, scraping with a wooden spoon, and stir in the tarragon. Season.
- Cut the tortilla into squares and serve warm or cold alongside the chicken and tarragon jus.

643

SERVES 4

Chicken Legs with Tomatoes

PREPARATION TIME:
5 MINUTES

COOKING TIME:
20–25 MINUTES

....

INGREDIENTS

2 tbsp oil
4 chicken legs
1 tsp dried oregano
8 cherry tomatoes
2 green peppers, deseeded and sliced
2 cloves of garlic, finely sliced
salt and pepper

- Heat the oil in a pan and brown the chicken legs on all sides.
- Add the oregano, tomatoes, peppers and garlic and a glass of water and cook gently until the chicken is cooked through and the peppers are tender.
- Season and serve hot.

644

SERVES 3–4

Chicken Pizza

PREPARATION TIME:
45 MINUTES

COOKING TIME:
8–10 MINUTES

....

INGREDIENTS

FOR THE PIZZA DOUGH

400 g / 13 ½ oz / 1 ½ cups strong white bread flour
100 g / 3 ½ oz / ½ cup fine ground semolina flour
*If you can't find semolina flour, simply make up the whole amount with strong white bread flour
½ tbsp salt
1 x 7 g sachet dried yeast
½ tbsp caster (superfine) sugar
approx 350 ml / ½ pint / ⅓ cup lukewarm water

FOR THE TOPPING: PER PIZZA

6 tbsp passata
2 chicken breasts, cooked and sliced
½ ball mozzarella, sliced
handful fresh spinach leaves
extra virgin olive oil
black pepper

- Make the pizza: Pour the flour(s) and salt into a bowl and make a well in the centre. Add the yeast and sugar to the water, mix with a fork and leave for a few minutes. When frothing, pour into the well. Using a fork in a circular movement, slowly bring in the flour from around the insides and mix into the water.
- Bring in all the flour, working your way towards the outer edges, mixing well. When it starts to come together, use your hands and pat it into a ball.
- Knead the dough by pushing it away from you with the heel of your hand for around 10 minutes until the dough is smooth and elastic. Flour the dough, cover with cling film and leave to rest for 30 minutes.
- Roll the pizzas out about 30 minutes before you want to cook them. Preheat the oven to 240°C (220°C fan) / 475F / gas 9. Flour the surface, tear off a piece of dough and roll into a rough circle about 0.5 cm thick. Dust each one with a little flour and lay out on the surface.
- Spread the base of each pizza with the passata, then with chicken. Scatter over the garlic and spinach, then lay over the mozzarella.
- Place either directly on the bars of the oven or on a preheated baking sheet for 8–10 minutes until golden and crisp. Drizzle with extra virgin olive oil, grind over some pepper and serve hot.

645
SERVES 4

Chicken and Avocado Fajitas

- Coat the chicken in half the spices and leave to marinate for 30 minutes.
- Heat half the oil in a pan until nearly smoking, then cook the peppers until golden and tender. Remove from the pan, keep warm and set aside.
- Add the remaining oil and reheat, then add the meat and sprinkle over the remaining spices. Stir briskly for a 2–3 minutes until the chicken is just cooked through.
- Squeeze the lime juice over the avocado.
- Wipe out the pan and use to warm the tortillas through.
- Serve the chicken and avocado and peppers wrapped in tortillas with the sauces to accompany.

PREPARATION TIME:
35 MINUTES

COOKING TIME: 10–15 MINUTES

INGREDIENTS

2 chicken breasts, skinned and
    thinly sliced
2 tsp ground cumin
2 tsp ground coriander
pinch dried chilli (chili) flakes
salt and pepper
4 tbsp olive oil
1 red pepper, deseeded and sliced
1 avocado, peeled, stoned and sliced
1 lime, juiced
8 tortilla wraps
sour cream, tomato salsa

Creamy Chicken with Mushrooms

646
SERVES 4

PREPARATION TIME:
10 MINUTES

COOKING TIME:
40 MINUTES

INGREDIENTS

40 g / 1 oz butter
1 tbsp olive oil
4 chicken legs
1 shallot, finely chopped
1 clove of garlic, crushed
200 g / 7 oz / ¾ cup morel mushrooms,
    cleaned
4 sprigs tarragon
150 ml / 5 fl. oz / ⅔ cup dry
    white wine
½ head cauliflower, broken
    into florets
150 ml / 5 fl. oz / ⅔ cup
    crème fraiche
salt and pepper

- Heat the butter and oil in a large pan and brown the chicken legs on all sides, then remove.
- Sweat the shallot and garlic without colouring for a few minutes, then add the mushrooms, tarragon and cauliflower florets. Season and cook for 5–7 minutes until tender.
- Deglaze with the white wine, then add the chicken back to the pan, cover with a lid and leave to simmer gently for 20–25 minutes until the chicken is cooked.
- Stir through the crème fraiche, reheat gently, adjust the seasoning and serve.

Chicken and Vegetable Stir Fry

647
SERVES 4

PREPARATION TIME:
10 MINUTES

COOKING TIME:
10–12 MINUTES

INGREDIENTS

2 tbsp vegetable oil
350 g / 12 oz / 1 ½ cups chicken thigh
    meat, diced
1 onion, peeled and finely sliced
2 cloves of garlic, finely sliced
1 tsp fresh ginger, grated
1 green pepper, deseeded and finely
    sliced
100 g / 3 ½ oz / ¼ cup mangetout
½ bunch spring onions (scallions), sliced
200 g / 7 oz / ¾ cup baby sweetcorn
75–100 ml / 2 ½–3 ½ fl. oz / ⅓–½ cup
    soy sauce
2–3 tbsp oyster sauce
2–3 tbsp sweet chilli (chili) sauce
salt and pepper

- Heat the oil in a wok until nearly smoking, then add the chicken. Stir fry over a high heat until golden all over and the fat crisp. Remove from the pan with a slotted spoon.
- Add the onion, garlic and ginger and stir fry for 2 minutes. Add the vegetables and cook until crisp-tender. Add the meat back to the pan and stir in the sauces.
- Leave to bubble for a few minutes then check and adjust the seasoning if necessary.

648

SERVES 6

Guinea Fowl with Chanterelle Stuffing

**PREPARATION TIME:
20 MINUTES**

**COOKING TIME:
1 HOUR 30 MINUTES**

INGREDIENTS

1 guinea fowl
40 g / 1 oz butter
salt and pepper

FOR THE STUFFING

2 tbsp butter
200 g / 7 oz / ¾ cup chicken
    livers, trimmed
500 g / 1lb / 2 cups chanterelles
1 onion, finely chopped
1 clove of garlic, chopped
½ bunch thyme
1 slice bread, soaked in milk
1 egg, beaten

- Preheat the oven to 200°C (180°C fan) / 400F / gas 6.
- Melt the butter in a pan and cook the chicken livers briskly until brown on the outside. Add the onion, garlic and chanterelles and sauté until softened, then stir in the thyme leaves and season.
- Spoon into a bowl, crumble in the bread and stir in the egg until thoroughly combined.
- Stuff the cavity of the guinea fowl and place in a roasting tin. Roast for 20 minutes then turn the oven down to 180°C (160°C fan) / 350F / gas 4.
- Roast for a further 45 minutes then check to see if the juices run clear when pierced with a toothpick. If not return to the oven for 10 minutes.
- Rest for 15–20 minutes before carving.

Guinea Fowl with Bacon Stuffing

649

- Add chopped streaky bacon and prunes to the stuffing mixture for richness.

650

SERVES 4

Crunchy Asian Chicken Salad

**PREPARATION TIME:
25 MINUTES**

INGREDIENTS

2 chicken breasts, cooked
2 carrots, peeled and cut into
    fine batons
½ white cabbage, cored and
    finely shredded
2 courgettes (zucchini), cut into
    fine batons
½ bunch coriander (cilantro), chopped
4 tbsp cashew nuts or peanuts, chopped
2 tbsp fish sauce
½ red chilli (chili), finely chopped
1 lime, juiced
1 tbsp soy sauce
1 tsp sugar

- Shred the chicken and toss in a large serving bowl with the vegetables and coriander.
- Add the nuts and toss again.
- Whisk together the fish sauce, chilli, lime, soy, sugar and taste. Adjust the seasoning if necessary.
- Spoon over the salad and toss thoroughly to coat. Leave for 5 minutes to soak up the flavours, then serve.

Asian Seafood Salad

651

- Add prawns, squid and even crab, all of which eat well with the dressing.

652

SERVES 4–6

Pot Roast Chicken with Vegetables

- Preheat the oven to 200°C (180°C fan) / 400F / gas 6.
- Place the chicken in a casserole. Smear the butter over the skin, sprinkle with fennel seeds and seasoning. Roast in the oven for 20 minutes.
- Reduce the heat to 180°C (160°C fan) / 350F / gas 4.
- Add the vegetables to the pot with the wine, cover with a lid and return to the oven for 1 hour or until the chicken is cooked through. Remove the lid for 10 minutes to crisp the skin again if necessary.
- Serve in the pot at the table.

PREPARATION TIME:
10 MINUTES

COOKING TIME:
1 HOUR 30 MINUTES

INGREDIENTS

1 oven-ready chicken
40 g / 1 oz butter, softened
1 tbsp fennel seeds
salt and pepper
1 head of broccoli, separated
    into florets
200 g / 7 oz / ¾ cup green beans
250 g / 9 oz / 1 cup mushrooms, sliced
1 red pepper, deseeded and
    finely sliced
200 ml / 7 fl. oz / ¾ cup white wine

Pot Roast Chicken with Apples and Potatoes

653

- Try using halved waxy potatoes, wedges of apple and cider in place of the wine.

654

SERVES 4–6

Chicken, Almond and Honey Tart

- Preheat the oven to 200°C (180°C fan) / 400F / gas 6.
- Roll the pastry out on a floured surface and use to line a pie dish, pushing into the corners. Prick the base all over with a fork and bake in the oven for 10 minutes until pale gold. Leave to cool.
- Meanwhile heat the oil in a pan and gently cook the onion until golden and sweet. Add the chicken and spices, increase the heat slightly and cook until the chicken is golden.
- Add the almonds and honey and stir well to combine. Tip into the pie dish, cover with the remaining puff pastry sheet, crimping well around the edges to seal. Brush with beaten egg and bake in the oven for 25–30 minutes until dark gold.
- Serve hot or cold.

PREPARATION TIME:
10 MINUTES

COOKING TIME:
40–45 MINUTES

INGREDIENTS

2 x 375 g / 13 oz sheets ready-rolled
    puff pastry
2 tbsp olive oil
1 onion, peeled and sliced
4 chicken thighs, skinned,
    deboned and diced
1 tsp ground cumin
1 tsp ground coriander
150 g / 5 oz / ⅔ cup almonds, skinned
2 tbsp runny honey
1 egg, beaten

Chicken and Chickpea Pie

655

- Adding a 400 g / 14 oz can of drained chickpeas would stretch this pie even further.

656

SERVES 6

Mediterranean Chicken Tart

Mozzarella Chicken and Vegetable Tart

657

- Once the tart has nearly cooked, add slices of mozzarella to ooze slowly across the top.

Chicken and Parma Ham Tart

658

- Layer very thin slices of Parma ham on top before baking to crisp in the oven.

PREPARATION TIME:
10 MINUTES

COOKING TIME:
35–40 MINUTES

INGREDIENTS

1 x 375 g / 13 oz pack ready-rolled shortcrust pastry
1 egg, beaten

FOR THE FILLING
olive oil
1 onion, peeled and finely chopped
2 cloves of garlic, finely sliced
1 aubergine (eggplant), cut into thin rounds
2 courgettes (zucchini), cut into thin rounds
1 jar roasted red peppers
2 chicken thighs, skinned, deboned and chopped
salt and pepper

- Preheat the oven to 180°C (160°C fan) / 350F / gas 4.
- Roll out the pastry and use to line a pie dish. Blind bake in the oven for 10 minutes until pale gold. Remove and leave to cool.
- Heat the oil in a pan and cook the onion and garlic until slightly golden. Remove from the pan to a bowl with a slotted spoon.
- Add the aubergine and a little more oil and cook until tender, taking care to try to keep the sliced intact. Remove to kitchen paper. Repeat with the courgette and chicken.
- Layer the vegetables with the peppers in the base of the pie dish, alternating the layers so they will look attractive when cut.
- Bake in the oven for about 20 minutes until the pastry is golden. Serve warm.

659

SERVES 4

Chicken, Potato and Mushroom Pie

- Sieve flour and salt into a bowl, work in butter until the mix resembles breadcrumbs. Work in 2 tbsp water, bring mixture together to make a ball of dough. Wrap in cling film, refrigerate for 30 minutes.
- Preheat the oven to 200°C (180°C fan) / 400F / gas 6.
- Heat the butter in a pan and fry the chicken pieces until golden in patches. Remove with a slotted spoon.
- Sweat the shallot and mushrooms with the parsley. Return the chicken to pan, season and add potatoes.
- Divide the pastry in half. Roll the pastry out on a floured surface to slightly larger than the pie dish and sit it in the base. Blind bake for 15 minutes.
- Tip chicken mixture into the pastry base. Roll the remaining pastry to slightly larger than the pie dish and sit on top of the filling.
- Brush with beaten egg, make a hole in the pastry to let the steam escape, bake in oven for 30 minutes.

PREPARATION TIME:
50 MINUTES

COOKING TIME:
30 MINUTES

INGREDIENTS

2 tbsp butter
3–4 chicken thighs, deboned and
    skinned, cut into chunks
1 shallot, finely chopped
200 g / 7 oz / ¾ cup chestnut
    mushrooms, sliced
3 large floury potatoes, peeled
    and diced, parboiled
100 g / 3 ½ oz / ½ cup frozen peas
¼ bunch parsley, chopped
salt and pepper
1 egg, beaten

FOR THE PASTRY

120 g / 4 oz / ½ cup plain
    (all-purpose) flour
60 g / 2 oz / ¼ cup butter
pinch salt
cold water

Chicken, Swede and Mushroom Pie

660

- The earthy sweet flavour of swede makes a good alternative to potato.

661

SERVES 2

Grilled Chicken and Tofu Skewers

- Marinate the chicken, tofu and vegetables with the rest of the ingredients for 30 minutes.
- Thread alternately onto soaked wooden skewers and griddle over high heat until stripy and cooked through – about 8 minutes.
- Serve with a squeeze of lemon juice.

PREPARATION TIME:
5 MINUTES

COOKING TIME:
8–10 MINUTES

INGREDIENTS

2 chicken breasts, skinned and cubed
200 g / 7 oz / ¾ cup firm tofu, cut into
    squares
1 courgette (zucchini), chopped
1 red pepper, deseeded and roughly
    chopped
1 green pepper, deseeded and roughly
    chopped
½ lemon, juiced and zested
1 tbsp olive oil
salt and pepper

Grilled Chicken and Halloumi Skewers

662

- Substitute the tofu for a pack of halloumi, cubed and cooked just the same.

663

SERVES 4

Chicken and Mango Fajitas

PREPARATION TIME:
35 MINUTES

COOKING TIME:
10–15 MINUTES

INGREDIENTS

4 chicken breasts, skinned and
    thinly sliced
2 tsp paprika
2 tsp ground cumin
2 tsp ground coriander
pinch dried chilli (chili) flakes
salt and pepper
4 tbsp olive oil
1 mango, peeled, stoned and sliced
1 lime, juiced
4 ripe tomatoes, cored and diced
2 tbsp extra virgin olive oil
hot sauce
3 spring onions (scallions),
    finely chopped
½ lime, juiced
8 tortilla wraps

- Coat the chicken in half the spices and leave to marinate for 30 minutes.
- Heat half the oil in a pan until nearly smoking, then cook the chicken until tender, then sprinkle over the rest of the spices.
- Stir briskly for a 2–3 minutes until either the chicken is just cooked through. Squeeze over the lime juice. Remove and keep warm.
- Toss the tomatoes in a bowl with oil, hot sauce to taste, spring onions, lime juice and seasoning.
- Wipe out the chicken pan and use to warm the tortillas through.
- Serve the chicken with the slices mango to fill the tortillas and tomato salsa alongside.

Fajitas with Avocado and Tomato Salsa

664

- Avocado is the perfect accompaniment – stir cubed avocado into the tomatoes for creamy contrast.

665

SERVES 4

Sweet and Sour Chicken Fajitas

PREPARATION TIME:
5 MINUTES

COOKING TIME:
15–20 MINUTES

INGREDIENTS

1 tbsp vegetable oil
4 chicken breasts, skinned and cubed
1 onion, peeled and sliced
125 ml / 4 fl. oz / ½ cup pineapple juice
splash dry sherry or Shaoxing
    rice wine
2 tbsp ketchup
2 tbsp soy sauce
2 tbsp Chinese vinegar or red
    wine vinegar
1 tsp cornflour (cornstarch)
1 mango or ½ pineapple, diced
8 tortillas
lettuce leaves

- Heat the oil in a pan or wok and stir fry the chicken and onion until golden.
- Add the sauce ingredients and bubble up until thickened. Stir in the mango or pineapple.
- Warm the tortillas briefly in a dry pan.
- Wrap the chicken mix in the tortillas with lettuce leaves.

Sweet and Sour Fajitas with Rice

666

- Serve alongside Mexican Fried Rice.

667

SERVES 6

Chicken Cannelloni

Light Chicken Cannelloni
668

- Use canned tomatoes in place of the cream.

Chicken Lasagne
669

- Use lasagne sheets and layer with the chicken mix in a gratin dish, sprinkle with cheese and bake.

PREPARATION TIME:
20 MINUTES

COOKING TIME:
20 MINUTES

....

INGREDIENTS

3 tbsp olive oil
2 shallots, finely chopped
1 onion, finely chopped
1 clove of garlic, finely chopped
500 g / 1 lb / 2 cups wild mushrooms
4 chicken thighs, skinned, deboned
    and diced
1 bunch parsley, chopped
300 ml / 10 fl. oz / 1 ¼ cups double
    (heavy) cream
12–18 cannelloni tubes
40 g /1 oz butter
3 tbsp Parmesan, grated
salt and pepper

- Preheat the oven to 200°C (180°C fan) / 400F / gas 6.
- Heat the oil in a pan and add the shallot and onion. Cook for a few minutes, stirring regularly.
- Add the mushrooms, chicken and garlic and cook until the liquid has evaporated. Season, then add the parsley and half the double cream. Reduce until the cream has thickened, then remove from the heat.
- Cook the cannelloni tubes in boiling salted water according to packet instructions. Drain thoroughly and pat dry.
- Stuff the cannellonis with the mixture – either use a piping bag or a teaspoon.
- Place in a buttered baking dish, pour over the cream and sprinkle with Parmesan and a few dots of butter.
- Cook in the oven for 20 minutes then serve.

670

SERVES 4

Grilled Chicken with Saffron Vegetable Rice

PREPARATION TIME:
10 MINUTES

COOKING TIME:
15–20 MINUTES

INGREDIENTS

2 tbsp olive oil
4 chicken breasts, sliced in half
salt and pepper
250 g / 9 oz / 1 cup basmati rice
2 cups water infused with pinch saffron
40 g / 1 oz butter
1 courgette (zucchini), diced
150 g /5 oz / ⅔ cup mushrooms, finely
    sliced
1 carrot, peeled and diced

- Tip the rice into a pan with the water and cook covered with a lid for 10 minutes. Remove from the heat and leave covered for 5 minutes.
- Griddle the chicken breasts on both sides until golden for about 3–4 minutes per side.
- Heat the butter in a pan and sauté the vegetables until tender. Season.
- Toss the vegetables with the saffron rice and adjust the seasoning.
- Spoon the rice onto plates and top with griddled chicken.

Oven-cooked Chicken and Rice

671

- For a one-pot dish, put everything in a casserole, pour over the saffron water and bake in a hot oven for 20 minutes until cooked and tender.

672

SERVES 4

Basque Chicken with Rice

PREPARATION TIME:
10 MINUTES

COOKING TIME:
30 MINUTES

INGREDIENTS

2 tbsp olive oil
4 rashers streaky bacon, chopped
1 onion, chopped
2 cloves of garlic, chopped
4 chicken breasts, skinned and chopped
1 red pepper, 'cheeks' cut off and
    chopped
1 yellow pepper, 'cheeks' cut off
    and chopped
400 g / 14 oz / 1 ½ cups canned tomatoes
1 tsp sugar
1 tsp smoked paprika
salt and pepper
1 bunch basil
cooked rice to serve

- Heat the oil in a pan and cook the bacon, onion and garlic until golden.
- Add the peppers and chicken and cook until golden in patches.
- Add the tomatoes, sugar, paprika and seasoning and allow to simmer for about 15–20 minutes until reduced to the desired consistency. Adjust the seasoning.
- Serve hot with the rice.

Basque Pie

673

- Top the sauce with puff pastry and bake in a hot oven for 20 minutes for a Basque-style chicken pie.

674

SERVES 4

Chicken and Leek Pie

- Sieve the flour and salt into a bowl, then work the butter into the flour with your fingers. Work in 2 tbsp water, bring mixture together to make a ball of dough. Wrap in cling film and refrigerate.
- Preheat the oven to 200°C (180°C fan) / 400F / gas 6.
- Heat the butter and fry the chicken until golden. Remove. Sweat the shallot and leeks with tarragon. Stir in flour to make a paste, whisk in milk a little at a time. Return chicken to pan, season, simmer for 10 minutes.
- Divide the pastry in half. Roll the pastry out on a floured surface to slightly larger than the pie dish and sit it in the base. Blind bake for 15 minutes.
- Tip the chicken mixture into the pastry base. Roll the remaining pastry out to slightly larger than the pie dish and sit on top of the filling. Brush with beaten egg, make a hole in pastry to let the steam escape, bake in the oven for 30 minutes.

Chicken Pie with Vegetables   675

- Try purple sprouting broccoli simply steamed or green beans tossed in butter and lemon to serve with.

PREPARATION TIME:
50 MINUTES

COOKING TIME:
30 MINUTES

INGREDIENTS

2 tbsp butter
3–4 chicken thighs, deboned
  and skinned, cut into chunks
1 shallot, finely chopped
2 leeks, trimmed and finely sliced
2 sprigs tarragon leaves
1 ½ tbsp plain (all-purpose) flour
300 ml / 10 fl. oz / 1 ¼ cups milk
salt and pepper
1 egg, beaten

FOR THE PASTRY
120 g / 4 oz / ½ cup plain
  (all-purpose) flour
60 g / 2 oz / ¼ cup butter
pinch salt
cold water

676

SERVES 4

Herby Chicken Pie

- Preheat the oven to 200°C (180°C fan) / 400F / gas 6.
- Heat the butter in a pan and fry the chicken pieces until golden in patches. Remove with a slotted spoon.
- Sweat the shallots with the herbs. Stir in the flour to make a paste, then whisk in the milk a little at a time. Return the chicken to the pan, add the peas and carrot, then season and leave to simmer for 10 minutes.
- Divide the pastry in half. Roll the pastry out on a floured surface to slightly larger than the pie dish and sit it in the base, pushing it into the corners. Prick the base and bake for 15 minutes, then leave to cool.
- Tip the chicken mixture into the pastry base. Roll the remaining pastry out to slightly larger than the pie dish and sit on top of the filling.
- Brush with beaten egg, make a hole in the pastry to let the steam escape and bake in the oven for about 25–30 minutes.

Herby Chicken and Leek Pie   677

- Add 3 sliced leeks to the other ingredients for allium sweetness.

PREPARATION TIME:
20 MINUTES

COOKING TIME:
30 MINUTES

INGREDIENTS

2 sheets (225 g / 8 oz) puff pastry, ready
  rolled
2 tbsp butter
6 chicken thighs, deboned and skinned,
  cut into chunks
2 shallots, finely chopped
100 g / 3 ½ oz / ½ cup frozen peas
1 carrot, diced
6 sprigs thyme
2 sprigs tarragon leaves
1 tsp Herbes de Provence
1 ½ tbsp plain (all-purpose) flour
250 ml / 9 fl. oz / 1 cup milk
salt and pepper
1 egg, beaten

678

SERVES 4

Pesto Chicken with Roast Tomatoes

Chicken with Slow–Roast Tomatoes

679

- Roast tomatoes at an even lower temperature overnight, then store under olive oil in sterilised jars in the refrigerator.

Chicken and Tomatoes Roasted with Anchovies

680

- If you like them, add finely chopped anchovies under the pesto mix to be absorbed into the tomatoes.

PREPARATION TIME:
10 MINUTES

COOKING TIME:
2 HOURS 20 MINUTES

INGREDIENTS

4 ripe tomatoes
2 tbsp olive oil
salt and pepper
4 chicken breasts
2 tbsp olive oil
cooked pasta, to serve

FOR THE PESTO

2 handfuls pine nuts
1 clove of garlic, peeled and chopped
2 bunches basil
80 g / 3 oz / ⅓ cup Parmesan, grated
extra virgin olive oil
salt and pepper

- Preheat the oven to 160°C (140°C fan) / 325F / gas 3.
- Place the tomatoes cut side up in a roasting tin, drizzle with oil, season and roast for 2 hours or even longer until shrivelled and deeply savoury. Set aside.
- Turn the oven up to 200°C (180°C fan) / 400F / gas 6.
- Rub the chicken with oil and seasoning and roast for 20 minutes until cooked through. Set aside to rest.
- Meanwhile add the pine nuts to a frying pan over medium heat and lightly toast for a few seconds until golden. Place in a food processor with the garlic, basil and Parmesan. Whiz the ingredients in a food processor until roughly blended, stirring in enough olive oil to loosen.
- Serve the chicken thickly sliced with the tomatoes all drizzled with pesto and pasta alongside.

681

SERVES 4–6

Chicken and Wild Mushroom Lasagne

- Heat the butter with a little oil in a pan and add the finely chopped vegetables, mushrooms and chicken and cook gently for about 10 minutes. Season.
- Add the wine and stir for about 5 minutes until it has evaporated. Add the herbs and ¾ of the passata and set aside.
- Preheat the oven to 190°C (170°C fan) / 375F / gas 5.
- Spread a third of the remaining passata in the base of a baking dish then top with 4 sheets of lasagne.
- Top the lasagne with the chicken tomato sauce, cover with more lasagne sheets and repeat. Then cover the top layer of lasagne with Parmesan.
- Bake in the oven for about 30–40 minutes until the pasta is tender. Leave to rest for 10 minutes before serving.

PREPARATION TIME:
30 MINUTES

COOKING TIME:
40 MINUTES

INGREDIENTS

40 g / 1 oz butter
1 onion, peeled and finely chopped
1 carrot, peeled and diced
1 celery stick, finely chopped
1 clove of garlic, finely sliced
350 g / 12 oz / 1 ½ cups wild mushrooms, cleaned and sliced
500 g / 1 lb / 2 cups chicken meat, diced
200 ml / 7 fl. oz / ¾ cup dry white wine
½ bunch parsley, chopped
salt and pepper
500 ml / 1 pint / 2 cups passata
12 fresh lasagne sheets
2 tbsp Parmesan, grated

Chicken and Mascarpone Lasagne

682

- 100 g / 3 ½ oz mascarpone cheese stirred into the tomato sauce will make a creamier version.

683

SERVES 4

Chicken Wraps

- Coat the chicken in half the spices and leave to marinate for 30 minutes.
- Heat half the oil in a pan until nearly smoking, then cook the onion and pepper and tomato until golden and tender. Remove from the pan, keep warm and set aside. Stir through the avocado, lime juice and chopped coriander.
- Add the remaining oil and reheat, then add the meat and sprinkle over the remaining spices.
- Stir briskly for a 2–3 minutes until the chicken is just cooked through. Squeeze over the lime juice. Remove and stir into the vegetable mixture.
- Wipe out the pan and use to warm the tortillas through.
- Spoon the chicken mixture into the centre of each tortilla, drizzle with mint yogurt, then wrap the tortillas around the mix and serve.

PREPARATION TIME:
35 MINUTES

COOKING TIME:
10–15 MINUTES

INGREDIENTS

2 chicken breasts, skinned and thinly sliced
2 tsp ground cumin
2 tsp ground coriander
salt and pepper
4 tbsp olive oil
1 onion, peeled and finely sliced
1 red pepper, deseeded and finely sliced
4 tomatoes, cored and finely diced
1 avocado, peeled, stoned and flesh diced
1 lime, juiced
¼ bunch coriander (cilantro)
8 tortilla wraps
mint yogurt, to serve

Chicken Enchiladas

684

- Enchiladas are very similar but baked in a gratin dish in a hot oven covered with a simple tomato sauce.

685
SERVES 2–3

Chicken Stir Fry with Pak Choi

PREPARATION TIME:
10 MINUTES

COOKING TIME:
15–20 MINUTES

INGREDIENTS

2 tbsp vegetable oil
350 g / 12 oz / 1 ½ cups chicken
   thigh meat, diced
1 onion, peeled and finely sliced
2 cloves of garlic, finely sliced
1 tsp fresh ginger, grated
100 g / 3 ½ oz / ½ cup mangetout
1 red pepper, deseeded and
   finely sliced
2 tbsp soy sauce
2 tbsp oyster sauce
2 heads pak choi, leaves separated
2 tbsp cashew nuts
1 tbsp sesame seeds

- Heat the oil in a wok and stir fry the chicken until golden.
  Remove with a slotted spoon and set aside.
- Add the onion, garlic and ginger and fry quickly until golden,
  then return the chicken to the pan with the mangetout and
  peppers. Cook for a few minutes until tender.
- Add the sauces and bubble up.
- Meanwhile briefly steam the pak choi for 2–3 minutes until the
  stems are tender. Add to the wok, toss in the cashews and sesame
  seeds and serve hot.

Chicken and Mushroom Stir Fry   686

- Add more meatiness with sliced mushrooms.

687
SERVES 6

Pot-roast Chicken with Apricots

PREPARATION TIME:
15 MINUTES

COOKING TIME:
40 MINUTES

INGREDIENTS

40 g / 1 oz butter
1 tbsp flour, seasoned
1 chicken, jointed and cut into large
   pieces
1 onion, peeled and sliced
2 cloves of garlic, whole and lightly
   flattened
60 g / 2 oz dried apricots
handful chives, chopped
200 ml / 7 fl. oz / ¾ cup white wine
salt and pepper

- Preheat the oven to 160°C (140°C fan) / 325F / gas 3.
- Heat the butter in a casserole. Dust the chicken pieces with
  seasoned flour and brown in batches in the butter over a medium
  heat then transfer to a plate.
- Add the onion and garlic and cook gently until golden, then add
  the chicken back to the pan. Add the wine, apricots, chives and
  seasoning, bubble up, cover with a lid and cook in the oven for
  40 minutes until the chicken is cooked through.
- Serve with cooked cauliflower and broccoli.

All-in-one Pot-roast   688

- Add halved waxy potatoes to the pot with
  the chicken for an all-in-one supper and less
  washing up.

SERVES 4–6 # Roast Chicken with Stuffing

Honey-glazed Roast Chicken

690

- Rub the chicken all over with honey for a sweeter taste.

Roast Chicken with Stuffing Balls

691

- Roll the stuffing ingredients into tiny balls and roast around the chicken for the last 20 minutes for a crisp finish.

PREPARATION TIME:
15 MINUTES

COOKING TIME:
1 HOUR 30 MINUTES

INGREDIENTS

1 oven ready chicken
500 g / 1 lb / 2 cups sausages,
   any flavour you like
75 g / 2 ½ oz / ⅓ cup breadcrumbs
1 apple, peeled and cored
2 tbsp herbs such as rosemary
   or thyme, chopped
3 cloves of garlic, crushed
salt and pepper
40 g / 1 oz butter, softened
zest of 1 orange
handful thyme sprigs

- Preheat oven to 220°C (200°C fan) / 425F / gas 7.
- Slit the sausage skins and squeeze the middles out into a bowl. Dice the apple and add with the breadcrumbs, herbs garlic and seasoning and use your hands to combine thoroughly.
- Smear the chicken with the butter, orange zest and thyme, then season generously. Stuff the cavity with the sausage stuffing, place in a roasting tin and roast for 20 minutes.
- After 20 minutes lower the heat to 180°C (160°C fan) / 350F / gas 4 and return to the oven for another hour or until the chicken is cooked through and the juices run clear when pierced with a toothpick.
- Leave to rest loosely covered with foil for 15–20 minutes before carving.

692

SERVES 6

Classic Roast Chicken

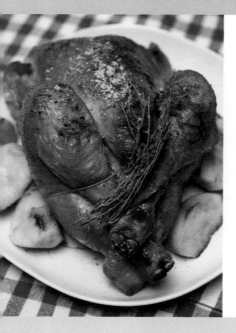

PREPARATION TIME:
20 MINUTES

COOKING TIME:
1 HOUR 30 MINUTES

INGREDIENTS

1 oven-ready chicken
1 kg / 2 lb / 4 ¼ cups floury
    potatoes, peeled
1 tbsp flour
4 tbsp goose fat, duck fat or olive oil

FOR THE STUFFING

2 tbsp butter
1 onion, finely chopped
1 clove of garlic, chopped
2 eating apples, diced
1 lemon, zested
½ bunch parsley
1 slice bread, soaked in milk
1 egg, beaten
salt and pepper

- Preheat the oven to 220°C (200°C fan) / 425F / gas 7.
- Heat the butter in a pan and cook the onions until soft. Add the garlic. Transfer to a bowl and mix in the zest, parsley, crumble in the bread then mix in the egg.
- Stuff the chicken and place in a roasting tin. Season, drizzle with oil and roast for 20 minutes then reduce the heat to 180°C (160°C fan) / 350F / gas 4 and cook for 1 hour.
- Meanwhile cut the potatoes and cook in boiling water for 8 minutes. Drain, return to the pan and dry briefly.
- Heat the fat in a roasting tin in the oven. Sprinkle the flour over the potatoes and toss to coat, then tip carefully into the hot fat and roast in the oven for 45 minutes–1 hour until dark gold and crisp.
- Once the chicken is cooked and is resting, turn the heat up on the oven and give the potatoes another 20 minutes.

693

Classic Roast Chicken and Vegetables

- If you're less fussy about crisp vegetables, make life easier by roasting the potatoes and perhaps carrots and parsnips around the chicken.

694

SERVES 4–6

Ultimate Roast Chicken

PREPARATION TIME:
10 MINUTES

COOKING TIME:
1 HOUR 30 MINUTES

INGREDIENTS

1 oven-ready roast chicken
2 tbsp goose or duck fat
salt and pepper
4 sprigs thyme or rosemary

- Preheat oven to 220°C (200°C fan) / 425F / gas 7.
- Smear the skin of the chicken with goose fat, season very generously and push the herbs into the cavity. Place in a roasting tin and roast for 20 minutes.
- After 20 minutes lower the heat to 180°C (160°C fan) / 350F / gas 4 and return to the oven for another hour or until the chicken is cooked through and the juices run clear when pierced with a toothpick.
- Leave to rest loosely covered with foil for 15–20 minutes before carving.

Ultimate Roast Chicken with Lemon

695

- Place a lemon inside the chicken before roasting for a citrus twist.

Crisp Chicken with Parsley Sauce

696

SERVES 4

- Place the chicken in a bowl with the buttermilk. Refrigerate for at least 2 hours or even overnight.
- When ready to cook, whizz the parsley in a blender with the garlic and olive oil. You may not need all of it to make a loose sauce so add it a little at a time.
- Dip the chicken breasts one at a time into the flour, egg then breadcrumbs and lay on a rack to dry slightly.
- Heat 1 cm (½ in) depth oil in a pan and fry the chicken in batches until golden on both sides and cooked through.
- Squeeze a little lemon into the parsley sauce, season and serve with the hot chicken.

PREPARATION TIME:
10 MINUTES

COOKING TIME:
15–20 MINUTES

INGREDIENTS

4 chicken breasts, skinned
300 ml / 10 fl. oz / 1 ¼ cups buttermilk
100 g / 3 ½ oz / ½ cup plain
   (all-purpose) flour
2 eggs, beaten
200 g / 7 oz / ¾ cup breadcrumbs,
vegetable oil
1 bunch parsley
1 clove of garlic, peeled
150 ml / 5 fl. oz / ⅔ cup extra
   virgin olive oil
½ lemon, juiced
salt and pepper

Stuffed Chicken Breasts

697

- Make the parsley sauce as above using just enough oil to bind, then use this to stuff the chicken breasts, before coating and frying.

Chestnut Stuffed Chicken and Timbale

698

SERVES 6

- Preheat the oven to 190°C (170°C fan) / 375F / gas 5.
- Heat the butter in a pan and cook the mushrooms and onions until soft. Add the garlic and chestnuts and stir well. Transfer to a bowl and mix in the parsley, crumble in the bread then mix in the egg. Use your hands to combine everything.
- Lay the chicken skin-side down on a work surface and spoon the stuffing into the centre. Truss with kitchen string and place in a roasting tin. Season and roast in the oven for about 1 ½ hours until the juices run clear when pierced with a toothpick. Leave the chicken to rest for 10 minutes.
- Meanwhile tip the mashed potatoes into a bowl and mix in the remaining ingredients until combined.
- Spoon into ring moulds and reheat gently in an oiled frying pan, using a spatula to turn – they will crisp slightly on the cooked sides, adding texture.

PREPARATION TIME:
20 MINUTES

COOKING TIME:
1 HOUR 30 MINUTES

INGREDIENTS

1 whole chicken, deboned
   (ask your butcher)

FOR THE STUFFING
2 tbsp olive oil
½ tsp caster (superfine) sugar
350 g / 12 oz / 1 ½ cup sliced
basil, to garnish

FOR THE TIMBALE
500 g / 1 lb / 2 cups floury
   potatoes, mashed
60 g / 2 oz butter, melted
400 g / 14 oz / 1 ½ cups canned puréed
   chestnuts
1 tbsp rosemary leaves,
   finely chopped
100 ml / 3 ½ fl. oz / ½ cup double
   (heavy) cream

Chestnut Apple Timbales

699

- Add 2 diced eating apples to the mix for a fruity taste.

SERVES 6

Stuffed Roast Chicken with Apples

Stuffed Roast Chicken with Pears

701

- Replace the apples with pears.

Chicken with Duchesse Potato Gratin

702

- The potato mix can be piped on top of any pie for a rich version of mashed potato.

PREPARATION TIME:
40 MINUTES

COOKING TIME:
I HOUR 30 MINUTES

INGREDIENTS

1 oven-ready chicken
1.5 kg / 3 lb / 6 cups potatoes, peeled and cut into chunks
150 ml / 5 fl. oz / ⅔ cup milk
100 g / 3 ½ oz / ½ cup butter
3 eggs, beaten
salt and pepper
150 g / 5 oz / ⅔ cup flaked (slivered) almonds

FOR THE STUFFING

2 tbsp butter
1 onion, finely chopped
1 clove of garlic, chopped
2 eating apples, diced
1 lemon, zested
½ bunch parsley
1 slice bread, soaked in milk
1 egg, beaten

- Preheat the oven to 220°C (200°C fan) / 425F / gas 7.
- Heat the butter in a pan and cook the onions until soft. Add the garlic and stir well. Transfer to a bowl and mix in the zest, parsley, crumble in the bread then mix in the egg. Use your hands to combine everything.
- Spoon the stuffing into the cavity of the chicken and place in a roasting tin. Season, drizzle with oil and roast in the oven for 20 minutes then reduce the heat to 180°C (160°C fan) / 350F / gas 4 and cook for 1 hour or until the juices run clear.
- Meanwhile cook the potatoes in boiling salted water until tender to the point of a knife. Drain thoroughly and return briefly to the heat to drive off any excess water. Mash the potatoes thoroughly with a potato ricer or hand–held masher.
- Heat the milk and butter until the butter has melted, then stir into the potatoes with 2 of the beaten eggs and season well.
- Spoon into a piping bag with a 1.25 cm (½ in) star nozzle and pipe into pyramid shapes onto a greased baking tray. Brush with the remaining egg and sprinkle on the almonds, patting them on to help them stick.
- When the chicken has cooked turn the oven back up to 220°C (200°C fan) / 425F / gas 7 and bake in the oven for 15 minutes or until golden.
- Carve the chicken and serve with the potatoes.

CLASSIC MAINS

703

SERVES 4–6 # Chicken Hashis

- Preheat the oven to 180°C (160°C fan) / 350F / gas 4.
- Heat the oil in a large pan and sweat the vegetables until soft. Add the chicken and cook for 3 minutes until white.
- Stir in the tomato purée and cook out for 2 minutes, before adding the herbs and pouring over the stock. Simmer until the stock has reduced and there is just a little liquid left in the bottom of the pan.
- Meanwhile cook the potatoes in boiling salted water until tender to the point of a knife. Drain thoroughly, then mash until completely smooth with the butter and season well.
- Spread a third of the potato into the bottom of a gratin dish, then spoon in the chicken mixture. Top with the remaining mashed potato. Run a fork down the length of the potato to create edges that will crisp in the oven.
- Bake for 30 minutes until bubbling and golden.

Cheesy Chicken Hashis   704
- Top with grated cheese before baking.

PREPARATION TIME:
25 MINUTES

COOKING TIME:
30 MINUTES

INGREDIENTS

2 tbsp vegetable oil
450 g / 1 lb / 2 cups chicken, chopped
1 onion, peeled and finely chopped
2 carrots, peeled and finely chopped
2 sticks celery, finely chopped
2 tbsp tomato purée
1 bay leaf
1 sprig rosemary
350 ml / 12 fl. oz / 1 ½ cups chicken stock
salt and pepper
900 g / 2 lb / 3 ½ cups floury potatoes, peeled and cut into chunks
100 g / 3 ½ oz / ½ cup butter

705

SERVES 2 # Chicken and Aubergine Rosemary Stack

- Preheat the oven to 190°C (170°C fan) / 375F / gas 5.
- Slice the chicken in half through the middle. Slice the aubergine thinly along its length, giving you two long slices.
- Place a chicken escalope on the counter, top with a slice of aubergine, season, then top with the second piece of chicken. Season the top slice of chicken, press a rosemary sprig into the meat then tie together to form a parcel. Repeat.
- Sit in a roasting tin, add half the cherry tomatoes, drizzle with half the oil and roast in the oven for 20–25 minutes.
- Meanwhile heat the remaining oil in a pan. Finely dice the reserved tomatoes and fry with the onion.
- When the chicken is cooked, remove from oven and cut off the string. Serve the stacks with the roasted tomatoes and the tomato sauce.

Chicken and Courgette Stack   706
- Replace the aubergine (eggplant) with courgette (zucchini).

PREPARATION TIME:
15 MINUTES

COOKING TIME:
25 MINUTES

INGREDIENTS

2 chicken breasts, skinned
1 aubergine (eggplant)
2 sprigs rosemary
4 tbsp olive oil
salt and pepper
8 cherry tomatoes
½ red onion, finely chopped

707

SERVES 6

Chicken with Lemon and Olives

PREPARATION TIME:
15 MINUTES

COOKING TIME:
1–1 HOUR 30 MINUTES

....

INGREDIENTS

40 g / 1 oz butter, softened
1 chicken
1 red onion, peeled and sliced
I head of garlic, cloves separated
100 g / 3 ½ oz / ½ cup mixed olives
1 lemon, cut into wedges
200 ml / 7 fl. oz / ¾ cup white wine
small bunch herbs, such as sage,
    rosemary or thyme
salt and pepper

- Preheat the oven to 160°C (140°C fan) / 325F / gas 3.
- Smear the butter all over the chicken and season generously. Sit in a large lidded casserole, then add the remaining ingredients.
- Cover with a lid and cook in the oven for 1–1 ½ hours until the chicken is cooked through. Remove the lid for the last 10 minutes of cooking to brown the skin.
- Serve hot or warm.

Chicken with Lemon and Tomatoes

708

- Replace the olives with sun-dried tomatoes.

709

SERVES 2

Mushroom Chicken with Sautéed Apples

PREPARATION TIME:
10 MINUTES

COOKING TIME:
20 MINUTES

....

INGREDIENTS

40 g / 1 oz butter
2 chicken breasts or 4 thighs, skinned
    and cut into chunks
1 eating apple, cored and cut into thick
    slices
150 g / 5 oz / ⅔ cup button or chestnut
    mushrooms, sliced
100 ml / 3 ½ fl. oz / ½ cup dry
    white wine
150 ml / 5 fl. oz / ⅔ cup double (heavy)
    cream
salt and pepper
cooked rice, to serve

- Heat the butter in a pan and sauté the apples and chicken together until golden and softened and the chicken is cooked through. Remove from the pan with a slotted spoon and keep warm.
- Add the mushrooms and season, then sauté until any excess liquid has evaporated, then deglaze the pan with the white wine. Reduce until syrupy then add the cream and bubble up. Return the chicken to the sauce to heat through and adjust the seasoning.
- Serve with the sautéed apple wedges and cooked rice.

Chicken Mushroom Tart

710

- Tip the chicken mushroom mixture (use only half the cream) onto a part-baked puff pastry sheet and bake in the oven for 20 minutes or until golden.

711

SERVES 4

Chicken Waldorf Papillote

Chicken Papillote

712

- You could use any diced or thinly cut vegetables to ring the changes, such as broccoli, carrots, celeriac (celery root) etc.

Chicken with Aioli

713

- Make a simple garlicky mayonnaise tinged with saffron and serve alongside.

PREPARATION TIME:
15 MINUTES

COOKING TIME:
25–30 MINUTES

INGREDIENTS

2 eating apples, diced
4 sticks celery, diced
4 sprigs tarragon
4 chicken breasts, skinned
120 ml / 4 fl. oz / ½ cup dry
    white wine
2 tbsp butter
salt and pepper

- Preheat the oven to 180°C (160°C fan) / 350F / gas 4.
- Take 8 large pieces of foil and lay 4 out on a work surface, then top with the other 4 to make a double layer.
- Tip the apple, celery, herbs into the centre of each parcel, then sit a chicken breast on top. Top with a knob of butter and some seasoning, pour over a little wine then carefully seal each parcel, ensuring there are no gaps and the foil does not tear.
- Place on a baking tray and bake in the oven for 25–30 minutes or until the chicken is just cooked through. Leave to rest for 5–10 minutes before serving the entire parcel at the table for people to open.

714

SERVES 4

Chicken in Red Wine Mushroom Sauce

PREPARATION TIME:
20 MINUTES

COOKING TIME:
45 MINUTES

INGREDIENTS

50 g / 2 oz dried mushrooms
300 ml / 10 fl. oz / 1 ¼ cups chicken
    stock
2 tbsp olive oil
4 chicken legs, skin on
1 onion, peeled and finely chopped
2 cloves of garlic, finely chopped
100 g / 3 ½ oz / ½ cup chanterelles
200 ml / 7 fl. oz / ¾ cup red wine
¼ bunch parsley
salt and pepper
500 g / 1 lb / 2 cups ready
    made gnocchi
40 g / 1 oz butter

- Soak the dried mushrooms in the hot stock.
- Heat the oil in a pan and brown the chicken legs on both sides, then remove and set aside.
- Add the onion and garlic and cook until softened, then add the chanterelles. Remove the dried mushrooms with a slotted spoon and add to the pan and cook all for 5–10 minutes until the mushrooms are tender.
- Deglaze with the red wine and reduce by half, then add the chicken stock, reserving the last little bit as there may be grit from the mushrooms. Add the parsley stalks and chicken back to the pan and simmer for 30 minutes until the chicken is cooked through.
- Meanwhile cook the gnocchi in boiling salted water according to packet instructions, then drain and toss with butter.
- Serve alongside the chicken and mushroom sauce.

715

SERVES 4

Chicken Bouchees

PREPARATION TIME:
10 MINUTES

COOKING TIME:
20 MINUTES

INGREDIENTS

4 chicken thighs, skinned,
    deboned and opened out
4 slices ham
1 ball mozzarella, sliced
75 g / 2 ½ oz / ⅓ cup plain
    (all-purpose) flour
2 eggs, beaten
250 g / 9 oz / 1 cup breadcrumbs
vegetable oil
salt and pepper

- Open the chicken thighs out like a book.
- Place a piece of ham on top, then cheese and fold over and press the edges together to seal.
- Place the flour, eggs and breadcrumbs on separate plates. Season the flour. Dip each chicken breast into the flour, eggs, then breadcrumbs, coating thoroughly each time.
- Heat the oil in a thin layer in the base of a pan then add 2 chicken breasts and cook, turning regularly for about 20 minutes until cooked through.
- Keep warm in a low oven while you cook the remaining chicken. Serve hot.

716

SERVES 4

Basil and Lemon Chicken with Ratatouille

- Preheat the oven to 200°C (180°C fan) / 400F / gas 6.
- Marinate the chicken with oil, lemon zest and a little juice and basil for 30 minutes.
- Meanwhile heat the oil in a pan and cook the onions.
- Add the aubergines and cook for 2 minutes, then add the garlic and cook for 2 minutes, then add the courgettes and peppers and cook for 5 minutes.
- Add the tomatoes and coriander seeds and leave to simmer for at least 30 minutes over a very low heat, stirring occasionally, until the vegetables are very soft. Season and sprinkle over the basil.
- Meanwhile heat a griddle or frying pan and cook the chicken for 6 minutes each side until golden and cooked through. Season and squeeze over a little more lemon juice.
- Serve the chicken with the ratatouille.

PREPARATION TIME:
10 MINUTES

COOKING TIME: 45 MINUTES

INGREDIENTS

4 chicken breasts
2 tbsp olive oil
½ lemon, juiced and zested
½ bunch basil
4–6 tbsp olive oil
2 onions, peeled and finely sliced
2 aubergines (eggplant), diced
2 garlic cloves, finely chopped
3 courgettes (zucchini), diced
3 red peppers, seeded and sliced
    400 g / 14 oz / 1 ½ cups tomatoes
1 tsp coriander seeds, crushed

717

Pineapple Chicken Colombo

SERVES 4

PREPARATION TIME:
15 MINUTES

COOKING TIME:
30 MINUTES

INGREDIENTS

1 tbsp vegetable oil
4 chicken thighs, skinned, deboned and cubed
salt and pepper
1 onion, peeled and chopped

3 cloves of garlic, crushed
2 tbsp curry powder
6 sprigs thyme leaves
1 tsp ground allspice
½ tsp ground cinnamon
2 bay leaves
1–2 Scotch Bonnet chillies (chilies)
    (depending on how hot you want it)
500 ml / 1 pint / 2 cups chicken stock
400 g / 14 oz / 1 ½ cups chopped tomatoes
200 g / 7 oz / ¾ cup pineapple, chopped
1 lime, quartered

- Heat the oil and sear the chicken on all sides until golden. Remove with a slotted spoon and set aside.
- Add the onion and cook until softened, then add the garlic and spices and cook for 2 minutes.
- Add the chillies, stock and tomatoes and bring to a simmer. Add the chicken back to the pan, reduce the heat, cover with a lid and cook for 20 minutes until the chicken is cooked.
- Remove the chillies, adjust the seasoning and add the pineapple to heat through.
- Serve with white rice.

Chicken with Roast Vegetables

718

SERVES 4

PREPARATION TIME:
10 MINUTES

COOKING TIME:
25–40 MINUTES

INGREDIENTS

4 chicken breasts or legs, skin on
2 courgettes (zucchini), thickly sliced

2 red peppers, deseeded and roughly chopped
1 onion, peeled and thickly sliced
4 cloves of garlic, whole
8 cherry tomatoes
200 g / 7 oz / 1 cup passata
1 bunch basil leaves
salt and pepper

- Preheat the oven to 200°C (180°C fan) / 400F / gas 6.
- Arrange the chicken and vegetables in a roasting tin and drizzle over the passata. Toss to coat. Season well and roast for 25 minutes or until all is cooked through and tender. If using legs, they will take another 10 minutes.
- If the vegetables are still a little pallid-looking, remove the chicken and keep warm and return the tin to the oven for 10 minutes until they start to char appetisingly.
- Serve topped with torn basil.

719

SERVES 4

Chicken Stuffed with Ham and Apple

Chicken With Cream Cheese Stuffing

720

- Swap the apple sauce for cream cheese and sprinkle with chives before adding the ham.

Chicken with Pesto and Stuffing

721

- Try using a little pesto instead if apple sauce.

PREPARATION TIME:
50 MINUTES

COOKING TIME:
20–25 MINUTES

INGREDIENTS

4 chicken breasts
100 g / 3 ½ oz / ½ cup apple sauce
8 slices of cooked ham
salt and pepper
2 tbsp olive oil

- Preheat the oven to 180°C (160°C fan) / 350F / gas 4.
- Open the chicken out like a book by slicing nearly all the way through horizontally and folding back the meat.
- Spoon the apple sauce inside, then lay slices of ham over the top. Fold the chicken back over to seal the filling inside. You can secure with toothpicks if necessary.
- Place in a roasting tin, drizzle with oil, season the skin and roast for 20 minutes or until cooked through.
- Leave to rest for 10 minutes before slicing and serving.

722

SERVES 4

Indian Chicken Goujons

- Mix the breadcrumbs with the spices and seasoning.
- Dip the chicken breasts one at a time into the flour, egg then spiced breadcrumbs and lay on a rack to dry slightly.
- Heat 1 cm (½ in) depth oil in a pan and fry the chicken in batches until golden on both sides and cooked through.
- Drain briefly on kitchen paper before serving with mango chutney.

PREPARATION TIME:
10 MINUTES

COOKING TIME:
20 MINUTES

INGREDIENTS

4 chicken breasts, skinned and
  batted out slightly
100 g / 3 ½ oz / ½ cup plain
  (all-purpose) flour
2 eggs, beaten
200 g / 7 oz / ¾ cup breadcrumbs
1 tsp ground cumin
1 tsp ground coriander
½ tsp ground ginger
½ tsp chilli (chili) powder
salt and pepper
vegetable oil
mango chutney

Garam Masala Chicken Goujons

723

- Use 1 tbsp garam masala in the breadcrumbs if you don't have the above spices for an authentic Indian flavour.

724

SERVES 4

Thai-scented Chicken in Banana Leaves

- Lay the banana leaves out on a surface and a halved stick of lemongrass and a chicken thigh on each one.
- Drizzle over a little honey, then top with ginger and seasoning, then wrap completely in the banana leaf.
- Steam over simmering water for 25–35 minutes until the chicken is cooked through.
- Sprinkle with sesame seeds before serving for crunch.

PREPARATION TIME:
10 MINUTES

COOKING TIME:
25–35 MINUTES

INGREDIENTS

4 chicken thighs, skinned
  and deboned
2 stalks lemongrass, halved lengthways
2 tbsp honey
1 tbsp fresh ginger, finely sliced
salt and pepper
4 banana leaves
1 tbsp sesame seeds

Thai-scented Chicken Parcels

725

- If you can't find banana leaves, wrap in foil or baking parchment and bake in the oven for the same amount of time.

SPECIAL & SPICY

726

SERVES 4

Chicken Tikka

**PREPARATION TIME:
20 MINUTES**

**COOKING TIME:
30–35 MINUTES**

INGREDIENTS

4 chicken breasts, skinned and chopped
3 tbsp plain yogurt
2 tbsp tandoori paste
2 tbsp vegetable oil
1 onion, peeled and finely sliced
2 cloves of garlic, finely sliced
knob of ginger, finely sliced
1 cinnamon stick
4 cardamom pods, lightly crushed
1 tsp ground cumin
1 tsp ground coriander
½ tsp turmeric, 2 tsp paprika
400 g / 14 oz / 1 ½ cup tomatoes
100 ml / 3 ½ fl. oz / ½ cup chicken stock
½ lemon, juiced
salt and pepper
250 g / 9 oz / 1 cup basmati rice

- Chop and marinate the chicken for at least 1 hour in the yogurt and tandoori paste.
- Heat the oil in a pan and fry the onion until golden. Add the garlic, ginger and spices and fry for 2–3 minutes.
- Add the chicken, shaking off any excess marinade, and sauté over high heat until patchily golden, then add the tomatoes and stock and simmer for 20 minutes.
- Once thickened, stir in the remaining marinade and heat through but do not allow to boil.
- Tip the rice into a pan with the water and cook covered with a lid for 10 minutes. Remove from the heat and leave covered for 5 minutes.
- Season the tikka with lemon juice and salt and pepper and serve with rice.

Minted Chicken Tikka

727

- Stir fresh mint leaves through the tikka once cooked for a refreshing kick.

728

SERVES 4

Moroccan Chicken Couscous

**PREPARATION TIME:
10 MINUTES**

COOKING TIME: 55 MINUTES

INGREDIENTS

2 tbsp olive oil
1 onion, peeled and finely sliced
2 cloves of garlic, finely sliced
small knob fresh ginger
4 chicken drumsticks, skinned
2 carrots, peeled and chopped
1 tsp ras-el-hanout spice mix
2 cinnamon sticks
1 tsp ground cumin
1 large pinch dried chilli (chili) flakes
400 g / 14 oz / 1 ½ cups canned
    chickpeas, drained
400 ml / 14 fl. oz / 1 ½ cups
    chicken stock
200 g / 7 oz / ¾ cup prunes
1 lemon, juiced
sprigs of mint
salt and pepper
250 g / 9 oz / 1 cup couscous
250 ml / 9 fl. oz / 1 cup chicken

- Heat the oil in a large pan and cook the onions.
- Peel and grate the ginger. Add the garlic and ginger and cook for a few minutes, then remove all from the pan with a slotted spoon.
- Increase the heat and brown the chicken thighs on all sides, then tip the onions back into the pan with the carrot and sprinkle over the spices.
- Pour over the stock, add the chickpeas and prunes and season, lower the heat and cook gently for about 45 minutes or until the sauce has thickened and the chicken is cooked. Stir in the lemon juice and mint.
- While the chicken is cooking place the couscous in a bowl, add the raisins, cover with the hot stock and cling film the bowl. Leave for 10 minutes or so until tender, then fork through the grains and add the lemon.
- Spoon the couscous onto a large serving platter, then spoon the stew on top and serve.

Cheesy Chicken Couscous

729

- Add 100 g of grated cheese to the couscous.

730

SERVES 2–3

Stir Fried Sesame Chicken

- Heat the oil in a wok and stir fry the chicken until golden. Remove with a slotted spoon and set aside.
- Add the onion, garlic and ginger and fry quickly until golden, then return the chicken to the pan with the vegetables. Cook for a few minutes until tender.
- Add the sauces and bubble up.
- Sprinkle in the sesame seeds and serve immediately.

PREPARATION TIME:
15 MINUTES

COOKING TIME:
15–20 MINUTES

INGREDIENTS

2 tbsp vegetable oil
350 g / 12 oz / 1 ½ cups chicken
    thigh meat, diced
1 onion, peeled and finely sliced
2 cloves of garlic, finely sliced
1 tsp fresh ginger, grated
100 g / 3 ½ oz / ½ cup beansprouts
1 red pepper, deseeded and finely sliced
100 g / 3 ½ oz / ½ cup green beans,
    blanched in boiling water
2 carrots, peeled and cut into thin
    batons
2 tbsp soy sauce
2 tbsp oyster sauce
1 tbsp chinese rice wine or mirin
2 tbsp sesame seeds

Stir Fry with Palm Hearts

731

- Canned palm hearts, widely available, make an interesting addition to the stir fry added at the last minute.

732

SERVES 4

Chicken Lemon and Olive Tagine

- Heat the oil in a large pan and cook the onions until golden and tender.
- Add the garlic and cook for a few minutes, then remove all from the pan with a slotted spoon.
- Increase the heat and brown the chicken on all sides, then tip the onions back into the pan and sprinkle over the spices. Add the lemons.
- Pour over the stock and season, lower the heat and cook gently for about 45 minutes or until the sauce has thickened and the chicken is cooked.
- Add the olives to warm through, adjust the seasoning and sprinkle with parsley.

PREPARATION TIME:
15 MINUTES

COOKING TIME:
45 MINUTES

INGREDIENTS

2 tbsp olive oil
1 onion, peeled and thickly sliced
2 cloves of garlic, finely sliced
4 chicken legs, skinned
1 tsp ras-el-hanout spice mix
1 tsp ground (cilantro) coriander seeds
1 tsp cumin
4 preserved lemons, chopped
1 lemon, chopped
400 ml / 14 fl. oz / 1 ½ cups chicken
    stock
2 tbsp olives
½ bunch parsley, chopped
salt and pepper

Chicken Chorizo Tagine

733

- Add chunky slices of chorizo sausage with the onions for colour and spice.

Chicken with Mushrooms and Asparagus

Chicken with Truffle Sauce

735

- You don't need to use foie gras, but you could enrich the sauce with double cream or even some sliced truffles.

Chicken with Mushrooms and Baby Corn

736

- Replace the asparagus with baby corn.

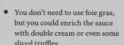

PREPARATION TIME:
20 MINUTES

COOKING TIME:
45 MINUTES

INGREDIENTS

4 chicken breasts, skinned
1 carrot, chopped
½ onion
1 stick celery, chopped
6 black peppercorns
1 bay leaf
50 g / 2 oz butter
50 g / 2 oz plain (all-purpose) flour
50 g / 2 oz butter
50 g / 2 oz button mushrooms, halved
50 g / 2 oz porcini mushrooms
1 bunch asparagus, trimmed
100 g / 3 ½ oz / ½ cup vacuum-packed chestnuts, chopped
salt and pepper
50 g / 2 oz foie gras

- Poach the chicken breasts in a pan with the vegetables, just covered with water, for about 20 minutes, or until just cooked through.
- Remove from the liquid, keep warm and set aside. Drain the vegetables, reserving the poaching liquor.
- Melt the first amount of butter in the pan and whisk in the flour to make a 'roux'. Slowly whisk in 300 ml of the poaching liquor to make a smooth thick sauce then leave to simmer for 10 minutes.
- Melt the second amount of butter in a pan and cook the mushrooms for 10 minutes or until just tender. Steam the asparagus until tender.
- Cube the foie gras and whisk into the sauce. Adjust the seasoning.
- Serve the chicken sliced with the asparagus, mushrooms and chestnuts and the sauce poured over.

737

SERVES 4

Chicken, Artichoke and Olive Tagine

- Heat the oil in a large pan and cook the onions until golden and tender.
- Add the garlic and cook for a few minutes, then remove all from the pan with a slotted spoon.
- Increase the heat and brown the chicken on all sides, then tip the onions back into the pan and sprinkle over the spices.
- Pour over the stock and season, lower the heat and cook gently for about 45 minutes or until the sauce has thickened and the chicken is cooked.
- Add the vegetables to warm through, adjust the seasoning.
- Serve with the basmati rice.

PREPARATION TIME:
15 MINUTES

COOKING TIME:
45 MINUTES

INGREDIENTS

2 tbsp olive oil
1 onion, peeled and finely sliced
2 cloves of garlic, finely sliced
4 chicken legs, skinned
1 tsp ras-el-hanout spice mix
1 tsp ground (cilantro) coriander seeds
4 preserved lemons, chopped
400 ml / 14 fl. oz / 1 ½ cups chicken stock
200 g / 7 oz / ¾ cup globe artichokes in oil, drained
150 g / 5 oz / ⅔ cup broad beans, blanched and podded
2 tbsp green olives
salt and pepper
basmati rice, cooked, to serve

Chicken, Artichoke and Sun-dried Tomatoes

738

- Replace the olives with sun-dried tomatoes.

739

SERVES 2

Chicken with Chinese Mushroom Broth

- Rehydrate the black mushrooms in the chicken stock for 20 minutes.
- Heat the oils in a pan and gently fry the onion without colouring. Add the carrot, garlic and ginger and cook for 2 minutes.
- Add the chicken and morels and cook until white. Scoop the rehydrated mushrooms from the stock and fry for 1 minute, then pour over the stock, discarding the last little bit as there may be grit. Add the soy and simmer for 5 minutes, then add the noodles and cook for a further 5 minutes.
- Sprinkle with coriander and serve.

PREPARATION TIME:
20 MINUTES

COOKING TIME:
15–20 MINUTES

INGREDIENTS

200 g / 7 oz / ¾ cup dried Chinese black mushrooms
500 ml / 1 pint / 2 cups chicken stock
1 tbsp groundnut oil
1 tsp sesame oil
1 onion, peeled and finely sliced
1 carrot, peeled and cut into fine batons
1 clove of garlic, finely sliced
1 tsp fresh ginger, grated
2 chicken breasts, skinned and chopped
200 g / 7 oz / ¾ cup morels or Chinese morels, cleaned
2 tbsp soy sauce
2 nests of noodles
¼ bunch coriander (cilantro), chopped

Chicken with Mushroom Broth

740

- If Chinese mushrooms are hard to find, use dried wild mushrooms and chestnut mushrooms for good flavour.

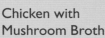

741

SERVES 4

Indian-marinated Chicken

PREPARATION TIME:
10 MINUTES

COOKING TIME:
15 MINUTES

....

INGREDIENTS

4 chicken breasts, skinned and cubed
1 red chilli (chili), finely chopped,
    deseeded if preferred
½ bunch coriander (cilantro) leaves
½ tsp ground turmeric
½ tsp ground coriander
½ tsp ground cumin
½ lemon, juiced
vegetable oil
salt and pepper
basmati rice, cooked, to serve
basil, to garnish

- Whizz the chilli and spices in a food processor with lemon juice and enough vegetable oil to make a paste.
- Toss the chicken in the paste and leave to marinate for up to 1 hour in the refrigerator.
- Heat a frying pan with a little oil then wipe off any excess marinade and cook the chicken until golden and sizzling.
- Scrape in any remaining marinade with a little water to make a sauce.
- Serve hot with the basmati rice alongside.

Spiced Chicken with Mustard Seeds

742

- ½ tsp mustard seeds with the spice paste add a strong authentic flavour to the marinade.

743

SERVES 4

Chicken Creole

PREPARATION TIME:
15 MINUTES

COOKING TIME:
30 MINUTES

....

INGREDIENTS

2 tbsp olive oil
1 onion, peeled and chopped
1 green (bell) pepper, seeded and
    chopped
1 stock celery, finely chopped
2 cloves of garlic, finely chopped
1cm piece fresh ginger, finely chopped
1 tbsp flour
4 chicken breasts, skinned, cubed
1 tsp paprika
½ tsp cayenne pepper
400 g / 14 oz / 1 ½ cups chopped
    tomatoes
100 ml / 3 ½ fl. oz / ½ cup chicken stock
1 bay leaf
salt and pepper
2 mangos, peeled, stoned and cubed
½ lime, juiced
basmati rice, cooked

- Heat the oil in a large pan and sauté the onion, peppers and celery until softened.
- Add the garlic, ginger and flour and cook out for a few seconds, then add the chicken and brown.
- Sprinkle over the spices, then pour in tomatoes and stock. Add the bay leaf and season, then simmer for about 20 minutes over a low heat until the sauce has thickened and the chicken is cooked.
- Serve with the mango tossed with lime juice and the rice alongside.

Chicken Creole with Pistachios

744

- Try using 2 tbsp ground pistachios in the sauce to thicken.

745

SERVES 4

Indian Chicken Curry

Fruity Indian Chicken Curry

746

- Add a couple of handfuls of dried apricots to the sauce to add sweetness and richness.

Creamy Indian Curry

747

- Add 100 ml / 3 ½ fl. oz plain yogurt at the end of cooking, off the heat.

PREPARATION TIME:
15 MINUTES

COOKING TIME:
40 MINUTES

INGREDIENTS

2 tbsp vegetable oil
500 g / 1 lb / 2 cups chicken thigh meat, cubed
1 onion, peeled and finely sliced
2 cloves of garlic, finely sliced
1cm piece fresh ginger, grated
1 green chilli (chili), finely chopped
1 tbsp tomato purée
1 tbsp ground coriander
1 tbsp ground cumin
1 tsp turmeric
1 tsp paprika
½ tsp ground cinnamon
400 g / 14 oz / 1 ½ cups canned chopped tomatoes
200 ml / 7 fl. oz / ¾ cup chicken stock
salt and pepper

- Heat the oil in a large pan and sear the chicken on all sides until golden. Remove from the pan and set aside.
- Add the onion, garlic and ginger to the pan and cook until golden. Add the chilli, tomato purée and spices and cook out for 2 minutes.
- Add the chicken back to the pan, then cover with tomatoes and stock.
- Bring to the boil, reduce the heat and simmer very gently for at least 30 minutes until the chicken is cooked through and the sauce has thickened.
- Season well and serve with nan bread.

748

SERVES 4

Chicken, Chestnut, Prune and Fig Tagine

PREPARATION TIME:
10 MINUTES

COOKING TIME:
55 MINUTES

INGREDIENTS

2 tbsp olive oil
1 onion, peeled and finely sliced
2 cloves of garlic, finely sliced
small knob fresh ginger, peeled
    and grated
4 chicken thighs
1 tsp ras-el-hanout spice mix
1 tsp ground cumin
1 tsp ground cinnamon
1 large pinch dried chilli (chili) flakes
400 ml / 14 fl. oz / 1 ½ cups
    chicken stock
200 g / 7 oz / ¾ cup prunes
150 g / 5 oz / ⅔ cup dried figs
100 g / 3 ½ oz / ½ cup vacuum packed
    cooked chestnuts
1 orange, juiced
salt and pepper

- Heat the oil in a large pan and cook the onions until golden and tender.
- Add the garlic and ginger and cook for a few minutes, then remove all from the pan with a slotted spoon.
- Increase the heat and brown the chicken thighs on all sides, then tip the onions back into the pan with the sweet potato and sprinkle over the spices.
- Pour over the stock, add the prunes, figs and chestnuts and season, lower the heat and cook gently for about 45 minutes or until the sauce has thickened and the chicken is cooked. Stir in the orange juice and heat through.
- Serve with couscous.

Chicken and Date Tagine 749

- Replace the prunes with dates.

750

SERVES 4

Chilli Lemon Chicken

PREPARATION TIME:
5 MINUTES

COOKING TIME:
25–30 MINUTES

INGREDIENTS

4 chicken breasts, skinned
1 pinch saffron
1 tbsp olive oil
1 lemon, juiced
1 red chilli (chili), finely chopped
spring onions (scallions)
black olives
salt and pepper

- Place the chicken in a pan and pour in enough boiling water to cover. Add the saffron and poach very gently for about 15–20 minutes until cooked through.
- Heat the oil in a pan and add the chilli, then add the chicken and fry for a couple of minutes each side until lightly golden. Squeeze over the lemon juice off the heat.
- Serve with the spring onions and olives, seasoned with salt, pepper and a little more lemon juice.

Chilli Orange Chicken 751

- Replace the lemon with orange.

SERVES 4 — 752

Chicken with Chorizo and Tomatoes

- Preheat the oven to 200°C (180°C fan) / 400F / gas 6.
- Place the chicken in a large roasting tin with the chorizo, new potatoes, tomatoes, seasoning and drizzle over the oil.
- Roast in the oven for 30–40 minutes or until the chicken is cooked through, adding a splash of water or white wine if it looks a little dry after 20 minutes.
- Serve sprinkled with coriander.

PREPARATION TIME:
10 MINUTES

COOKING TIME:
40 MINUTES

INGREDIENTS

4 tbsp olive oil
4 chicken drumsticks, skin on
75 g / 2 ½ oz / ⅓ cup cooking chorizo sausage, sliced
200 g / 7 oz new potatoes
8 tomatoes, quartered
salt and pepper
1 tbsp coriander (cilantro) leaves

Chicken with Potatoes, Chorizo and Tomatoes — 753

- Adding quartered waxy potatoes to the oven dish makes this a more substantial supper.

SERVES 4 — 754

Chicken and Seafood Stew

- First cook the mussels: Place in a large pan with a splash of water or white wine and steam with a lid on until all the mussels have opened. Discard any that remain closed and carefully drain off and reserve the mussel liquor, bring careful of any grit at the bottom.
- In a large pan sweat the onion, celery, carrot and garlic in the oil until softened, then increase the heat and cook the chicken until golden on all sides. Remove with a slotted spoon.
- Add the mussel liquor, tomatoes and stock and simmer for 15–20 minutes until the flavour has intensified.
- Add the fish, prawns, peas and chicken, simmer until cooked – about 10 minutes.
- Add the mussels and adjust the seasoning. Serve with good bread.

PREPARATION TIME:
15 MINUTES

COOKING TIME:
50 MINUTES

INGREDIENTS

400 g / 14 oz / 1 ½ cups mussels, cleaned and debearded
2 tbsp olive oil
1 onion, peeled and finely sliced
1 stick celery, finely chopped
1 carrot, peeled and finely sliced
2 cloves of garlic, finely sliced
2 chicken thighs, deboned and cubed
200 g / 7 oz / ¾ cup firm white fish, cut into chunks, such as haddock
200 g / 7 oz / ¾ cup shell-on king prawns, raw
400 g / 14 oz / 1 ½ cups chopped tomatoes
500 ml / 1 pint / 2 cups chicken or fish stock
1 pinch saffron
1 bay leaf
1 sprig thyme
salt and pepper
100 g / 3 ½ oz / ½ cup peas

Shellfish and Chicken Stew — 755

- Try adding half clams, half mussels for a more intense flavour.

756

SERVES 4

Chicken Fricassee

Chicken Fricassee with Rice

757

- Serve on a bed of boiled rice.

Fricassee Sandwiches

758

- Use the leftovers in packed lunch sandwich.

PREPARATION TIME:
10 MINUTES

COOKING TIME:
45–50 MINUTES

....

INGREDIENTS

2 tbsp olive oil
4 chicken drumsticks or thighs
1 onion, peeled and finely sliced
2 cloves of garlic, finely sliced
2 red peppers, deseeded and finely sliced
1 bulb fennel, cored and thickly sliced
4 sprigs thyme
200 ml / 7 fl. oz / ¾ cup white wine
salt and pepper

- Heat the oil in a deep sided pan and fry the chicken on all sides until golden.
- Add the onion and garlic and continue to cook until deep gold and sweet.
- Add the peppers and fennel and cook for a few minutes, then add the thyme and wine, season and cover with a lid.
- Cook over a low heat for 20–25 minutes until the chicken is cooked through.
- Serve with crusty bread

759

SERVES 4

Tandoori-style Chicken

- Prepare the tandoori marinade by mixing together all the ingredients for the marinade in a mixing bowl. Add the chicken, mix well, then cover and chill for at least 1 hour.
- Scrape off any excess marinade and add to a hot wok. When sizzling, add the tomatoes and chicken stock and simmer for 10 minutes. Set aside and keep warm.
- Bring double the volume of water to rice to the boil in a large saucepan and add the rice. Bring back to the boil, then cover and simmer for 10–12 minutes.
- Remove from the heat and keep the lid in place and set to one side.
- Grill or roast the drumsticks until golden and sticky, then add to the sauce and simmer for 5 minutes to cook through completely.
- Serve the tandoori chicken with the rice, sprinkled with coriander.

PREPARATION TIME:
25–30 MINUTES

COOKING TIME:
30 MINUTES

INGREDIENTS

8 chicken drumsticks
400 g / 14 oz / 1 ½ cups chopped
    tomatoes
200 ml / 7 fl. oz / ¾ cup chicken stock
1 tsp paprika
200 ml / 7 fl. oz / ¾ cup basmati rice
fresh coriander (cilantro) leaves
300 ml / 10 fl. oz / 1 ¼ cups plain yogurt
1 tsp ground cumin
1 tsp ground coriander
1 tsp garam masala
1 tsp ground cinnamon
1 ½ tsp tandoori chilli (chili) powder
1 tsp caster (superfine) sugar
1 clove garlic, minced
salt and pepper

Tandoori Yogurt
Chicken Skewers

760

- Use cubed chicken in the marinade and grill on skewers for a BBQ version.

761

SERVES 4–6

Chicken with Truffles and Sage Butter

- Preheat oven to 220°C (200°C fan) / 425F / gas 7.
- Push the handle of a wooden spoon between the skin and flesh of the chicken breast to create a pocket. Mix the butter with seasoning and truffles and push the butter into the pockets to create a stuffing.
- Roast the chicken in the oven for 20 minutes, then reduce the heat to 200°C (180°C fan) / 400F / gas 6 and roast for a further hour. Set aside to rest for 15 minutes.
- Meanwhile, heat the butter and olive oil in a pan and sauté the potatoes whole until golden and tender – about 25 minutes.
- Transfer the chicken to a carving board and set the pan full of juices on the hob. Simmer and add the sage leaves and lemon juice, deglazing with a wooden spoon. Adjust the seasoning.
- Carve the chicken and serve with the potatoes, spooning over the truffled sage juices.

PREPARATION TIME:
10 MINUTES

COOKING TIME:
45 MINUTES

INGREDIENTS

1 x ready-to-roast chicken
    (weighing about 1.5kg / 3 lbs)
60 g / 2 oz / ¼ cup butter, softened
1 truffle, sliced
salt and pepper
1 kg / 2 lb / 4 ¼ cups new potatoes
30 g / 1 oz butter
olive oil
½ bunch sage leaves
½ lemon, juiced

Chicken with Herb
Butter Stuffing

762

- If your budget doesn't run to truffles, use thyme leaves or basil for the butter stuffing.

763

SERVES 2

Chicken and Prawn Chop Suey

PREPARATION TIME:
20 MINUTES

COOKING TIME:
15 MINUTES

....

INGREDIENTS

1 chicken breast, skinned and
   thinly sliced
225 g / 8 oz / 1 cup raw king prawns
½ tsp salt
1 egg white
1 tbsp cornflour mixed with 1 tbsp
   water to a paste
100 ml / 3 ½ fl. oz / ½ cup
   vegetable oil
2 cloves of garlic, crushed
1 tbsp fresh ginger, grated
1 red pepper, deseeded and
   finely sliced
8 asparagus spears, trimmed
1 tsp sugar
1 tbsp soy sauce
1 tbsp mirin or Chinese rice wine
100 ml / 3 ½ fl. oz / ½ cup chicken stock
1 tsp sesame oil

- Toss the chicken slices and prawns with the salt, egg and enough cornflour to coat. If you have any left, reserve.
- Heat the oil in a wok and when very hot, cook the prawns and chicken in batches until golden. Remove with a slotted spoon and discard most of the oil, leaving about 1 tbsp.
- Sauté the garlic, ginger, pepper and asparagus until crisp-tender, then add the sugar, soy, mirin, stock and stir in any remaining cornflour paste. Bubble up to thicken.
- Toss the prawns and chicken in the sauce and serve immediately.

Chop Suey with Rice or Noodles

764

- Add cooked noodles for a substantial meal.

765

SERVES 4

Caramelised Chicken with Beans

PREPARATION TIME:
10 MINUTES

COOKING TIME:
2 HOURS

....

INGREDIENTS

250 g / 9 oz / 1 cup dried
   cannellini beans
3 tbsp extra virgin olive oil
2 cloves of garlic, whole
4 sage leaves
3 black peppercorns
salt and pepper
4 chicken legs
2 tbsp runny honey
pinch dried chilli (chili) flakes
½ orange, juiced

- Sort through the beans carefully, discarding any small stones. Place in a pan, cover with cold water and soak for at least 4 hours or overnight.
- Drain and return to the pan. Cover with 3 pints / 6 cups of water and add the garlic, sage and peppercorns. Bring to a brisk simmer and leave for 1 hour.
- Reduce the heat to a 'blip' season very lightly and leave to simmer gently for another hour. When the beans are tender, leave to cool in the liquid.
- Preheat the oven to 180°C (160°C fan) / 350F / gas 4.
- Roll the chicken legs in the honey, chilli flakes and orange juice then place in a foil-lined roasting tin. Roast for about 30 minutes until sticky and golden and cooked through.
- Reheat the beans gently in the liquid, then remove to plates with a slotted spoon. Sit the caramelised chicken on top and serve.

Caramelised Chicken with Carrots

766

- Replace the beans with honey glazed carrots.

767

SERVES 2

Thai Chicken Salad

Thai Chicken and Squid Salad

768

- Rings of squid, tossed with curry paste and quickly fried, would make a good addition.

Crunchy Thai Salad

769

- Add a generous handful of chopped toasted peanuts for authentic Thai crunch and flavour.

PREPARATION TIME:
15 MINUTES

COOKING TIME:
10 MINUTES

INGREDIENTS

2 chicken breasts, skinned and thickly sliced
2 tbsp Thai yellow or red curry paste
200 g / 7 oz / ¾ cup vermicelli noodles or glass noodles
1 carrot, peeled
1 courgette (zucchini)
1 tsp sesame oil
2 tbsp vegetable oil

- Toss the chicken with the curry paste and marinate for at least 1 hour.
- Soak the noodles according to packet instructions.
- Cut the carrot and courgette into very fine matchsticks. One way to do this is to peel off ribbons using a vegetable peeler, then slice finely lengthways.
- Heat the oils in a pan or wok and fry the chicken until golden and cooked through. Toss with the vegetable batons.
- Twist the noodles into nests, then top with the chicken and vegetables.

770

SERVES 4

Green Peppercorn Chicken and Rice

PREPARATION TIME:
10 MINUTES

COOKING TIME:
15 MINUTES

INGREDIENTS

4 chicken breasts, skinned
2 tbsp bottled green peppercorns
2 tbsp olive oil
250 g / 9 oz / 1 cup basmati rice
2 cups water infused with pinch saffron
salt
basil, to garnish

- Lightly crush the peppercorns with the back of a knife and marinate with the chicken for 1 hour.
- Griddle the chicken over medium heat until golden on both sides and cooked through.
- Tip the rice into a pan with the water and cook covered with a lid for 10 minutes. Remove from the heat and leave covered for 5 minutes.
- Serve the chicken sliced with peppercorns scattered over for heat on top of the rice.

Popping Peppercorn Chicken
771

- For real colour, use a mixture of pink, green, black and white peppercorns.

772

SERVES 4

Chicken Almond and Prune Tagine

PREPARATION TIME:
10 MINUTES

COOKING TIME:
55 MINUTES

INGREDIENTS

2 tbsp olive oil
1 onion, peeled and finely sliced
2 cloves of garlic, finely sliced
small knob fresh ginger, peeled and grated
4 chicken drumsticks, skinned
2 sweet potatoes, peeled and roughly chopped
1 tsp ras-el-hanout spice mix
2 cinnamon sticks
1 tsp ground cumin
1 large pinch dried chilli (chili) flakes
400 ml / 14 fl. oz / 1 ½ cups chicken stock
200 g / 7 oz / ¾ cup prunes
60 g / 2 oz flaked (slivered) almonds
1 lemon, juiced
salt and pepper

- Heat the oil in a large pan and cook the onions until golden and tender.
- Add the garlic and ginger and cook for a few minutes, then remove all from the pan with a slotted spoon.
- Increase the heat and brown the chicken thighs on all sides, then tip the onions back into the pan with the sweet potato and sprinkle over the spices.
- Pour over the stock, add the prunes and season, lower the heat and cook gently for about 45 minutes or until the sauce has thickened and the chicken is cooked. Stir in the almonds, lemon juice and mint and heat through.
- Serve with couscous.

Butternut Squash Tagine
773

- Use butternut squash for a similar sweetness but firmer texture.

774
SERVES 4 Peruvian Spicy Chicken

- Poach the chicken in the stock for about 10 minutes, or until just cooked. Remove and reserve 500 ml stock. Cut the chicken into bite-sized pieces.
- Soak the bread in the milk.
- Place the peppers and chilli in a food processor with the oil and purée until smooth.
- Heat the oil in a pan and cook the onions and garlic until golden, then add the peppers and cook until all is soft.
- Whiz the bread/milk until smooth with the walnuts and cheese then add the pepper mixture and combine well.
- Return to the pan, add the reserved chicken stock then add the chicken and heat gently until hot.
- Serve with cooked rice.

PREPARATION TIME:
30 MINUTES

COOKING TIME:
20 MINUTES

INGREDIENTS

750 g / 1 ½ lb / 3 cups chicken breasts, skinned
1 l / 2 ¼ pints / 4 ¼ cups chicken stock
4 slices white bread
200 ml / 7 fl. oz / 1 ¼ cups milk
3 yellow peppers, deseeded and chopped
1 red chilli (chili), deseeded (optional) and chopped
vegetable oil
2 tbsp olive oil
1 onion, peeled and finely sliced
2 cloves of garlic, crushed
3 tbsp walnuts, finely chopped
3 tbsp Parmesan cheese, grated

Spicy Peruvian Chicken with Almonds   775

- Almonds would thicken the sauce as well as walnuts without being as strong in flavour.

776
SERVES 2 Timbale of Vegetables with Chicken

- Preheat the oven to 200°C (180°C fan) / 400F / gas 6.
- Drizzle the chicken with oil, season and roast in the oven for 20 minutes. Leave to rest.
- Meanwhile cut each of the vegetables into equal-sized tiny dice – try to make sure they are as even as possible.
- Blanch the vegetables in boiling salted water for 1 minute, scooping them out with a slotted spoon and refreshing immediately in iced water to retain the colour and stop the cooking.
- Once the vegetables have cooled, dry on kitchen paper. Mix each of the vegetables with a little mayonnaise, just enough to bind and season.
- Set a ring mould on the plate, then layer in the vegetables one at a time. Remove the mould.
- Thinly slice the chicken and carefully sit equal slices on top of the timbales. Top with any remaining mayonnaise and serve.

PREPARATION TIME:
25 MINUTES

COOKING TIME:
20 MINUTES

INGREDIENTS

1 chicken breast, skin on
1 tbsp olive oil
salt and pepper
2 carrots, peeled
200 g / 7 oz / ¾ cup green beans, topped and tailed
150 g / 5 oz / ⅔ cup peas
200 g / 7 oz / ¾ cup baby turnips, peeled and trimmed
100 g / 3 ½ oz / ½ cup mayonnaise
salt and pepper

Timbale of Vegetables with Chicken and Rice   777

- Serve on a bed of white boiled rice.

SERVES 4

Prune-stuffed Chicken and Carrot Mash

Chicken Parcels with Herbs

779

- For a less rich stuffing, use whatever herbs you like and butter before rolling up the escalopes.

Chicken with Apricot Tarragon Stuffing

780

- Use the same quantity of dried apricots with a few sprigs chopped tarragon.

PREPARATION TIME:
20 MINUTES

COOKING TIME:
25 MINUTES

INGREDIENTS

4 chicken escalopes, batted out
    to 1 cm (½ in) thickness
100 g / 3 ½ oz / ½ cup dried prunes
8 red plums, halved and stoned
1 lemon, sliced
1 grapefruit, sliced
olive oil

FOR THE CARROT PURÉE

30 g / 1 oz butter
1 onion, peeled and finely chopped
1 garlic clove, finely chopped
500 g / 1 lb / 2 cups carrots, peeled
    and diced
1 tsp ground cumin
300 ml / 10 fl.oz / 1 ½ cups vegetable
    stock
a little orange zest
salt and pepper

- Preheat the oven to 180°C (160°C fan) / 350F / gas 4.
- Lay a few prunes and plum halves in the centre of each chicken escalope and roll up to form a sausage shape. Secure with toothpicks.
- Lay 4 pieces greaseproof paper out and place on lemon and grapefruit slices. Sit the chicken rolls on top, drizzle with olive oil then loosely wrap each roll in the paper and scrunch to seal in the heat. Bake in the oven for 25 minutes or until the chicken is cooked.
- Meanwhile heat the butter in a pan and sweat the onion and garlic for about five minutes until soft and translucent.
- Add the carrots and cumin and just cover with vegetable stock – you may not need all of it. Cook until the carrots are very soft, then drain in a sieve over a bowl to catch the stock.
- Place the carrots in a food processor and add a little stock and the orange zest. Blitz until smooth, adding more stock if necessary to make a smooth purée.
- Remove from the blender and return to the pan. Season and reheat gently before serving with the chicken parcels, to be unwrapped at the table.

781

SERVES 4–6 # Roast Chicken with Spicy Coconut Milk

- Preheat the oven to 220°C (200°C fan) / 425F / gas 7.
- Mix the coconut milk with chilli, lime juice and fish sauce and pour over the chicken. Leave to marinate for 30 minutes.
- Line a roasting tin with foil, then sit the chicken in it and pour over the marinade. Roast for 20 minutes then reduce the heat to 180°C (160°C fan) / 350F / gas 4 and cook for a further hour, basting with the marinade occasionally.
- Meanwhile heat the oil in a pan and sauté the potatoes until golden, then season well and keep warm.
- Rest the chicken for 15 minutes after cooking, then serve with the potatoes.

PREPARATION TIME:
10 MINUTES

COOKING TIME:
1 ½ HOURS

INGREDIENTS

1 x oven-ready chicken
400 ml / 14 fl. oz / 1 ½ cups
    coconut milk
1 red chilli (chili), chopped
1 lime, juiced
2 tbsp fish sauce
1 kg / 2 lb / 4 ¼ cups new potatoes,
    thickly sliced
4 tbsp olive oil
salt and pepper

Spicy Coconut Chicken

782

- Try whizzing the chilli, lime, fish sauce and a little coconut milk to a paste to make a more intense spicy marinade.

783

SERVES 4 # Chicken, Fig and Cinnamon Tagine

- Heat the oil in a large pan and cook the onions until golden and tender.
- Add the garlic and cook for a few minutes, then remove all from the pan with a slotted spoon.
- Increase the heat and brown the chicken thighs on all sides, then tip the onions back into the pan and sprinkle over the spices.
- Pour over the stock, add the dried figs and season, lower the heat and cook gently for about 45 minutes or until the sauce has thickened and the chicken is cooked. Stir in the fresh figs and heat through.
- Serve with couscous or a salad.

PREPARATION TIME:
10 MINUTES

COOKING TIME:
45 MINUTES

INGREDIENTS

2 tbsp olive oil
1 onion, peeled and finely sliced
2 cloves of garlic, finely sliced
4 chicken thighs, skinned
1 tsp ras-el-hanout spice mix
2 cinnamon sticks
1 large pinch dried chilli (chili) flakes
400 ml / 14 fl. oz / 1 ½ cups
    chicken stock
200 g / 7 oz / ¾ cup dried figs
8 fresh figs
salt and pepper

Chicken and Preserved Lemon Tagine

784

- If you can find preserved lemons, add a couple to the tagine for freshness.

785

SERVES 4

Caramel Ginger Chicken

PREPARATION TIME:
15 MINUTES

COOKING TIME:
30–40 MINUTES

INGREDIENTS

1 tbsp vegetable oil
1 shallot finely chopped
2 cloves of garlic, finely chopped
5 cm (1 in) piece ginger, grated
1 lemon, juiced and zested
150 g / 5 oz / ⅔ cup granulated sugar
175 ml / 6 fl. oz / ¾ cup water
2 tbsp soy sauce
8 chicken drumsticks or wings
salt and pepper
sesame seeds, to serve

- Preheat the oven to 180°C (160°C fan) / 350F / gas 4.
- Heat the oil in a pan and gently sweat the shallot and garlic. Add the ginger and cook for 2 minutes, then add the remaining ingredients, apart from the chicken, and simmer until thick and syrupy.
- In another pan, sear the chicken until golden on all sides, then place in a foil–lined roasting tin. Tip the marinade over the chicken, coat thoroughly and roast for about 30–40 minutes until dark, sticky and cooked through.
- Serve sprinkled with sesame seeds

Ginger Chicken with Crunchy Vegetables

786

- Souse shredded carrot and courgette in 1 tbsp salt, 2 tbsp vinegar and 1 tsp sugar, then drain and serve alongside.

787

SERVES 4

Tarragon Mustard Chicken

PREPARATION TIME:
5 MINUTES

COOKING TIME:
30 MINUTES

INGREDIENTS

2 tbsp grain mustard
1 tbsp Dijon mustard
1 bunch tarragon
2–3 tbsp olive oil
salt and pepper
½ lemon, juiced

- Preheat the oven to 200°C (180°C fan) / 400F / gas 6.
- Mix together the mustards, half the bunch of tarragon, chopped, oil and seasoning and use to coat the chicken. Leave to marinate for 30 minutes.
- Roast in a foil-lined tin for 30 minutes, until cooked through.
- Serve hot or cold sprinkled with tarragon and a squeeze of lemon juice.

Tarragon Mustard and Yogurt Chicken

788

- Make a milder version by adding 2 tbsp yogurt to the marinade.

789

SERVES 2

Paprika Chicken with Sautéed Vegetables

Creamy Paprika Chicken

790

- Stir in 150 ml / 5 fl. oz / ⅔ cup sour cream for a quick goulash-style sauté.

Slow Cooked Casserole

791

- Use chicken legs and 400 ml / 14 fl. oz / 1 ½ cups stock and slow cook in the oven for a winter dish.

PREPARATION TIME:
10 MINUTES

COOKING TIME:
10 MINUTES

INGREDIENTS

2 tbsp olive oil
2 chicken breasts, skinned and sliced
2 tsp smoked paprika
salt and pepper
100 g / 3 ½ oz / ½ cup chestnut
    mushrooms, sliced
100 g / 3 ½ oz / ½ cup mangetout
½ lemon, juiced

- Heat the oil in a pan and add the chicken and paprika. Sauté until golden, then add the mushrooms and seasoning and cook until the mushrooms are tender.
- Steam the mangetout over simmering water for 2 minutes, then add to the pan with lemon juice and a splash of water.
- Serve hot.

Chicken Tagine with Sumac and Olives

PREPARATION TIME:
15 MINUTES

COOKING TIME:
45 MINUTES

INGREDIENTS

2 tbsp olive oil
1 onion, peeled and thickly sliced
2 red peppers, deseeded and sliced
2 cloves of garlic, finely sliced
4 chicken legs, skinned
1 tbsp ground sumac
1 tsp ras-el-hanout spice mix
1 tsp ground (cilantro) coriander seeds
1 tsp cumin
4 preserved lemons, chopped
400 ml / 14 fl. oz / 1 ½ cups chicken stock
2 tbsp green olives
½ bunch parsley or coriander (cilantro), chopped
salt and pepper

- Heat the oil in a large pan and cook the onions and peppers until golden and tender.
- Add the garlic and cook for a few minutes, then remove all from the pan with a slotted spoon.
- Roll the chicken in the sumac making sure it's thoroughly coated.
- Increase the heat and brown the chicken on all sides, then tip the onions back into the pan and sprinkle over the spices.
- Pour over the stock and season, lower the heat and cook gently for about 45 minutes or until the sauce has thickened and the chicken is cooked.
- Add the olives to warm through, adjust the seasoning and sprinkle with herbs.

Chinese Chicken and Vegetables with Rice

PREPARATION TIME:
30 MINUTES

COOKING TIME: 20 MINUTES

INGREDIENTS

4 chicken breasts, skinned
2 carrots, peeled and sliced
knob of fresh ginger, peeled and sliced
2 tbsp vegetable oil
1 tsp sesame oil
100 ml / 3 ½ fl .oz / ½ cup chicken stock
1–2 tsp sugar
splash soy sauce
splash dry sherry
1 tsp cornflour (cornstarch)
2 tbsp vegetable oil
1 onion, peeled and finely chopped
1 garlic clove, finely chopped
3 eggs, beaten
500 g / 1 lb / 2 cups cooked white rice
3–4 spring onions (scallions), sliced
soy sauce
handful bean sprouts
handful cooked peas
salt and pepper

- Slice the chicken into strips.
- Heat the oils in a wok until smoking, then add the chicken and carrots and stir fry over a high heat until the chicken turns white.
- Remove the chicken from the pan and set aside. Discard the oil. Add the stock, sugar and soy and sherry/wine and bring to a rapid boil.
- Whisk in the cornflour until thickened then return the chicken to the pan for a few minutes to cook through.
- To make the rice: Heat the oil in a wok until nearly smoking then add the onion and garlic and stir fry briskly for 1 minute. Push to one side and add the eggs and cook for a couple of minutes until starting to set. Add the rice and meat and combine thoroughly. Stir in some soy sauce and the bean sprouts and peas and combine until everything is heated through.
- Serve the rice with the chicken and sprinkle with seasoning.

794

SERVES 4

Chicken Curry

- Heat the oil in a pan and sauté the onion for about 15–20 minutes or until golden-brown.
- Add the garlic and ginger and fry for another minute.
- Add the spices and stir well, then add 200ml water and cook gently for 10 minutes or so.
- Add the chicken to the sauce and top up with 300ml water. Cook at a simmer for around 20 minutes until the chicken and pumpkin are tender.
- Stir in the yogurt and heat through without boiling.
- Season before serving.

PREPARATION TIME:
15 MINUTES

COOKING TIME: 50 MINUTES

INGREDIENTS

3 tbsp vegetable oil
1 onion, peeled and finely sliced
2 cloves of garlic, chopped
1 tsp fresh ginger, grated
1 tsp ground coriander
pinch turmeric
½ tsp ground cumin
½ tsp garam masala, 1 tsp paprika
450 g / 1 lb / 2 cups chicken thigh meat, skinned and diced
100 g / 3 ½ oz / ½ cup plain yogurt
salt

795

SERVES 4

Chicken Masala

PREPARATION TIME:
20 MINUTES + MARINATING TIME

COOKING TIME:
30–35 MINUTES

INGREDIENTS

4 chicken breasts
3 tbsp plain yogurt
2 tbsp tandoori paste

2 tbsp vegetable oil
1 onion, 2 cloves of garlic
knob of ginger, cinnamon stick
4 cardamom pods
1 tsp ground cumin
1 tsp ground coriander
½ tsp turmeric, 1 tsp paprika
400 g / 3 ½ fl. oz / ½ cup chicken stock
salt and pepper
flaked (slivered) almonds, to serve

- Skin and chop the chicken, then marinate for at least 1 hour in the yogurt and tandoori paste.
- Peel and finely slice the onion, garlic and ginger. Lightly crush the cardamom pods.
- Heat the oil in a pan and fry the onion until golden. Add the garlic, ginger and spices and fry for 2–3 minutes.
- Add the chicken, shaking off any excess marinade, and sauté over high heat until almost golden, then add the remaining marinade, chopped tomatoes and stock, and simmer for 20 minutes.
- Season with salt and pepper, then sprinkle with flaked almonds and serve.

796

SERVES 4–6

Gingerbread and Port Chicken

PREPARATION TIME:
20 MINUTES

COOKING TIME:
1 HOUR 40 MINUTES

INGREDIENTS

1 oven-ready chicken
30 g / 1 oz butter, softened
salt and pepper

thyme sprigs, 1 star anise
8 shallots, peeled
2 cloves of garlic, unpeeled
2 tbsp olive oil
1–2 tsp flour
200 ml / 7 fl. oz / ¾ cup port
400 ml / 14 fl. oz / 1 ½ cups chicken stock
100 g / 3 ½ oz / ½ cup gingerbread
basil, to garnish

- Preheat oven to 220°C (200°C fan) / 425F / gas 7.
- Rub the chicken all over with the butter, season well and push the thyme inside the cavity. Place in a roasting tin and roast for 20 minutes.
- Turn the heat down to 180°C (160°C fan) / 350F / gas 4 and add the shallots and garlic and roast for another hour or so until the juices run clear. Check the shallots occasionally to check they aren't burning – if so, remove.
- Transfer the chicken to a platter to rest, covered with foil and place the pan on the heat. Add the shallots back into the pan if necessary.
- Stir in the flour and cook out for a couple of minutes, then whisk in the port. Simmer until reduced by half, then whisk in the stock and star anise. Leave to simmer for 10–15 minutes.
- Sprinkle the gingerbread crumbs over the chicken and serve with the port sauce.

797

SERVES 4

Martinique-style Chicken Fricassee

**PREPARATION TIME:
10 MINUTES**

**COOKING TIME:
30–40 MINUTES**

INGREDIENTS

40 g / 1 oz butter
1 tbsp vegetable oil
4 chicken legs
2 large onions, peeled and sliced
2 cloves of garlic, finely sliced
1 tsp ground allspice
16 chestnut mushrooms, halved
2 carrots, chopped
3 sprigs rosemary
1 tsp paprika
4 tomatoes, quartered
200 ml / 7 fl. oz / ¾ cup chicken stock

- Heat the butter and oil in a large pan and brown the chicken legs on both sides. Add the onions, garlic and allspice and cook until softened and golden.
- Add the mushrooms, carrots, rosemary and paprika and sauté until the mushrooms have started to soften, then add the tomatoes and stock.
- Simmer for 15 minutes or until the chicken is cooked through.
- Serve with white rice.

Creamy Chicken Fricassee   798

- Add 100 ml / 3 ½ fl. oz / ½ cup coconut milk for a creamy finish.

799

SERVES 4

Chicken Korma Bake

**PREPARATION TIME:
15 MINUTES**

**COOKING TIME:
15–20 MINUTES**

INGREDIENTS

40 g / 1 oz butter
1 onion, peeled and finely sliced
2 cloves of garlic, finely chopped
3 chicken breasts, skinned and chopped
3–4 tbsp korma paste
250 ml / 9 fl. oz / 1 cup fromage frais
¼ bunch fresh coriander (cilantro)
½ lemon, juiced
salt and pepper

- Preheat the oven to 180°C (160C° fan) / 350F / gas 4.
- Heat the butter in a pan and cook the onion and garlic until golden.
- Add the chicken and korma paste and cook until the chicken is golden.
- Stir in the fromage frais, coriander and lemon juice and season, then tip into a gratin dish.
- Bake in the oven for 15–20 minutes until bubbling.

Korma Bake with Broccoli   800

- Adding florets of steamed broccoli adds vitamins and colour.

801

SERVES 4

Chicken Cari

- Heat the oil in a pan and brown the chicken legs on both sides, then transfer to a dish.
- Whiz the garlic and ginger to a paste with a little water.
- Add the onion to the pan and cook until golden, then add the garlic paste and cook for a few minutes.
- Add the chicken back to the pan with the tomatoes, thyme, saffron and seasoning and cook for 15–20 minutes until cooked through, adding a splash of water if the pan looks fry.
- Serve with white rice.

PREPARATION TIME:
5 MINUTES

COOKING TIME:
30–35 MINUTES

INGREDIENTS

2 tbsp vegetable oil
4 chicken legs
2 onions, peeled and finely chopped
3 cloves of garlic, finely chopped
knob of fresh ginger, finely chopped
10 tomatoes, chopped
3 sprigs thyme
pinch saffron, soaked in 1 tbsp water
salt and pepper

Chicken Cari with Roasted Aubergine

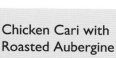

802

- Roast a roughly chopped aubergine in the oven with a little chilli and dried oregano and serve alongside.

803

SERVES 4

Potted Chicken with Turmeric

- Preheat the oven to 160°C (140°C fan) / 325F / gas 3.
- Place the chicken legs in a roasting tin, pour over the oil, season and cover with foil and slowly cook for about 45–60 minutes until cooked through and falling off the bone. Set aside to rest.
- Meanwhile heat the butter in a pan and gently cook the celery.
- Blanch the runner beans briefly in boiling salted water, then drain and add to the celery.
- Shred the chicken meat finely and stir into the pan with turmeric. Season generously.
- Pack into small ramekins and chill until needed.

PREPARATION TIME:
10 MINUTES

COOKING TIME:
60 MINUTES

INGREDIENTS

4 chicken legs
100 ml / 3 ½ fl. oz / ½ cup olive oil
salt and pepper
60 g / 2 oz butter
1 stick celery, finely chopped
½ tsp turmeric
150 g / 5 oz / ⅔ cup runner beans, finely sliced

Potted Chicken with Mango Chutney

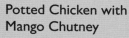

804

- Try stirring 1 tbsp mango chutney into the chicken before chilling for a fruity backnote.

805

SERVES 4

Chicken with Tarragon Tomato Sauce

Chicken with Herbed Tomato Sauce

 806

- Adding sprigs of rosemary and parsley will add extra heft to the herby flavour.

Chicken with Mascarpone Tomato Sauce

807

- Add 2 large tbsp mascarpone for a creamy sauce and toss with pasta.

PREPARATION TIME:
10 MINUTES

COOKING TIME:
40 MINUTES

INGREDIENTS

2 tbsp olive oil
1 onion, peeled and finely sliced
2 cloves of garlic, finely sliced
1 stick celery, finely sliced
4 chicken legs
3 carrots, peeled and cut into
    short lengths
12 baby turnips, scrubbed
400 ml / 14 fl. oz / 1 ½ cups passata
300 ml / 10 fl. oz / 1 ¼ cups chicken
    stock
salt and pepper
2 large sprigs tarragon

- Heat the oil in a large pan and sweat the onion, garlic and celery until softened.
- Add the chicken legs, increase the heat and brown on both sides.
- Add the carrots and turnips, cook for a few minutes, then pour in the passata and stock.
- Simmer for 25–30 minutes or until the chicken is cooked and the vegetables are tender.
- Season and stir through the tarragon before serving.

808

SERVES 4

Chicken Colombo with Bulghur

- Heat the oil and sear the chicken on all sides until golden. Remove with a slotted spoon and set aside.
- Add the onions and carrots and cook until softened, then add the garlic and spices and cook for 2 minutes.
- Add the chillies, cubed sweet potatoes, spring onions stock and tomatoes and bring to a simmer. Return the chicken to the pan.
- Reduce the heat, cover with a lid and cook for 25 minutes until the potatoes are tender.
- Meanwhile soak the bulghur wheat in the hot stock for 25–30 minutes until tender. Drain off any excess liquid and season.
- Serve the chicken with the bulghur on the side.

PREPARATION TIME:
20 MINUTES

COOKING TIME:
35 MINUTES

INGREDIENTS

1 tbsp vegetable oil
4 chicken thighs
1 onion, peeled and chopped
2 carrots, peeled and cut into batons
3 cloves of garlic, crushed
2 tbsp curry powder
6 sprigs thyme leaves
1 tsp ground allspice
½ tsp ground cinnamon
2 bay leaves
1–2 Scotch Bonnet chillies (chilies)
8 spring onions (scallions), ends trimmed
750 g / 1 ⅓ lb sweet potatoes, peeled
500 ml / 1 pint / 2 cups chicken stock
400 g / 14 oz / 1 ½ cups canned tomatoes
300 g / 10 oz / 1 ¼ cups bulghur wheat
400 ml / 14 fl. oz / 1 ½ cups chicken stock
salt and pepper

Chicken with Herby Bulghur Wheat

809

- Adding 1 bunch parsley or some mint to the soaked bulghur will add herby freshness.

810

SERVES 4

Chicken Ratatouille

- Preheat the oven to 200°C (180°C fan) / 400F / gas 6.
- Roast the chicken legs in the oven with a little oil and seasoning for 25–30 minutes until cooked. Set aside to rest.
- Meanwhile heat the oil in a pan and cook the onions until deep gold and sweet.
- Add the aubergines and courgettes, then cook for 2 minutes. Add the garlic and cook for 2 minutes, then add the peppers and cook for 5 minutes.
- Add the tomatoes and coriander seeds and leave to simmer for at least 30 minutes over a very low heat, stirring occasionally, until the vegetables are very soft. Season.
- Serve the chicken with the ratatouille and sprinkle with rosemary sprigs.

PREPARATION TIME:
10 MINUTES

COOKING TIME:
50 MINUTES

INGREDIENTS

4 chicken legs
2 tbsp olive oil
4–6 tbsp olive oil
2 onions, peeled and finely sliced
2 aubergines (eggplant), cut in half lengthways and finely sliced
2 courgettes (zucchini), chopped
2 garlic cloves, finely chopped
3 red peppers, seeded and cut into strips
400 g / 14 oz / 1 ½ cups chopped tomatoes
1 tsp coriander seeds, crushed
salt and pepper
rosemary sprigs, to serve

Chicken Ratatouille Tart

811

- Use a sheet of ready-rolled puff pastry as a base, top with the ratatouille and shredded cooked chicken, then bake in the oven for 20–25 minutes until golden.

812

SERVES 4

Tandoori Chicken with Herbed Yogurt

PREPARATION TIME:
25–30 MINUTES

COOKING TIME:
30 MINUTES

INGREDIENTS

4 chicken drumsticks
1 cucumber, thickly sliced
1 tsp salt
150 ml / 5 fl. oz / ⅔ cup plain yogurt
½ bunch mint leaves, finely sliced
1 clove of garlic, crushed
flatbreads, to serve

FOR THE MARINADE

300 ml / 10 fl. oz / 1 ¾ cups plain yogurt
1 tsp ground cumin
1 tsp ground coriander
1 tsp garam masala
1 tsp ground cinnamon
1 ½ tsp tandoori chilli (chili) powder
1 tsp caster (superfine) sugar
1 clove garlic, minced
salt and pepper

- Prepare the tandoori marinade by mixing together all the ingredients for the marinade in a mixing bowl. Add the chicken, mix well, then cover and chill for at least 1 hour.
- Preheat the oven to 200°C (180°C fan) / 400F / gas 6.
- Roast the drumsticks in a foil-lined roasting tin for about 30 minutes until golden and cooked through.
- Meanwhile toss the cucumber with the salt and leave to drain in a sieve to draw out excess water.
- Mix the yogurt with the mint, garlic and seasoning and set aside.
- Pat the cucumber dry, then serve on a platter with the drumsticks and the herby yogurt and flatbreads alongside.

Tandoori Chicken with Potatoes

813

- Roast wedges of potatoes alongside the chicken so they soak up all the flavours.

814

SERVES 4

Chicken in Squid Ink with Pappardelle

PREPARATION TIME:
15 MINUTES

COOKING TIME:
30–40 MINUTES

INGREDIENTS

2 tbsp olive oil
4 chicken breasts, skin on
1 onion, peeled and finely sliced
2 cloves of garlic, finely sliced
4 rashers streaky smoked bacon, chopped
8 baby carrots, peeled and trimmed
1 red chilli (chili), deseeded and finely chopped
1 sachet squid ink, from your fishmonger
300 ml / 10 fl. oz / 1 ¼ cups chicken stock
salt and pepper
300 g / 10 oz pappardelle pasta
40 g /1 oz butter
½ bunch parsley, finely chopped

- Heat the oil in a pan and brown the chicken skin side down until golden, then remove and set aside.
- Add the onion and garlic to the pan and cook until lightly golden, then add the bacon and cook until golden.
- Add the carrots, chilli, squid ink and stock and chicken breasts and simmer for about 20 minutes, or until the chicken is cooked through.
- Remove the chicken and carrots with a slotted spoon and reduce the sauce until thickened and to your liking. Season.
- Cook the pasta in boiling salted water according to packet instructions, then drain and toss with butter.
- Thickly slice the chicken and serve on top of the pappardelle with the carrots and sauce spooned around. Sprinkle with parsley.

Chicken Seafood Pappardelle

815

- Adding raw prawns 5 minutes before the end of cooking adds a burst of seafood flavour.

SERVES 4

Chicken, Prune and Sweet Potato Tagine

Chicken with Grated Carrot Salad   817

- Toss 2 grated carrots with the juice of 1 orange, 1 tsp mustard seeds and extra virgin olive oil and serve alongside for zingy freshness.

Chicken Tagine Wraps   818

- Use any leftovers in tortilla wraps and drizzle with plain yogurt.

PREPARATION TIME:
10 MINUTES

COOKING TIME:
55 MINUTES

....

INGREDIENTS

2 tbsp olive oil
1 onion, peeled and finely sliced
2 cloves of garlic, finely sliced
small knob fresh ginger, peeled
    and grated
4 chicken drumsticks, skinned
2 sweet potatoes, peeled and
    roughly chopped
1 tsp ras-el-hanout spice mix
2 cinnamon sticks
1 tsp ground cumin
1 large pinch dried chilli (chili) flakes
400 ml / 14 fl. oz / 1 ½ cups chicken
    stock
200 g / 7 oz / ¾ cup prunes
1 lemon, juiced
sprigs of mint
salt and pepper

- Heat the oil in a large pan and cook the onions until golden and tender.
- Add the garlic and ginger and cook for a few minutes, then remove all from the pan with a slotted spoon.
- Increase the heat and brown the chicken thighs on all sides, then tip the onions back into the pan with the sweet potato and sprinkle over the spices.
- Pour over the stock, add the prunes and season, lower the heat and cook gently for about 45 minutes or until the sauce has thickened and the chicken is cooked. Stir in the lemon juice and mint and heat through.
- Serve with couscous.

819

SERVES 4

Roast Chicken with Spiced Risotto

PREPARATION TIME:
10 MINUTES

COOKING TIME:
25 MINUTES

INGREDIENTS

4 chicken breasts, skin on
2 tbsp olive oil
2 tbsp olive oil
40 g /1 oz butter
1 onion, peeled and finely chopped
2 cloves of garlic, finely chopped
1 cinnamon stick
1 star anise
320 g / 11 oz / 1 ⅓ cups risotto rice
100 ml / 3 ½ fl. oz / ½ cup dry
    white wine
1 l / 2 ¼ pints / 4 ¼ cups chicken or
    vegetable stock with pinch saffron
    threads soaking
salt and pepper
3 tbsp butter
120 g / 4 oz / ½ cup Mimolette cheese,
    grated

- Preheat the oven to 200°C (180°C fan) / 400F / gas 6.
- Place the chicken in a roasting tin, drizzle with oil, season and roast for 20 minutes.
- Heat the oil and butter in a large pan and add the onion and garlic. Cook until soft and translucent. Add the rice and stir to coat in the butter and add the spices. Pour in the wine and stir the rice while the wine is absorbed.
- Once the wine has cooked in, reduce the heat a little and add the hot stock, a ladleful at a time, stirring fairly continuously.
- Keep stirring in the stock and tasting the rice. After about 15–20 minutes the rice should be soft but with a slight bite.
- Season and remove from the heat. Add the butter and cheese and leave to melt into the risotto. Serve immediately with the chicken.

Chicken with Spiced Couscous

820

- Replace the risotto with couscous.

821

SERVES 4

Thai Chicken Curry with Rice

PREPARATION TIME:
10 MINUTES

COOKING TIME:
20–25 MINUTES

INGREDIENTS

1 tbsp vegetable oil
2 banana shallots, finely chopped
1 tsp fresh ginger, grated
1 stalk lemongrass, finely chopped
100 g / 3 ½ oz / ½ cup fine green beans,
    cut into thirds
2–3 tbsp Thai red curry paste
400 ml / 14 fl. oz / 1 ½ cups coconut
    milk
2 chicken breasts, skinned
1–2 tbsp fish sauce
1–2 tsp sugar
1 lime, juiced
Thai sticky rice, cooked

- Heat the oil in a wok and fry the shallots, ginger and lemongrass for 2 minutes until softened.
- Add the green beans and fry for a further 2 minutes.
- Stir in the curry paste and cook out for 2 minutes, stirring. Add the coconut milk and leave to simmer for 10 minutes until thickened.
- Slice the chicken breasts into 1cm thick slices and add to the curry. Stir in the fish sauce and sugar and simmer until the chicken is cooked.
- Adjust the seasoning and add the lime juice.
- Serve with Thai sticky rice.

Banana Leaf Parcels

822

- If you can source them, wrap a spoonful of rice and curry in a leaf then steam or bake for 10 minutes for people to open at the table.

823

SERVES 2

Chicken Vegetable Noodles

- Cook the noodles in boiling salted water according to packet instructions.
- Heat the oils in a wok and sauté the chicken over high heat until patchily golden.
- Add the carrots, mushrooms, garlic and ginger and stir fry for 2–3 minutes until the mushrooms are tender.
- Add the noodles to the pan with a little cooking water and toss to combine, then add the sauces and spring greens. Heat through until bubbling and the greens are wilted, then serve.

PREPARATION TIME:
10 MINUTES

COOKING TIME:
10 MINUTES

INGREDIENTS

2 nests of dried egg noodles
1 tbsp groundnut oil
1 tsp sesame oil
2 chicken thighs, skinned, deboned and chopped
1 carrot, peeled and cut into thin batons
200 g / 7 oz / ¾ cup field or Chinese mushrooms, cleaned
2 cloves of garlic, finely sliced
1 tsp fresh ginger, grated
3–4 tbsp soy sauce
2 tbsp oyster sauce
100 ml / 3 ½ fl. oz / ½ cup chicken stock
150 g / 5 oz / ⅔ cup spring greens, shredded

Chilli Chicken Noodles

824

- Finely chopped red chilli (chili) or 1 tsp chilli oil will add fire.

825

SERVES 4

Stuffed Chicken Breast and Lettuce Flan

- Preheat the oven to 200°C (180°C fan) / 400F / gas 6.
- Season the outside of the chicken and lay on a board.
- Heat the butter in a pan and sweat the leeks until soft but not coloured. Leave to cool for 5 minutes, then stir through the cream cheese, seasoning and lemon zest.
- Spoon the leek stuffing down the middle of the chicken, roll the meat into a sausage shape and tie with cooking string to secure. Roast in the oven for 30–45 minutes. Leave to rest before carving.
- Meanwhile heat the butter in a pan and sweat the shallots for a few minutes. Stir in the lettuces and season.
- Whisk together the eggs, cream and water and a little salt. Stir the lettuce and shallots into the mixture then pour into greased muffin tins.
- Bake in the oven for 20 minutes until puffed and golden. Serve alongside slices of chicken.

PREPARATION TIME:
15 MINUTES

COOKING TIME:
45 MINUTES

INGREDIENTS

1 chicken, boned out (ask your butcher)
50 g / 1 ¾ oz / ¼ cup butter
2 leeks, trimmed and finely sliced
200 g / 7 oz / ¾ cup cream cheese
salt and pepper
½ lemon, zested
30 g / 1 oz butter
2 shallots, finely chopped
2 little gem lettuces, shredded
12 eggs
120 ml / 4 fl. oz / ½ cup double (heavy) cream
120 ml / 4 fl. oz / ½ cup water

Chicken stuffed with Mushroom Flan

826

- Substitute 200 g / 7 oz / ¾ finely sliced chestnut mushrooms for the lettuces for a more substantial accompaniment.

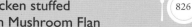

827

SERVES 4

Chicken and Beef Kebabs

Balsamic Meat Kebabs 828

- Try drizzling the meats with balsamic instead for a sweet sharp flavour.

Surf and Turf 829

- Alternate large prawns with the other ingredients.

PREPARATION TIME:
10 MINUTES

COOKING TIME:
10 MINUTES

INGREDIENTS

4 chicken breasts, skinned and cubed
1 tbsp thyme leaves
1 tbsp olive oil
400 g / 14 oz rump steak, cubed
2 tbsp teriyaki sauce
8–12 cherry tomatoes
1 green pepper, deseeded and roughly chopped
1 onion, peeled and cut into large chunks
salt and pepper

- Mix the chicken with thyme olive oil and seasoning. Mix the steak with teriyaki and pepper.
- Thread onto soaked wooden skewers alternating with the vegetables.
- Griddle or barbecue over high heat – the chicken will take about 10 minutes, the steak much less, if you like it pink.
- Serve hot or warm.

830

SERVES 2–4 # Tandoori Chicken

- Heat the oil in a wok and sauté the chicken over high heat until golden.
- Mix together the ingredients for the tandoori sauce.
- Place a banana leaf in each bowl, spoon chicken into the centre and spoon over the tandoori sauce. Serve with lime wedges.

PREPARATION TIME:
10 MINUTES

COOKING TIME:
10 MINUTES

INGREDIENTS

4 chicken thighs, skinned, deboned
    and cubed
1 tbsp groundnut oil
banana leaves
lime wedges

FOR THE SAUCE

1 tsp ground cumin
1 tsp ground coriander
1 tsp garam masala
1 tsp ground cinnamon
1 ½ tsp tandoori chilli (chili) powder
1 tsp caster (superfine) sugar
1 tsp paprika
1 clove of garlic, minced
salt and pepper
200 ml / 7 fl. oz / ¾ cup plain yogurt

Tandoori Parathas

831

- Roll the chicken and sauce into ready-made parathas or chapattis for a filling snack.

832

SERVES 4 # Chicken, Sweet Potato and Grape Stew

- Heat the oil in a large pan and cook the onions until golden and tender.
- Add the garlic and ginger and cook for a few minutes, then remove all from the pan with a slotted spoon.
- Increase the heat and brown the chicken thighs on all sides, then tip the onions back into the pan with the sweet potato and sprinkle over the spices.
- Pour over the stock, add the grapes and season, lower the heat and cook gently for about 45 minutes or until the sauce has thickened and the chicken is cooked. Stir in the almonds, lemon juice and mint and heat through.
- Serve with couscous.

PREPARATION TIME:
10 MINUTES

COOKING TIME:
55 MINUTES

INGREDIENTS

2 tbsp olive oil
1 onion, peeled and finely sliced
2 cloves of garlic, finely sliced
small knob fresh ginger, peeled
    and grated
4 chicken drumsticks, skinned
2 sweet potatoes, peeled and
    roughly chopped
1 tsp ras-el-hanout spice mix
2 cinnamon sticks
1 tsp ground cumin
1 large pinch dried chilli (chili) flakes
400 ml / 14 fl. oz / 1 ½ cups chicken
    stock
200 g / 7 oz / ¾ cup green grapes,
    seedless
2 tbsp whole almonds, skinned
1 lemon, juiced
sprigs of mint
salt and pepper

Grated Courgette Salad

833

- Grate a courgette (zucchini) into a bowl and mix with lemon juice and toasted black onion seeds and serve alongside.

834

SERVES 4

Grilled Chicken with Paprika

PREPARATION TIME:
10 MINUTES

COOKING TIME:
50 MINUTES

INGREDIENTS

4 chicken drumsticks, skin on
2 tbsp olive oil
1 tbsp smoked paprika
4–6 tbsp olive oil
2 onions, peeled and finely sliced
2 aubergines (eggplant), cut in half
    lengthways and finely sliced
1 courgette (zucchini), diced
2 garlic cloves, finely chopped
3 red peppers, seeded and cut
    into strips
400 g / 14 oz / 1 ½ cups chopped
    tomatoes
1 tsp coriander seeds, crushed
salt and pepper
handful fresh basil leaves
½ lemon, juiced

- Preheat the oven to 200°C (180°C fan) / 400F / gas 6.
- Roast the chicken legs in the oven rubbed with the oil and paprika and seasoning for 25–30 minutes until cooked. Set aside to rest.
- Meanwhile heat the oil in a pan and cook the onions until deep gold and sweet.
- Add the aubergines and cook for 2 minutes, then add the courgettes and cook for 2 minutes, then add the peppers and garlic and cook for 5 minutes.
- Add the tomatoes and coriander seeds and leave to simmer for at least 30 minutes over a very low heat, stirring occasionally, until the vegetables are very soft. Season and sprinkle over the basil
- Squeeze the lemon over the chicken and serve with the ratatouille.

Chilli Chicken with Ratatouille 835

- Spicy chilli (chili) paste or even harissa can be rubbed onto the chicken before roasting.

836

SERVES 2

Chinese Chicken with Noodles

PREPARATION TIME:
5 MINUTES

COOKING TIME:
25 MINUTES

INGREDIENTS

2 chicken breasts, skinned
500 ml / 1 pint / 2 cups weak
    chicken stock
2 nests vermicelli noodles
1 tbsp vegetable oil
1 tbsp sesame oil
1 bunch spring onions (scallions), finely
    chopped
1 carrot, peeled and diced
1 courgette (zucchini), diced
1 cm (½ in) piece ginger, grated
2 cloves of garlic, finely sliced
4 tbsp soy sauce

- Poach the chicken in the stock very gently for about 20 minutes or until cooked through. Set aside to rest, reserving the chicken stock.
- Soak the noodles in the chicken stock according to packet instructions and drain when tender.
- Meanwhile heat the oils in a wok and sauté the carrots, courgettes, spring onions, ginger and garlic over a high heat, then add the noodles and soy sauce.
- Toss well to heat through and serve topped with sliced chicken.

Chinese Chicken Noodle Soup 837

- You could serve this in deep bowls with the reserved chicken stock ladled over piping hot.

838

SERVES 4

Chicken with Chilli Prawns

Chicken with Seafood **839**

- Chicken works well with all seafood – try adding squid rings, mussels or clams for briny savour.

Chicken Chilli Prawn Pasta **840**

- Toss with spaghetti and sprinkle with more parsley.

PREPARATION TIME:
5 MINUTES

COOKING TIME:
30 MINUTES

···

INGREDIENTS

80 ml / 2 ½ fl. oz / ⅓ cup olive oil
4 chicken legs, skin on
2 cloves of garlic, finely sliced
1 red chilli (chili), finely sliced
16 large prawns (shrimps),
    raw and shell on
½ bunch parsley, finely chopped
salt and pepper
½ lemon, juiced

- Heat the oil in a deep–sided pan and brown the chicken on all sides.
- Lower the heat and leave to cook until the juices run clear when pierced with the point of a knife.
- Add the garlic and chilli and cook briefly, then add the prawns and toss until the prawns turn pink and are cooked.
- Sprinkle over parsley and seasoning, then squeeze over the lemon juice and serve in bowls with crusty bread.

841

SERVES 4

Sweet and Sour Chicken Soup

PREPARATION TIME:
15 MINUTES

COOKING TIME: 20 MINUTES

....

INGREDIENTS

500 g / 1 lb / 2 cups chicken thigh meat,
    sliced
1 tbsp vegetable oil
1 yellow pepper, deseeded and
    finely sliced
1 red onion, peeled and thickly sliced
100 g / 3 ½ oz / ½ cup dried apricots,
    halved

FOR THE SAUCE

125 ml / 4 fl. oz / ½ cup pineapple juice
Splash dry sherry or Shaoxing
    rice wine
2 tbsp ketchup
2 tbsp soy sauce
2 tbsp Chinese vinegar or red
    wine vinegar
400 ml / 14 fl. oz / 1 ½ cups chicken
    stock
1 tsp cornflour (cornstarch)

- Heat the vegetable oil in a wok until smoking, then add the chicken and stir fry over a high heat until the chicken turns white.
- Remove the chicken from the pan and set aside. Discard the oil.
- Heat the oil in the wok again and stir fry the vegetables over a high heat for 4 minutes.
- Mix together the sauce ingredients with the cornflour. Add the chicken back to the pan with the sauce and apricots, bubble up until thickened and serve hot.

Sweet and Sour Noodle Soup

842

- Add a nest of noodles to the soup.

843

SERVES 4

Spicy Skewers and Vegetable Ratatouille

PREPARATION TIME:
20 MINUTES

COOKING TIME:
30 MINUTES

....

INGREDIENTS

4 chicken breasts, skinned and cubed
2 tbsp olive oil
1 tbsp garam masala
1 tbsp sesame seeds
1 red onion, peeled

FOR THE RATATOUILLE

100 ml / 3 ½ fl. oz / ½ cup olive oil
1 onion, peeled and chopped
1 large carrot, peeled and diced
300 g / 10 oz / 1 cup waxy potatoes,
    quartered
½ swede, peeled and diced
2–3 cloves of garlic, finely sliced
1 aubergine (eggplant), diced
2 courgettes (zucchini), diced
½ tbsp ground cumin
salt and pepper

- Heat the oil in a large pan and gently cook the onion until pale gold, then add the carrots, potatoes and swede one at a time, cooking each for a few minutes before adding the next one.
- Add the garlic, aubergine and courgette, spices and salt and pepper, add a glass of water, partially cover with a lid and simmer gently for about 20 minutes. When the vegetables are completely tender, season and set aside to cool slightly.
- Meanwhile toss the chicken with the oil, spices and seasoning. Cut the onion into 8 small wedges and thread onto skewers alternating with the chicken. Griddle over high heat until golden and cooked through.
- Serve with the ratatouille at room temperature.

Spicy Skewers
with Tomato Ratatouille

844

- Add canned tomatoes for variation.

845
SERVES 4

Chicken with Juniper and Vegetables

- Heat the oil in a pan and brown skin side down until crisp and golden. Turn over, add the juniper berries, partially cover with a lid and cook gently on the other side.
- In a separate pan fry the field mushrooms with the butter and seasoning until tender.
- Once the chicken is cooked, remove from the pan and set aside to keep warm. Heat the remaining butter in a pan and sweat the onion, mushrooms and carrots until tender. Once the carrots are soft, stir in the sour cream and season. Stir through the parsley.
- Serve the chicken with the mushrooms and sautéed vegetables.

PREPARATION TIME:
10 MINUTES

COOKING TIME:
30 MINUTES

INGREDIENTS

4 chicken thighs
2 tbsp olive oil
salt and pepper
4 juniper berries, lightly crushed
30 g / 1 oz butter
4 flat field mushrooms
30 g / 1 oz butter
1 onion, peeled and finely chopped
200 g / 7 oz / ¾ cup chestnut
　mushrooms, quartered
2 carrots, peeled and finely diced
150 ml / 5 fl. oz / ⅔ cup sour cream
¼ bunch parsley, chopped

Chicken with Autumn Vegetables
846

- This tastes really good with diced sautéed swede, turnips or parsnips.

847
SERVES 4

Thai Red Chicken Curry

- Heat the groundnut oil in a large casserole dish over a moderate heat. Sauté the diced chicken in batches until golden brown all over. Remove and drain on a plate lined with kitchen paper.
- Add the onion, ginger and garlic to the dish and sauté over a reduced heat for 4–5 minutes, stirring occasionally. Add the paste and fry gently for 1–2 minutes, stirring occasionally.
- Add the chicken and potato back to the dish, then cover with the stock and add the peas. Simmer gently for 25–30 minutes until all is tender, then add the limes. Adjust the seasoning with the sugar, fish sauce and pepper.
- Serve with basil leaves.

PREPARATION TIME:
15–20 MINUTES

COOKING TIME:
30 MINUTES

INGREDIENTS

50 ml / 1 ½ fl. oz / ⅓ cup groundnut oil
500 g / 1 lb / 2 cups diced chicken thigh
　meat
1 onion, finely sliced
1 tbsp ginger, minced
3 cloves garlic, minced
110 g / 3 ½ oz / ½ cup Thai red
　curry paste
1 sweet potato, peeled and diced
750 ml / 1 ¼ pints / 3 cups chicken stock
100 g / 3 ½ oz / ½ cup frozen peas
1 tbsp palm or brown sugar
1 lime, quartered
2 tbsp fish sauce
salt and pepper
basil leaves

Thai Pork and Chicken Curry
848

- This curry works well with any meat – pork is particularly good with chicken.

849

MAKES 6

Chicken Crumble Blini

Chicken Crumble Pancakes

850

- Try wrapping normal pancakes around the chicken mixture, sprinkling with breadcrumbs and grilling until crisp.

Chicken Crumble

851

- Alternatively simply tip the chicken into a gratin dish, sprinkle with breadcrumbs and grill until golden.

PREPARATION TIME:
30 MINUTES

COOKING TIME:
30 MINUTES

....

INGREDIENTS

2 lemons, sliced into 8 thick slices
100 g / 3 ½ oz / ½ cup caster
    (superfine) sugar
1 clove of garlic
40 g / 1 oz buckwheat flour
40 g / 1 oz plain (all-purpose) flour
½ sachet easy-blend yeast
¼ tsp salt, ¼ tsp sugar
50 ml / 1 ¾ oz milk
1 tbsp crème fraiche or sour cream
30 g / 1 oz butter, 1 egg, separated
40 g / 1 oz butter
4 chicken thighs, deboned and chopped
1 shallot, finely chopped
1 clove of garlic, finely chopped
1 red chilli (chili), deseeded and chopped
salt and pepper
300 g / 10 oz / 1 ½ cups breadcrumbs
vegetable oil

- The day before, place the sliced lemons in a small pan with 150 ml salted water, boil, then remove from the heat and leave to cool. Drain.

- Simmer 100 ml water and sugar in a pan, then add the garlic and lemons and cook over the lowest possible heat for 12 hours. Store in a sterilised jar until needed.

- Mix the flours, yeast salt and sugar in a bowl. Pour the milk and sour cream into a measuring jug and top up to 250 ml / 9 fl. oz / 1 cup mark with water. Pour into a pan, add the butter and heat until the butter melts and the mixture is blood temperature.

- Whisk in the egg yolk, pour into the flours and leave covered for about 2–3 hours in a warm place. Whisk the egg whites to stiff peaks and fold into the batter.

- Meanwhile, fry the chicken with the shallot and garlic and chilli in the butter, then season and spoon into a gratin dish. Sprinkle over the breadcrumbs and dot with butter then grill until golden and crisp.

- Melt a little vegetable oil in a blini or frying pan and fry a large heaped tablespoon of batter at a time for about 2 minutes each side or until golden. Once cooked keep warm in a low oven.

- Serve the warm blini topped with chicken crumble and a slice of confit lemon.

852

SERVES 4

Chicken Biryani and Cardamom Rice

- Heat the oil in a pan and add the chicken, skin side down and cook until golden brown.
- Add the onions and cardamom and cook until golden.
- Add the rice and 800 ml water and the rest of the spices and leave to cook gently for about 25–30 minutes until the rice has cooked and the liquid evaporated. Check as you may need to add more water as the rice absorbs it.
- Adjust the seasoning and serve in the pan or in individual bowls.

PREPARATION TIME:
10 MINUTES

COOKING TIME:
50 MINUTES

INGREDIENTS

4 tbsp groundnut oil
4 chicken thighs, skin on
2 onions, peeled and finely chopped
2 cloves of garlic, chopped
4 cardamom pods
½ tsp ground ginger
1 tsp garam masala
½ tsp turmeric
500 g / 1 lb / 2 cups basmati rice
fresh coriander (cilantro)

Chicken Biryani with Peas and Potatoes

853

- Add diced potatoes and peas with the rice to make this even more substantial.

854

SERVES 4–6

Cameroon Chicken

- Marinate the chicken pieces with ginger, parsley, chilli and garlic and some seasoning for at least 1 hour.
- Heat the oil in a large pan and fry the onion until golden, then add the chicken pieces and cook until browned all over.
- Add the plantains and 300 ml water and simmer for 20 minutes, then add the tomatoes.
- Season and serve with coriander and rice.

PREPARATION TIME:
10 MINUTES

COOKING TIME:
40 MINUTES

INGREDIENTS

1 oven-ready chicken, jointed
2 cm (½ in) piece fresh ginger, grated
1 tbsp parsley, finely chopped
1 green chilli (chili), finely sliced
1 clove of garlic, finely chopped
salt and pepper
2 tbsp groundnut oil
1 onion, peeled and finely chopped
3 plantains, peeled and chopped
4–6 ripe tomatoes, quartered
coriander (cilantro) sprigs

Cameroon Chicken with Peppers and Carrots

855

- It's traditional to add lots of vegetables, so add chopped peppers, carrots, peas and beans with the plantains.

856

SERVES 4

Pan-seared Chicken with Orange

PREPARATION TIME:
10 MINUTES

COOKING TIME:
20–30 MINUTES

INGREDIENTS

40 g / 1 oz butter
1 tbsp olive oil
4 chicken breasts
salt and pepper
100 g / 3 ½ oz / ½ cup caster (superfine)
    sugar
2 tbsp water
pinch saffron
2 oranges, zested
250 ml / 9 fl. oz / 1 cup orange juice
1 tbsp marmalade
75 g / 2 ½ oz / ⅓ cup butter,
    chilled and cubed
cooked white rice, to serve

- Heat the butter and oil in a pan and cook the chicken breasts over a medium heat until golden and cooked through. Remove from the pan and set aside, keeping warm.
- Place the sugar and water in a pan over a low heat and swirl until the sugar has melted. Do not stir. Allow to bubble up until golden. Once dark golden, remove from the heat and carefully, standing back, another 150 ml / 5 fl. oz juice and orange zest and saffron. Return to the heat and simmer gently for 10–15 minutes until thickened, stir in the marmalade then whisk in the butter a cube at a time until shiny.
- Add the chicken breasts and coat lightly in the sauce then serve with the cooked rice.

Pan-seared Citrus Chicken

857

- Try this dish with half grapefruit juice along with the orange for a zestier flavour.

858

SERVES 4

Oriental Chicken

PREPARATION TIME:
10 MINUTES

COOKING TIME:
20–25 MINUTES

INGREDIENTS

2 tbsp vegetable oil
4 chicken thighs
1 onion, peeled and finely sliced
1 thumb ginger, peeled and finely
    chopped
1 garlic clove, finely chopped
2 courgettes (zucchini), diced
2 tbsp Chinese cooking wine or
    dry sherry
1–2 tbsp garlic chilli (chili) sauce
1 tbsp soy sauce
1 tbsp honey
generous pinch dried chilli (chili) flakes
300 g / 10 oz / 1 ¼ cups white rice,
    cooked according to packet
    instructions

- Heat the oil in a wok until smoking, then stir fry the chicken until it turns golden.
- Add the onion, ginger and garlic and stir fry over a high heat. Add the courgettes and stir fry for 5 minutes.
- Add the wine/sherry then the sauces, honey and chilli and coat the vegetables, then cook partially covered for 10–15 minutes until the chicken is cooked through – add a splash of water if it looks dry.
- Serve piping hot with rice.

Oriental Chicken with Cashews

859

- A few tbsp of cashews in the sauce add crunch and flavour.

860

SERVES 4

Chicken Apple and Banana Curry

Chicken and Pineapple Curry

861

- Replace the banana with chunks of pineapple.

Light Chicken Curry

862

- Use yogurt or single cream in place of the double cream.

PREPARATION TIME:
10 MINUTES

COOKING TIME:
20–25 MINUTES

INGREDIENTS

2 tbsp vegetable oil
1 onion, peeled and finely sliced
1 tsp cumin seeds
1 tbsp curry powder
2 chicken breasts, skinned and
　cut into chunks
350 ml / 12 fl. oz / 1 ½ cups chicken
　stock
2 bananas, peeled and chopped
2 green apples, peeled and diced
100 ml / 3 ½ fl. oz / ½ cup double
　(heavy) cream
salt and pepper

- Heat the oil in a pan and sweat the onion, cumin seeds and curry powder for about 5 minutes until softened.
- Add the chicken, cook until starting to turn golden, then add the stock and simmer gently for 10–15 minutes until the chicken is cooked.
- Add the fruit and cream, reheat and season, then serve with rice.

863

SERVES 4–6

Chicken with Pineapple and Lime

PREPARATION TIME:
10 MINUTES

COOKING TIME:
30 MINUTES

INGREDIENTS

1 chicken, jointed
1 tbsp olive oil
1 tbsp honey
1 lime, zested
½ tsp cayenne pepper
salt
1 pineapple, peeled, cored and
 cut into large chunks
1–2 limes, juiced
1 red onion, peeled and finely sliced
cooked rice, to serve

- Coat the chicken with the oil, honey, lime zest and cayenne.
- Cook over a barbecue for 20–30 minutes until golden and cooked through – turning often so the honey does not burn. Season well.
- Meanwhile, thread the pineapple onto skewers and cook alongside the chicken for 5 minutes. Sprinkle with lime juice.
- Serve the cooked chicken with the pineapple chunks, doused in lime juice and sprinkled with red onion, on a bed of rice.

864

SERVES 4

Indian Chicken Soup

PREPARATION TIME:
15 MINUTES

COOKING TIME:
40–45 MINUTES

INGREDIENTS

2 tbsp groundnut oil
2 onions, peeled and sliced
1 carrot, peeled and sliced
2 cloves of garlic, finely sliced
4 chicken thighs, skinned,
 deboned and cubed
1 tbsp garam masala
½ tsp black onion seeds
4 curry leaves
2 tbsp tomato purée
400 g / 14 oz / 1 ½ cups canned tomatoes
300 ml / 10 fl. oz / 1 ¼ cups chicken
 stock
salt and pepper
200 g / 7 oz / ¾ cup spinach leaves,
 washed

- Heat the oil in a large pan and fry the onions until very dark gold.
- Add the carrot and garlic and fry for 2 minutes, then add the chicken and cook until the chicken is patchily golden.
- Add the spices and tomato purée and cook out for 2 minutes, stirring to coat the chicken, then add the tomatoes and stock and leave to simmer for 20 minutes.
- Season and stir in the spinach and leave to wilt for 5 minutes.
- Serve with naan bread.

865 · SERVES 6 · Yassa Chicken

- Marinate the chicken in the lemon juice, onions, seasoning, chilli and a little oil for at least 4 hours.
- Preheat the oven to 200°C (180°C fan) / 400F / gas 6.
- Shake off any excess marinade and roast the chicken pieces in the oven for 20 minutes or so until golden.
- Meanwhile cook the onions from the marinade in 1 tbsp oil in a pan until tender, then add the remaining marinade and heat through. Add the browned chicken, habanero, olives, carrots, mustard and 100 ml water and simmer for 20 minutes until the chicken is cooked through.
- Remove the habanero and serve with the rice.

PREPARATION TIME: 5 MINUTES

COOKING TIME: 40 MINUTES

INGREDIENTS

2 tbsp lemon juice
2 onions, peeled and finely sliced
salt and pepper
1 red chilli (chili), finely chopped
1 chicken, jointed into 6 pieces
2 tbsp peanut or groundnut oil
1 habanero chilli (chili), pricked with a fork
100 g / 3 ½ oz / ½ cup green olives
4 carrots, peeled and finely sliced
1 tbsp Dijon mustard
Cooked white rice, to serve

866 · Chicken with Gratin Dauphinois · SERVES 4–6

PREPARATION TIME: 20 MINUTES

COOKING TIME: 1 ½–2 HOURS

INGREDIENTS

50 g / 1 ¾ oz butter, softened
1 kg / 2 ¼ lb / 4 ¼ cups floury potatoes, peeled
2 cloves of garlic, crushed
salt and pepper
½ bunch thyme
500 ml / 1 pint / 2 cups double (heavy) cream
milk
1 oven-ready chicken
4 cloves of garlic
4 sprigs of thyme
40 g / 1 oz butter, softened

- Preheat oven to 160°C (140°C fan) / 300F / gas 2.
- Use the softened butter to generously grease a large baking dish.
- Slice the potatoes as thinly as possible.
- Layer the potatoes in individual gratin dishes, seasoning and sprinkling with thyme leaves and garlic as you go.
- Pour the cream over the potatoes – it should come to the top of the potatoes. Push the potatoes down into the cream, place on a baking tray and bake for 1 ½ hours until the potatoes are completely tender.
- Meanwhile stuff the cavity of the chicken with garlic and thyme, rub the butter over the skin and season. Place in a roasting tin and roast in the oven with the gratins
- Remove the gratins from the oven and leave to settle before serving. Grill the chicken until the skin is crisp and golden.
- Leave the chicken to rest then carve and serve with the gratins.

867 · Chicken with Vodka and Bulghur · SERVES 6

PREPARATION TIME: 20 MINUTES

COOKING TIME: 40 MINUTES

INGREDIENTS

2 tbsp olive oil
1 chicken, jointed
100 ml / 3 ½ fl. oz / ½ cup vodka
1 onion, peeled and thickly sliced
2 peppers, deseeded and roughly chopped
2 cloves of garlic, finely sliced
300 g / 10 oz / 1 ¼ cups bulghur wheat
400 ml / 14 fl. oz / 1 ½ cups chicken stock
mint leaves
salt and pepper

- Preheat the oven to 180°C (160°C fan) / 350F / gas 4.
- Heat the oil in an oven-proof casserole and brown the chicken on all sides, in batches so as not to overcrowd the pan. Remove from the pan.
- Add the onion, peppers and garlic and cook for 10 minutes until softened, then remove from the pan with a slotted spoon. Deglaze with vodka, scraping with a wooden spoon.
- Return the chicken and vegetables to the pan with the bulghur and stock and simmer. Transfer to the oven and bake for 30–40 minutes until the chicken is cooked through and the bulghur is tender – check periodically as you may need to add more water if it looks dry.
- Stir through mint leaves and seasoning and serve.

868

SERVES 4

Chicken Curry with Yogurt

PREPARATION TIME:
15 MINUTES

COOKING TIME:
45 MINUTES

....

INGREDIENTS

3 tbsp vegetable oil
1 bunch spring onions (scallions), finely
    sliced
2 cloves of garlic, chopped
1 tsp fresh ginger, grated
1 tsp ground coriander
1 tsp ground cumin
4 chicken breasts, skinned and thickly
    sliced
100 g / 3 ½ oz / ½ cup plain yogurt
salt
coriander (cilantro) leaves,
    to garnish
250 g / 9 oz / 1 cup rice

- Heat the oil in a pan and sauté the onions for about 10 minutes or until golden-brown. Add the garlic and ginger and fry for another minute.
- Add the spices and stir well, then add 200 ml water and cook gently for 10 minutes or so.
- Add the chicken to the sauce and top up with 300 ml water. Cook at a simmer for around 15 minutes until the chicken is tender.
- Meanwhile cook the rice according to packet instructions. Drain thoroughly.
- Stir the yogurt into the curry and heat through without boiling.
- Season and sprinkle with coriander leaves before serving.

Spicy Chicken Yogurt Curry

 869

- This is a very gentle curry – turn up the volume with chopped red chilli (chili) and mint leaves for contrast.

870

SERVES 2

Chicken in Spiced Crust

PREPARATION TIME:
15 MINUTES

COOKING TIME:
10–15 MINUTES

....

INGREDIENTS

2 chicken escalopes
3 tbsp flour, seasoned
1 egg, beaten
75 g / 2 ½ oz / ⅓ cup breadcrumbs
1 tsp dried thyme
1 tsp fennel seeds, crushed
1 tsp cumin seeds, crushed
½ tsp cayenne pepper
salt
2 tbsp vegetable oil
1 tbsp olive oil
1 yellow pepper, deseeded and sliced
100 g / 3 ½ oz / ½ cup mangetout
1 onion, peeled and sliced

- Mix the breadcrumbs with the spices and a little salt.
- Dredge the escalopes in flour, then egg, then the spiced breadcrumbs and lay on a rack to dry a little.
- Heat the oil in a pan and cook for 5 minutes on each side until golden and crisp.
- Meanwhile, heat the oil in a pan and sauté the vegetables until just tender. Season.
- Serve the crisp chicken on a bed of vegetables.

Crusty Chicken with Rice

871

- Serve on a bed of boiled rice.

872

SERVES 2

Chicken with Black Sesame Paste

- Paint the chicken on both sides with a mixture of soy and mirin.
- Heat a griddle pan and cook on both sides for 2–3 minutes until stripy, golden and cooked through.
- Serve with cucumber slices, spring onions sliced lengthways and a spoon of black sesame paste.

PREPARATION TIME:
10 MINUTES

COOKING TIME:
8–10 MINUTES

INGREDIENTS

2 chicken escalopes
1 tbsp soy sauce
1 tbsp mirin (rice wine)
salt and pepper
4 tbsp black sesame paste
1 cucumber, halved lengthways and
    sliced into half moons
1 bunch spring onions (scallions)

Sesame Chicken with Wild Rice

873

- Serve on a bed of wild rice.

874

SERVES 4

Chicken and Fennel Tagine

- Heat the oil in a large pan and cook the onions until golden and tender.
- Add the garlic and cook for a few minutes, then remove all from the pan with a slotted spoon.
- Increase the heat and brown the chicken on all sides, then add the fennel and cook until lightly caramelised. Tip the onions back into the pan and sprinkle over the spices, then add the olives, apricots and lemons.
- Pour over the stock and season, lower the heat and cook gently for about 45 minutes or until the sauce has thickened and the chicken is cooked.
- Adjust the seasoning and sprinkle with coriander to serve.

PREPARATION TIME:
15 MINUTES

COOKING TIME:
45 MINUTES

INGREDIENTS

2 tbsp olive oil
1 onion, peeled and thickly sliced
2 cloves of garlic, finely sliced
4 chicken legs, skinned
2 bulbs of fennel, cored and cut
    into quarters
1 tsp ras-el-hanout spice mix
1 tsp ground (cilantro) coriander seeds
1 tsp cumin
1 tsp turmeric
handful green olives
handful apricots
4 preserved lemons, chopped
400 ml / 14 fl. oz / 1 ½ cups chicken
    stock
½ bunch coriander (cilantro), chopped
salt and pepper

Chicken and Raisin Tagine

875

- Add a handful of raisins to the stock for a sweeter taste.

876

SERVES 2

Spicy Beer-roasted Chicken

Quick Chicken Stir Fry

877

- Use chopped chicken and mushrooms and stir fry in a wok, using half the beer and soy to make a quick simple version.

Rice Wine Stir Fry

878

- Use the same amount of rice wine instead of beer for a different flavour.

PREPARATION TIME:
10 MINUTES

COOKING TIME:
50 MINUTES

INGREDIENTS

2–4 chicken drumsticks
2 tbsp vegetable oil
4 tbsp soy sauce
2 tsp sugar
300 ml / 10 fl. oz / 1 ¼ cups Asian lager
8 large shiitake or field mushrooms
1 onion, peeled
100 ml / 3 ½ fl. oz / ½ cup Asian lager
75 ml / 2 ½ fl. oz / ⅓ cup soy sauce
1 green chilli (chili), chopped
juice of ½ lime (optional)
black pepper

- Preheat the oven to 200°C (180°C fan) / 400F / gas 6.
- Place the drumsticks in a roasting tin. Mix together the oil, soy and sugar and coat the drumsticks thoroughly. Pour the beer into the roasting tin and add the mushrooms and the onion cut into 8 wedges. Roast for 30–40 minutes until the chicken is cooked through and all is sticky and golden.
- Remove the contents from the pan to a plate and place the roasting tin on the heat. Deglaze the pan with the beer and reduce until syrupy with the chilli and the soy. Taste and adjust the seasoning, adding the lime if desired.
- Serve the chicken and mushrooms with the sauce spooned over.

879

SERVES 4

Chicken and Tarragon Sausage

- Peel and core the apples and cut into chunks. Place in a pan with the sugar, cloves and water and cover with a lid. Cook over a low heat for 10–15 minutes until the apples are a fine purée and are soft. Beat, remove the cloves and set aside.
- Place the chicken in a food processor and blend, adding a tbsp of cream and blending until combined. Add the cream, blend well, scrape into a bowl, season and add the tarragon. Cover with cling film and chill.
- Cut 4 large squares of cling film and divide the chicken mixture equally between them. Wrap the film tightly around the chicken to form a sausage shape.
- Poach in simmering water for 8–10 minutes.
- Heat the butter and fry the garlic and mushrooms until the mushrooms are tender. Season.
- Unwrap the sausages and serve with mushrooms and apple sauce.

PREPARATION TIME:
45 MINUTES

COOKING TIME:
20 MINUTES

INGREDIENTS

250 g / 9 oz / 1 cup Bramley apples
250 g / 9 oz / 1 cup Cox apples
1 tbsp sugar (optional, depending on tartness of apples and usage)
2 cloves
2 tbsp water
2 chicken breasts, skinned
200 ml / 7 fl. oz / ¾ cup double (heavy) cream
2 tbsp tarragon leaves, chopped
salt and pepper
40 g / 1 oz butter
200 g / 7 oz / ¾ cup chanterelle mushrooms, cleaned
1 clove of garlic, crushed

Chicken Mousse Stuffing

880

- You could use this mousse as a stuffing for pork, rabbit or even mushrooms as it will cook within the meat you have wrapped it in.

881

SERVES 4

Chicken with Fennel, Olives and Lemons

- Heat the oil in a large casserole and brown the chicken legs on both sides until golden – you may need to cook them 2 at a time. Remove to a plate.
- Add the onion and garlic to the pan and cook gently until softened and gold. Add the fennel and cook for 2 minutes, before adding the cumin, lemons and chicken back to the pan. Cover with the stock, reduce the heat and simmer gently for 30–40 minutes until the chicken has cooked through.
- 5 minutes before the end of cooking, stir in the olives. When cooked, adjust the seasoning carefully – olives are salty – and serve.

PREPARATION TIME:
10 MINUTES

COOKING TIME:
45 MINUTES

INGREDIENTS

3 tbsp olive oil
4 chicken legs
1 onion, peeled and sliced
2 cloves of garlic, finely sliced
2 fennel bulbs, cored and sliced
1 tsp ground cumin
3 preserved lemons, chopped
300 ml / 10 fl. oz / 1 ¼ cups chicken stock
100 g / 3 ½ oz / ½ cup green olives
salt and pepper

Chicken with Fennel and Rice

882

- You could add 150 g / 5 oz rice in with the chicken to cook in the stock to stretch this dish further – you might need a fraction more stock.

883

SERVES 4

Chicken à la Nage

PREPARATION TIME:
15 MINUTES

COOKING TIME:
10–15 MINUTES

....

INGREDIENTS

2 chicken breasts, skinned
1 stick celery, finely sliced
1 leek, trimmed and finely sliced
2 carrots, peeled and cut into
  matchsticks
2 red peppers, deseeded and
  finely sliced
8 black peppercorns
1 bay leaf
1 bunch parsley stalks, leaves reserved
400 ml / 14 fl. oz / 1 ½ cups hot chicken
  stock
½ bunch chives, finely chopped
salt and pepper

- Finely slice the chicken breasts and place in a large pan with the vegetables, peppercorns, bay leaf and parsley stalks. Pour over the stock, simmer and skim off any scum that floats to the surface.
- Poach the chicken and vegetables until just tender – 10–15 minutes.
- Ladle into deep bowls and stir through the chives and seasoning. Serve hot.

Chicken à la Nage with Thai Flavourings

884

- Try adding a chopped chilli, 2 tbsp fish sauce and a squeeze of lime for a fresh take on this soup.

885

SERVES 4–6

Chicken and Sweet Potato Mafé

PREPARATION TIME:
20 MINUTES + MARINATING
TIME

COOKING TIME:
45 MINUTES

....

INGREDIENTS

1 chicken, jointed into 6 pieces
250 g / 9 oz / 1 cup plain yogurt
250 g / 9 oz / 1 cup tomatoes, chopped
1 cinnamon stick
3 cardamom pods, lightly crushed
4 cloves
6 black peppercorns
1 tsp cumin seeds
2–3 green chillies (chilies), chopped
½ tsp turmeric
1 tsp cayenne pepper (optional)
1 tsp paprika
2 tsp fresh ginger, grated
salt and pepper
3 tbsp vegetable oil
2 onions, peeled and finely sliced
2 red peppers, deseeded and finely sliced
3 sweet potatoes, peeled and diced

- Place the chicken in a large non–reactive bowl.
- Mix together the yogurt, tomatoes, spices, chillies and some salt and coat the chicken thoroughly. Refrigerate for 1–2 hours to marinate.
- Meanwhile heat the oil in a pan and cook the onions gently until golden. Add the peppers and cook for 5–8 minutes until tender.
- Add the chicken and the marinade and cook gently until the chicken is cooked all the way through – you will need to add a little water every now and then to prevent the sauce sticking. It should take about 25–35 minutes.
- Meanwhile steam the sweet potatoes for about 10 minutes until tender.
- Serve the chicken spooned over the sweet potatoes.

Fruity Chicken Curry

886

- This sauce lends itself well to the addition of fruit such as dried apricots, prunes or even diced apples.

887

SERVES 4

Traditional Paella

Pork, Chicken and Seafood Paella

888

- Add pork to the paella for a meatier dish.

Pepper Paella

889

- Add a mix of coloured peppers to the paella .

PREPARATION TIME:
20 MINUTES

COOKING TIME:
40 MINUTES

INGREDIENTS

5 tbsp olive oil
1 onion, peeled and finely sliced
2 cloves of garlic, finely chopped
1 celery stick, finely chopped
1 red pepper, seeded and sliced
300 g / 10 oz / 1 ¼ cups paella rice
4 chicken thighs
1 l / 2 ¼ pints / 4 ¼ cups chicken
    or vegetable stock
pinch saffron threads
1 tsp paprika
4 ripe tomatoes, chopped
50 g / 1 ¾ oz / ¼ cup frozen peas
12 raw prawns, shell on
1 lemon
salt and pepper

- Heat the olive oil in a large shallow pan and cook the onion, garlic and celery until softened.
- Add the pepper, cook for a further 5 minutes, then stir in the chicken and paella rice and coat thoroughly in the oil.
- Stir the saffron into the stock then pour it over the rice. Add the paprika. Simmer uncovered for 15 minutes. Add more stock if it looks dry.
- Add the tomatoes, peas and prawns and cook for a further 8–10 minutes until everything is just cooked through.
- Stir through the lemon juice, season well and serve.

890

SERVES 4

Saffron Chicken with Sorrel Sauce

PREPARATION TIME:
5 MINUTES

COOKING TIME:
20 MINUTES

....

INGREDIENTS

4 chicken breasts
600 ml / 1 pint / 2 ½ cups chicken stock
1 pinch saffron
500 g / 1 lb / 2 cups new potatoes,
    in their skins
250 g / 9 oz / 1 cup sorrel leaves
1 tbsp butter
120 ml / 4 fl. oz / ½ cup crème fraiche
salt and pepper

- Simmer the chicken in gently simmering stock infused with the saffron for 20 minutes or until cooked.
- Cook the potatoes whole in boiling salted water for 20 minutes until tender to the point of a knife. Drain thoroughly.
- Meanwhile wilt the sorrel in a non–reactive pan with the butter, then stir in the crème fraiche. Transfer to a food processor and blitz until smooth.
- When ready to serve, transfer the sauce back to the pan and reheat gently, correcting the seasoning (if you do this before you are ready, the sauce will turn grey).
- Serve the chicken and potatoes on top of the sauce.

Saffron Rice with Spinach Sauce

891

- If sorrel is hard to get hold of, use the same amount of spinach with a squeeze of lemon juice and a little grated nutmeg.

892

SERVES 4

Tandoori Chicken Drumsticks

PREPARATION TIME:
10 MINUTES + MARINADING TIME

COOKING TIME:
30 MINUTES

....

INGREDIENTS

8 chicken drumsticks
salad leaves, to serve

FOR THE MARINADE
300 ml /10 fl. oz / 1 ¼ cups plain yogurt
1 tsp ground cumin
1 tsp ground coriander
1 tsp garam masala
1 tsp ground cinnamon
1 ½ tsp tandoori chilli (chili) powder
1 tsp paprika
1 tsp caster (superfine) sugar
1 clove garlic, minced
salt and pepper

- Prepare the tandoori marinade by mixing together all the ingredients for the marinade in a mixing bowl. Add the chicken, mix well, then cover and chill for at least 1 hour.
- Preheat the oven to 200°C (180°C fan) / 400F / gas 6.
- Tip the chicken and marinade into a foil–lined roasting tin and roast for 25–30 minutes until the chicken is dark gold and cooked through.
- Serve with a fresh salad.

Tandoori Kebabs with Peppers

893

- Use diced chicken and thread onto skewers with green peppers.

894

SERVES 4

Chicken Cooked with Cola

- Put the Coca-Cola and flavourings in a large saucepan and simmer for 5 minutes.
- Add the chicken breasts and carrots and poach gently for 20 minutes or until the chicken is just cooked.
- Remove from the poaching liquor with a slotted spoon and serve, perhaps with creamy mashed potato.

PREPARATION TIME:
5 MINUTES

COOKING TIME:
20 MINUTES

INGREDIENTS

1 red chilli (chili)
6 black peppercorns
1 tsp fennel seeds, lightly crushed
500 ml / 1 pint / 2 cups Coca-Cola
4 chicken breasts, skinless
2 carrots, peeled and cut into
    thin batons

Chicken with Cherry Cola

895

- Replace the cola with cherry cola for a sweeter taste.

896

SERVES 4

Chicken and Vegetable Skewers

- Toss the chicken chunks with quatre epices, oil and seasoning. Leave to marinate for 20 minutes.
- Thread the chicken onto soaked wooden skewers alternating with the peppers, courgette and onion.
- Grill or griddle until the chicken is golden and just cooked through – about 8–10 minutes.
- Serve with lemon juice squeezed over and a little more salt.

PREPARATION TIME:
30 MINUTES

COOKING TIME:
10 MINUTES

INGREDIENTS

4 chicken breasts, skinned and
    cut into chunks
1 tbsp quatre epices
4 tbsp olive oil
salt and pepper
1 yellow pepper, deseeded and roughly
    chopped
½ courgette (zucchini), thickly sliced
1 red onion, peeled and thickly sliced
½ lemon, juiced

Chicken and Prawn Brochettes

897

- Raw king prawns make a good meaty addition to the kebabs.

898

SERVES 4

Mexican-style Chicken Hash

Chicken Chilli 899

- This is only a few steps away from chilli. Use canned tomatoes, a little sliced chorizo and 1 tsp cocoa powder all simmered for 30 minutes.

Chicken Chilli Tortilla Tower 900

- Layer the mix between warmed tortilla wraps in a tower to serve at the table.

PREPARATION TIME:
15 MINUTES

COOKING TIME:
30–35 MINUTES

INGREDIENTS

2 tbsp olive oil
1 onion, peeled and chopped
4 chicken thighs, skinned, deboned and chopped
2 red peppers, deseeded and chopped
1 yellow pepper, deseeded and chopped
1 green pepper, deseeded and chopped
2 cloves of garlic, finely sliced
400 g / 14 oz / 1 ½ cups red kidney beans or black beans, drained
6 ripe tomatoes, cored and chopped
2 tsp smoked paprika
1 lime, juiced
2–3 dried chillies (chilies), rehydrated and chopped (or less if you want it milder)
salt and pepper

- Heat the oil in a large pan and cook the onion until golden. Add the chicken thighs, increase the heat slightly and cook until patchily golden.

- Add the peppers and fry for 4 minutes or until starting to soften, then add the garlic and cook for another minute.

- Add the beans, tomatoes, paprika, lime juice and chillies and a glass of water and simmer for 10–15 minutes until the chicken is cooked and all is tender.

- Season well and serve hot with crusty bread.

901

SERVES 4

Chicken Tandoori Escalopes

- Place the chicken breasts between 2 pieces of cling film and bash with a rolling pin until about 1 cm thick.
- Mix together all the spices and oil and coat the chicken thoroughly. Marinade for 4 hours or overnight.
- When ready to cook, heat a little oil in a pan and cook the escalopes in batches until golden and just cooked through – 2–3 minutes per side.
- Serve with lime wedges and cooked rice, if desired.

PREPARATION TIME:
10 MINUTES

COOKING TIME:
6–7 MINUTES

INGREDIENTS

4 skinless chicken breasts

FOR THE MARINADE
2 tbsp groundnut oil
1 tsp ground cumin
1 tsp ground coriander
1 tsp garam masala
1 tsp ground cinnamon
1 ½ tsp tandoori chilli (chili) powder
1 tsp caster (superfine) sugar
1 clove garlic, minced
salt and pepper
lime wedges

Chicken Tandoori Pizza

902

- Cut the marinated chicken into small pieces, add to a traditional pizza and crumble feta over the top before baking.

903

SERVES 2–4

Two Chicken Stews

- Divide the chicken equally so half the pieces will go in each stew and set aside. Add the saffron to the stock.
- Heat the oil in a casserole and sweat the onion and garlic for 5–10 minutes until softened. Increase the heat, add half the chicken pieces and brown on all sides.
- Add the peas, mangetout, almonds, lemon and saffron infused stock and simmer for 30 minutes or until the chicken is cooked through and liquid reduced. Season.
- Repeat the same process for the second stew, adding the potatoes, almonds and the stock and simmering until the chicken is cooked. Season to taste.
- Serve in 2 serving bowls with crusty bread.

PREPARATION TIME:
10 MINUTES

COOKING TIME:
45 MINUTES

INGREDIENTS

1 chicken, jointed into 6 pieces

FOR THE PEA STEW
2 tbsp olive oil
1 onion, peeled and finely sliced
1 clove of garlic, finely sliced
100 g / 3 ½ oz / ½ cup peas
100 g / 3 ½ oz / ½ cup mangetout
60 g / 2 oz whole skinned almonds
½ lemon, sliced
400 ml / 14 fl. oz / 1 ½ cups chicken stock
pinch saffron, salt and pepper

FOR THE SWEET POTATO STEW
2 tbsp olive oil
1 onion, peeled and finely sliced
1 clove of garlic, finely sliced
2 sweet potatoes, peeled and diced
60 g / 2 oz whole skinned almonds
400 ml / 14 fl. oz / 1 ½ cups chicken stock

Chicken Stew with Vegetables

904

- This basic process can be followed to make any kind of vegetable chicken stew – try using celeriac (celery root), quartered fennel, broccoli or carrots.

905

SERVES 4

Chicken Stir Fry

PREPARATION TIME:
10 MINUTES

COOKING TIME:
10–12 MINUTES

....

INGREDIENTS

2 tbsp vegetable oil
350 g / 12 oz / 1 ½ cups chicken
   thigh meat, diced
1 onion, peeled and finely sliced
2 cloves of garlic, finely sliced
1 tsp fresh ginger, grated
1 red pepper, deseeded and
   finely sliced
1 yellow pepper, deseeded and
   finely sliced
1 green pepper, deseeded and
   finely sliced
200 g / 7 oz / ¾ cup beansprouts
75–100 ml / 2 ½–3 ½ fl. oz / ⅓–½ cup
   soy sauce
2–3 tbsp oyster sauce
2–3 tbsp sweet chilli (chili) sauce
salt and pepper

- Heat the oil in a wok until nearly smoking, then add the chicken.
  Stir fry over a high heat until golden all over and the fat crisp.
  Remove from the pan with a slotted spoon.
- Add the onion, garlic and ginger and stir fry for 2 minutes.
  Add the vegetables and cook until crisp–tender. Add the meat
  back to the pan and stir in the sauces.
- Leave to bubble for a few minutes then check and adjust the
  seasoning if necessary.

Chicken Noodle Stir Fry

906

- Add ready-cooked or soaked noodles to the wok
  for a more substantial supper.

907

SERVES 2

Chicken with Pomegranate

PREPARATION TIME:
10 MINUTES

COOKING TIME:
15 MINUTES

....

INGREDIENTS

2 tbsp olive oil
2 chicken thighs, deboned and
   meat diced
1 clove of garlic, crushed
150 ml / 5 fl. oz / ⅔ cup chicken stock
2 tbsp pomegranate molasses
salt and pepper
1 pomegranate, halved

- Heat the oil in a pan and sauté the chicken over high heat
  until golden.
- Add the garlic, lower the heat, then add the stock and pomegranate
  molasses and simmer for 10 minutes until the chicken is cooked
  through. Season.
- Tip into a serving bowl. Hold the pomegranate cut side down over
  the bowl and bash with a wooden spoon to release the seeds – be
  careful as the juice will spurt out. Serve.

Pomegranate Chicken
with Flatbreads

908

- This would be delicious as a filling for pitta breads,
  rolled flatbreads or even with white rice.

909

SERVES 4

Vietnamese Chicken Skewers

Vietnamese Skewers with Rice

910

- Serve on a bed of wild rice.

Vietnamese Chicken Noodles

911

- Toss the chicken with soaked rice noodles.

PREPARATION TIME:
10 MINUTES

COOKING TIME:
10 MINUTES

INGREDIENTS

4 chicken thighs, skinned, deboned and
    cut into chunks
1 stalk lemongrass, bruised
2 cloves of garlic, finely chopped
1 tbsp fish sauce
1 lime, juiced and zested
1 tsp sugar
1 red chilli (chili), deseeded and finely
    chopped
8 basil leaves, torn
2 tbsp groundnut oil

- Whisk together all the ingredients apart from the chicken and
  lime juice in a bowl.
- Marinate the chicken for at least 1 hour.
- Thread the chicken onto soaked wooden skewers and barbecue
  or griddle, turning every so often, until cooked – 8–10 minutes.
  Brush frequently with any remaining marinade.
- Serve hot with lime juice squeezed over.

912

SERVES 4

Vietnamese Chicken Curry

PREPARATION TIME:
10 MINUTES

COOKING TIME:
35–40 MINUTES

INGREDIENTS

1 tbsp groundnut oil
4 chicken thighs, skinned
2 onions, peeled and sliced
1 red chilli (chili), deseeded and finely chopped
3 cloves of garlic, finely chopped
3 stalks lemongrass, bruised
2 tsp ground coriander
1 tsp turmeric
400 ml / 14 fl. oz / 1 ½ cups coconut milk
200 ml / 7 fl. oz / ¾ cup chicken stock
2 tbsp fish sauce
1 tbsp soft dark brown sugar
salt and pepper
1 bunch basil leaves (or Thai holy basil, if you can get it)

- Heat the oil in a wok and brown the chicken thighs on all sides.
- Add the onions, chilli, garlic and lemongrass and cook for 5 minutes until the onions are golden.
- Add the coriander and turmeric, stir to coat, then add the coconut milk and stock, fish sauce, sugar and a little seasoning and simmer for 20–25 minutes until the chicken is cooked through.
- Stir in the basil and serve with cooked rice.

Vietnamese Noodles **913**

- Make the recipe the same way with chopped chicken, but only use half the amount of coconut milk and toss with cooked rice noodles.

914

SERVES 4

Chicken Cakes with Chilli Sauce

PREPARATION TIME:
15 MINUTES

COOKING TIME:
35 MINUTES

INGREDIENTS

500 g / 1 lb / 2 cups chicken, minced
1 onion, peeled and grated
2 cloves of garlic, crushed
½ bunch coriander (cilantro), chopped
salt and pepper
1 egg, beaten, 2 tbsp olive oil
1 onion, peeled and finely chopped
2 cloves of garlic, finely chopped
1–2 red chillies (chilies), deseeded and chopped
1 tsp smoked paprika
2 tbsp tomato purée
400 g / 14 oz / 1 ½ cups canned tomatoes
1 tsp sugar
1 tbsp red wine vinegar
4 flatbreads
1 bunch spring onions (scallions)
200 ml / 7 fl. oz / ¾ cup plain yogurt
2 tbsp olive oil
1 clove of garlic, crushed

- Tip the minced chicken into a bowl and use your hands to combine with the onion, garlic, coriander and seasoning. Mix in the egg and form into 4 large patties. Refrigerate for 30 minutes.
- Heat the oil in a pan and sauté the onion and garlic with the chillies until golden. Add the paprika and purée and cook out for 2 minutes, stirring, then add the tomatoes and sugar and simmer gently for 20–25 minutes until very thick. Season and stir in the vinegar.
- Heat a little oil in a pan and fry the patties in batches until golden on both sides and cooked through.
- Griddle the spring onions over high heat until limp and blackened.
- Mix the yogurt with the oil, garlic and seasoning. Serve warmed flatbreads topped with the chicken cakes, spoon over yogurt and serve the spring onions alongside.

Chicken Pittas **915**

- Alternatively push the cakes, onions and sauces into warmed split pittas.

916

SERVES 4

Jerk Chicken with Okra

- Blitz the marinade ingredients in a food processor until smooth.
- Coat the chicken thighs and leave to marinate in the refrigerator overnight or for at least four hours.
- Pour off any excess marinade and reserve.
- Roast or barbecue the chicken thighs until cooked through and there are no pink juices when pierced with a skewer – 20–30 minutes.
- Bring the reserved marinade to the boil in a small pan and reduce a little. Add a little salt if necessary.
- Halve the okra lengthways and toss lightly in the seasoned flour and shake off any excess. Heat a thin film of oil in a pan and shallow-fry in batches until crisp-tender.
- Serve the chicken with the lime wedges, fried okra and extra hot sauce for dunking.

PREPARATION TIME:
10 MINUTES

COOKING TIME:
20–30 MINUTES

INGREDIENTS

4 chicken thighs, bone in
2 limes, halved
200 g / 7 oz / ¾ cup okra
2 tbsp flour, seasoned
vegetable oil

FOR THE MARINADE

4 onions, peeled and sliced
1 scotch bonnet or red chilli (chili), sliced
2 tbsp fresh ginger, grated
1 tsp ground allspice
½ tsp grated nutmeg
½ tsp ground cinnamon
3 garlic cloves, chopped
½ orange, juiced
120 ml / 4 fl. oz / ½ cup white wine vinegar
2 tbsp vegetable oil
salt

Jerk Chicken Wraps

917

- Use tortilla wraps to wrap the shredded meat with lettuce, tomato and a dollop of mayo.

918

SERVES 4

Spicy Indian Chicken Soup

- Heat the olive oil in a large saucepan set over a medium heat. Fry the chicken until golden then remove with a slotted spoon.
- Sweat the onion, carrots, garlic and ginger for 6–8 minutes until soft. Add the ground spices and some salt and pepper. Stir well and cook for a few minutes over a reduced heat.
- Add the tomatoes, stir well then cover with the stock. Simmer for 20–25 minutes until thickened.
- Remove from the heat and purée roughly using a stick blender, then return to the heat, add the chicken back to the pan and adjust the seasoning to taste.
- Ladle into serving bowls and garnish with coriander before serving.

PREPARATION TIME:
15 MINUTES

COOKING TIME:
35–40 MINUTES

INGREDIENTS

50 ml / 1 ½ fl. oz / ¼ cup olive oil
2 chicken breasts, skinned and chopped
1 large onion, finely chopped
2 carrots, peeled and diced
2 cloves garlic, minced
3.5 cm (1 in) piece of ginger, peeled and minced
1 tbsp ground coriander
2 tsp ground cumin
1 tsp Madras curry powder
½ tsp chilli (chili) powder
½ tsp turmeric
400 g / 14 oz / 1 ½ cups canned tomatoes
1 l / 2 pints / 4 cups chicken stock
salt and pepper
coriander (cilantro) leaves, to garnish

Indian Lentil Soup

919

- Use 250 g / 9 oz lentils instead of the chicken for a vegetarian version, or as well as for a more substantial soup.

SERVES 4

Thai Chicken Cakes

Easy Chicken Cakes

921

- If you are short of time, 1–2 tbsp red or green thai curry paste will add instant zing to your chicken cakes.

Little Gem Chicken Wraps

922

- Serve drizzled with sweet chilli sauce and wrapped in individual little gem leaves.

PREPARATION TIME:
15 MINUTES + REFRIGERATION TIME

COOKING TIME:
16–20 MINUTES

INGREDIENTS

500 g / 1 lb / 2 cups chicken, minced
1 shallot, finely chopped
1 lime, zested
1 red chilli (chili), deseeded and finely
    chopped
2 tbsp fish sauce
1 tsp sugar
1 tsp dried shrimp paste (optional)
1 egg, beaten
vegetable oil
2 heads pak choi, leaves separated

- Tip the chicken into a bowl and add the shallot, lime zest, chilli, fish sauce, sugar and shrimp paste and use your hands to mix thoroughly. Mix in the egg.
- Form into equal-sized cakes – you should get 4 large-ish patties, place on a plate, cover with cling film and refrigerate for 30 minutes.
- Heat a thin film of oil in a pan and fry the patties 2 at a time for 4 minutes each side or until golden.
- Steam the pak choi leaves over simmering water for 3 minutes until the stems are tender.
- Serve the cakes with the pak choi.

923

SERVES 2

Chicken with Ginger and Cardamom

- Heat the oil in a pan and cook the onion until golden and tender.
- Add the garlic, ginger, chicken and peppered and cook until the chicken is golden in patches.
- Add the spices and fry for 1 minute, then add the tomatoes and 100 ml / 3 ½ fl. oz water and simmer for 20 minutes until thickened.
- Remove the cinnamon stick before sprinkling with chopped coriander.

PREPARATION TIME:
10 MINUTES

COOKING TIME:
30 MINUTES

INGREDIENTS

2 tbsp vegetable oil
1 onion, peeled and finely sliced
2 cloves of garlic, finely sliced
1 tbsp fresh ginger, finely chopped
2–4 chicken thighs, skinned, deboned and diced
1 green pepper, deseeded and sliced
4 cardamom pods, lightly crushed
1 cinnamon stick
4 curry leaves
400 g / 14 oz / 1 ½ cups canned tomatoes
salt and pepper
coriander (cilantro) leaves, finely chopped

Chicken with Ginger, Cardamom and Squash

924

- Butternut squash, peeled and diced, would sit well with the spices in this dish and add substance.

925

SERVES 4

Tom Kai

- Heat the oil in a wok or large pan and fry the onion until deep gold and sweet.
- Add the garlic and galangal and the cubed chicken and allow to colour on all sides.
- Stir in the tamarind and fish sauce, then pour over the coconut milk and chicken stock. Stir in the lime leaves and peppers. Lower the heat and leave to simmer for 15–20 minutes until the chicken is cooked through.
- Adjust the seasoning and stir in the lime juice just before serving.

PREPARATION TIME:
15 MINUTES

COOKING TIME:
25–30 MINUTES

INGREDIENTS

3 tbsp vegetable oil
1 onion, peeled and finely sliced
2 cloves of garlic, finely chopped
3–4 chicken breasts, skinned and cubed
1 knob galangal, peeled and grated
2 tsp tamarind paste
2 tbsp fish sauce
3 lime leaves
400 ml / 14 fl. oz / 1 ½ cups coconut milk
200 ml / 7 fl. oz / ¾ cup chicken stock
salt and pepper
1–2 limes, juiced
1 red pepper, deseeded and sliced

Thai Tom Kai

926

- A spoonful or two of Thai curry paste would add a rich red colour.

927

SERVES 4

Chicken Pappardelle with Peas

PREPARATION TIME:
10 MINUTES

COOKING TIME:
10–12 MINUTES

....

INGREDIENTS

4 chicken breasts, skinned and cubed
1 tsp smoked paprika
1 tsp oregano
2 tbsp olive oil
1 clove of garlic, finely sliced
320 g / 11 oz / 1 ¼ cups pappardelle
    pasta
100 g / 3 ½ oz / ½ cup frozen peas
salt and pepper
Parmesan, to serve

- Rub the chicken breasts in smoked paprika and oregano, then season with salt and freshly ground black pepper.
- Heat the oil in a pan and cook the chicken until golden and nearly cooked through – about 7 minutes.
- Add the garlic and cook over a low heat.
- Meanwhile cook the pasta in boiling salted water according to packet instructions. Drain thoroughly, reserving the pasta water.
- Cook the peas in the reserved water on a low heat, according to packet instructions.
- Toss the pasta with the peas and a little cooking water, then top with slices of the cooked chicken. Season and serve.

Chicken Pasta with Pesto Sauce

928

- Mix pesto with ricotta and spoon over the top before serving.

929

SERVES 4

Chicken Osso Bucco

PREPARATION TIME:
10 MINUTES

COOKING TIME:
55 MINUTES

....

INGREDIENTS

2 tbsp olive oil
4–6 chicken drumsticks
1 onion, chopped
2 cloves of garlic, chopped
1 red pepper, deseeded and sliced
1 green pepper, deseeded and sliced
1 tsp sugar
1 tsp smoked paprika
1 piece orange peel, without
    white pith
400 g / 14 oz / 1 ½ cups canned tomatoes
250 ml / 9 fl. oz / 1 cup chicken stock
2 bay leaves
1 sprig rosemary
salt
cooked polenta or mashed potato, to
    serve

- Preheat the oven to 180°C (160°C fan) / 350F / gas 4.
- Heat the oil in a pan and brown the thighs until golden. Remove to a plate and set aside.
- Add the onion and garlic and cook gently until golden, then add the chicken back to the pan and add the peppers, sugar, paprika and seasoning and cook for 5 minutes.
- Pour over the canned tomatoes and stock, add the bay leaves, rosemary and some salt, cover with a lid and cook in the oven for 45 minutes until the chicken is cooked.

Gremolata

930

- Finely chop ½ bunch parsley and 1 clove of garlic with some salt and add zest of ½ lemon. Sprinkle over before serving.

931

SERVES 2

Imperial Chicken

Chinese-style Chicken

932

- Try grated ginger; crushed Szechuan peppercorns; cashew nuts; the choice is endless.

Chicken with Szechuan Peppercorns

933

- Szechuan peppercorns add a traditional lip-numbing lick of heat – sprinkle over to serve.

PREPARATION TIME:
10 MINUTES

COOKING TIME:
10–15 MINUTES

INGREDIENTS

2 tbsp vegetable oil
2 chicken breasts, skinned and chopped
2 tsp cornflour (cornstarch)
½ onion, peeled and roughly chopped
1 green pepper, deseeded and roughly chopped
1 yellow pepper, deseeded and roughly chopped
½ bunch spring onions (scallions), chopped
100 g / 3 ½ oz green beans
2–4 dried chillies (chilies), chopped
1 clove of garlic, finely sliced
2 tbsp Chinese rice wine
4 tbsp soy sauce
100 ml / 3 ½ fl. oz / ½ cup chicken stock
handful cashew nuts

- Heat the oil in a wok until smoking. Toss the chicken in cornflour, shake off the excess and fry quickly until golden.
- Add the onion, pepper, spring onions, green beans and chillies, then the garlic and stir fry for 2 minutes.
- Add the rice wine, reduce, then the soy, stock and cashew nuts and simmer for 5 minutes.
- Serve in deep bowls.

934

SERVES 4

Chilli Chicken Wings

PREPARATION TIME:
10 MINUTES

COOKING TIME:
35–40 MINUTES

INGREDIENTS

16 chicken wings
100 g / 3 ½ oz / ½ cup butter
1 red chilli (chili), finely chopped
OR ½ Habanero chilli (chili), chopped
2 tbsp honey
salt and pepper

- Preheat the oven to 200°C (180°C fan) / 400F / gas 6.
- Melt the butter in a pan and add chilli, honey and salt. Coat the chicken thoroughly in the butter.
- Place the chicken wings in a roasting tin and roast in the oven for 20 minutes. Turn them over, then roast for another 15–20 minutes until sticky, golden and cooked through.
- Serve hot.

Spicy Wings with Mint Yogurt

935

- Habanero is very spicy. To cool things down stir fresh chopped mint into yogurt to dip.

936

SERVES 4

Spicy Chicken with Peppers

PREPARATION TIME:
5 MINUTES

COOKING TIME:
30–40 MINUTES

INGREDIENTS

8 chicken pieces such as thighs
2 tbsp olive oil
1 tsp paprika
½ tsp cayenne pepper
1 tsp ground cumin
salt and pepper
1 red pepper, deseeded and sliced

- Preheat the oven to 200°C (180°C fan) / 400F / gas 6.
- Whisk the oil with paprika, cayenne, cumin and seasoning and thoroughly coat the chicken.
- Roast in the oven for 30–40 minutes until cooked through and golden.
- Serve with fresh crunchy red pepper slices.

Spicy Chicken with Sweet Potatoes

937

- Add diced sweet potato around the chicken to roast to make this go further.

Chicken and Shiitake Mushroom Noodles

938

SERVES 2

- Cook the noodles in boiling salted water according to packet instructions.
- Heat the oils in a wok and sauté the chicken over high heat until patchily golden.
- Add the mushrooms, garlic and ginger and stir fry for 2–3 minutes until the mushrooms are tender.
- Add the noodles to the pan with a little cooking water and toss to combine, then add the sauces and sesame seeds. Heat through until bubbling and serve.

PREPARATION TIME:
10 MINUTES

COOKING TIME:
10 MINUTES

INGREDIENTS

1 tbsp groundnut oil
1 tsp sesame oil
2 chicken thighs, skinned, deboned and chopped
200 g / 7 oz / ¾ cup shiitake mushrooms, cleaned
2 cloves of garlic, finely sliced
1 tsp fresh ginger, grated
2 tbsp soy sauce
1 tbsp teriyaki sauce
1 tbsp sesame seeds
2 nests of dried egg noodles

Chicken with Teriyaki Mushrooms

939

- Meaty teriyaki sauce goes really well with mushrooms – try a few drops on baked field mushrooms.

Mexican-style Chicken

940

SERVES 4

- Preheat the oven to 200°C (180°C fan) / 400F / gas 6.
- Place the chicken in a foil-lined roasting tin. Whisk the remaining ingredients together and coat the chicken thoroughly.
- Roast for about 35 minutes until golden and cooked through.

PREPARATION TIME:
10 MINUTES

COOKING TIME:
35 MINUTES

INGREDIENTS

4 chicken thighs
2 tsp paprika
½ lime, juiced
1 tsp cayenne pepper
1 tsp ground cumin
1 tsp ground coriander
1 clove of garlic, finely sliced
3 tbsp olive oil

Chicken with Refried Beans

941

- Serve on a bed of spicy refried beans.

942

SERVES 4

Chicken Curry with Rice

PREPARATION TIME:
15 MINUTES

COOKING TIME:
45 MINUTES

INGREDIENTS

3 tbsp vegetable oil
1 onion, peeled and finely sliced
1 red pepper, deseeded and finely
  chopped
2 cloves of garlic, chopped
1 tsp fresh ginger, grated
1 tsp ground coriander
½ tsp turmeric
1 tsp ground cumin
1 tbsp garam masala
1 tsp paprika
4 chicken breasts, skinned
  and thickly sliced
100 g / 3 ½ oz / ½ cup plain yogurt
salt
coriander (cilantro) leaves,
  to garnish
250 g / 9 oz / 1 cup rice
100 g / 3 ½ oz / ½ cup frozen peas

- Heat the oil in a pan and sauté the onion and pepper for about 10 minutes or until golden–brown. Add the garlic and ginger and fry for another minute.
- Add the spices and stir well, then add 200 ml water and cook gently for 10 minutes or so.
- Add the chicken to the sauce and top up with 300 ml water. Cook at a simmer for around 20 minutes until the chicken is tender.
- Meanwhile cook the rice according to packet instructions, adding the peas for the last 5 minutes of cooking. Drain thoroughly.
- Stir the yogurt into the curry and heat through without boiling.
- Season and sprinkle with coriander leaves before serving.

943

SERVES 2

Chicken Artichoke Tagine

PREPARATION TIME:
10 MINUTES

COOKING TIME:
45 MINUTES

INGREDIENTS

2 globe artichokes, prepared
  and halved
1 lemon, juiced
2 tbsp olive oil
1 onion, peeled and finely sliced
2 cloves of garlic, finely sliced
4 chicken thighs, skinned
1 tsp ras-el-hanout spice mix
1 tsp ground (cilantro) coriander seeds
4 preserved lemons, chopped
300 ml / 10 fl. oz / 1 ¼ cups chicken
  stock
4 ripe tomatoes, quartered
salt and pepper

- Prepare the artichokes: Remove around 4–5 of the toughest outer leaves. Place the artichoke at the edge of the table so the stalk hangs over the edge. Snap away the stem, removing some of the tough fibres running into the base.
- Remove the inedible choke: Spread the leaves apart until you come to the central thinner, lighter leaves. Pull this cone out in one piece and underneath will be the hairy choke – scrape out with a teaspoon.
- Rinse the artichokes with water and place immediately in a bowl of water with lemon juice to prevent discolouring.
- Heat the oil in a large pan and cook the onions until golden and tender.
- Add the garlic and cook for a few minutes, then remove all from the pan with a slotted spoon.
- Increase the heat and brown the chicken on all sides, then tip the onions back into the pan and sprinkle over the spices. Add the artichoke halves into the pan with the tomatoes.
- Pour over the stock and season, lower the heat and cook gently for about 45 minutes or until the sauce has thickened and the chicken is cooked.
- Add the vegetables to warm through, adjust the seasoning. Serve with bulghur wheat.

944

SERVES 6

Chicken Yassa with Rice

- Marinate the chicken in the lemon juice, onions, seasoning, chilli and a little oil for at least 4 hours.
- Preheat the oven to 200°C (180°C fan) / 400F / gas 6.
- Shake off any excess marinade and roast the chicken pieces in the oven for 20 minutes or so until golden.
- Meanwhile cook 2 onions from the marinade in 1 tbsp oil in a pan until tender, then add the remaining marinade and heat through. Add the browned chicken, habanero, olives, mustard and 100 ml water and simmer for 20 minutes until the chicken is cooked through.
- Heat the oil in a separate pan and gently fry the remaining onion with turmeric and sugar until caramelised.
- Remove the habanero from the curry. Serve the rice with the caramelised onion on top and the rice alongside.

PREPARATION TIME:
5 MINUTES

COOKING TIME: 40 MINUTES

INGREDIENTS

2 tbsp lemon juice, salt and pepper
3 onions, peeled and finely sliced
1 red chilli (chili), finely chopped
1 chicken, jointed into 6 pieces
2 tbsp peanut or groundnut oil
1 habanero chilli (chili), pricked with a fork
100 g / 3 ½ oz / ½ cup green olives
1 tbsp Dijon mustard
2 tbsp olive oil
½ tsp turmeric, ½ tsp sugar
cooked white rice

945

SERVES 4

Chicken and Almond Curry

PREPARATION TIME:
15 MINUTES

COOKING TIME:
30 MINUTES

INGREDIENTS

2 tbsp olive oil
4 chicken thighs, skinned
1 onion
1 green (bell) pepper
1 stick celery, 2 cloves of garlic
1 cm piece fresh ginger
4 tomatoes, cored and diced
1 tbsp flour, 1 tsp paprika
1 tsp cayenne pepper
400 g / 14 oz / 1 ½ cups coconut milk
100 ml / 3 ½ fl. oz / ½ cup chicken stock
100 g / 3 ½ oz / ½ cup flaked (slivered) almonds
1 bay leaf, salt and pepper

- Peel and chop the onion. Seed and chop the pepper, and finely chop the celery, garlic and ginger.
- Heat the oil in a large pan and cook the chicken on all sides until golden then remove and set aside. Sauté the onion, peppers and celery until softened.
- Add the garlic, ginger and flour and cook out for a few seconds, then add the chicken back to the pan.
- Sprinkle over the spices, then pour in coconut milk and stock. Add the bay leaf and season, then simmer for about 20 minutes over a low heat until the sauce has thickened and the chicken is cooked.
- Serve decorated with the almonds.

946

SERVES 4

Teriyaki Chicken with Asparagus

PREPARATION TIME:
25 MINUTES

COOKING TIME:
20 MINUTES

INGREDIENTS

2 chicken breasts, skinned and sliced
4 tbsp teriyaki sauce
1 tbsp soy sauce
1 tsp sugar
300 g / 10 oz / 1 ¼ cups Japanese rice, washed
500 ml / 1 pint / 2 cups water
1 tbsp vegetable oil
1 tsp sesame oil
1 tbsp sesame seeds
1 bunch asparagus, trimmed

- Toss the chicken in the sauces and sugar and leave for 20 minutes.
- Meanwhile place the rice and water in a pan, cover and simmer for 15 minutes. Turn the heat to low and simmer for about 5 minutes with the lid off to evaporate all the water. Taste and check the rice is cooked.
- Heat the oils in a wok and stir fry the chicken until cooked through – about 5–6 minutes, then toss in the sesame seeds.
- Steam the asparagus over simmering water for 4 minutes until just tender.
- Serve the chicken on top of the rice, the asparagus alongside.

947

SERVES 2

Chicken with Broccoli

PREPARATION TIME:
10 MINUTES

COOKING TIME:
15 MINUTES

INGREDIENTS

1 tbsp vegetable oil
2 chicken breasts, skinned and roughly
    chopped
1 head of broccoli, separated
    into florets
1 bunch of spring onions
    (scallions), sliced
2 cloves of garlic, finely sliced
2 tbsp soy sauce
½ tsp cornflour (cornstarch) dissolved
    in 1 tbsp water
1 star anise
black pepper
cooked rice, to serve

- Heat the oil in a wok and stir fry the chicken briskly until golden. Add the vegetables, garlic, soy, dissolved cornflour and star anise and reduce the heat.
- Bubble up until the sauce is slightly thickened and glossy and the chicken is cooked. The broccoli should retain some bite.
- Serve the chicken with the vegetables on top of cooked rice.

Chicken with Mangetout   **948**

- Replace the broccoli with mangetout.

949

SERVES 2

Chicken and Spring Vegetables

PREPARATION TIME:
10 MINUTES

COOKING TIME:
25–30 MINUTES

INGREDIENTS

2 chicken breasts, skin on
400 g / 14 oz / 1 ½ cups waxy potatoes,
    halved
1 bunch baby carrots, scrubbed
    and trimmed
3 tbsp olive oil
40 g / 1 oz butter
2 sprigs thyme
salt and pepper
150 g / 5 oz / ⅔ cup sugar snap peas
500 g / 1 lb / 2 cups spinach leaves

- Preheat the oven to 200°C (180°C fan) / 400F / gas 6.
- Arrange the chicken, potatoes and carrots in a roasting tin, dot with butter and oil, sprinkle over thyme leaves, season and roast for 25 minutes until golden and caramelised.
- Meanwhile steam the sugar snap peas over simmering water for 4–5 minutes until tender.
- Wilt the spinach in a pan with 1 tbsp water.
- You could serve this all in one pot: thickly slice the chicken and toss all the vegetables gently together with the roasting juices from the pan.

Chicken with Spring Vegetables and Rice   **950**

- Serve on a bed of boiled rice.

951

SERVES 4

Summer Chicken and Vegetable Crumble

- Heat the butter in a pan and sauté the chicken, onion, courgette and peppers until golden. Add the tomatoes, simmer for 20 minutes until thickened then season and set aside.
- Meanwhile rub the butter and semolina or couscous together with your fingertips to resemble large breadcrumbs, then stir through the pine nuts and season well.
- Spoon the chicken mixture into a gratin dish, then top lightly with the crumble. Grill or bake until bubbling and the topping is golden and crunchy.

PREPARATION TIME:
15 MINUTES

COOKING TIME:
30–40 MINUTES

INGREDIENTS

40g / 1 oz butter
4 chicken breasts, skinned and cubed
1 onion, peeled and chopped
1 yellow pepper, deseeded and roughly chopped
1 red pepper, deseeded and roughly chopped
1 courgette (zucchini), sliced
100 g / 3 ½ oz / ½ cup mangetout
400 g / 14 oz / 1 ½ cups canned tomatoes
salt and pepper
120 g / 4 oz / ½ cup semolina or couscous
100 g / 3 ½ oz / ½ cup butter, cold and cubed
50 g / 1 ¾ oz / ¼ cup pine nuts, chopped

Creamy Chicken Crumble

 952

- Stir in 2 tbsp cream cheese or crème fraiche for an indulgent version on a cool night.

953

SERVES 4

Chicken Tagine with Oranges and Olives

- Heat the oil in a large pan and cook the onions until golden and tender.
- Add the garlic and cook for a few minutes, then remove all from the pan with a slotted spoon.
- Increase the heat and brown the chicken on all sides, add the courgette, then tip the onions back into the pan and sprinkle over the spices. Add the orange peel.
- Pour over the stock and season, lower the heat and cook gently for about 45 minutes or until the sauce has thickened and the chicken is cooked.
- Add the orange to warm through, adjust the seasoning and serve.

PREPARATION TIME:
15 MINUTES

COOKING TIME:
45 MINUTES

INGREDIENTS

2 tbsp olive oil
1 onion, peeled and finely sliced
2 cloves of garlic, finely sliced
4 chicken legs, skinned
1 courgette (zucchini), chopped
1 tsp ras-el-hanout spice mix
1 tsp ground (cilantro) coriander seeds
1 orange, segmented + 1 piece orange peel
400 ml / 14 fl. oz / 1 ½ cups chicken stock
2 tbsp olives
salt and pepper

Chicken with Lemon and Olives

 954

- Replace the orange with lemon.

SERVES 6

Moroccan Chicken Tortilla

Chicken Merguez and Potato Tortilla 956

- Substitute the chickpeas for chunks of boiled potato.

Pepper Tortilla 957

- Add mixed chopped red and yellow peppers.

PREPARATION TIME:
20 MINUTES

COOKING TIME:
35 MINUTES

INGREDIENTS

2 tbsp olive oil
1 onion, peeled and finely sliced
100 g / 3 ½ oz / ½ cup merguez sausage, sliced
2 chicken thighs, skinned, deboned and diced
1 clove of garlic, crushed
1 tsp ground cumin
1 tsp ground coriander
400 g / 14 oz / 1 ½ cups canned chickpeas, drained
8 eggs
1 tbsp crème fraiche
olive oil
salt and pepper

- Preheat the oven to 190°C (170°C fan) / 375F / gas 5.
- Heat the oil in a pan and gently fry the onion until golden and soft.
- Add the sausage, chicken and garlic and fry for a few minutes until the chicken is cooked.
- Beat the eggs with the crème fraiche in a large bowl. Add the chicken mixture and chickpeas and season then mix together carefully.
- Oil a large frying pan, then pour the mixture in and bake for about 35 minutes until puffed and golden. The egg should be cooked through.
- Cut into squares and serve warm or cold.

958

SERVES 4

Ginger Chinese Chicken Soup

- Heat the oil in a large pan and gently cook the onion, garlic and ginger without colouring.
- Add the chicken, stock and sauces and simmer gently for 20 minutes until cooked.
- Adjust the seasoning, stir in the grated carrot and palm hearts and serve hot.

PREPARATION TIME:
15 MINUTES

COOKING TIME:
25 MINUTES

INGREDIENTS

2 tbsp vegetable oil
1 onion, peeled and sliced
2 cloves of garlic, finely sliced
1 tsp fresh ginger, grated
4 chicken thighs, skinned, deboned and cut into chunks
500 ml / 1 pint / 2 cups chicken stock
2 tbsp oyster sauce
1 tbsp soy sauce
1 carrot, peeled and grated
200 g / 7 oz / ¾ cup canned palm hearts, drained

Chinese Chicken Soup with Pak Choi

959

- Pak choi will cook quickly in the stock and make it even healthier.

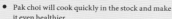

960

SERVES 4

Chicken and Leek Crumbles

- Poach the chicken in the stock for 5 minutes until just cooked through. Drain, reserving the stock.
- Heat the butter in a pan and sauté the onion and tomatoes until golden, then add the chicken. Add the basil and enough poaching liquor to loosen a little, then season and set aside.
- Meanwhile rub the butter and flour together with your fingertips to resemble breadcrumbs, then stir through the chopped walnuts and season well.
- Spoon the chicken mixture into a gratin dish, then top lightly with the crumble. Grill or bake until bubbling and the topping is golden and crunchy.
- To make the leek crumble, proceed as above, gently frying the onion and leek until soft and slithery but not coloured. Add the cream and season generously.
- Make the crumble as above and assemble as above. Grill or bake similarly.

PREPARATION TIME:
30 MINUTES

COOKING TIME:
30 MINUTES

INGREDIENTS

FOR THE CHICKEN CRUMBLE
4 chicken breasts, skinned and cubed
500 ml / 1 pint / 2 cups chicken stock
40 g / 1 oz butter
1 onion, peeled and chopped
8 cherry tomatoes, halved
½ bunch basil, salt and pepper
120 g / 4 oz / ½ cup plain flour
100 g / 3 ½ oz / ½ cup butter
50 g / 1 ¾ oz / ¼ cup walnuts

FOR THE LEEK CRUMBLE
40 g / 1 oz butter
1 onion, peeled and chopped
2 leeks, trimmed and chopped
200 ml / 7 fl. oz / ¾ cup double (heavy) cream
120 g / 4 oz / ½ cup plain (all-purpose) flour
100 g / 3 ½ oz / ½ cup butter
50 g / 1 ¾ oz / ¼ cup Parmesan cheese, grated

Leek Cheese Crumble

961

- Add caerphilly cheese to the leeks, crumbled in, for extra flavour.

962

SERVES 2

Vietnamese Chicken Fricassee

PREPARATION TIME:
10 MINUTES

COOKING TIME:
10–15 MINUTES

INGREDIENTS

1 tbsp vegetable oil
1 onion, peeled and finely sliced
2 cloves of garlic, finely sliced
2 chicken breasts, skinned and cubed
1–2 green chillies (chilies), chopped
2 tbsp soy sauce
1–2 tsp sugar
½ bunch Thai basil
steamed rice, to serve

- Heat the oil in a wok and stir fry the onion until deep gold. Add the garlic, chillies and chicken and stir fry until the chicken is cooked through.
- Add the soy and sugar and reduce until caramelised and sticky and coating the chicken.
- Stir through the basil and serve with the rice.

Vietnamese Prawn and Chicken Fricassee

963

- Add raw king prawns to the wok as well as the chicken.

964

SERVES 4

Chicken with Padron Peppers

PREPARATION TIME:
10 MINUTES

COOKING TIME:
35–40 MINUTES

INGREDIENTS

2 tbsp olive oil
4 chicken drumsticks
1 onion, peeled and sliced
2 cloves of garlic, finely sliced
200 g / 7 oz / ¾ cup padron peppers (available online) or green peppers, chopped
8 ripe tomatoes, cored and diced
salt and pepper

- Heat the oil in a casserole and brown the chicken on all sides.
- Add the onion and garlic, fry until golden, then add the padron peppers. Cook until everything is slightly caught and golden, then add the tomatoes, a glass of water and seasoning, cover with a lid and simmer for 20 minutes or until the chicken is cooked.
- Adjust the seasoning and serve

Chicken with Peppers and Couscous

965

- Serve on a bed of couscous.

966

SERVES 4

Chicken with Peppers and Sesame Seeds

Chicken with Steamed Rice

967

- Steamed rice would stretch this meal even further for unexpected company.

Stuffed Aubergines

968

- Hollow out halved aubergines, bake in the oven until tender then stuff with the mixture.

PREPARATION TIME:
10 MINUTES

COOKING TIME:
10–12 MINUTES

INGREDIENTS

2 tbsp vegetable oil
1 tsp sesame oil
350 g / 12 oz / 1 ½ cups chicken thigh meat, diced
2 cloves of garlic, finely sliced
1 tsp fresh ginger, grated
1 red pepper, deseeded and finely sliced
1 green pepper, deseeded and finely sliced
200 g / 7 oz / ¾ cup bamboo shoots
2–3 tbsp oyster sauce
2–3 tbsp black sesame seeds
salt and pepper

- Heat the oils in a wok until nearly smoking, then add the chicken. Stir fry over a high heat until golden all over. Remove from the pan with a slotted spoon.
- Add the garlic and ginger and stir fry for 2 minutes. Add the vegetables and cook until crisp-tender. Add the meat back to the pan and stir in the sauce.
- Leave to bubble for a few minutes then, toss in the sesame seeds, check and adjust the seasoning if necessary.

969

SERVES 4

Sweet and Sour Chicken

PREPARATION TIME:
15 MINUTES

COOKING TIME:
20 MINUTES

INGREDIENTS

500 g / 1 lb / 2 cups chicken thigh meat,
    sliced
1 tbsp vegetable oil
1 carrot, peeled and cut into matchsticks
1 red pepper, deseeded and finely sliced
1 red onion, peeled and thickly sliced
50 g / 1 ¾ oz / ¼ cup pineapple chunks

FOR THE SAUCE

125 ml / 4 fl. oz / ½ cup pineapple juice
splash dry sherry or Shaoxing
    rice wine
2 tbsp ketchup
2 tbsp soy sauce
2 tbsp Chinese vinegar or red
    wine vinegar
1 tsp cornflour (cornstarch)

- Heat the vegetable oil in a wok until smoking, then add the chicken and stir fry over a high heat until the chicken turns white.
- Remove the chicken from the pan and set aside. Discard the oil.
- Heat the oil in the wok again and stir fry the vegetables over a high heat for 4 minutes.
- Mix together the sauce ingredients with the cornflour. Add the chicken back to the pan with the sauce, bubble up until thickened and serve with white rice.

Sweet and Sour Chicken and Prawns

970

- Add king prawns as well as the chicken.

971

SERVES 4

Spicy Chicken with Herbs

PREPARATION TIME:
10 MINUTES

COOKING TIME:
20–25 MINUTES

INGREDIENTS

4 chicken breasts, roughly chopped
2 tbsp vegetable oil
1 shallot, finely chopped
1 clove of garlic, finely chopped
1–2 green chillies (chilies), sliced
1 bay leaf
1 cinnamon stick
½ bunch coriander (cilantro), chopped
400 ml / 14 fl. oz / 1 ½ cups coconut
    milk
½ lime, juiced
salt and pepper

- Heat the oil in a wok and stir fry the chicken until golden.
- Add the shallot, garlic and chillies and fry for 2 minutes, then add the coriander and coconut milk and simmer for 10–15 minutes until the chicken is cooked through.
- Squeeze over the lime, adjust the seasoning and serve, removing the cinnamon stick if you can find it.

Spicy Chicken with Chilli Sauce

972

- Drizzle with sweet chilli sauce before serving for an extra kick.

973

SERVES 4

Chicken Jambalaya

- Heat the oil in a pan and fry the onion, garlic and celery until golden.
- Add the chorizo and fry until the fat starts to run, then add the chicken, chilli and rice and stir to coat thoroughly.
- Pour over the stock, bring to a simmer, turn down the heat and leave to cook for about 15 minutes.
- Stir in the tomatoes and peas and cook until the peas are tender – about 5–6 minutes.
- Season with Tabasco, lemon juice and salt and pepper before serving.

PREPARATION TIME:
10 MINUTES

COOKING TIME:
30 MINUTES

INGREDIENTS

2 tbsp olive oil
1 onion, peeled and finely sliced
2 cloves of garlic, finely chopped
2 stalks of celery, finely chopped
100 g / 4 oz / ⅓ cup chorizo sausage, diced
2 chicken breasts, skinned and diced
1 chilli (chili), deseeded and finely chopped
200 g / 7 oz / ¾ cup white basmati rice
600 ml / 1 ¼ pints / 2 ½ cups chicken stock
2 ripe tomatoes, chopped
50 g / 1 ¾ oz ¼ cup frozen peas
hot sauce
1 lemon, juiced
salt and pepper

Jambalaya Chicken and Prawns

974

- Add cooked king prawns as well as the chicken.

975

SERVES 4

Creamy Chicken with Rice

- Heat the oil in a pan and fry the chicken until white on both sides. Remove with a slotted spoon.
- Add the shallot and sweat without colouring, then return the chicken to the pan with the curry powder, mango chutney and cream. Simmer for 5–10 minutes until the chicken is cooked. Season to taste.
- Tip the rice into a pan with the water and cook covered with a lid for 10 minutes. Remove from the heat and leave covered for 5 minutes.
- Serve the chicken with the sauce spooned over and peppercorns sprinkled on top.

PREPARATION TIME:
5 MINUTES

COOKING TIME:
15–20 MINUTES

INGREDIENTS

2 tbsp vegetable oil
4 chicken breasts, skin on
1 shallot, finely diced
1 tbsp curry powder
1 tbsp mango chutney
200 ml / 7 fl. oz / ¾ cup double (heavy) cream
salt and pepper
250 g / 9 oz / 1 cup basmati rice
2 cups water
1 tbsp Szechuan peppercorns

Old-school Chicken Curry

 976

- Add sultanas, a handful of shaved coconut and almonds for a flashback to the 70s.

977

SERVES 4

Chicken Tikka Masala

Chicken Tikka
Sandwiches

978

- This is excellent the next day served in warm crunchy baguettes.

Chicken Tikka
with Dal

979

- Lentil Dal – cooked lentils with spices – make a refreshing alternative to rice.

PREPARATION TIME:
20 MINUTES

COOKING TIME:
30–35 MINUTES

INGREDIENTS

4 chicken breasts, skinned and chopped
3 tbsp plain yogurt
2 tbsp tandoori paste
2 tbsp vegetable oil
1 onion, peeled and finely sliced
2 cloves of garlic, finely sliced
knob of ginger, finely sliced
1 cinnamon stick
4 cardamom pods, lightly crushed
1 tsp ground cumin
1 tsp ground coriander
½ tsp turmeric
2 tsp paprika
400 g / 14 oz / 1 ½ cup chopped
    tomatoes
100 ml / 3 ½ fl. oz / ½ cup chicken stock
½ lemon, juiced
salt and pepper

- Marinate the chicken for at least 1 hour in the yogurt and tandoori paste.
- Heat the oil in a pan and fry the onion until golden. Add the garlic, ginger and spices and fry for 2–3 minutes.
- Add the chicken, shaking off any excess marinade, and sauté over high heat until patchily golden, then add the remaining marinade, tomatoes and stock and simmer for 20 minutes.
- Season with lemon juice and salt and pepper and serve with rice.

980

SERVES 4

Spicy Sticky Chicken

- Mix together the marinade ingredients, tasting as you go – adjust as you wish – you may want it spicier or sweeter.
- Coat the chicken thoroughly and marinate for 30 minutes.
- Preheat the oven to 190°C (170°C fan) / 375F / gas 5.
- Cook the chicken in a foil-lined roasting tin for about 30 minutes or until dark golden and sticky.
- Serve with lime wedges.

PREPARATION TIME:
10 MINUTES

COOKING TIME:
30 MINUTES

INGREDIENTS

4 chicken thighs
2 tbsp runny honey
1–2 tbsp Worcestershire sauce
1 tbsp Dijon mustard
tabasco
salt and pepper
1 tbsp vegetable oil
lime wedges to serve

Szechuan Sticky Chicken

981

- Add 1 tbsp crushed szechuan peppercorns to the chicken for their lip-tingling heat.

982

SERVES 4

Spicy Chicken Kebabs

- Marinate the chicken in a bowl with chilli, oregano, lemon juice and oil for 30 minutes.
- Heat the oil in a pan and sauté the vegetables until just tender, then toss in the balsamic vinegar. Season and keep warm.
- Thread the chicken onto soaked wooden skewers, then griddle over high heat for 6–8 minutes until cooked through and golden.
- Serve the kebabs with the balsamic glazed vegetables.

PREPARATION TIME:
10 MINUTES

COOKING TIME:
15 MINUTES

INGREDIENTS

4 chicken thighs, skinned,
    deboned and chopped
1 red chilli (chili), finely chopped
2 tsp dried oregano
½ lemon, juiced
2 tbsp olive oil
salt
2 tbsp olive oil
1 courgette (zucchini), cut into
    thin batons
1 red pepper, deseeded and sliced
1 yellow pepper, deseeded and sliced
1 tbsp balsamic vinegar

Balsamic Chicken Kebabs

983

- Swap the flavourings over: Marinate the chicken in balsamic and sauté the vegetables with chilli, oregano and lemon – equally delicious.

984

SERVES 2

Soy-glazed Chicken

PREPARATION TIME:
10 MINUTES

COOKING TIME:
20 MINUTES

··

INGREDIENTS

1 tbsp vegetable oil
2 chicken breasts, skinned
   and roughly chopped
2 cloves of garlic, finely sliced
2 tbsp soy sauce
1–2 tsp sugar
1 star anise
black pepper
basil leaves, to serve

- Heat the oil in a wok and stir fry the chicken briskly until golden.
- Add the garlic, soy, sugar and star anise and reduce the heat.
- Spoon the sauce repeatedly over the chicken for 5–10 minutes until the chicken is cooked and sticky.
- Serve topped with basil leaves.

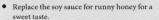

Honey Glazed Chicken

985

- Replace the soy sauce for runny honey for a sweet taste.

986

SERVES 4

Roast Chicken Supreme

PREPARATION TIME:
20 MINUTES

COOKING TIME:
30–40 MINUTES

··

INGREDIENTS

4 chicken supremes, skin on
2 tbsp olive oil
salt and pepper
400 g / 14 oz / 1 ½ cups Jerusalem
   artichokes, peeled and chopped
½ lemon
1 tbsp butter
1–2 tbsp double (heavy) cream
1 satsuma, peeled and segmented

FOR THE SAUCE

100 g / 3 ½ oz / ½ cup caster (superfine)
   sugar
2 tbsp water
2 oranges, zested
250 ml / 9 fl. oz / 1 cup orange juice
75 g / 2 ½ oz / ⅓ cup butter, chilled
   and cubed
candied orange zest, to serve

- Preheat the oven to 200°C (180°C fan) / 400F / gas 6.
- Drizzle the chicken with oil, season and roast in the oven for 25 minutes or until cooked through. Set aside.
- Cook the artichokes in boiling water with the squeezed out lemon half until completely tender. Drain, remove the lemon, then tip into a food processor with the butter and cream and whizz until smooth. Season.
- Make the sauce: set the sugar and water in a pan over a low heat and swirl until the sugar has melted. Do not stir. Allow to bubble up until golden.
- Once dark golden, remove from the heat and add the juice and orange zest. Return to the heat and simmer gently for 10–15 minutes, whisk in the butter a cube at a time.
- Sit the chicken on a plate with the sauce spooned over and topped with candied zest. Serve with the purée.

Lemon Chicken Supreme

987

- Replace the oranges with lemons.

988

SERVES 4

Tandoori Grilled Chicken

Tandoori Chicken with Coconut Milk

989

- For a richer dish, substitute the yogurt for coconut milk. This will temper the spice and make it sweeter.

Tandoori Chicken Kebab

990

- Use the marinade on diced chicken meat and grill on skewers, drizzle with yogurt to serve.

PREPARATION TIME:
15 MINUTES + MARINATING TIME

COOKING TIME:
30 MINUTES

INGREDIENTS

4 chicken legs
200 ml / 7 fl. oz / ¾ cup basmati rice
fresh coriander (cilantro) leaves

FOR THE RUB

1 tsp ground cumin
1 tsp ground coriander
1 tsp garam masala
1 tsp paprika
1 tsp ground cinnamon
1 ½ tsp tandoori chilli (chili) powder
1 tsp caster (superfine) sugar
1 clove garlic, minced
salt and pepper
1 tbsp vegetable oil
400 g / 14 oz / 1 ½ cups chopped tomatoes
300 ml / 10 fl. oz / 1 ¼ cups plain yogurt

- Prepare the tandoori rub by mixing together all the ingredients for the marinade in a mixing bowl. Add the chicken, mix well, then cover and chill for at least 1 hour.

- Heat the oil in a pan and brown the chicken legs. Add the tomatoes and paprika and simmer for 20 minutes or until the chicken has cooked. Remove the chicken legs and keep warm.

- Meanwhile bring double the volume of water to rice to the boil in a large saucepan and add the rice. Bring back to the boil, then cover and simmer for 10–12 minutes. Remove from the heat and keep the lid in place and set to one side.

- Stir the yogurt into the sauce and reheat gently without boiling otherwise the yogurt will split. Season.

- Serve the tandoori chicken with the sauce and rice, sprinkled with coriander.

SERVES 4

Grilled Spicy Chicken in Lemon Leaves

PREPARATION TIME:
10 MINUTES

COOKING TIME:
20–30 MINUTES

....

INGREDIENTS

4 chicken thighs, skinned and deboned
1 red chilli (chili), finely sliced
1 tbsp fresh ginger, finely sliced
2 cloves of garlic, finely sliced
2 tbsp huoc nam or fish sauce
1–2 tsp sugar
1 lime, juiced
lemon or banana leaves

- Mix together the chilli, ginger, garlic, huoc nam and sugar with some lime juice and taste – you need a balance of hot, sharp and sweet.
- Toss the chicken in the marinade and refrigerate for 1 hour.
- Wrap the chicken in the leaves. Heat a griddle pan until hot.
- Griddle the parcels over the heat until charred and the chicken is cooked through.
- You could bubble up any remaining marinade in a small pan to serve as a dipping sauce.

Griddled Chicken with Lime 992

- Add sliced lime tucked under the chicken for extra freshness.

SERVES 4

Basque Chicken

PREPARATION TIME:
10 MINUTES

COOKING TIME:
30 MINUTES

....

INGREDIENTS

2 tbsp olive oil
4 chicken drumsticks
1 onion, chopped
2 cloves of garlic, chopped
1 red pepper, deseeded and sliced
1 green pepper, deseeded and sliced
6 ripe vine tomatoes, cored and chopped
2 bay leaves
1 tsp sugar
1 tsp smoked paprika
salt and pepper
rice or mashed potato, to serve

- Heat the oil in a pan and brown the drumsticks until golden. Remove to a plate and set aside.
- Add the onion and garlic and cook gently until golden, then add the chicken back to the pan and add the peppers and tomatoes, bay leaves, sugar, paprika and seasoning and allow to simmer for about 10–15 minutes until all is combined. Adjust the seasoning.
- Serve hot with your choice of accompaniment.

Oven Baked Basque Chicken 994

- Add 100 ml / 3 ½ oz water or stock, some chopped carrots and transfer to a lidded casserole dish and cook slowly for an hour.

995

SERVES 4

Chicken with Spices and Cocoa

- Heat the oil in a pan and fry the chicken skin side down until crisp and golden.
- Turn over, add the onion and spices and cook until the onion is golden and the chicken just cooked through. Remove from the pan with a slotted spoon.
- Pour in the cream, bubble up and add the chocolate cut into chunks. Stir until thickened and smooth, season carefully and serve alongside the chicken.

PREPARATION TIME:
10 MINUTES

COOKING TIME:
20 MINUTES

INGREDIENTS

4 chicken breasts, skin on
2 tbsp vegetable oil
1 onion, peeled and finely sliced
1 stick cinnamon
1 red chilli (chili), finely sliced
150 ml / 5 fl. oz / ⅔ cup single cream
75–100 g / 2 ½–3 ½ oz / ⅓–½ cup dark chocolate
salt and pepper

Chicken with Chocolate Sauce

996

- Try serving with a little chocolate sauce and grilled halloumi cheese.

997

SERVES 4

Chicken Stir-fry Salad

- Heat the oil in a wok until nearly smoking, then add the chicken. Stir fry over a high heat until golden all over and the fat crisp. Remove from the pan with a slotted spoon.
- Meanwhile steam the broccoli florets and carrots for 2 minutes, then remove from the heat.
- Add the onion, garlic and ginger to the wok and stir fry for 2 minutes. Add the remaining vegetables including the broccoli and carrots and cook until crisp–tender.
- Add the meat back to the pan and stir in the sauces. Leave to bubble for a few minutes then check and adjust the seasoning if necessary.
- Serve warm or at room temperature.

PREPARATION TIME:
10 MINUTES

COOKING TIME:
10–12 MINUTES

INGREDIENTS

2 tbsp vegetable oil
350 g / 12 oz / 1 ½ cups chicken thigh meat, diced
1 head broccoli, separated into florets
2 carrots, peeled and sliced
1 onion, peeled and finely sliced
2 cloves of garlic, finely sliced
1 tsp fresh ginger, grated
1 red pepper, deseeded and finely sliced
150 g / 5 oz / ⅔ cup mushrooms, sliced
200 g / 7 oz / ¾ cup beansprouts
75–100 ml / 2 ½ –3 ½ fl. oz / ⅓–½ cup soy sauce
2–3 tbsp oyster sauce
salt and pepper

Chicken and Squid Stir-fry

998

- Rings of squid, added with the chicken, would add texture and interest to the dish.

999

SERVES 2

Bulgarian Chicken Salad

PREPARATION TIME:
10 MINUTES

COOKING TIME:
20 MINUTES

INGREDIENTS

2 chicken breasts
½ red onion, peeled and finely diced
1 yellow pepper, deseeded and
   finely diced
400 g / 14 oz / 1 ½ cups baby
   spinach leaves
1 lemon
salt and pepper

- Poach the chicken breasts in simmering water very gently for about 20 minutes until just cooked through. Set aside to cool.
- Mix the diced onion and peppers with spinach. Use a zester to take the yellow rind off a lemon – no white pith – and add to the vegetables. Toss with a little of the juice.
- Slice the chicken and serve with the salad.

1000

SERVES 4

Spicy Chicken with Lassi

PREPARATION TIME:
20 MINUTES

COOKING TIME:
20 MINUTES

INGREDIENTS

4 chicken thighs, skinned, deboned and
   cut into chunks
½ onion, peeled and chopped
2–3 green chillies (chilies), deseeded,
   chopped
3 cloves of garlic, peeled
2 tsp fresh ginger, chopped
1 tsp ground cumin
1 tsp ground coriander
1 tbsp dried mint
80 g / 2 ½ oz / ⅓ cup plain yogurt
250 g / 9 oz / 1 cup basmati rice
2 cups water with pinch saffron

FOR THE LASSI

200 ml / 7 fl. oz / ¾ cup single cream
400 ml / 14 fl. oz / 1 ½ cups milk
800 ml / 1 ¾ pints / 3 ⅓ cups plain
   yogurt
400 g / 14 oz / 1 ½ cups fruit pulp, such
   as mango

- Pat the chicken dry with kitchen paper.
- Whiz the ingredients for the marinade in a food processor until smooth. Use the yogurt for a creamier, less spicy version. Toss the chicken in the paste and leave to marinate in the refrigerator for at least 1 hour or overnight.
- When ready to serve, whizz the ingredients for the lassi in a blender until smooth – taste to see how much sugar you need. Chill in the refrigerator.
- Tip the rice into a pan with the water and cook covered with a lid for 10 minutes. Remove from the heat and leave covered for 5 minutes.
- Shake off any excess marinade from the chicken and thread onto skewers and cook either on a barbecue or very hot griddle pan until charred on the outside and pink in the centre – about 5–6 minutes.
- Serve with the saffron rice and lassi.

1001

SERVES 4

Basque Chicken Stew

- Preheat the oven to 180°C (160°C fan) / 350F / gas 4.
- Chop the onion and garlic.
- Heat the oil in a pan and brown the thighs until golden. Remove to a plate and set aside.
- Add the onion and garlic and cook gently until golden, then add the chicken back to the pan and add the peppers, sugar, paprika and seasoning and cook for 5 minutes.
- Pour over the canned tomatoes and stock, add the bay leaves and some salt, cover with a lid and cook in the oven for 45 minutes until the chicken is cooked.

PREPARATION TIME:
10 MINUTES

COOKING TIME:
55 MINUTES

INGREDIENTS

2 tbsp olive oil
4–6 chicken thighs
1 onion, 2 cloves of garlic
1 red pepper, deseeded and sliced
1 green pepper, deseeded and sliced
1 tsp sugar
1 tsp smoked paprika
1 tsp Espelette pepper
400 g / 14 oz / 1 ½ cups canned tomatoes
250 ml / 9 fl. oz / 1 cup chicken stock
2 bay leaves, salt
rice or mashed potato

Coconut Milk Chicken Soup

1002

SERVES 4

PREPARATION TIME:
15 MINUTES

COOKING TIME:
25–30 MINUTES

INGREDIENTS

3 tbsp vegetable oil
1 onion, peeled and finely sliced
2 cloves of garlic, finely chopped
1 red chilli (chili), finely sliced

3–4 chicken breasts, skinned and cubed
2 tsp tamarind paste
2 tbsp fish sauce
400 ml / 14 fl. oz / 1 ½ cups coconut milk
200 ml / 7 fl. oz / ¾ cup chicken stock
salt and pepper
1–2 limes, juiced
½ bunch coriander (cilantro), finely chopped, stalks reserved

- Heat the oil in a wok or large pan and fry the onion until deep gold and sweet.
- Add the garlic and chilli and cook out for 2 minutes.
- Add the cubed chicken and allow to colour on all sides.
- Stir in the tamarind and fish sauce, then pour over the coconut milk and chicken stock and add the coriander stalks.
- Lower the heat and leave to simmer for 15–20 minutes until the chicken is cooked through.
- Adjust the seasoning and stir in the lime juice and chopped coriander just before serving.

Chicken and Pear Curry

1003

SERVES 4

PREPARATION TIME:
10 MINUTES

COOKING TIME:
30 MINUTES

INGREDIENTS

2 tbsp vegetable oil
4 chicken thighs, skin on

1 onion, peeled and finely sliced
4 pears, halved and cored
2 yellow peppers, deseeded and finely sliced
½ tsp turmeric
1 tsp ground cinnamon
1 tsp ground cumin
350 ml / 12 fl. oz / 1 ½ cups chicken stock
salt and pepper

- Heat the oil in a pan and brown the chicken thighs on all sides, then remove to a plate.
- Add the onion and cook until golden and soft, then add the pears and peppers and cook for 5 minutes until softening.
- Add the chicken back to the pan with the spices and stir to coat, then pour in the stock. Simmer for 20 minutes or until the chicken is cooked through.
- Adjust the seasoning and serve.

1004

SERVES 4

Chicken with Couscous

**PREPARATION TIME:
10 MINUTES COOKING TIME:
1 HOUR 20 MINUTES**

....

INGREDIENTS

olive oil
2 onions, peeled and sliced
4 cloves of garlic, finely sliced
4 merguez sausages
2 carrots, peeled and sliced
3 preserved lemons
400 g / 14 oz / 1 ½ cups chickpeas
400 g / 14 oz / 1 ½ cups tomatoes
500 ml / 1 pint / 2 cups chicken stock
50 g / 1 ¾ oz / ¼ cup dates
2 tbsp honey
1 bunch coriander (cilantro)
225 g / 8 oz / 1 cup couscous
225 ml / 8 fl. oz / 1 cup chicken stock
½ tsp cayenne, 1 tbsp paprika
1 tsp turmeric, salt and pepper
2 tsp ground cinnamon
1 tbsp ground cumin
4 chicken legs

- Preheat the oven to 160°C (140°C fan) / 325F / gas 3.
- Mix the spices together in a bowl and toss the chicken legs in half of the spice mix. Marinade overnight.
- The next day heat 2 tbsp oil in a large casserole or tagine and cook the onions and garlic gently for at least 15 minutes. Add the spice mix and stir well.
- Add the vegetables and cook until softening, then add the sausages and chicken. Tip in the preserved lemons and chickpeas and increase the heat to brown.
- Add the tomatoes, stock and dates with the honey and season. Cover with a lid and bake in the oven for 1 hour.
- Meanwhile soak the couscous in the boiling stock and cover with cling film for 5 minutes. Remove and separate the grains with a fork.
- When the chicken is cooked, season and stir in the coriander. Serve with the couscous.

Chicken with Wild Rice

1005

- Replace the couscous with cooked wild rice.

1006

SERVES 4

Creole Chicken Coconut Curry

**PREPARATION TIME:
15 MINUTES**

**COOKING TIME:
30 MINUTES**

....

INGREDIENTS

2 tbsp olive oil
4 chicken drumsticks
1 onion, peeled and chopped
1 green (bell) pepper, seeded
  and chopped
1 stick celery, finely chopped
2 cloves of garlic, finely chopped
1 cm piece fresh ginger, finely chopped
4 tomatoes, cored and diced
1 tbsp flour
1 tsp paprika
1 tsp cayenne pepper
400 g / 14 oz / 1 ½ cups coconut milk
100 ml / 3 ½ fl. oz / ½ cup chicken stock
1 bay leaf
salt and pepper
1 bunch spring onions (scallions), finely
  sliced lengthways

- Heat the oil in a large pan and cook the drumsticks on all sides until golden then remove and set aside. Sauté the onion, peppers and celery until softened.
- Add the garlic, ginger and flour and cook out for a few seconds, then add the chicken back to the pan.
- Sprinkle over the spices, then pour in coconut milk and stock. Add the bay leaf and season, then simmer for about 20 minutes over a low heat until the sauce has thickened and the chicken is cooked.
- Serve decorated with the spring onions.

Light Creole Curry

1007

- Use the same amount canned tomatoes as coconut milk for a fresher dish.

SERVES 4–6 1008

Roast Chicken with Pan-fried Foie Gras

Roast Chicken and Foie Gras on Brioche 1009

- For a different way of serving, try serving the pan-fried foie on slices of lightly toasted brioche.

Roast Chicken with Fried Black Pudding 1010

- If you don't fancy foie gras, try fried slices of black pudding alongside which will add similar earthy richness.

PREPARATION TIME:
10 MINUTES

COOKING TIME:
1 HOUR 30 MINUTES

INGREDIENTS

1 oven-ready roast chicken
40 g / 1 oz butter
salt and pepper
4 sprigs thyme or rosemary
400 g / 14 oz foie gras, cut into
    4–6 thick slices

- Preheat oven to 220°C (200°C fan) / 425F / gas 7.
- Smear the skin of the chicken with butter, season very generously and push the herbs into the cavity. Place in a roasting tin and roast for 20 minutes.
- After 20 minutes lower the heat to 180°C (160°C fan) / 350F / gas 4 and return to the oven for another hour or until the chicken is cooked through and the juices run clear when pierced with a toothpick.
- Leave to rest loosely covered with foil for 15–20 minutes.
- Heat a frying pan till quite hot. Lightly salt the foie gras slices and sear on each side for 30 seconds, then cook for 1 minute more. Remove from the pan.
- Serve the carved chicken alongside the pan-fried tranches of foie gras.

1011

SERVES 4

Moroccan Chicken with Couscous

TIME:
15 MINUTES

COOKING TIME:
30 MINUTES

....

INGREDIENTS

2 tbsp olive oil
4 chicken thighs, skinned and deboned,
    cut into chunks
1 yellow pepper, deseeded and
    finely sliced
1 red pepper, deseeded and
    finely sliced
1 courgette (zucchini), chopped
1 ½ tsp ras-el-hanout spice mix
100 g / 3 ½ oz / ½ cup black olives
400 g / 14 oz / 1 ½ cups canned tomatoes
salt and pepper
250 g / 9 oz / 1 cup couscous
250 ml / 9 fl. oz / 1 cup chicken
    or vegetable stock
60 g / 2 oz raisins
squeeze of lemon juice

- Heat the oil in a pan and fry the chicken until golden, then remove with a slotted spoon and set aside.
- Add the vegetables and sauté until starting to soften, then add the spice mix and cook for 1 minute. Add the chicken back to the pan, toss to coat, then add the olives and tomatoes and simmer for 20 minute or until all is tender. Season.
- Place the couscous in a bowl, add the raisins, cover with the hot stock and cling film the bowl. Leave for 10 minutes or so until tender, then fork through the grains and add the lemon.
- Serve the hot stew with the couscous alongside.

Chicken with Baked Potato

1012

- Serve the chicken on top of a baked potato.

1013

SERVES 4

Wok-fried Chicken and Vegetables

PREPARATION TIME:
10 MINUTES

COOKING TIME:
10–12 MINUTES

....

INGREDIENTS

2 tbsp vegetable oil
350 g / 12 oz / 1 ½ cups chicken
    thigh meat, diced
1 head broccoli, separated into florets
2 carrots, peeled and sliced
2 cloves of garlic, finely sliced
1 tsp fresh ginger, grated
½ bunch spring onions (scallions),
    finely sliced
150 g / 5 oz / ⅔ cup mushrooms, sliced
200 g / 7 oz / ¾ cup beansprouts
75–100 ml / 2 ½ – 3 ½ fl. oz / ⅓– ½ cup
    soy sauce
2–3 tbsp oyster sauce or hoisin sauce
salt and pepper

- Heat the oil in a wok until nearly smoking, then add the chicken. Stir fry over a high heat until golden all over and the fat crisp. Remove from the pan with a slotted spoon.
- Meanwhile steam the broccoli florets and carrots for 2 minutes, then remove from the heat.
- Add the spring onions, garlic and ginger to the wok and stir fry for 2 minutes. Add the remaining vegetables including the broccoli and carrots and cook until crisp-tender.
- Add the meat back to the pan and stir in the sauces. Leave to bubble for a few minutes then check and adjust the seasoning if necessary.
- Serve immediately.

Wok-fried Chicken and Noodles

1014

- Serve on a bed of cooked noodles.

1015

SERVES 4

Chicken, Galangal and Lemongrass Soup

- Heat the oil in a pan and sweat the onion and garlic without colouring.
- Add the spices and cook for a few minutes until the scent is released, then pour in the coconut milk and stock.
- When simmering, add the chicken pieces and simmer gently for 15 minutes or until the chicken is cooked.
- Season the soup with the fish sauce and lime juice and serve sprinkled with coriander.

PREPARATION TIME:
10 MINUTES

COOKING TIME:
25 MINUTES

INGREDIENTS

1 tbsp vegetable oil
1 onion, peeled and finely sliced
2 cloves of garlic, finely sliced
2 cm piece galangal, finely sliced
1 stalk lemongrass, bruised
3 curry leaves
2 lime leaves
1 red chilli (chili), finely sliced
400 ml / 14 fl. oz / 1 ½ cups coconut milk
250 ml / 9 fl. oz / 1 cup chicken stock
2 chicken breasts, skinned and sliced
2 tbsp fish sauce
1 lime, juiced
½ bunch fresh coriander (cilantro), chopped

Chicken Galangal Curry

1016

- Reduce the liquid by half and serve over white rice as a curry.

1017

SERVES 4

Chicken Tikka Kebab Bites

- Cube the chicken, toss with the curry paste, yogurt and seasoning, then leave to marinate in the refrigerator for 30 minutes.
- Thread the chicken pieces onto skewers, wipe off excess marinade, then grill until golden and cooked through.
- In the centre of each tortilla, arrange the lettuce, cucumber and onions. Top with the chicken kebabs and drizzle over some lemon juice and coriander leaves. Remove the skewers before eating.

PREPARATION TIME:
5 MINUTES + MARINATING TIME

COOKING TIME:
10 MINUTES

INGREDIENTS

4 chicken breasts, skinned
4 tbsp tikka masala paste
200 ml / 7 fl.oz / ¾ cup plain yogurt
salt and pepper
4 tortillas
1 iceberg lettuce, shredded
cucumber slices
1 red onion, thinly sliced
½ lemon, juiced
coriander (cilantro) leaves, chopped

Chicken Tikka with a Mint Yogurt

1018

- For cooling dip, stir a few tbsp plain yogurt with chopped mint, a crushed clove of garlic and some grated cucumber.

Index

Chicken and Potato Tortilla 189
Chicken and Prawn Brochettes 263
Chicken and Prawn Chop Suey 226
Chicken and Prawn Open Sandwiches 84
Chicken and Prawn Pancakes 23
Chicken and Prawn Pizza 144
Chicken and Preserved Lemon Tagine 231
Chicken and Prune Parcels 77
Chicken and Pumpkin Soup 50
Chicken and Raisin Tagine 257
Chicken and Red Pepper Meatballs 103
Chicken and Red Pepper Skewers 73
Chicken and Red Wine Fricassee 117
Chicken and Rice Courgette 72
Chicken and Rice Sesame Salad 74
Chicken and Sage Terrine 107
Chicken and Salsify Pie 167
Chicken and Serrano Ham Croquettes 86
Chicken and Shiitake Mushroom Noodles 275
Chicken and Spring Vegetable Pasta 105
Chicken and Spring Vegetable Stew 97
Chicken and Spring Vegetables 278
Chicken and Squid Stir Fry 291
Chicken and Summer Fruit Tagine 125
Chicken and Sweet Potato Colombo 138
Chicken and Sweet Potato Mafé 260
Chicken and Swiss Chard Terrine 80
Chicken and Tarragon Cake 150
Chicken and Tarragon Sausage 259
Chicken and Tarragon Skewers 99
Chicken and Tomato Coconut Soup 37
Chicken and Tomato Crostini 80
Chicken and Tomato Fromage Frais Pie 146
Chicken and Tomato Lasagne 185
Chicken and Tomato Pasta 158
Chicken and Tomato Rolls 22
Chicken and Tomato Terrine 46
Chicken and Tomatoes Roasted with Anchovies 200
Chicken and Vegetable Brochettes 34
Chicken and Vegetable Penne 162
Chicken and Vegetable Pizza 144
Chicken and Vegetable Salad 49
Chicken and Vegetable Skewers 263
Chicken and Vegetable Stir Fry 191
Chicken and Vegetable Tagliatelle 162
Chicken and White Wine Fricassee 117
Chicken and Wild Mushroom Lasagne 201
Chicken and Wild Rice Salad 74
Chicken and Winter Fruit Tagine 125
Chicken, Apple and Banana Curry 253

Chicken Artichoke Tagine 276
Chicken Aubergine Cannelloni 106
Chicken Aubergine Colombo 138
Chicken Aubergine Pastries 172
Chicken Avocado Salad with Fennel 33
Chicken Basquaise 184
Chicken Biryani and Cardamom Rice 251
Chicken Biryani with Peas and Potatoes 251
Chicken Bites in Boats 56
Chicken Bites with Fresh Mint 10
Chicken Bouchees 210
Chicken Breast with Chestnuts and Stuffing 163
Chicken Broccoli Quiche 137
Chicken Brochettes and Cannelloni 101
Chicken Brochettes and Tomato Cannelloni 101
Chicken Brochettes with Peach Chutney 34
Chicken Brochettes with Plum Chutney 34
Chicken Broth with Mixed Greens 142
Chicken Broth with Mushrooms 142
Chicken Burger 164
Chicken Burger with Avocado 97
Chicken Burgers with Pepper and Basil 182
Chicken Caesar Salad with Grapefruit 91
Chicken Caesar Tuiles 171
Chicken Caesar with Soft–Boiled Egg 91
Chicken Cakes with Chilli Sauce 268
Chicken Canneberg 186
Chicken Cannelloni 197
Chicken Cari 237
Chicken Cari with Roasted Aubergine 237
Chicken Carrot and Salsify Pie 167
Chicken Cheddar Fondants 52
Chicken, Cheese and Herb Empanadas 32
Chicken Chilli 264
Chicken Chilli Prawn Pasta 247
Chicken Chilli Tortilla Tower 264
Chicken Chorizo Tagine 217
Chicken Colombo with Basmati Rice 145
Chicken Colombo with Bulghur 239
Chicken Colombo with Green Beans 145
Chicken Cooked in Coconut 147
Chicken Cooked with Cola 263
Chicken Courgette Kebabs 11
Chicken Creole 220
Chicken Creole with Pistachios 220
Chicken Croquettes 78
Chicken Croquettes with Tomato Sauce 78
Chicken Crumble 250
Chicken Crumble Blini 250
Chicken Crumble Pancakes 250
Chicken Crumble with Hazelnuts and Pumpkin 127

Chicken Curry 235
Chicken Curry Filo Parcels 9
Chicken Curry Parcels with Sauce 9
Chicken Curry with Rice 276
Chicken Curry with Yogurt 256
Chicken Cushions with Pistachio Couscous 152
Chicken Enchiladas 201
Chicken Escalope with Caper Berries 179
Chicken Escalope with Exotic Kebabs 180
Chicken Fajitas 93
Chicken Fajitas with Rice 93
Chicken Feta Pittas 94
Chicken Feta Tart 157
Chicken Fig Salad with Pomegranate 90
Chicken Fricassee 224
Chicken Fricassee with Green Beans 185
Chicken Fricassee with Rice 224
Chicken Fromage Frais Quiche 137
Chicken Fruit Salad 100
Chicken, Galangal and Lemongrass Soup 297
Chicken Galangal Curry 297
Chicken Galettes 148
Chicken Goats' Cheese Skewers 62
Chicken Hashis 207
Chicken in Red Wine Mushroom Sauce 210
Chicken in Spiced Crust 256
Chicken in Squid Ink with Pappardelle 240
Chicken in White Wine 19
Chicken in White Wine Sauce 128
Chicken Jambalaya 285
Chicken Kebabs with Apricots 81
Chicken Kebabs with Garlic Sauce 35
Chicken Kebabs with Lemon Satay 88
Chicken Kebabs with Lime Satay 88
Chicken Kebabs with Tabbouleh 35
Chicken Korma Bake 236
Chicken Lasagne 197
Chicken Legs with Tomatoes 190
Chicken Lemon and Olive Tagine 217
Chicken Liver and Caper Terrines 91
Chicken Liver and Olive Cake 41
Chicken Liver and Pine Nut Cake 41
Chicken Liver Terrine with Gingerbread 72
Chicken Liver Terrine with Pine Nuts 72
Chicken Lollipop Salad 98
Chicken Masala 235
Chicken Meatballs 38
Chicken Meatballs with Baby Spinach 76
Chicken Merguez and Potato Tortilla 280
Chicken Mimolette Fondants 44
Chicken Mousse Stuffing 259

Index

Chicken with Ginger Caramel Sauce 129

Chicken with Ginger, Cardamom and Squash 271

Chicken with Grated Carrot Salad 241

Chicken with Gratin Dauphinois 255

Chicken with Grilled Courgette 175

Chicken with Ham & Basil 118

Chicken with Herb Butter Stuffing 225

Chicken with Herbed Tomato Sauce 238

Chicken with Herby Bulghur Wheat 239

Chicken with Herby Tortilla 189

Chicken with Homardine Sauce 121

Chicken with Honey, Tomato and Almonds 173

Chicken with Juniper and Vegetables 249

Chicken with Lemon and Olives 208

Chicken with Lemon and Olives 279

Chicken with Lemon and Tomatoes 208

Chicken with Lime and Mint 87

Chicken with Mangetout 278

Chicken with Mango 166

Chicken with Mascarpone Tomato Sauce 238

Chicken with Mashed Potatoes 118

Chicken with Mixed Vegetable Mash 127

Chicken with Mozzarella Salad 171

Chicken with Mushroom Broth 219

Chicken with Mushroom Couscous 175

Chicken with Mushroom Sauce 183

Chicken with Mushrooms & Asparagus 218

Chicken with Mushrooms 133

Chicken with Mushrooms and Baby Corn 218

Chicken with Olives and Preserved Lemons 132

Chicken with Orange and Sesame Seed 48

Chicken with Padron Peppers 282

Chicken with Peppers and Couscous 282

Chicken with Peppers and Sesame Seeds 283

Chicken with Pesto Stuffing 212

Chicken with Pineapple and Lime 254

Chicken with Plums 81

Chicken with Pomegranate 266

Chicken with Port and Red Wine Sauce 186

Chicken with Potatoes and Pumpkin 123

Chicken with Potatoes, Chorizo and Tomatoes 223

Chicken with Prawns and Spaghetti 130

Chicken with Prunes and Oranges 69

Chicken with Raisin Couscous 175

Chicken with Ravioli 142

Chicken with Refried Beans 275

Chicken with Rice Noodles 166

Chicken with Roast Tomatoes 181

Chicken with Roast Vegetables 211

Chicken with Roasted Vegetables 126

Chicken with Saffron Rice 104

Chicken With Sautéed Fennel 123

Chicken with Sautéed Turnips 123

Chicken with Seafood 247

Chicken with Serrano Ham 22

Chicken with Slow-roast Tomatoes 200

Chicken with Spiced Couscous 242

Chicken with Spiced Parsnip Sauce 154

Chicken with Spices and Cocoa 291

Chicken with Spicy Caramel Sauce 129

Chicken with Spring Vegetables 148

Chicken with Spring Vegetables and Herbs 97

Chicken with Spring Vegetables and Rice 278

Chicken with Steamed Rice 283

Chicken with Stuffed Roasted Peppers 126

Chicken with Szechuan Peppercorns 273

Chicken with Tabbouleh 155

Chicken with Tarragon Cream Sauce 136

Chicken with Tarragon Tomato Sauce 238

Chicken with Teriyaki Mushrooms 275

Chicken with Thyme and Lime 177

Chicken with Thyme Yogurt Sauce 136

Chicken with Truffle Sauce 218

Chicken with Truffles and Sage Butter 225

Chicken with Vanilla and Carrot Mash 127

Chicken with Vodka and Bulghur 255

Chicken with Walnut Pesto 132

Chicken with Wild Mushroom Mash 135

Chicken with Wild Mushrooms 135

Chicken with Wild Rice 294

Chicken Wraps 201

Chicken Yakitori 70

Chicken Yassa with Rice 277

Chicken, Almond and Coconut Brochettes 29

Chicken, Almond and Honey Tart 193

Chicken, Apple and Peanut Skewers 62

Chicken, Apple and Rocket Wrap 60

Chicken, Artichoke and Olive Tagine 219

Chicken, Artichoke and Sun-dried Tomatoes 219

Chicken, Cheese and Bacon Rolls 100

Chicken, Cheese and Spinach Muffins 45

Chicken, Cheese and Sun-dried Tomato Fondants 44

Chicken, Chestnut, Prune and Fig Tagine 222

Chicken, Chickpea and Asparagus Salad 67

Chicken, Corn and Vegetable Rice 152

Chicken, Courgette and Walnut Crumble 127

Chicken, Feta and Beetroot Salad 176

Chicken, Fig and Cinnamon Tagine 231

Chicken, Fig and Mangetout Salad 90

Chicken, Ham and Apple Bagel 58

Chicken, Lemon and Olive Fricassee 185

Chicken, Mango and Rocket Wrap 60

Chicken, Mascarpone and Pancetta Soufflé 61

Chicken, Mushroom and Leek Soup 82

Chicken, Mushroom and Tarragon Soup 82

Chicken, Olive and Tomato Sandwiches 40

Chicken, Orange and Pepper Kebabs 78

Chicken, Pepper and Bacon Tagine 150

Chicken, Pistachio 42

Chicken, Potato and Mushroom Pie 195

Chicken, Prune and Sweet Potato Tagine 241

Chicken, Raisin and Almond Salad 108

Chicken, Swede and Mushroom Pie 195

Chicken, Sweet Potato and Grape Stew 245

Chicken, Tomato and Cheese Muffins 45

Chicken, Tomato and Gouda Melt 68

Chicken, Vegetable & Cheese Wok–Bake 133

Chicken, Vegetable and Cheese Gratin 133

Chilli Chicken Meatballs 87

Chilli Chicken Noodles 243

Chilli Chicken Wings 274

Chilli Chicken with Ratatouille 246

Chilli Lemon Chicken 222

Chilli Orange Chicken 222

Chinese Chicken and Vegetables with Rice 234

Chinese Chicken Baguettes 149

Chinese Chicken Noodle Soup 246

Chinese Chicken Soup 26

Chinese Chicken Soup with Pak Choi 281

Chinese Chicken Stir Fry 149

Chinese Chicken with Noodles 246

Chinese Flavoured Pâté 15

Chinese-style Chicken 273

Chop Suey with Rice or Noodles 226

Cider Chicken with Apples 139

Citrus Chicken Salad 102

Citrus Chicken with Cantonese Rice 144

Citrus Chicken with Sesame Seeds 48

Citrus Salad 100

Classic Roast Chicken 204

Classic Roast Chicken and Vegetables 204

Coconut Chicken Fondue 46

Coconut Chicken Pasta 147

Coconut Milk Chicken Soup 293

Cold Picnic Pie 146

Colombo Style Chicken Legs 14

Colombo Style Chicken Wings 14

Coq au Vin 178

Coq au Vin Blanc 178

Index

Index